This volume offers a unique record of India's role in multilateral trade negotiations. As importantly, it offers an invaluable analysis and template of negotiating strategies and tactics that will be indispensable reading for negotiators from across the Global South.

—Dr. Rob Davies, Former Minister of Trade and Industry, South Africa

Abhijit Das masterfully draws back the veil on the complex and largely invisible world of trade negotiations to examine developing countries' attempts to protect and advance their interests, successfully and otherwise, in the face of the systemic asymmetries and power politics of the WTO. There's no hyperbole, just an exceptionally lucid and insightful analysis of actual events and insiders' accounts over several decades. Das's guidelines to negotiators will empower developing countries and civil society alike as they confront an even more fractured WTO.

—Prof. Jane Kelsey, Emeritus Professor, University of Auckland

Trade negotiation is a complex art, where an in-depth understanding of the subject under negotiation is as important as insights into the relevant political economy. I have not encountered literature that touches on the theory and practice of international trade negotiations in such depth. Abhijit has the distinct advantage of having been an insider to a national trade establishment and yet having seen trade negotiations from the unbiased position of a trade academician. It is not surprising, therefore, that this book draws theoretical nuggets from a strong experiential foundation. A must-read for all practitioners and enthusiasts of trade negotiations.

—Rajeev Kher, Former Commerce Secretary of India

The book fills a very important void in international trade law and practice, providing comprehensive guidance on issues related to WTO negotiations. It approaches some very technical and complex subjects related to international trade and the WTO in a simple, lucid, and engaging way, bringing out their essence without burdening the reader with unnecessary details and technicalities. It is commendable for its comprehensive sweep and depth as well as its analytical rigour.

—J.S. Deepak, India's former ambassador to the WTO

This will be an invaluable go-to book, and a must read for trade policy practitioners, economists, political scientists, academics, and just about anyone interested in understanding why international trade negotiations are so complex and take a long time to conclude.

—Dr. Jayant Dasgupta, India's former ambassador to the WTO

The book provides excellent conceptual, empirical, and practical arguments to demonstrate that despite the limited room to manoeuvre for the developing world in multilateral trade negotiations, it can still better its outcomes through careful use of many negotiation strategies and tactics. The narrative is rich in experiences and histories of negotiations.

—Prof. J.P. Singh, Distinguished University Professor,
Schar School of Policy and Government, George Mason University;
Richard von Weizsäcker Fellow, Robert Bosch Academy, Berlin

This is a book that has been sorely missing in my bookshelf. Abhijit Das must be congratulated for offering a comprehensive analysis of strategies and tactics deployed by key players at the GATT/WTO negotiations. The most exciting aspect of the book is the analysis of action behind the scenes. It closes the gap on how the strategies and tactics work out in the real world of international trade negotiations.

—Prof. Diana Tussie, Director of International Relations Area,
Facultad Latinoamericana de Ciencias Sociales, Argentina

Strategies in GATT and WTO Negotiations

ABHIJIT DAS

OXFORD
UNIVERSITY PRESS

OXFORD
UNIVERSITY PRESS

Great Clarendon Street, Oxford, OX2 6DP,
United Kingdom

Oxford University Press is a department of the University of Oxford.
It furthers the University's objective of excellence in research, scholarship,
and education by publishing worldwide. Oxford is a registered trade mark of
Oxford University Press in the UK and in certain other countries

Published in the United States of America by Oxford University Press
198 Madison Avenue, New York, NY 10016, United States of America

British Library Cataloguing in Publication Data
Data available

Library of Congress Control Number: 2024948812

ISBN 9780198934400

DOI: 10.1093/9780198934431.001.0001

Printed and bound in India by
Replika Press Pvt. Ltd.

To my parents

Chandra Das and Bhagirath Lal Das

Preface

While participating in international trade negotiations, I felt the need of a book which would have explained to me in simple terms the strategies used by countries for securing their negotiating objectives. Some classic books had been written on negotiating strategies, but these discussed issues related to commercial negotiations. No doubt, excellent articles in some academic journals analysed in detail a few strategies used by countries in multilateral trade negotiations. However, searching for a comprehensive book on negotiating strategies in the context of GATT and WTO negotiations, especially from the perspective of developing countries, proved to be an elusive and futile exercise. From this frustration emerged the idea of this book.

Negotiations are at the core of WTO's functioning and decision-making—be it the appointment of the Director General of the organization, appointment of panellists to resolve trade disputes, or decisions and declarations finalized at various ministerial meetings. However, it is in the negotiations for new rules to govern international trade that the complexities involved in this process come to the fore. It is this aspect of negotiations, and the underlying strategies, which is the theme of this book.

Some of the terminologies and broad ideas underpinning this book need to be clarified upfront. At many places, the book uses the term 'developing countries' to refer collective to a large number of countries in the GATT/WTO negotiations. Why is it relevant to do so? No doubt, developing countries differ in terms of the size of their economies and markets, resource endowments, participation in international trade, sectors of competitive advantage, domestic instabilities, etc. However, what is common to most of these countries is that while many of them were active participants in some of the rounds of multilateral of trade negotiations at the GATT and subsequently in the WTO negotiations, it did not result in these countries decisively shaping the negotiating agenda and the negotiated outcomes. Although they succeeded, to some extent, in securing special and differential treatment during the GATT era and subsequently in some of the agreements at the WTO, their negotiating efforts could not mould the substantial content of the multilateral trade rules. The few occasions when they were successful in securing their negotiating objectives are mostly exceptions to the general trend of the developed countries being significantly more influential at the negotiating table. It may, thus, not be inappropriate to treat the developing countries as a collective, which is distinct from the USA, the European Union, Japan, Australia, Canada, etc.—countries that have exercised decisive influence in the GATT and the WTO negotiations. It is also important to note that while many of the negotiating episodes analysed in the book relate to India, Brazil and a few other developing countries, the lessons on negotiating strategies would be applicable for most developing countries and, in some instances, even the developed countries.

In academic literature and popular media, developing countries are often depicted as naysayers at the negotiating table, lacking a positive agenda and also being against international trade. This perception is neither accurate nor fair. It ignores the large number of issues on which the developing countries had a positive agenda in the WTO negotiations, but they were repeatedly thwarted by the powerful at the negotiating table—negotiations on movement of professionals for delivering services abroad, Implementation Issues, permanent solution for addressing the problem of public stockholding for food security purposes and the Covid-19 TRIPS waiver being some illustrations of this trend. Further, it would be incorrect to equate the opposition of many developing countries to negotiating *rules* in new and emerging area with being against international trade. Most developing countries would readily agree that international trade can have a positive impact on economic development and be a force for good. However, it is also true that negotiating rules at the WTO in areas such as digital trade, labour issues, and environment are not likely to be beneficial for the economic prospects of many developing countries. Often, the distinction between international trade and the impact of rules on international trade on many developing countries is not sufficiently recognized; thereby resulting in incorrect perception and inaccurate depiction. Hopefully, the discussion on negotiating strategies will set right some of these distortions.

This book would not have been possible without the generosity of a large number of persons who agreed to be interviewed and shared insights about the GATT and WTO negotiations. Needless to say, I am responsible for any shortcoming in the book. I am grateful to S.P. Shukla,

India's ambassador to the GATT during the early years of the Uruguay Round, for elaborating the intricate dynamics behind the launch of the Uruguay Round of negotiations under the GATT. Rajeev Kher, India's former Commerce Secretary, and three of India's former ambassadors to the WTO—S. Narayanan, Jayant Dasgupta, and J.S. Deepak—shared details of how negotiations under the Doha Round commenced and proceeded subsequently, including on the crucial issues of the Singapore Issues and agriculture. They also readily agreed to review an earlier version of the manuscript and provided many useful suggestions. I cannot thank these stalwarts enough for their efforts in seeking to ensure that this book provides a robust account of developments at the negotiating table, as well as the associated events in the domestic arena. Rajesh Aggarwal, India's Counsellor to the WTO, and Gabriel Taboada, delegate for Agriculture of the Permanent Mission of Argentina to the WTO, deserve a special appreciation for sharing invaluable information on how the G-20 was established and what went behind the scenes in the Agriculture negotiations during the Doha Round. I am grateful to Rob Davies, South Africa's Minister of Trade and Industry at the Bali Ministerial Conference for confirming the facts of the crucial role which he played on the issue of food security at that meeting. I would be remiss in not gratefully acknowledging the contribution of many persons who provided fascinating details about the Doha Round negotiations, but chose to remain anonymous for the sake of confidentiality.

If the book is not a dry narration of facts and strategies, it is mainly on account of the candid feedback and constructive suggestions provided by the following on various versions of the manuscript: Ajay Srivastava, Anu Mathai, Atul Kaushik, J.P. Singh, Mukesh Bhatnagar, Pallavi Arora, R.V. Anuradha, Sachin Sharma, Sangeeta Godbole, Shailja Singh, Shishira Johny, and Sunayana Sasmal. V.S. Seshadri not only gave useful comments on the manuscript, but also provided sagacious advice regarding publication of the book. I am grateful to him for all his help and suggestions.

I had the good fortune to benefit from discussions with many persons on different aspects of WTO negotiations, including negotiating strategies and domestic imperatives of these negotiations. I happily acknowledge with gratitude the following persons for enriching my understanding of these issues: Agneshwar Sen, Aileen Kwa, Amit Yadav, Anil Bhardwaj, Anjali Prasad, Anup Wadhawan, Anwarul Hoda, Ashwani Mahajan,

Augustine Peter, Biraj Patnaik, Chandni Raina, Devinder Sharma, Gopal Pillai, Harsha Vardhana Singh, K.M. Chandrasekhar, Madhukar Sinha, Manab Mazumdar, Manoj Joshi, Mohan Kumar, Monika, Murali Kallummal, Neeraj R.S., P.K. Srivastava, Pralok Gupta, Pranav Kumar, Rahul Khullar, Rajan S. Ratna, Ranja Sengupta, Rita Teaotia, S.N. Menon, Sajal Mathur, Shashank Priya, Sudhakar Dalela, Sumanta Chaudhuri, Sunil Bhartwal, Vandana Aggarwal, and Vivek Johri. Each of them has, knowingly or even unknowingly, made an important contribution to the book. Thanks to Vipin Sharma and Santosh Kumar at the Centre for WTO for their help in many ways, including finding many books and journal articles that I had to read for this book. Martin Khor, unfortunately no longer with us, deserves a special appreciation. I had the privilege of interacting with him for over a decade and seeing him in action provided many valuable lessons in negotiating strategy.

I am grateful to the team at Oxford University Press, in particular Dhiraj Pandey and Amrita Brahmo and her team, for taking forward this publication in a professional manner. I gratefully acknowledge the efforts of Robert Wilkinson as the copy editor and the support provided by Radhika Rajendren.

It would not be incorrect to describe this book as a family venture. My father, Bhagirath Lal Das, was a former ambassador of India to the GATT. He is a font of wisdom on many issues, including the GATT and the WTO. Our long hours of discussion on technical details related to the GATT and the WTO, as well as strategy, has shaped and improved the book beyond measure. In respect of certain negotiating episodes, I have relied on his recollection and personal papers. No words are enough to thank him for all his efforts in helping me bring the book to a fruition. My wife, Sucharita, has been the rock of support in my life. This book is as much hers as it is mine. She and Isha (my daughter) were understanding beyond reasonable expectations. This ensured that I could persist with writing the book, even if it meant occasionally ignoring domestic responsibilities. Isha also helped in researching some of the issues discussed in the book. Thank you, Sucharita and Isha. Without your encouragement and support the book would have remained a pie in the sky. I am grateful to my sisters, Supreeti and Shipra, their respective spouses, Raghav and Shantanu, and the most recent addition to our family, my son-in-law Aditya, for contributing in multiple ways during the long years of writing this book.

Contents

Abbreviations

ACP countries	African, Caribbean and Pacific countries
AD	Anti-dumping
AGOA	African Growth and Opportunity Act
AMS	Aggregate Measure of Support
AOA	Agreement on Agriculture
APEC	Asia-Pacific Economic Cooperation
ASCM	Agreement on Subsidies and Countervailing Measures
ASEAN	Association of South East Asian Nations
BATNA	Best alternative to a negotiated agreement
BISD	Basic instruments and selected documents
BIT	Bilateral Investment Treaties
BoP	Balance of Payments
CAP	Common Agricultural Policy
CARICOM	Caribbean Community
CBD	Convention on Biological Diversity
CEI	Confederation of Engineering Industry
CGE	Computable General Equilibrium
CSO	Civil Society Organization
CTE	Committee on Trade and Environment
CVD	Countervailing duty
DDR	Doha Development Round
DG	Director General
DSB	Dispute Settlement Body
EC	European Community
EEC	European Economic Community
EFPIA	European Federation of Pharmaceutical Industries and Associations
ERP	External Reference Price
EU	European Union
FAO	Food and Agriculture Organization
FICC	Federation of Indian Chambers of Commerce
FTA	Free Trade Agreement
G20	Group of Twenty, intergovernmental forum comprising 19 countries and the European Union
G-4	Negotiating configuration during the Doha Round comprising Brazil, EU, India and USA

G-20	Coalition of developing countries led by Brazil and India, which was active in agriculture negotiations during the Doha Round of the WTO
G-33	Coalition of developing countries led by Indonesia and India, which was active in agriculture negotiations during the Doha Round of the WTO. It focussed on issues related to food security, farm livelihood, and rural development
GATS	General Agreement on Trade in Services
GATT	General Agreement on Tariffs and Trade
GC	General Council
GDP	Gross Domestic Product
GP	Government Procurement
GPA	Government Procurement Agreement
GSP	Generalized System of Preferences
GVC	Global Value Chains
HOD	Heads of delegation
IBM	International Business Machines Corporation
IIA	International Investment Agreement
ILO	International Labour Organization
IMF	International Monetary Fund
IPC	Intellectual Property Committee
IPR	Intellectual Property Rights
ITA	Information Technology Agreement
ITES	IT-Enabled Services
ITO	International Trade Organization
LDC	Least-Developed Country
LMG	Like-Minded Group
MAI	Multilateral Agreement on Investment
MC12	12th Ministerial Conference of the WTO
MEA	Multilateral Environmental Agreement
MFN	Most-Favoured Nation
MM82	Ministerial Meeting of GATT held in 1982
MNC	Multi-National Corporation
MRA	Mutual Recognition Agreements
NGO	Non-governmental Organization
NT	National Treatment
NTB	Non-tariff Barriers
OECD	Organization for Economic Cooperation and Development
OTDS	Overall Trade Distorting Support
PCTF	Preparatory Committee on Trade Facilitation
RTA	Regional Trade Agreement
S&D treatment	Special and Differential Treatment
SMEs	Small and Micro Enterprises

SSM	Special Safeguard Mechanism
SSG	Special Safeguards
TFA	Trade Facilitation Agreement
TPP or TPP Agreement	Trans-Pacific Partnership Agreement
TRIMs	Trade-related Investment Measures
TRIPS	Trade-Related Aspects of Intellectual Property Rights
UNCTAD	United Nations Conference on Trade and Development
UNDP	United Nations Development Programme
UNECOSOC	United Nations Economic and Social Council
UNEP	United Nations Environment Programme
UNHCR	United Nations High Commissioner for Refugees
UK	United Kingdom
US or USA	United States of America
USTR	United States Trade Representative
WHO	World Health Organization
WIPO	World Intellectual Property Organization
WTO	World Trade Organization

Chronology of Events

Date/Month	Event
September 1946	USA presents a Suggested Charter for an International Trade Organisation of the United Nations for consideration.
April–October 1947	Intense negotiations on the GATT text held in Geneva.
30 October 1947	Negotiators produce the final GATT text along with the outcome of tariff negotiations.
1 January 1948	GATT, with 23 countries as the contracting parties, enters into force on a provisional basis.
21 November 1947–24 March 1948	International Conference on Trade and Employment meets in Havana and draws up the Havana Charter for an International Trade Organization. Fifty-three countries sign the Havana Charter for finalizing the ITO.
1950	President Truman of the USA announces that he would not submit the Havana Charter for Congressional ratification. Without the participation of the USA, the ITO could not come into existence.
1955	At the request of the USA, the GATT Contracting Parties grant a waiver to the USA in order to enable it to impose quantitative restrictions on imports of agricultural products, otherwise not permitted under provisions of Article XI:1 of GATT.
1960	At the request of the USA, a GATT Working Party established to deliberate on the problem of market disruption in the textiles and clothing sector. This provided the basis for imposition of quotas on exports of these products, and hit a large number of developing countries for almost forty-five years.
1973	Launch of the Tokyo Round of Multilateral Trade Negotiations at the GATT.
1979	Conclusion of the Tokyo Round of Multilateral Trade Negotiations at the GATT. It resulted in a fragmentation of GATT rules.
November/ December 1982	GATT Ministerial Meeting held. Attempt by the USA to initiate Multilateral Trade Negotiations on new issues, such as Services and trade in high technology, fails.
September 1986	Launch of Multilateral Trade Negotiations at Punte del Este, commonly referred to as the Uruguay Round. It included mandates on services and intellectual property rights.

Date/Month	Event
April 1989	Resistance of India to negotiating standards of protection of intellectual property rights collapses.
December 1991	Arthur Dunkel, Director General of GATT, tables his text, the draft 'Final Act' (commonly referred to as the Dunkel Draft) which formed the substantial basis for concluding the Uruguay Round.
November 1992	Blair House accord between the EC and the USA for resolving some of the contentious issues related to agriculture during the Uruguay Round. The bilateral accord formed the basis of some of the obligations in the Agreement on Agriculture.
15 December 1993	Negotiations under the Uruguay Round concluded.
15 April 1994	Marrakesh Agreement Establishing the WTO signed by 123 governments at Marrakesh (Morocco).
January 1995	WTO comes into existence.
December 1996	Working Groups established to study issues on Investment, Competition, and Government Procurement during the 1st Ministerial Conference of the WTO held in Singapore. Further, the Council for Trade in Goods was mandated to undertake exploratory work on trade facilitation. These four issues are collectively called Singapore Issues. In addition, some WTO Members agreed to eliminate customs duties in IT products, popularly called the Information Technology Agreement.
May 1998	Temporary moratorium on customs duties on electronic transmissions agreed at the 2nd Ministerial Conference of the WTO held in Geneva.
October/November 2001	Stormy meeting of General Council of the WTO held for deliberating on the Draft Ministerial Declaration prepared by the Chairman of the GC and the DG WTO on their own responsibility for the WTO Ministerial Conference to be held in Doha.
November 2001	Doha Round of Multilateral Trade Negotiations (formally called the Doha Work Programme) launched at the 4th Ministerial Conference of the WTO held in Doha.
13 August 2003	Joint proposal on issues in the Agriculture negotiations under the Doha Round submitted by the USA-EU.
20 August 2003	Coalition of developing countries led by Argentina, Brazil, India, and South Africa created and its counter-proposal to the USA-EU joint proposal submitted in Agriculture negotiations.
10–14 September 2003	5th Ministerial Conference of the WTO held at Cancun (Mexico). A coalition of fifty-two developing countries created opposing the Singapore Issues. The meeting collapses without taking any substantive decision. At the last stage of the meeting, the EU proposes to drop two of the four Singapore Issues from the negotiating agenda under the Doha Work Programme.

Date/Month	Event
11–12 December 2003	G-20 meeting organized at Brasilia, Brazil, which conveys a strong signal about the cohesion of the coalition and its continued relevance.
31 July–1 August 2004	General Council of the WTO decides to take 3 issues—Investment, Competition, and Government Procurement—off the negotiating agenda under the Doha Work Programme.
December 2005	6th Ministerial Conference of the WTO held at Hong Kong. Progress made in various areas of the negotiations under the DWP.
December 2008	Draft Modalities Text in Agriculture includes a provision allowing subsidies on account of procurement of food stocks not to be included in the Amber Box, provided the procurement is for supporting low-income or resource-poor farmers.
2009–2011	With the exception of trade facilitation, very little progress in negotiations on most of the other issues under the DWP.
November 2012	G-33 seeks to revive issues related to public stockholding for food security purposes by making a submission proposing an amendment to the AOA.
January–May 2013	Trade facilitation negotiations make some progress. Link between this issue and food security established. On the issue of food security, the EU signals its willingness to work towards a peace clause.
3–7 December 2013	The IX Ministerial Conference of the WTO, held in Bali (Indonesia), adopts the Bali Peace Clause. Negotiations concluded on the Trade Facilitation Agreement. General Council mandated to meet by 31 July 2014 to adopt a Protocol of Amendment to the Marrakesh Agreement to include the TFA in the WTO family of agreements.
2 July 2014	Citing lack of progress on the issue of public stockholding for food security purposes, India declines to join the consensus on the Protocol of Amendment on the TFA.
27 November 2014	General Council adopts the decisions on public stockholding for food security purposes and the TFA Protocol. This provides satisfaction to India on the former issue, while unblocking the inclusion of the TFA in the WTO agreements.
December 2015	The X Ministerial Conference of the WTO, held in Nairobi (Kenya), fails to endorse by consensus continuing the Doha Round.
December 2017	The XI Ministerial Conference of the WTO, held in Buenos Aires (Argentina) collapses without any concrete outcome. Joint Statement Initiatives launched without multilateral consensus for initiating negotiations on some issues including Electronic commerce, Investment Facilitation, and Domestic Regulation in Services

Date/Month	Event
2 October 2020	India and South Africa submit a proposal at the WTO seeking a temporary waiver from certain provisions of the TRIPS Agreement for prevention, containment and treatment of Covid-19.
12–17 June 2022	XII Ministerial Conference of the WTO held in Geneva. A partial agreement on Fisheries Subsidies finalized. Ministerial Decision on the TRIPS Agreement adopted.
26 February–2 March 2024	XIII Ministerial Conference of the WTO held in Abu Dhabi. A non-multilateral initiative related to investment facilitation finalized by 124 WTO members.

1

Studying Negotiating Strategies

An Introduction

1.1 Introduction

Since time immemorial, negotiations have played a significant role in resolving conflicts between nations. In a fast-changing modern world, fractured by deep political strife and economic friction, negotiations remain an indispensable part of statecraft. While issues may vary, the core of each negotiation remains partly a struggle over distribution of gains and losses—who gets what and how much.[1] In this context an important question needs to be addressed—what factors determine the final outcome of negotiations? Relative political and economic power among the countries at the negotiating table is crucial in determining the distribution of gains from negotiations. A sound understanding of negotiating strategies, backed by the wisdom to use the appropriate one according to the situation, is another important determinant of the eventual success at the negotiating table. In terms of diversity of issues and their complexity, as well as their far-reaching economic impacts on nations, few state-to-state negotiations over the past eight decades can match the multilateral trade negotiations at the erstwhile Agreement on Tariffs and Trade (GATT) and subsequently the World Trade Organization (WTO).[2] These negotiations have not only created an overarching framework of rules for the conduct of international trade among more than 160 countries today, but have also imposed constraints in many areas of domestic policymaking. This book is a modest attempt at exploring the strategies deployed by the developed countries in multilateral trade negotiations at the GATT and the WTO (collectively referred to as GATT/WTO), and the response of developing countries at the negotiating table.

No doubt there are many informative books on negotiating strategies, which are also relevant for trade negotiations. However, as these books

Strategies in GATT and WTO Negotiations. Abhijit Das, Oxford University Press. © Abhijit Das 2025.
DOI: 10.1093/9780198934431.003.0001

do not focus on international trade in a comprehensive manner, they fail to capture many of the unique characteristics and dynamics of multilateral trade negotiations. How are GATT/WTO negotiations different from commercial negotiations, which are the subject matter of most of the books on negotiations? First, unlike commercial negotiations which are among private entities, multilateral trade negotiations at GATT/WTO involve sovereign governments. Second, while GATT/WTO negotiations involve more than a hundred countries, it is unlikely that any commercial negotiation would have so many parties at the negotiating table. Third, as GATT/WTO negotiations are undertaken on the basis of consensus, theoretically, each negotiating party can exercise a veto power. Fourth, the conduct, conclusion, and entry into force of the outcomes of the international trade negotiations are treated as parts of a single undertaking, whereby nothing is agreed until everything is agreed. In the light of these unique features of GATT/WTO negotiations, it may not always be relevant to mechanically extend the lessons and strategies discussed in the context of commercial negotiations to international trade negotiations. A few books that delve into negotiating strategies in the context of multilateral trade negotiations at the GATT/WTO provide deep insights and learnings about strategies—but mainly from the perspective of the developed countries.[3] While a comprehensive analysis of negotiating strategies from the perspective of developing countries is mostly missing, a few accounts stand in sharp contrast.

Based on his personal experience, T.S.R. Subramanian provides a witty account of policymaking and administration in India in multiple spheres and different contexts. In respect of trade policymaking in India, he provides insightful anecdotes which illustrate some of the strategies deployed by the United States of America (USA) and other developed countries in international trade negotiations.[4] There is a feeling of deja vu, as the strategies mentioned by Subramanian in the context of GATT negotiations in early 1980s, continue to be effectively deployed by the developed countries many decades down the line.

The personal papers and published writings of Bhagirath Lal Das, India's former ambassador to the GATT, provide a detailed account of happenings at this forum during the early 1980s. As he was an influential player at the negotiating table, his personal account is of immense value. He provides a graphic description of the push by the USA and the

European Economic Community (EEC) to initiate a comprehensive round of multilateral trade negotiations during the GATT Ministerial Meeting held in 1982. He has made some pithy and insightful observations about negotiating strategies that were deployed by some countries. The strategies used by him, as the chairman of GATT Council in 1982, provide many practical lessons in reconciling vastly divergent negotiating positions and striking compromises among countries.[5] In addition, he has provided detailed suggestions on how developing countries should engage in multilateral negotiations.[6] These contain valuable ideas on negotiating strategies for developing countries.

In trying to deduce some of the strategies deployed in multilateral trade negotiations from a general description of events at the negotiating table and developments outside it, a few other books are worth mentioning. The memoir of Celso Amorim, the sagacious Foreign Minister of Brazil during 2003–2010, provides insights into the negotiating dynamics during the crucial years when the Doha Round of the WTO was active. Some of his candid observations shed light on the strategies deployed by the key players at the negotiating table. To illustrate, he provides a fascinating account of the game of shifting alliances between Brazil, the European Union (EU), India, and the USA. His analysis of the internal dynamics within G-20, an influential coalition of developing countries spearheaded by Brazil and India, provides important clues to the strategies deployed to retain the cohesion and effectiveness of the coalition.[7] Mohan Kumar, a long-standing Indian trade negotiator of repute, has provided detailed accounts of the developments and dynamics at the negotiating table during the Uruguay Round of multilateral trade negotiations at the GATT, and subsequently at the WTO. Some interesting negotiating strategies can be inferred from the rich details contained in his books.[8] K.M. Chandrasekhar, who was India's ambassador to the WTO during the initial years of the Doha Round, provides a peek into some of the strategies behind important developments at the negotiating table.[9] Tussie (2009) provides indirect evidence of how research can become an indispensable part of a larger negotiating strategy of developing countries.[10] A chapter of this book analyses the influence of research in the coalition strategy of some developing countries in the context of negotiations on agriculture during the Doha Round of the WTO.[11] Bilal et al. (2011) examine the asymmetries in trade negotiations, including on aspects such as forum selection, agenda setting, issue selection, and participation in negotiations.[12] Some negotiating strategies can be gleaned from this book as well.

In the overall context of studying negotiating strategies at the GATT/WTO, the following questions are likely to arise: first, why study negotiating strategies; and second, why study negotiating strategies at the GATT/WTO, particularly at a time when the multilateral trading system seems to be retreating and supposedly losing its relevance? Answers to these questions will partly explain the relevance of this book.

1.2 Rationale for Studying Strategies in Multilateral Trade Negotiations at GATT/WTO

The importance and role of strategy in securing favourable outcomes in negotiations cannot be denied. There are at least four reasons for studying negotiating strategies. First, skills relevant for negotiations can be acquired and enhanced by studying negotiating strategies. Second, a study of strategies deployed by negotiators in the past can prepare the negotiators of today to be more effective at the negotiating table. Third, even in vastly different contexts, just a handful of variables determine success at the negotiating table. Lessons at the negotiating table in one context can become highly relevant for negotiations in another setting. Fourth, many strategies are deployed repeatedly. By acquiring insights into strategies used in the past, negotiators would be better prepared to respond, if they are confronted with similar strategies from others at the negotiating table.

Turning to the question regarding the continuing relevance of the GATT/WTO, trade agreements throughout history have 'affected the lives, either for better or for worse, of billions of people around the world and across generations'.[13] Rules of the GATT and the WTO are no different. While the rules under the GATT were applicable mainly to international merchandise trade, the rules under the WTO cover larger categories of economic activities. These include rules on services (e.g., banking, construction, education, telecommunications, transportation, tourism, etc.) and protection of intellectual property (e.g., patents, copyrights, trademarks, industrial designs, etc.). Further, the rules that countries negotiate have a bearing not only on international trade, but also on many areas of domestic policymaking not directly linked to international trade. While formulating any new policy or implementing new schemes, governments have to be mindful that these do not fall foul of WTO rules. Given the far-reaching impact of WTO rules on government functioning in many areas, it is in the interest of all countries, particularly the developing countries, to seek to ensure that the rules that they negotiate promote their development objectives. As the strategies adopted by the key players have influenced the outcomes of the GATT/WTO negotiations, this clearly establishes the relevance of studying strategies deployed in the past for drawing lessons for future negotiations at the WTO. However, on account of the deadlock in WTO negotiations under the Doha Round and the protests against globalization worldwide, doubts could be raised whether the WTO would continue to remain relevant.

In a world of increasing inter-dependence among nations in commercial and economic relations, international trade cannot be conducted efficiently without an overarching framework of rules applicable to a large number of countries. In the absence of any such overarching framework, in order to trade with other countries in a predictable manner, a country would need to sign bilateral agreements with each of its trading partners. Clearly, this is not an efficient solution. It is, therefore, unlikely that the comity of nations can dispense with a common framework of rules to which a large number of countries subscribe.

We must not completely rule out the possibility of the WTO being replaced by another inter-governmental organization performing functions similar to that of the WTO, but with the rules covering many economic activities that are presently missing from the WTO rulebook. In this context, it is relevant to note that the ambit of the GATT, whose rules were largely confined to merchandise trade, got expanded to include services and intellectual property rights (IPR) at the WTO. This template of preserving existing rules, while negotiating additional disciplines in new areas, could be replicated in the future. A successor organization to the WTO, if it gets established, is likely to include most of the substantive rules of the WTO. In addition, it could include rules on certain new issues being strongly pushed by the developed countries. What these new issues could be is a matter of detail. As such an organization will have to provide for future negotiations on trade and many other related economic matters, the relevance of studying strategies at the WTO gets further enhanced, and not diminished, even if the WTO were to be replaced by a successor organization.

Having established the utility and relevance of studying negotiating strategies at the GATT/WTO, it is pertinent to get a flavour of negotiating strategies from some commonly heard statements at the negotiating table. Multilateral trade negotiations frequently involve the art of conveying messages laden with multi-layered meanings. Often, these messages are a part of the strategy deployed by parties to meet their negotiating objectives—a subject discussed in the next section.

1.3 Discerning Negotiating Strategies from Statements Commonly Heard at the Negotiating Table

While we may have an intuitive understanding of strategic thinking, nevertheless it is useful to provide a non-technical description of this concept. In most situations in life, we do not take decisions in a vacuum. We are surrounded by decision-makers whose choices and aims could conflict with ours. But they also include some potential allies. Our decisions and choices must allow for the conflict and also leverage the co-operation. Such interactive decisions are called strategic and the plan of action appropriate to them is called a strategy.[14] While there is considerable literature which differentiates between strategy and tactics, for the purposes of this book the two terms have been used inter-changeably.

Negotiators thrive on strategies. Shrewd negotiators may purposely misrepresent their preferences in order to secure a greater share of gains from negotiations. Negotiators may feign surprise, dissimulate, and display other behaviour patterns that may be a part of the strategy to steer the negotiations in their favour.[15] Thus, statements commonly heard at the negotiating table can capture the state of negotiation, and also reflect the thrust and parry of strategies of the parties. It is relevant to briefly discuss the significance and the meaning latent in some of the statements and conversations made at the negotiating table, which would be familiar to experienced negotiators.

I am willing to agree to X provided you agree to Y: This represents bargaining in conditional terms. A party is willing to commit but with strings attached. Its commitment is contingent on the other party providing reciprocal concessions. While conditional commitments allow negotiations to move forward, this is a useful mechanism to link outcomes on different issues. It shows an openness to move ahead, but also retains the possibility for a party to claw-back from its stand without losing face, if the other is unable to meet the demands made on it. It would come as no surprise that the party making this statement may itself be offering less, but demanding more from others.

If I lower my demand on this issue, what are you willing to give me in return? This commonly heard remark captures the essence of a negotiation—showing flexibility in one area in order to garner gains in another. However, before responding to the offer as conveyed in the remark, an astute negotiator must make a judgment based on three aspects. First, did the other party initially pitch its demand high so that it could secure concessions from other parties by lowering its demand as the negotiation progresses? Second, how crucial is the issue for the party that is offering to lower its demand? Third, how crucial is the issue for meeting the negotiating objectives of the responding party? If the responding party judges that the party offering to lower its demand would actually provide a significant, relevant, and meaning concession, it could consider reciprocating with a matching concession from its side.

I wish I could agree to what you want, but this would create a crisis in my firm/country. In the interest of being constructive, I would have given up this demand, but my stakeholders back home attach high priority to this issue: These remarks demonstrate how a skilful negotiator can use its domestic constraints in order to strike a hard bargain. As observed by a scholar, 'lamenting domestic constraints under which one operates is the natural thing to say at the beginning of a tough negotiation'.[16] This is often resorted to by negotiators from the EU, who are hesitant to show much flexibility at the negotiating table on the plea that their hands are tied by their Member States.

While I am fully on board with your demands, I will need to get the green light from my superiors: On hearing such a statement, a negotiator must immediately become alert that the person articulating it is not empowered or authorized to make concessions. Parties that grant concessions to such negotiators, often fail to secure reciprocal concessions from the other party. It is also possible that the need to refer the matter to superior authorities may merely be a ruse for seeking more time to examine the issue.

Since the negotiations are not moving ahead, let us lower our expectations and split the difference: On the face of it, this statement appears to be a constructive and fair way of resolving deadlocks in negotiations. However, more often than not, the party making the offer has already set up the situation in such a way that splitting the difference would skew the distribution of gains in its favour. This is best illustrated with an example. I wish to buy a second-hand car and approach the car owner with an offer of $10,000. The owner refuses to accept anything less than $20,000. If at this stage the difference between the offer and demand were to be split, the negotiated price would have been $15,000. However, neither side offers to split the difference. After many rounds of bargaining, I raise my offer to $16,000 and the owner has come down to $18,000. If at this stage the owner makes the offer to split the difference, the negotiated price would be $17,000. Clearly, the owner has been strategic in starting with a high demand but being parsimonious in making concessions during the negotiation. By splitting the difference, he has skewed the distribution of the negotiated outcome in his favour. The initial position of the contesting parties, and their respective pace of concessions, determine who gains more from splitting the difference.

If you continue to rigidly stick to your stand, we may as well close the discussions and return home empty handed: While this remark might suggest an imminent breakdown in the negotiations, often the reality may be different. The party making this statement has assessed that the other party is desperate to secure a deal, but is unwilling to make concessions. The statement is intended to exploit the downside for the other party of collapse of the negotiation, in order to compel it to show more flexibility. If the lease of my house is expiring within a week and I am desperate to get it extended, I would be willing to show flexibility and raise my offer under the threat of the owner to call off the negotiation.

This is not the only game in town; I have other options outside this negotiating table: Similar to the previous statement, this statement is also intended to compel other parties to move from their rigid positions and show more flexibility. The party making the statement seeks to exploit the fact that it may have a more attractive option outside the negotiating table—commonly referred to as 'best alternative to a negotiated agreement' (BATNA) in the theory on negotiation. A party with higher payoffs from alternatives outside the negotiations table is likely to play hardball at the negotiating table and succeed in influencing other parties to become more accommodative to its interests. Overall, a party's bargaining power depends on the alternatives available to it.[17] Further, availability of alternatives may influence the type of strategies and tactics that parties may choose to deploy.[18] When developing countries lack alternatives, their approach might be confined to accommodate or confront. They may not engage fully in the negotiation. However, if alternatives are available, they may actually have an interest in engaging constructively in the negotiation process.[19] Alternatives may also help developing countries to implement value-creating strategies.[20]

Are you sure what you are asking is in your interest? While I may not be affected if all of us agree to what you want, but surely this would hurt the interest of XYZ parties: Such remarks are made to create doubts in minds of other parties about their true interest in negotiation. It is not always that the parties have a clear idea about what is in their own interest.[21] These remarks may, in some situations, also be aimed at exploiting inadequate understanding of the issues among some parties for securing an agreement. Similar remarks may also be made to discredit the negotiating position of some of the other parties, or to create fissures among coalition of parties. In a multi-party setting, by pretending to be indifferent to the outcome of the negotiation, a party can skilfully use the interests of other parties as a strategy for promoting its own interest.

I am not demanding this concession. It is in the interest of some of your stakeholders: This statement seeks to exploit the conflicting interests among certain stakeholders in a country. This is best comprehended through an example. In many developing countries while manufacturers of a product normally seek protection against imports, downstream users of that product generally lobby their government for liberalizing its imports. In such a situation of conflict, exporters of the product from other countries leverage this opportunity by getting their negotiators to argue for the interests of the downstream users of the product in the importing country. By disguising the interests of its exporters and instead presenting it as being in the interest of some stakeholders of the other country, experienced negotiators can get the better of others at the negotiating table.

Our industry is quite upset that we are giving you concession in X. As we need to mollify them, you would have to give us more concessions in Y: Using supposed pressure from domestic constituencies as a justification for extracting concessions from others at the negotiating table is a strategy commonly used by the developed countries. By exaggerating the value of the concession which it has made in X, the party articulating the above statement is seeking to achieve two latent objectives. By granting concessions in X, it has got the other side hooked onto the negotiating table. It is also confident that after securing the concession in X, the other side would be more willing to grant concessions in Y. It cannot be ruled out that the concession granted in X may have been of little or no significance to the first party, but it has used the excuse of domestic pressure to secure concessions in other areas.

We welcome your step, which is in the right direction: The party making this statement is actually not appreciating the move by the other side. In fact, it is conveying a clear message that it expects more concessions from the other side.

1.4 Role of State Strength in Determining Negotiating Outcomes

Not all countries are equally influential in shaping the outcome of multilateral treaties. It is often acknowledged that US negotiators enjoy certain built-in advantages, including the power of military, size of its economy, and the historical influence of the country.[22] The party that has more time and options will have the edge over others at the negotiating table.[23] Relative power of parties at the negotiating table is often crucial in determining the final outcome, particularly in the context of state-to-state negotiations. But what exactly constitutes relative power at the negotiating table? According to one view 'distribution of power implies a hierarchical distribution of resources and abilities simultaneously across many issue areas that almost always result in outcomes favourable to those at the top of the hierarchy'.[24] It can also be viewed as the ability to bring to the negotiating table other countries with the objective of extracting concessions from them.

The traditional realist conception of international relations defines a state's power in terms of its economic and military capabilities[25]—often viewed as the essential sources of 'raw' or 'hard' power that determine the position of states within an overarching global power hierarchy.[26] According to an eminent scholar 'international organizations mirror the distribution of power in the international system and act as vehicles for the interests of the most economically and militarily powerful states'.[27] This further entrenches the relative distribution of power in favour of the powerful. As more powerful states have better resources and greater diplomatic capacity, hence they are more influential in addressing the problem at hand. Conventional wisdom dictates that parties with more relative power are successful in imposing their solutions to the problems at the negotiating table in different negotiating contexts and across all issues. Most of the other parties are left with little choice, other than silently acquiescing to the wishes of the powerful. However, in two respects, this might be changing.

First, many scholars have identified a shift in global power relations as one of the most important transformations in modern history.[28] In the context of global economic governance, it is widely assumed in literature that the rise of new powers, including India and Brazil, can be explained by their growing economic might.[29] However, there is another dimension to this debate. It was not the economic might of these two countries, but their leadership of developing countries coalitions, which enabled them to exercise influence in the negotiation.[30] Second, it is no longer possible to predict the outcome of negotiations based exclusively upon global distribution of power.[31] Some studies posit that weak powers or developing countries can influence negotiated outcomes in their favour by following strategies such as taking advantage of negotiation sequences and procedures[32], following well-informed and skilful technocratic strategies[33], finding loopholes in great power protectionism towards them[34], or taking advantage of competitors for their resources or markets.[35] These studies suggest that while developing countries and developed countries may not be on an equal footing, by using suitable negotiating strategies, the developing countries can reduce the odds arrayed against them at the negotiating table. In the context of diffusion of power among state and non-state actors, coercive strategies by the strong may no longer be effective.[36] The twin developments—rise of new powers and diffusion of power—create opportunities and challenges at the negotiating table. A great power may no longer use or be able to use its authority to stamp its will and impose solutions in negotiations through take-it-or-leave-it dictum. Instead, the negotiated outcome is more likely to be based on creative problem-solving, which requires convergence of interests of dominant powers, rising powers, and weaker players. However, this can also lead to negotiating gridlocks and longer negotiation periods.[37] It may not be inaccurate to conclude that while the dominant powers are no longer able to close negotiations in line with their preferences and interest, the rising powers do not yet have the clout to clinch state-to-state deals based on their interests.

Before concluding the discussion on the role of state strength in determining outcomes, it is useful to note that this variable can result in unbalanced and asymmetric agreements at the negotiating table. It is relevant to recall the sagacious words of Francois de Callieres articulated more than 300 years ago:

> 'There is no durable treaty which is not founded on reciprocal advantage, and indeed a treaty which does not satisfy this condition is no treaty at all, and is apt to contain the seeds of its own dissolution. Thus, the great secret of negotiation is to bring out prominently the common advantage to both sides and to link these advantages that they may appear equally balanced to both parties. For this purpose, when negotiations are on foot between two sovereigns, one the greater and the other the less, the more powerful of those two should make the first advance, and even undertake a large outlay of money to bring about the union of interests with his lesser neighbor . . . The secret of negotiation is to harmonize the interests of the parties concerned.'[38]

1.5 Domestic Determinants of International Economic Negotiations

The role of power of a state relative to others at the negotiating table looks at the external dimension. What about variables within a country that are crucial in influencing the negotiating approach of a country?

State-to-state economic diplomacy negotiations now involve state-firm and firm-firm negotiations, thereby adding multiple layers of complexities to the dynamics of negotiations. In most negotiations a state has to contend simultaneously with international and domestic pressures.[39] It is now generally accepted that any international negotiation is accompanied with parallel domestic negotiations among different stakeholders within a negotiating party. Negotiations being a two-level game evocatively captures the reality that governments have to negotiate simultaneously with domestic and international actors in order to strike deals.[40] Reality of the two-level game has been attested to by many experienced negotiators. In the words of Robert Strauss, a key negotiator during the Tokyo Round of GATT negotiations: 'During my tenure as Special Trade Representative, I spent as much time negotiating with domestic constituents (both industry and labor) and members of the US Congress as I did negotiating with our foreign trading partners.'[41] Thus, the outcome of negotiations has to be acceptable not only to the other parties at the negotiating table, but also to the domestic stakeholders within the party.

Domestically, different groups of stakeholders might pull in different directions and exert pressure on the state to pursue negotiating approaches that would promote their interest. In turn, at the negotiating table at the international level, negotiators seek ways to maximize the satisfaction of their domestic pressure groups. How does the two-level game play out, and what are its implications for negotiations? In this section we look at how the two-level game requires the state to resolve conflicting domestic interests while seeking to maximize domestic interests at the negotiating table.

1.5.1 Resolving Multiplicity of Conflicting Domestic Interests

States are rarely monoliths in terms of domestic interest on various issues. On many issues that are the subject of negotiations, different groups of stakeholders within a country may get arrayed against each other. To illustrate, lowering import tariffs on silk fabrics would be beneficial for the domestic apparel industry. However, if the country also has a domestic industry producing silk fabric, that industry would oppose lowering of tariffs. If reduction in import tariffs is a subject matter of negotiation, the state would need to balance the conflicting interests of apparel industry and fabric industry. In such a situation of conflict, whose interest prevails in the negotiation depends on several factors, the key being which stakeholders are mobilized and which are not. This affects the balance of forces between actors in situations of conflict. In an effort to overcome failure of competing groups to mobilize themselves, some countries have even created institutional mechanisms to actively reach out to different groups of stakeholders. These efforts also help negotiators address what has been described as 'a risk from not knowing stakeholder preferences and, therefore, their reactions to a future agreement'.[42] In the context of international trade negotiations, it is not merely different business and industry groups that lobby with the state to push their interests in the negotiations. Many government and non-government actors seek to influence policymaking and negotiating stance. These include national parliaments, regulatory bodies, interest groups with economic objectives, consumer organizations, sub-federal level government entities, and civil society organizations. The presence of a large number of domestic players with varying interests, at times even conflicting with each other, makes the reality of negotiations as a two-level game extremely complicated.

1.5.2 How Do Interactions at the Domestic Level Affect Negotiating Flexibility

It is relevant to note that as more domestic players start to have a greater say in policymaking, negotiating flexibility is likely to diminish.[43] It is also likely that involvement of more departments of the government, apart from the ministry responsible for trade negotiations, makes negotiation positions more protectionist.[44] Thus, with a view to expediting the negotiations, there may be a tendency in the ministry responsible for undertaking international trade negotiations to seek inputs only from a limited number of ministries. Another perspective is that deals between core actors can, in fact, potentially enhance negotiating flexibility.[45] Further, regular interaction between negotiators and their domestic stakeholders reduces asymmetry on the part of stakeholders and also allows the stakeholders to monitor the negotiators' actions.[46] This can also reduce the risk of the final agreement being rejected by the stakeholders.

Interaction between negotiators and domestic stakeholders creates options for negotiators. It is not unusual for negotiators to deliberately bemoan, and perhaps exaggerate, the rigid stance of their domestic constituents, in order to tilt the negotiation in their favour. Negotiators with accommodating constituencies have to make concessions in negotiations, while negotiators with unyielding stakeholders garner greater distribution of gains.[47] This tendency is often exploited by American negotiators to drive a hard bargain.[48] As noted by a scholar 'the power of a negotiator often rests on a manifest inability to make concessions and meet demands'.[49] The main theme running through the views of these scholars is that lamenting domestic constraints and highlighting domestic pressures can be gainfully leveraged by skilled negotiators to strike a more favourable bargain.

1.6 Chapter Scheme of the Book

While strategy is often discussed in developing countries, it is rarely pursued at the WTO negotiating table in a systematic manner. Without any formal training in negotiations, most trade diplomats are compelled to rely on their inherent skills, observation, and occasional mentoring. Perhaps a paucity of scholarship dealing with negotiating strategies at the GATT/WTO from the perspective of developing countries has contributed to this malaise. This book is a modest attempt at blending academic literature with first-hand account of negotiators for comprehending strategies used by different countries in multilateral trade negotiations at the GATT/WTO. Based on unparalleled access to detailed first-hand accounts of key negotiators from India and other developing countries spanning four decades, it discerns and analyses a large number of strategies deployed at the negotiating table. Many strategies discussed in it appear to have escaped the attention of researchers. Further, the 'insider' contribution adds value to the known knowledge about how some of the well-known strategies are practised, which is often lacking in most theoretical accounts from academics who stand at an arms-length from these negotiations. First-hand accounts are valuable, but these come with the concomitant risk of memory being selective and the negotiators attempting to distort events to put themselves in a better light. In most instances, the outcomes of the negotiations bear out the account of the negotiators discussed in the book. In some cases, the accounts were verified from others who were either present at the negotiating table or were aware of the developments. However, not all the accounts mentioned in this book could be verified from other sources.

With a view to enhancing the understanding of the role of strategy in trade negotiations among countries, particularly multilateral trade negotiations, this book seeks to address the following four related questions: what strategies have been used by the developed countries in striking deals in multilateral trade negotiations and finalizing agreements at the GATT/WTO, what has been the response of developing countries to these strategies, what strategies were used by some developing countries in securing their negotiating interests in a few exceptional episodes and what should developing countries do in order to be more strategic in multilateral trade negotiations? While comprehending these issues, the reader will also get answers to many intriguing questions including the following: why is it that before a trade agreement is finalized at the WTO, most of the contesting countries at the negotiating table articulate strong misgivings which magically vanish after the deal is sealed; how was it that a minister who perhaps lacked many of the textbook qualities of an effective negotiator, changed the course of multilateral trade negotiations on some issues; how did it come about that the country, which was responsible for the collapse of negotiations, was never blamed for it, but other countries were censured for the failure; after having refused to even negotiate face-to-face with a party on a particular issue for more than one year, what compelled a powerful party to concede to the core demand of the other side within an hour of the first meeting? By exploring the strategies deployed in multilateral trade negotiations at the GATT/WTO, this book seeks to answer these questions, as well as many others. Consequently, the readers would appreciate how developing countries can think strategically and put their best foot forward in multilateral trade negotiations.

In order to understand the strategies in trade negotiations it is relevant to know from a theoretical perspective what is meant by the term 'negotiation', what are the different types of negotiations, stages of negotiation, and strategies. Most analysis of negotiating strategies are confined to examining distributive and integrative strategies. The former is often referred to as value-claiming strategy, which treats negotiations as a zero-sum game where gain for one party necessarily involves a loss for others. On the other hand, integrative strategies seek to attain goals that create gains for many parties at the negotiating table. While these are useful concepts, nevertheless an in-depth study of negotiating strategies has necessarily to go beyond these two approaches at the extreme ends of the spectrum. Chapter 2 seeks to address these fundamental aspects of negotiations. This sets the stage for providing an overview of the negotiating process at the GATT/WTO and analysing the participation and role of developing countries in these negotiations. Chapter 3 traces the origin and evolution of the multilateral trading system from the days of the negotiations for the International Trade Organization during 1946–1947 to the present day of the WTO. It highlights how the outcome of the multilateral trade negotiations are increasingly setting limits on government policymaking in many areas, including those not directly related to international trade.

Chapters 4 and 5 describe the negotiating strategies and tactics deployed by the developed countries in GATT/WTO negotiations. Chapter 4 focuses on strategies away from the negotiating table, while Chapter 5 discusses the strategies used at the negotiating table. These chapters provide a deeper understanding of what strategies have worked and at times the limitations of certain strategies. Chapter 6 shifts attention to the developing countries and examines the constraints faced by them in GATT/WTO negotiations. The chapter also discusses their response to challenges posed by the strategies of the developed countries.

Despite facing challenges on multiple fronts, there have been episodes during the Doha Round of multilateral trade negotiations at the WTO where some developing countries were able to secure their negotiating objectives, albeit in limited areas. Chapters 7–9 describe three episodes in which favourable outcomes were achieved by certain developing countries during the Doha Round negotiations at the WTO. As these were accomplished despite the odds being stacked against the developing countries, these episodes should rightly be considered to be impressive and striking. While in only one of the three episodes discussed in these chapters was a negotiated solution finally achieved, this does not diminish the importance of the outcomes in the other two cases. In fact, the specific developing countries that were the protagonists in these two episodes achieved most of their negotiating objectives. Thus, the two episodes also merit inclusion as illustrations of striking deals.

Success of a large number of developing countries in achieving many of their negotiating objectives in these three episodes cannot be attributed to luck and fluke; strategy appears to have played a crucial role in their success. It would, thus, be relevant to examine the three episodes specifically from the perspective of negotiating strategies. Chapters 7–9 include a description of what a developing country, or a group of developing countries, sought to achieve on a limited set of issues at the negotiating table; how the negotiations in that area evolved; and finally looking back to identify and discuss the strategies deployed by the concerned developing countries in the negotiations. The three episodes provide important lessons for developing countries, while preparing to engage in negotiations and also at the negotiating table itself. The three chapters extend the framework used by Deveraux et al. for analysing negotiating strategies and dynamics.[50] Chapter 7 discusses the strategies deployed by India and other developing countries to remove three out of the four Singapore Issues from the Doha negotiating agenda. Chapter 8 focuses on how in a crisis situation, a coalition of developing countries, commonly referred to as the G-20, emerged. Formation of the G-20 compelled the USA, the EU, and other countries to confront a shifting negotiating landscape. The strategies adopted by this coalition for retaining its internal cohesion, as well as significantly influencing the progress in Agriculture negotiations after August 2003, are discussed in this chapter. Chapter 9 discusses strategies used by India at the last stage of the negotiations on public stockholding for food security purposes and its linkages with negotiations on the Trade Facilitation Agreement.

Chapter 10 discusses some implications for practice and theory of the negotiating episodes discussed in the book. Drawing on some of the strategies suggested by ancient scholars in the context of wars between kingdoms, it also provides an overview of the key points a strategic trade negotiator should bear in mind. Further, the chapter discusses theories in two areas—coalitions and forum shifting—and proposes how to bridge crucial gaps between theory and experience of countries in GATT/WTO negotiations. In order to foster strategic thinking, the chapter, and also the book, concludes by suggesting some questions that trade negotiators should ask throughout the negotiations.

It is hoped that trade negotiators who read this book will feel encouraged to adopt suitable strategies in the negotiating arena. Another objective of the book is to highlight how concepts of negotiation theory get applied in practice in multilateral trade negotiations and also discuss their limitations. This should not only motivate trade negotiators and practitioners of the craft to pay careful attention to what academics in this field have to say, but should also stimulate the latter to test their ideas and theories in the crucible of the experience of trade diplomats. This would be mutually rewarding for both groups. The efforts of the author would not be in vain if even a handful of persons strive towards either of these two objectives.

Notes

1. John S. Odell, 'Chairing a WTO Negotiation', *Journal of International Economic Law* 8, 2 (June 2005): 425–448.
2. It may be noted that the legal provisions of the GATT became subsumed in the WTO.
3. See, for example, Charan Devereaux, Robert Z. Lawrence, and Michael D. Watkins, *Case Studies in US Trade Negotiation Vol 1: Making the Rules* (Washington D.C.: Institute for International Economics, 2006).
4. T.S.R. Subramanian, *Journeys Through Babudom and Netaland: Governance in India* (New Delhi: Rupa publisher, 2004), 160–171.
5. Personal papers of Bhagirath Lal Das, available with the author.
6. Bhagirath Lal Das, *The WTO and the Multilateral Trading System: Past, Present and Future* (London and New York: Zed Books and Penang: Third World Network, 2003), 210–224.
7. Celso Amorim, *Acting Globally, Memoirs of Brazil's Assertive Foreign Policy*, trans. Michael Marsden (Maryland, MD: Hamilton Books, 2017).
8. See, Mohan Kumar, *Negotiation Dynamics of the WTO: An Insider's Account* (Singapore: Palgrave Macmillan, 2019); and Mohan Kumar, *India's Moment* (Gurugram: HarperCollins Publishers, 2023).
9. K.M. Chandrasekhar, *As Good as My Word: A Memoir* (Gurugram: HarperCollins Publishers, 2022).
10. Diana Tussie (ed.), *The Politics of Trade: The Role of Research in Trade Policy and Negotiation* (Dordrecht, Leiden and Boston: Republic of Letters Publishing BV, 2009).

11. Amrita Narlikar and Diana Tussie, 'Multiple Access Points: Knowledge Creation for the Group of Twenty', in *The Politics of Trade: The Role of Research in Trade Policy and Negotiation*, ed. Diana Tussie (Dordrecht, Leiden and Boston: Republic of Letters Publishing BV., 2009).
12. Bilal Sanoussi, Philippe De Lombaerde, and Diana Tussie (eds), *Asymmetric Trade Negotiations* (London and New York: Routledge Taylor and Francis Group, 2011).
13. Martin Guzman and Joseph E. Stiglitz, 'Post-Neoliberal Globalization: International Trade Rules for Global Prosperity', *Oxford Review of Economic Policy*, 40 (2024): 282–306.
14. Avinash K. Dixit and Barry J. Nalebuff, *Thinking Strategically: The Competitive Edge in Business, Politics, and Everyday Life* (New York and London: W.W. Norton and Company, 1991), 205.
15. Robert Putnam, 'Diplomacy and Domestic Politics: The Logic of Two-Level Games', *International Organization* 42, 3 (1988): 427–460.
16. Geoffrey W. Harrison, in *Successful Negotiation: Trieste 1954*, ed. John C. Campbell (Princeton, NJ: Princeton University Press, 1976), 62.
17. John S. Odell, *International Trade Bargaining Under Uncertainty: Cognitive Hypotheses and Evidence* (University of Southern California, 1993).
18. David A. Lax and James K. Sebenius, 'The Power of Alternatives or the Limits to Negotiation', *Negotiation Journal* (April 1985): 163–179.
19. I.William Zartman (ed.), *Positive Sum: Improving North-South Negotiations* (New Brunswick, NJ: Transaction Books, 1987).
20. J.P. Singh, 'Negotiating the Global Information Economy Weak Powers and Globalism: The Impact of Plurality on Weak-Strong Negotiations in the International Economy', *International Negotiation*, 5 (2000): 449–484.
21. Howard Raiffa, *The Art and Science of Negotiation* (Cambridge, MA: Harvard University Press, 1982), 274.
22. Richard Solomon and Nigel Quinney, 'Foreword' by Madeline Albright, in *American Negotiating Behavior: Wheeler-dealers, Legal Eagles, Bullies and Preachers*. (Washington, D.C.: United States Institute of Peace, 2010), ix.
23. Raymond Saner, *The Expert Negotiator* (Leiden/Boston: Martinus Nijhoff Publishers, 2012), 66.
24. J.P. Singh, 'Weak Powers and Globalism: The Impact of Plurality on Weak-Strong Negotiations in the International Economy', *International Negotiation*, 5 (2000): 449–484.
25. Paul Kennedy, *The Rise and Fall of the Great Powers: Economic Change and Military Conflict from 1500 to 2000* (New York: Random House, 1987).
26. A.F.K. Organski, *World Politics* (New York: Knopf, 1968).
27. Kristen Hopewell, 'Different Paths to Power: The Rise of Brazil, India and China at the WTO', *Review of International Political Economy* 22, 6 (2015): 1128–1158.
28. See, for example, Mark Beeson and Stephen Bell, 'The G-20 and International Economic Governance: Hegemony, Collectivism, or Both', *Global Governance*

15, (2009): 67. Andrew Hurrell, 'Hegemony, Liberalism and World Order: What Space for Would-Be Great Powers?' *International Affairs* 82, 1 (2006): 1–19; Matthew D. Stephen, 'Rising Regional Powers and International Institutions: The Foreign Policy Orientations of India, Brazil and South Africa', *Global Society* 26, 3 (2012): 289–309.

29. See, for example, Andrew Cooper, and Daniel Schwanen, 2009. Bill Emmott, *Rivals: How the Power Struggle Between China, India and Japan Will Shape Our Next Decade* (New York: Harcourt, 2008). Robert H. Wade, 'Emerging World Order? From Multipolarity to Multilateralism in the G20, the World Bank, and the IMF', *Politics & Society* 39, 3 (2011): 347–378. Fareed Zakaria, *The Post-American World* (New York: Norton, 2008).
30. Hopewell, 'Different Paths', 1128–1158.
31. John S. Odell, 'From London to Bretton Woods; Sources of Change in Bargaining Strategies and Outcomes', *Journal of Public Policy* 8, 3/4 (1990): 287–315.
32. William Zartman, *The Politics of Trade Negotiations between Africa and the European Economic Community: The Weak Confront the Strong* (Princeton, NJ: Princeton University Press, 1971).
33. John S. Odell, 1985. 'The Outcomes of International Trade Conflicts: The US and South Korea, 1960–1981', *International Studies Quarterly* 29 (1985): 263–286.
34. David B. Yoffie, *Power and Protectionism: Strategies of the Newly Industrializing Countries* (New York: Columbia University Press, 1983).
35. Joseph M. Grieco, 'Between Dependency and Autonomy: India's Experience with the International Computer Industry', *International Organization* 36 (Summer 1982): 609–632.
36. J.P. Singh, 'Diffusion of Power and Diplomacy: New Meanings, Problem Solving, and Deadlocks in Multilateral Negotiations', *International Negotiation* 20 (2015): 73–88.
37. J.P. Singh, 'Diffusion of Power', 73–88.
38. François de Callières, *On the Manner of Negotiating With Princes; On the Uses of Diplomacy; the Choice of Ministers and Envoys; and the Personal Qualities Necessary for Success in Missions Abroad* trans. A.F. Whyte (Boston and New York: Houghton Mifflin Co., 1919), 110.
39. See, for example, Peter J. Katzenstein, ed., *Between Power and Plenty: Foreign Economic Policies of Advanced Industrial States* (Madison, WI: University of Wisconsin Press, 1978); and Stephen D. Krasner, *Defending the National Interest: Raw Materials Investments and US Foreign Policy* (Princeton, NJ: Princeton University Press, 1978).
40. Putnam, 'Diplomacy and Domestic Politics', 427–460.
41. Robert S. Strauss, 'Foreword' in Joan E. Twiggs, *The Tokyo Round of Multilateral Trade Negotiations: A Case Study in Building Domestic Support for Diplomacy* (Washington, DC: Georgetown University Institute for the Study of Diplomacy, 1987), vii.

42. Jannie Lilja, 'Domestic-Level Factors and Negotiation (In)Flexibility in the WTO', *International Negotiation* 17, 1 (2012): 115–138.
43. Lilja, 'Domestic-Level Factors', 115–138.
44. Valentin Zahrnt, 'Domestic Constituents and the Formulation of the WTO Negotiating Positions', *World Trade Review* 7, 2 (2008): 393–421.
45. Amrita Narlikar, *International Trade and Developing Countries: Coalitions in the GATT and WTO* (London: Routledge, 2003).
46. Lilja, 'Domestic-Level Factors', 115–138.
47. John S. Odell, *International Trade Bargaining under Uncertainty*.
48. Putnam, 'Diplomacy and Domestic Politics', 427–460.
49. Thomas C. Schelling, 1960, *The Strategy of Conflict* (Cambridge, MA: Harvard University Press, 1960), 29.
50. Charan Devereaux, Robert Z. Lawrence, and Michael D. Watkins, *Case Studies in US Trade Negotiation Vol 1: Making the Rules* (Washington D.C.: Institute for International Economics, 2006).

2

Negotiation

Definition, Types, and Stages

2.1 Introduction

This chapter presents a brief overview of the theoretical literature on definition, categories, and stages of a negotiation. This will provide the lexicon and the framework for analysing the developments at multilateral trade negotiations and identifying strategies deployed by countries in these negotiations. However, a caveat is in order. Although there is no universally accepted definition of negotiation, its categories and stages, this does not have a significant bearing on the analysis contained in this book. For the purpose of this book, we adopt the stages of a negotiation as described by the eminent scholar Howard Raiffa in his classic titled *The Art and Science of Negotiation*.[1] Section 2.2 discusses a definition and categories of negotiation. Section 2.3 provides an overview of different stages of a negotiation. Sections 2.4–2.7 discuss the procedural and substantive aspects relevant to each stage of a negotiation, different behaviour patterns frequently encountered, and questions of strategy that confront the parties. These sections also provide the essential features of the procedural aspects of WTO negotiations and address a common strategy in multilateral negotiations—countries linking issues to advance their interests at the negotiating table. Section 2.8 summarizes the key messages of this chapter.

2.2 Negotiation: Definition and Categories

Think of a child crying, in order to extract an additional bar of chocolate from a parent. Envision a young boy attempting cartwheels and

Strategies in GATT and WTO Negotiations. Abhijit Das, Oxford University Press. © Abhijit Das 2025.
DOI: 10.1093/9780198934431.003.0002

similar other antics for attracting the attention of the girl whom he fancies. Imagine a fawning courtier, seeking to extend his influence over a king. Picture an executive from a steel firm haggling with an official from a mining company over the price of iron ore. Visualize a political personality threatening a civil servant with dire consequences if his desires are not fulfilled. Recall the image of the president of a country frowning at the prime minister of another nation, while ironing out differences in a trade deal. Our intuition tells us that in all these diverse situations one person, or a party, is seeking to secure something from another person, or the other side—a typical negotiating episode. It would not be incorrect to state that negotiations permeate almost all aspects of our life, both private and public. But what exactly constitutes a negotiation?

2.2.1 Negotiation: Definition

There is no commonly accepted definition of negotiation. In most situations, an intuitive understanding of negotiation—a means of resolving differences—is adequate for comprehending its broad objective. It is interesting to note that in the modern classic on negotiation—*The Art and Science of Negotiation*—the author, Howard Raiffa, chooses not to define this term explicitly. Instead, he focuses on disputes in different settings and contexts, involving varying degrees of complexity, to lucidly explain the objective, features, and process of a negotiation. However, an intuitive approach to understanding negotiation, without defining at least certain aspects of it, may not be adequate for our purpose. In order to understand the multi-dimensional nature of a 'negotiation', a comprehensive definition of this term is discussed in this sub-section.

According to Saner 'negotiation is a process whereby two or more parties seek an agreement to establish what each shall give or take, or perform and receive in a transaction between them'.[2] This definition suggests the following: a negotiation is not a one-off event, but a process involving two or more parties; the objective of a negotiation is an agreement establishing a relationship between the negotiating parties, which could be codified in a formal document, or be merely an informal word-of-mouth understanding; as the objective of a negotiation is to seek an agreement, the outcome is expected to be jointly determined by the negotiating parties involving give-and-take from a spectrum of options available to different parties; negotiated outcomes involve distribution of gains between two or more parties; and the negotiating process must provide some degree of satisfaction to each party.

Intrinsic in a negotiation is the assumption that parties are more anxious to agree than to disagree. While at the initial stage of a negotiation parties have expectations that may appear to be difficult to reconcile, mutual dependence among the parties becomes the pivot for them to reassess their expectations and resolve their differences. Without any give and take, negotiations would be difficult, if not totally impossible. As observed by former US president John F. Kennedy, 'we cannot negotiate with people who say what's mine is mine and what's yours is negotiable'. It may be an accurate characterization to state that negotiation is a process that seeks to harness cooperation in a situation of conflict for achieving a joint solution.

2.2.2 Types of Negotiation

While there is no universally recognized categorization of negotiations, some authors have used the following two parameters in this regard: number of parties and number of issues involved in a negotiation. Negotiating dynamics and strategies followed by the parties tend to be somewhat different, depending on the type of negotiation. In terms of the degree of complexity, negotiations involving just two parties and one issue are perhaps the simplest and negotiations involving many parties and multiple issues the more complicated. While a negotiation between two parties is usually undertaken without the intermediation of a chair, in multi-party negotiations it is common to appoint a chair for facilitating the negotiating process. Further, a two-party negotiation may require less of a formal and structured approach as compared to a multi-party negotiation. However, the most fundamental difference between two-party and multi-party negotiations is the interplay among shifting coalitions, which can have significant impact on how the gains of negotiation are distributed among the parties.[3] Finally, while multi-party negotiations involving multiple issues are no doubt complex, the possibility of trade-offs across issues increases considerably. This provides a fertile ground for achieving joint solutions through issue linkage, a topic that will be elaborated upon later in this chapter.

2.3 Stages of Negotiation

Why is it relevant to understand the different stages of a negotiation? As will be elaborated upon in this book, parties adopt different strategies depending on the stage of a negotiation. A strategy that might be useful to a party at the initial stage, might become counter-productive for it at later stages. Further, the amount of resources that are required to be allocated and the areas of expertise available in the negotiating team for negotiating effectively are not uniform throughout the entire course of most negotiations. This book uses the following four sequential stages of negotiation in its analytical framework as identified by Raiffa: setting the stage, opening gambit, negotiating dance, and end game (or end play, as Raiffa calls it).[4] It should be noted that there is no clear demarcation between different stages—each stage transitions into the subsequent stage almost seamlessly. The subsequent four sections of this chapter discuss the procedural and substantive aspects of what is involved in each stage of a negotiation and a few questions of strategy that confront the parties.

2.4 Setting the Stage

The first stage in the negotiating process is akin to warming up before the race actually begins. As the negotiating agenda influences the later phases of the negotiation, agenda setting becomes an important phase. Parties engage in an open discussion and bring on to the table all the issues they aspire to pursue in the negotiation. This provides an opportunity to all parties to assess the likely implications of the final outcome of the negotiation, which, in turn, might influence their strategy for deciding the issues to be included in the negotiating agenda. The importance of this stage should not be underestimated, as questions regarding the issues to be negotiated, procedural aspects of the negotiation including sequencing of issues for negotiation, and rules regarding conclusion of the negotiation and implementation of outcomes are addressed in this phase. It is also relevant to point out that where to negotiate—the forum itself—can also become a contentious issue.

At times, some parties may need to expend resources and implement strategies for getting other parties, who might otherwise be reluctant, on to the negotiating table. This becomes particularly relevant for some parties, if the reluctant parties are precisely those from whom favours and concessions will be eventually sought. At this stage how parties frame the issues for negotiation can have a crucial bearing on how these are perceived by other parties in terms of addressing their interests. This can become an effective strategy in convincing naysayers to come to the negotiating table. In sum, conflicts over the sequence and number of issues can compel states to devote scarce resources to pre-negotiation with the sole objective of arriving at a negotiable agenda.[5] Some of these aspects are discussed in the subsequent sub-sections.

2.4.1 Agenda Setting

Agenda setting entails jointly identifying the issues that would be discussed in greater detail during the subsequent phases of the negotiation. Agenda setting in negotiations involving a single contentious issue may be less complicated, but also extremely rare. In contrast, multi-party negotiations typically involve a mix of a large number of issues that are identified by parties during agenda setting. In some situations, a larger number of issues on the agenda, rather than just a handful of issues, can facilitate resolving the negotiating tangle. This counter-intuitive occurrence is explained by the fact that bargains and trade-offs between parties are easier to strike through the strategy of linking issues at the table—gains for a party in one area get tied to its concessions in another issue. Of course, the negotiating process may become unmanageable, if the agenda is overloaded with too many issues.

The normal practice at the GATT/WTO is to launch a round of multilateral trade negotiations through a consensus declaration by the trade ministers. The ministerial declaration identifies the issues for negotiation and their scope. While the initial trade rounds under the GATT were mainly about negotiating tariff reductions, subsequent rounds of multilateral trade negotiations have included a plethora of issues, many of which may not be directly related to trade. At this stage, issues are discussed in broad and general terms, without delving into technical details. The tendency of a party would be to push for inclusion of issues in which it has a deep interest and aspires to secure gains through the negotiation. On the other hand, if a party apprehends that it might have to grant concessions on certain issues, it might resist their inclusion in the negotiating agenda. If all parties at the negotiating table adopt a self-centred and narrow approach, this would frustrate their endeavour to arrive at joint solutions. It may, therefore, not be surprising to witness relatively more flexibility among the negotiating parties at GATT/WTO negotiations to accommodate interests of others at this stage, as compared to subsequent stages.

The declaration initiating a trade round is often preceded by intense negotiations for deciding the issues that would be on the negotiating agenda. To illustrate, on account of the insistence of the USA to include issues related to trade in services, intellectual property rights, and performance requirements, deciding the negotiating agenda for the Uruguay Round of the GATT in 1986 proved to be extremely divisive and time consuming. History was repeated in 2001 when the developed countries sought the inclusion of the four Singapore Issues (relationship between trade and investment, interaction between trade and competition policy, transparency in government procurement, and trade facilitation) in the negotiating agenda of the Doha Round. At the GATT/WTO, agreeing to a negotiating agenda may constitute a mini-negotiation encompassing all the stages of a negotiation.

Parties often pursue multiple strategies in order to get issues of their choice included in the agenda. While a party may strongly push for issues of its interest, it may not be unusual to find it also championing issues that others might not want on the agenda. By resorting to this strategy, a party exploits the weak points of others and gets its way by reluctantly agreeing to refrain from championing issues that others find uncomfortable to discuss. In return, the other parties agree to the issues of interest to the first party.[6]

How an issue is framed and what objective is ostensibly sought to be pursued through it, crucially influences outcomes in agenda setting.[7] The way a question is posed can make certain objectives of evaluation salient and thereby influence the outcome.[8] Further, 'ideas that are seen as legitimate, appropriate, or correct have a better chance of prevailing' in policy contests.[9] In the context of setting the agenda for the Uruguay Round of multilateral trade negotiations, protecting windfall profits and commercial interests of giant pharmaceutical companies was framed as a moral endeavour to prevent theft of intellectual property by developing countries. Through this clever framing, issues related to intellectual property rights were included in the agenda.

Deciding the issues for negotiation has to be accompanied with decisions on the procedural aspects in order to create an efficient and conducive environment for moving forward. The next sub-section turns to this crucial aspect.

2.4.2 Procedural Aspects of Negotiations

The stage of agenda setting is not confined to deciding the issues for negotiation, but also requires agreement among negotiating parties on many procedural questions—will the issues be negotiated simultaneously or sequentially; will negotiation proceed on the basis of a single text; who will prepare such a text; how will deadlocks be resolved; if partial agreements are reached on some issues can these be implemented, despite negotiations on other issues remaining inconclusive; is a chair envisaged for facilitation the negotiation; what role would the chair have; how will the final package of the negotiated outcomes be implemented etc.?

WTO negotiations follow the principle of 'single undertaking', which requires negotiations in different areas to be conducted in parallel, concluded at the same time and the outcomes enter into force simultaneously. However, agreements reached at an early stage may be implemented on a provisional or a definitive basis. Further, members have to mandatorily become party to all multilateral agreements. They cannot pick and choose to become a signatory to some multilateral agreements, while staying out of other agreements. Members have the flexibility to stay out of certain agreements, called plurilateral agreements in WTO parlance, that have been negotiated by only a handful of WTO members.

As achieving consensus among negotiating parties on these procedural issues can become contentious, thereby diverting attention from the substantive negotiating issues, efficiency demands that clear rules on the procedure be agreed to at an early stage of the negotiation. The choices made by parties on procedural aspects can influence the entire course of a negotiation. An important procedural aspect of most multi-party negotiations—role of the chairman—is discussed below.

The chairman's role is to grasp the core concerns of the differing countries/groups and assess the limits to which they are likely to converge to a compromise. Thereafter, the chairman has to balance these limits and come out with a position which, in his opinion, will not stretch any group beyond its tolerance limit. By becoming privy to privileged information acquired from parties through formal/informal processes, the chair can assess the true preferences of countries shorn of distortions and strategic behaviour. The chair often utilizes the privileged information available to it for suggesting compromises based on an assessment of the underlying zone of agreement.

The chair may also be required to filter proposals made by parties and consolidate some of them in a single negotiating text. This is based on the chair's subjective assessment of proposals that many parties might agree to and those that are likely to be rejected by most parties. The selection of proposals in the single negotiating text could be based on the convergence of views among parties, or in power-based setting it could be based on the interest of the dominant parties. As a chair's decisions and actions become crucial in determining how the gains of a negotiation will be distributed among the parties, they expect the chair to be objective and even-handed. How a constructive chair can facilitate making compromises in a situation fraught with deep divergences among parties on technically complex issues is discussed in Box 2.1. This relates to the preparation of the draft negotiating text for consideration of ministers at the GATT Ministerial Meeting (MM 82) in 1982.[10] After the Preparatory Committee (Prep Com) under the chairmanship of the ambassador of Canada had failed to produce a text on which all the countries could agree, disaster loomed large before the GATT Contracting Parties. In their desperation the DG of GATT, Arthur Dunkel, the USA and the EEC suggested that Bhagirath Lal Das, India's Ambassador to GATT and the chairman of the GATT Council, should undertake to prepare an agreed text for the MM 82.

Within a short span of two weeks, which included a punishing schedule of twenty hours of negotiations each day, Das salvaged a hopeless crisis

Box 2.1 Constructive Role of the Chair

What strategies did Bhagirath Lal Das, as chairperson of the GATT Council, adopt in bridging the divergences among the parties and striking compromises for producing a consensus text for MM 82?

First, Das took the bold decision to ignore the text prepared by the chairman of Prep Com, and instead opted to prepare a new text. Second, instead of working simultaneously on all contentious issues, he chose to take up relatively less complex subjects for discussion first and then move to more difficult subjects. The whiff of initial success on the less complex subjects demonstrated the value of the evolving document to the contracting parties. This created an incentive for them to remain engaged in the process and induced them to show flexibility when discussions progressed to more complex issues. Third, through a gentlemen's agreement, he persuaded countries that once the text on a subject had been agreed, they would not back-track and reopen the text in subsequent stages of the negotiation. This infused stability and certainty in the negotiating process. Fourth, and perhaps most important, Das combined his deep technical knowledge of each subject with political astuteness to comprehend where the balance of different interests lay. He could correctly assess how far a controversial point could be pushed without straining the opposite side beyond the breaking point. This created confidence in the process and facilitated bridging the divergence in differing views on each subject.

Fifth, while the process of creating an agreed text was being undertaken in the consultation group comprising fourteen contracting parties of GATT, the final text required consensus of the entire GATT membership. Das would keep ambassadors of key countries not included in the consultation group informed about the progress being made within the consultation group and also seek their inputs. Through these meetings with some of the ambassadors individually, Das created a sense of ownership and stake among countries not part of the consultation group. This helped minimize the possibility of failure when the final text was submitted to the full GATT membership for its endorsement. Sixth, Das persuaded the EEC and the USA to show flexibility and drop their demand for having a text on new issues, such as Services and High Technology. In a pragmatic move, the ambassador of the EEC agreed that there was no reason to jettison the entire agreed text on the pretext that no agreement could be reached on the new issues.

Source: Personal papers of Bhagirath Lal Das, India's former ambassador to the GATT, available with the author.

situation and crafted a finely balanced document that was approved by consensus by the entire GATT membership during the meeting of the GATT Council held on 16 November 1982 for further consideration by the ministers at MM 82. This effort and skill of Das in producing a consensus document and preventing MM 82 from collapsing without a ministerial declaration drew considerable appreciation from the GATT diplomats. As the GATT spokesman put it after the meeting of the GATT Council, 'while it is customary at such meetings for delegates to offer protocol congratulations to the chairman, there was no mistaking the warmth and sincerity of the statements from all delegates' for Das.[11] The value of this agreed document was heightened further when, after days of intense wrangling and heated discussions, the ministers adopted the 'Das Document', with minor changes and additions on the new issues, as the agreed outcome of MM 82[12].

2.4.3 Getting Recalcitrant Parties onto the Negotiating Table

At the initial stages of a negotiation, it is not unusual for a party to be confronted with a unique challenge—some of the other parties, which it views as potential sources for seeking concessions, may be unwilling to come on to the negotiating table. What strategies are adopted to bring the reluctant party on board? Four strategies can be identified. First, granting side payments to these parties in an unrelated area, on the condition that these parties join the negotiation. Second, with a view to luring the foot draggers, include issues of interest to them in the negotiating agenda. Third, frame the issues in the negotiating agenda in such a way that the naysayers anticipate gains for themselves from the negotiation. If none of these strategies succeed, then a powerful party may use credible threat and 'alter the balance of power in a significant way' compelling others to come to the negotiating table.[13] Thus, by increasing the cost for the reluctant parties of staying away from the negotiation, a powerful party is often able to get its way with the reluctant parties. Some of these strategies are discussed in detail in subsequent chapters of the book. With the agenda for negotiation being set, procedural rules decided and all relevant parties at the negotiating table, what happens next?

2.5 Opening Gambit

After warming up by setting the stage for the negotiations, parties com mence substantive negotiations by presenting their position and specifically stating what they expect from the negotiating process. While each party may privately assess what it really seeks to achieve, public disclosure may be a bit different. Further, each party privately decides its reservation price—the maximum price that the buyer is willing to pay, or the minimum price the seller will accept.

The key questions at this stage are the following: when should a party make the opening gambit and how should it determine where to aim; which party should make the first move; what happens when the seller aims too low in his initial demand; and is there any advantage for a party in letting other parties make the first move? These are often strategic questions, as the right opening move can prove to be decisive in determining the subsequent terms of engagement among parties.

A well thought out opening gambit—say, the price stated by a seller—provides the base for subsequent discussions. Often, the other parties use the opening gambit of the first mover as a cue for their response. If the buyer is not adequately prepared for the negotiation, its perception of the zone of possible agreement might get influenced by the opening bid of the first mover. If the seller has demanded \$3000, the buyer is likely to respond by offering a bit lower, say \$2500. It would be rare to find a buyer who responds with an offer of \$1000. The buyer has got trapped into bargaining on the terms offered by the seller!

The first mover faces two risks—aiming too high or setting its sight too low. In our example above, if the buyer perceives \$3000 to be an excessively high price, she may ignore the opening gambit of the seller and instead pitch her offer at \$1000. If the seller has indeed aimed too high, she would be compelled to bargain around $1000, and not around her own initial offer of $3000. Further, an extreme initial offer may require the first mover to make disproportionately larger concessions at later stages of the negotiation.[14] By over-pitching the initial demand, the seller has let the initiative slip into the hands of the buyer. In the process, the seller has also unwittingly conveyed her ignorance about the market situation to other parties. This fact can be exploited by other parties to beat down the first mover. Further, the seller might not be perceived as being serious in the negotiation.

Remaining silent, but absorbing everything that is happening at the negotiating table and outside it, and allowing other parties to take the initiative may suggest a lackadaisical and casual attitude in negotiation. At times, it may well be so. But before we reproach this behaviour, it is instructive for negotiators to draw lessons from military history going back to Napoleon's attack on Russia in 1812. Resisting the strong urgings of the Russian tsar, Alexander, and his courtiers, to launch a counter-offensive, the Commander-in-Chief of the Russian army, General Kutuzov, ostensibly chose inaction. His seemingly passive response lured Napoleon's army to advance deep into the Russian territory without encountering any resistance. Not being prepared for a winter campaign, Napoleon's army of 800,000 men was inflicted a crushing defeat by a raw Russian army of half its numerical strength. General Kutuzov, who believed that the two most powerful warriors and heroes of the battlefield are patience and time,[15] should remind negotiators that instead of being the first mover at the negotiating table, at times wisdom lies in playing the waiting game by letting others seize the initiative.

It is possible that on some contentious issues the negotiating mandate may include ambiguous language for bridging the gap between divergent positions. This creates the ground for protracted discussions at this stage on the scope of the negotiating mandate. During the Uruguay Round there was a stand-off for more than two and a half years on whether the ministerial declaration provided a mandate for negotiations on the standards of protection for intellectual property rights. Similarly, during the Doha Round, for more than two years there were contrasting views regarding the mandate on the four Singapore Issues.

In GATT/WTO negotiations, an important procedural step during this phase is the establishment of separate bodies, referred to as negotiating groups, where negotiations in various broad areas are undertaken. To illustrate, during the Doha Round, separate negotiating groups were constituted for issues related to market access in goods; agriculture; services; trade remedies (comprising anti-dumping and subsidies issues) etc. Participation in negotiations in each group is open to all WTO members. Further, the members appoint a chairman for each negotiating group, as well as for the Trade Negotiating Committee—the highest body for overseeing negotiations in all areas.

2.6 Negotiating Dance

After the parties have made known their initial position on the issues under negotiation, what happens next? The third stage of negotiations has been evocatively described as the negotiating dance.[16] During this stage, parties seek to defend their positions through detailed arguments and logic, but may also try to question and run down the stand of some others at the table. As compared to the previous stages, during the stage of negotiating dance there is greater information sharing among parties. The parties move away from their initial positions and through an iterative process of offers and counter-offers seek to come closer to a joint solution. Negotiation flexibility—defined as movement by a party from its initial position toward a compromise position[17]—is often evident during this stage of negotiation. If the gulf between aspiration of parties and their ability to make concessions cannot be bridged, the grace of negotiating dance may get replaced by acrimonious noise of a discordant orchestra. What is the fundamental dynamic that is evident at this stage?

At this stage parties try to align the negotiation with their reservation price or reservation point—the point beyond which a party may break off the negotiations.[18] In any negotiation, each party has a reservation point, which is also referred to as a 'bottom line'. If I am negotiating to buy a second-hand car, the maximum amount that I am willing to pay is my reservation point. The minimum amount that the seller is willing to accept is its reservation point. If the maximum price the buyer is willing to pay is lower than the minimum price the seller is ready to accept, there is no zone of agreement. In such a situation, negotiation will break down, unless the parties revise their reservation price.

Much of the action at the table during the phase of negotiating dance happens with three objectives centred around the reservation point: first, each party seeks to assess the reservation point of the other party, while keeping its own a secret; second, based on its reservation point and its assessment of the reservation point of the other parties, each party makes an educated guess about the zone of possible agreement; and third, each party tries to steer the compromise or joint solution as far away as possible from its reservation point, while staying within the zone of possible agreement. Thus, the buyer will seek to clinch the deal as far below as possible from its reservation point. On the other, the seller will aim to compromise at a price that is as high as possible from the minimum price it is willing to accept.

At this stage of negotiations at GATT/WTO an important milestone is reached when the chair of the negotiating group makes an assessment of the proposals that command consensus of the negotiating parties, proposals that are supported by a large number of parties and proposals that have the backing of very few members. Based on her personal assessment, the chair submits a consolidated text. Since the consolidated text usually becomes the basis for further negotiations, members have to be alert in evaluating the assessment of the chair. As negotiations proceed further, gaps in country positions on various issues are expected to get narrow. The convergence on various issues gets reflected in subsequent iterations of the chair's consolidated text. It contains rules for determining the concessions that each member would provide, as well as the rules that countries would be obligated to adhere to on various issues in the specific area of the negotiation. If considerable progress has been made in different areas of the negotiations, the negotiations move to the final phase.

In order to get a better understanding of the dynamics at this stage of a negotiation, some key questions need to be addressed. What are the broad types of strategic approaches pursued by parties? In a negotiation involving multiple issues, how do inter-connected issues influence the course of the negotiation?

There is no commonly accepted typology of different negotiating strategies. Most of the strategies adopted by parties during negotiations, and particularly at the stage of negotiating dance, can be described at the generic level as being either distributive or integrative strategy. Distributive strategy involves 'dividing a fixed resource between parties where one party's goals are in conflict with those of the other party'.[19] Distributive strategies come into play when one party can gain only at the expense of others. It is essentially a zero-sum game—gain for one party is a loss for the other. In situations of distributive strategy, parties have opposite interests. Bargaining over a single issue, say the sale of a second-hand car, involves distributive strategy. Higher the sale price, more is the gain garnered by the seller. On the other hand, the interest of the buyer is diametrically opposite to that of the seller. Lower is the price at which the deal is struck, higher is the buyer's gain. Distributive strategies figure prominently when negotiations centre around a single issue, or if multiple issues are negotiated sequentially. Distributive strategies are also referred to as value claiming strategies—insisting on an agreement under which one side gains at the expense of the other.[20]

In contrast to the zero-sum game of distributive strategies, integrative strategies aspire to create gains for the parties at the table. Integrative bargaining can be defined as 'attainment of objectives which are not in fundamental conflict with those of the other party'.[21] Integrative strategies become possible when several issues are negotiated simultaneously as a package. This creates opportunities for trade-offs involving different issues. A party may gain in some issues, while the other party may benefit in another set of issues. To illustrate, I may be willing to pay a price for a car slightly above my reservation price, provided I get after-sale service at a price significantly lower than what I may otherwise have to pay. This deal would not have matured if just the sale of the car was on the table, or the two issues—sale price of the car and the cost of after-sales service were negotiated sequentially one after another. Simultaneous negotiation on both the issues created new values, which helped in clinching the bargain. While each party seeks to maximize its gains, in integrative bargaining each party also attempts to limit the loss for the other. It is also referred to as value creating strategy. It involves attaining goals that are not in fundamental conflict.[22]

In state-to-state negotiations, integrative bargaining is facilitated by having a single negotiating text, which covers all issues on the table. Creativity at the negotiating table can be an important ingredient in recognizing potential linkages among issues for fostering integrative strategies.[23] The linkage between concessions in agriculture in return for concessions in industry has been identified as being crucial in successful conclusion of the Uruguay Round of multilateral trade negotiations at the GATT—an example of integrative bargaining.[24]

Apart from the distributive-integrative classification of negotiating strategies, it is also relevant to briefly mention two other categories commonly encountered in literature and also frequently used by negotiators—hard-soft strategies and offensive—defensive strategies. Strategies involving threats and public criticism are characterized as hard, while those involving publicly praising the other side, making conciliatory statements and attempting compromises are labelled as soft strategies. Offensive strategies involve demanding concessions and threatening harmful action. On the other hand, defensive strategies are reactions to another party's value claiming offensive strategy. It essentially requires a party to protect itself against granting concessions, or losing value, sought by the other party.[25]

An important strategy used by parties in negotiations is issue linkage—party X agrees to a particular demand of party Y, while party Y in turn agrees to a specific demand of party X in another issue area. In other words, success of party X in securing its negotiating objective on a particular issue is contingent on it accepting a demand of country Y in another area. Issues are said to be 'added', 'combined, or linked when they are simultaneously discussed for joint settlement'.[26] 'Linkage between unrelated or only loosely-related issues in order to gain increased leverage in negotiation is an ancient and accepted aspect of diplomacy.'[27] As observed by a scholar-diplomat 'the great secret of negotiation is to bring out prominently the common advantage to both sides and to link these advantages that they may appear equally balanced to both parties'.[28]

After edging closer during the negotiating dance, the denouement is about to be reached. What to look out for if it is a successful grand finale or a litany of shattered ambitions from a collapsed negotiation?

2.7 End Game

The end game is the final phase of a negotiation. This is a seize or freeze phase. Will the negotiators seize the moment and strike a deal; or will they freeze into inaction caused by their deeply entrenched negotiation positions? The long and numerous hours spent in coaxing, cajoling, arguing one's point, defending against thrusts from others at the table, standing firm in the face of attempts at arm-twisting, navigating around obstacles, finally meld together to either produce an agreement or result in a chaotic collapse. Normally shorter in duration as compared to the phase of negotiation dance, the end game is extremely tense and intense. As parties try to prevent the negotiated outcome from slipping through their grasp, much of the deal making and compromises happen at the last minute. Without having the luxury of referring issues for final decisions to their superiors, or promising to revert to the parties at a later date, negotiators have to do considerable thinking on their feet. As the deadline for concluding the agreement approaches, even a hardened negotiator is prone to committing errors. During the last stage of a negotiation, negotiators require considerable patience, persistence, and energy to stay the course.

The mask of posturing that might have been worn during the previous phases tends slip, revealing true interests, as parties scramble to extract concessions or make concessions, in an effort to strike bargains and conclude agreements. The iron fist behind the proverbial kid glove becomes evident as powerful parties use economic and political clout to achieve their objectives and close the negotiation. After successive days of almost round-the-clock negotiations, unless a sleep deprived and bleary-eyed negotiator is extremely careful, the temptation to be done with the negotiation and sign on to almost any agreement is difficult to resist. Differences are resolved by using ambiguous language, which allows contesting parties to interpret the agreement to their advantage. However, if parties fail to clinch a deal, acrimonious scenes—endless recriminations, bickering, spewing venom, and blaming others for the collapse of the negotiations—are quite common.

Success in the last phase of the negotiation normally depends on how the previous phases have proceeded. If most parties at the table are of the view that on many issues their interests have been addressed, they may be favourably inclined to endorse the final deal. However, if the negotiation has mostly addressed the interest of a handful of powerful countries in the previous phases, clinching the deal would require either a miracle, or a blatant demonstration of political and financial muscle by the few countries. What are some of the features of the end game in a successful negotiation? What should parties look out for in the emotion-laden concluding phase of a negotiation?

2.7.1 Strategic Hold-outs Until the Last Minute

In the last phase of a negotiation it is not unusual to witness a party granting concessions, which it had strongly resisted in the earlier stages. What explains this behaviour? If a party has secured most of its negotiating objectives, in an attempt to conclude the deal, it may be willing to concede some of the demands of other parties at the table. Irresolvable issues that were considered to be non-negotiable earlier, magically become non-issues.[29] Failure to provide concessions at the last stage may entail the risk of other parties walking off the table, thereby jeopardizing the agreement. Other parties may rightly guess this strategy and not back down from their demands. By holding out until the end, these parties may eventually extract some of the concessions, which they had sought earlier in the negotiation. However, this strategy runs the risk of failure, if some of the parties bring to bear their financial and political clout to conclude the negotiation, or the negotiation collapses on account of the hold-out parties.

2.7.2 Securing Insecure Contracts

The agreement has been successfully concluded, but can the parties remain assured that all the promises made during the negotiations will be respected and not prove to be brittle? Promises made by a party in the negotiations must not be taken at face value;[30] instead, they must be critically evaluated and formalized in a written document. Commitments that are oral, remain merely promises that cannot be enforced. As observed by an eminent scholar 'gentlemen's agreement that are not documented are fragile'.[31] A negotiator should also be cognizant that at times even commitments formalized in an agreement may prove difficult to implement. The following two commitments made by trade ministers at the Nairobi Ministerial Conference of the WTO in 2015 provide glaring evidence of this reality; first, members made a commitment to 'engage constructively to negotiate and make all concerted efforts to agree and adopt a permanent solution on the issue of public stockholding for food security purposes';[32] and second, it was agreed to pursue negotiations so that the developing country Members have the right to have recourse to a special safeguard mechanism (SSM).[33] Even nine years down the line, very little progress has been made by the WTO Members in fulfilling these commitments.

2.7.3 Avoiding Traps in Fine Print

Ensuring that the final legal text accurately reflects what was decided in the negotiating room, is an important task for negotiators during the final phase of a negotiation. Commonly referred to as 'legal scrubbing', it can sow seeds of subsequent disputes, if this is not carefully done. In this exercise, negotiators may have to resort to the formal record of the meetings in which key decisions regarding the legal texts were taken.

2.7.4 Requirement of Ratification of the Final Deal and Its Impact

Negotiators have toiled for long hours and the final agreement has been signed. But in the context of state-to-state negotiation, does signing of the treaty guarantee that the agreement would be implemented, or implemented without further modifications? A state-to-state treaty usually needs to be ratified by some, if not all, of the signatory countries, before it can be implemented. The process of ratification provides an opportunity to political groups and other stakeholders within a country to discuss the treaty before according approval. There are some prominent examples where the main country behind the negotiations eventually failed to ratify the final agreement. A relevant example in the trade context was the attempt by the USA to establish the International Trade Organization (ITO). However, this institution could not be established as the US president Truman failed to submit the final agreement for Congressional approval in 1950. This has been discussed in the next chapter.

2.7.5 Typical Behaviour Pattern in This Phase

During the final phase of negotiations, three behaviour patterns can be expected. First, some parties may, literally at the last minute, seek to extract additional concessions over and above what might have been agreed earlier by the parties at the negotiating table. A good illustration of such behaviour was the attempt during the final phase of the Uruguay Round by a developed country Member to seek some concessions on certain aspects of anti-dumping and countervailing duty investigations. Given its weight at the negotiating table, it was able to get its way even on some of its last-minute demands. However, not all parties at the negotiating table can pull off this strategy.

Second, the duration of future relationship between the parties is likely to determine the strategic behaviour at the end-game stage. If the parties are unlikely to interact in future after the deal has been sealed, some parties might adopt a hard-hitting approach. However, if the parties are expected to maintain long-term relationship, enlightened self-interest suggests that the powerful party should seek to be mindful of the interests of others at the negotiating table.

Third, amid self-congratulatory applause, in state-to-state negotiation even if a country has struck a bad deal, domestic political imperatives compel its minister or head of state to proclaim victory; rare is a political leader who can survive the backlash of the popular opinion domestically, if she openly confesses that the agreement is not favourable for the country. Everyone gives the appearance of being part of a large happy family, despite some parties seething with anger and discontentment internally at a lopsided deal. Evidently, the responses in public are aimed at creating a favourable impression on their domestic constituencies, despite the glaring deficiencies in the negotiated outcomes. At the conclusion of WTO ministerial conferences, it is not unusual to hear ministers and their high-level officials bombastically declaring the outcome to be 'stupendous', despite their countries having failed to secure any of their publicly articulated negotiating objectives.

2.8 Conclusions

This chapter has discussed various theoretical constructs that are relevant for understanding multilateral trade negotiations and gleaning insights about strategies deployed by parties to push their economic interests. These include a definition of negotiations, categories of negotiations, and stages of negotiations. In addition, the chapter has described certain typical behaviour patterns that a negotiator is likely to encounter at different stages of a negotiation. Further, this chapter has reflected on certain aspects that are crucial in multilateral negotiations involving multiple issues, including issue linkage, securing negotiated outcomes, requirement of ratification, etc. This sets the stage for a deeper analysis of strategies deployed at the multilateral trading system.

Notes

1. Howard Raiffa, *The Art and Science of Negotiation* (Cambridge, MA: Harvard University Press, 1982).
2. Raymond Saner, *The Expert Negotiator* (Leiden/Boston: Martinus Nijhoff Publishers, 2012), 21.
3. Raiffa, *Art and Science of Negotiation*, 255.
4. Raiffa, *Art and Science of Negotiation*, 126–130.
5. Janice G. Stein, ed., *Getting to the Table: The Processes of International Prenegotiation* (Baltimore, MD: Johns Hopkins University Press, 1989).
6. Saner, *Expert Negotiator*, 139.
7. Susan Sell and Assem Prakash, 'Using Ideas Strategically', *International Studies Quarterly*, 48, (2004): 143–175.
8. Raiffa, *Art and Science of Negotiation*.
9. Susan Sell, *Private Power, Public Law: The Globalization of Intellectual Property Rights* (Cambridge: Cambridge University Press, 2003).
10. The account of the preparatory work relating to MM 82 draws upon the personal papers of Bhagirath Lal Das available with the author.
11. Chakravarthi Raghavan, 'GATT Council recommends declaration for ministers', *SUNS- South North Development Monitor*, November 18 1982.
12. According to the WTO website MM 82 was 'widely regarded as a failure'. Source: https://www.wto.org/english/thewto_e/whatis_e/tif_e/fact5_e.htm. This view appears to be premised on the faulty assumption that lack of consensus on launching a new round of multilateral trade negotiations made MM 82 a failure.

13. Saner, *Expert Negotiator*, 49–50.
14. Raiffa, *Art and Science of Negotiation*, 127–128.
15. Leo Tolstoy, *War and Peace,* trans. Anthony Briggs (Penguin Books, 2009), 1139.
16. Raiffa, *Art and Science of Negotiation*, 128–129.
17. Daniel Druckman, 1995. 'Situational Levers of Position Change', *American Academy of Political and Social Science Annals*, 542 (November 1995): 61–80.
18. Raiffa, *Art and Science of Negotiation*, 128–129.
19. Richard E. Walton and Robert B. McKersie, 1965. *A Behavioral Theory of Labor Negotiations* (New York: McGraw-Hill Book Company, 1965).
20. John S. Odell, *Negotiating the World Economy* (Ithaca, NY: Cornell University Press, 2000).
21. Walton and McKersie, *Behavioral Theory of Labor Negotiations.*
22. Odell, *Negotiating World Economy.*
23. Saner, *Expert Negotiator*, 88.
24. Christina L. Davis, 'International Institutions and Issue-Linkage: Building Support for Agricultural Trade', *American Political Science Review*, 98, 1 (2004): 153–169.
25. Odell, *Negotiating World Economy.*
26. James K. Sebenius, 'Negotiation Arithmetic: Adding and Subtracting Issues and Parties', *International Organization*, 37, 2 (Spring, 1983): 281–316.
27. William Wallace, 1976. 'Atlantic Relations: Policy Coordination and Conflict', *International Affairs* 52 (April 1976): 16.
28. François de. Callières, *On the Manner of Negotiating With Princes; On the Uses of Diplomacy; the Choice of Ministers and Envoys; and the Personal Qualities Necessary for Success in Missions Abroad* trans. A.F. Whyte (Boston and New York: Houghton Mifflin Co., 1919), 110.
29. Raiffa, *Art and Science of Negotiation*, 254.
30. Saner, *Expert Negotiator*, 146.
31. Raiffa, *Art and Science of Negotiation*, 4.
32. WTO document WT/MIN(15)/44 dated 21 December 2015, Ministerial Decision of 19 December 2015 on Public Stockholding for Food Security Purposes.
33. WTO document WT/MIN(15)/43 dated 21 December 2015, Ministerial Decision of 19 December 2015 on Special Safeguard Mechanism for Developing Country Members.

3

Multilateral Trading System

Origin, Establishment, and Evolution

3.1 Introduction

In order to appreciate the challenges faced by developing countries in multilateral trade negotiations and derive lessons from the past, it is useful to start with the genesis of the multilateral trading system. The origins of the multilateral trading system, as initially embodied in the General Agreement on Tariffs and Trade (GATT), can be traced to the traumatic economic events during the 1920s and 1930s. The economic downturn and worldwide recession in 1929 triggered protectionism, which, in turn, precipitated the Great Depression of the 1930s. Trade restrictions imposed by many countries compounded the global problem, resulting in a collapse of international trade.[1] Although the USA sought to reverse the protectionist trend by concluding more than twenty bilateral trade agreements with various countries to reduce import tariffs, these initiatives had a 'limited effect in boosting world trade during the tumultuous 1930s'.[2]

While planning for postwar economic policy and global governance in the wake of the turmoil caused by the Second World War, the Trans-Atlantic partnership between the USA and the UK envisioned establishing the following three international institutions: the International Monetary Fund (IMF); the International Bank for Reconstruction and Development (the World Bank); and the International Trade Organization (ITO).[3] Within four years, the vision for an institutional arrangement for trade was realized, but with a twist. The ITO proved to be still-born on account of the refusal by US president Truman to submit the negotiated outcome, commonly referred to as the Havana Charter, for Congressional ratification.[4] However, on a parallel track, the ITO negotiations resulted in the creation of the GATT.

Strategies in GATT and WTO Negotiations. Abhijit Das, Oxford University Press. © Abhijit Das 2025.
DOI: 10.1093/9780198934431.003.0003

This agreement was initially signed by twenty-three countries, eleven of which were developing countries, and entered into force on 1 January 1948 on a provisional basis. This temporary agreement provided the bedrock of multilaterally determined framework of rules for conducting international trade. However, the GATT lacked a formal organization to enforce its rules. The framework of rules instituted by the GATT in 1948 for conducting international trade continues to remain applicable even seventy-five years later. With the establishment of the World Trade Organization in 1995, the GATT rules were subsumed into the WTO. Further, under the WTO, the scope of the rules have been expanded beyond goods trade, as was the situation under the GATT, to include trade in services and protection of intellectual property rights. WTO provides the common institutional framework for the conduct of trade relations between more than 160 countries.[5]

Given the crucial role of the erstwhile GATT, and now the WTO, in formulating rules for international trade, it is relevant to examine what were the main features of GATT; how did the transition from the GATT to the WTO come about; what have been some of the key influences on the GATT and WTO system; and how have the issues of interest and concern to the developing countries been addressed by it. The subsequent sections of this chapter address these questions. In addition, this chapter also briefly examines the implications of WTO rules on domestic policymaking in developing countries and seeks to explain why laypersons should care about the outcomes of WTO negotiations. Overall, this chapter will help the readers understand the key underpinnings of the multilateral trading system and its relevance for developing countries in their quest for economic prosperity.

3.2 Main Features of GATT

GATT established a system of rule of law, which the contacting parties were expected to respect. The rules-based system defined the rights and obligations of the contracting parties, created a forum for multilateral supervision of the system, established a mechanism for resolution of trade friction between countries and provided a platform for negotiations for further liberalization of international trade in goods. What are the main provisions of GATT and how was trade liberalization sought to be achieved through various rounds of multilateral trade negotiations? We address these two questions in this section.

The basic principle of the GATT system was that there should be free and open competition in trade. Towards this end, two provisions on non-discrimination form one of the main pillars of the system: Most-Favoured Nation (MFN) treatment and national treatment. MFN treatment mandates that there must not be any discrimination as between different Member countries in the matter of treatment that a Member extends to them. Thus, any concession given by a country to its most-favoured country was also to be extended to all. National treatment is the principle of non-discrimination as between an imported product and a 'like' domestic product. A country was prohibited from providing less favourable treatment to an imported product than that provided to a like domestic product. Under the rules of GATT, countries were forbidden from imposing any restrictions on international trade, apart from tariffs. However, there were multiple exceptions to this rule, including action against unfair trade practices,[6] general exceptions and security exception. GATT also contained rules to counter unfair trade practices such as dumping and subsidization. GATT established the tradition of decision-making by consensus. However, on certain rare occasions, the Contracting Parties resorted to voting.[7] GATT also provided a mechanism for amicably settling trade disputes between the contracting parties. However, as GATT followed the tradition of decision-making by consensus, the contracting party against which a complaint was made could block the adoption of the dispute settlement report.

GATT contracting parties pursued trade liberalization mainly through negotiating ceiling levels on various products, above which customs duties (also commonly referred to as import tariffs) would not be applied. The ceiling level for a particular product is technically called the 'bound rate'. Once tariff concession on a product was given by negotiating its bound rate, in normal circumstances the concession could not be withdrawn unilaterally by raising the bound rate.[8] In respect of bound rates, during various rounds of multilateral trade negotiations, trade liberalization was sought to be achieved through the following two channels: first, getting countries to expand the coverage of products on which concessions were provided by negotiating the bound rates; and second, lowering the bound rates on various products which had been bound during previous rounds of multilateral trade negotiations. The multilateral trade negotiations rounds were the following: (i) Geneva (1947); (ii) Annecy (1948); (iii) Torquay (1950); (iv) Geneva (1956); (v) Dillon (1960–1961); (vi) Kennedy (1964–1967); (vii) Tokyo (1973–1979) and (viii) Uruguay (1986–1994). While the first six rounds focused mainly on tariffs, the last two rounds covered wider areas.[9]

3.3 From GATT to WTO and Beyond: Reflecting Commercial Interests of the Developed Countries

The evolution of the multilateral trading system mirrors the changing commercial interests of the developed countries.[10] When the GATT was established in 1948, its rules were relevant for merchandise trade—also referred to as trade in goods. Over time, services-related economic activities, such as banking, insurance, cinema, telecommunications, information technology related activities, etc. acquired considerable salience in the developed countries. To illustrate, in 1980 services comprised 65 per cent, 59 per cent, and 58 per cent share of the Gross Domestic Product (GDP) in France, the USA, and Japan respectively. In contrast, the contribution of services sector was relatively lower in developing countries—45 per cent in Brazil and 40 per cent in India.[11] This provided a huge commercial opportunity to service providers from the developed countries to penetrate the markets in developing countries and expand their economic operations. In order to achieve this objective, the developed countries had to put fetters on the ability of developing countries to restrict imports of services and nurture their domestic service suppliers. This required multilateral rules on trade in services, a subject excluded from the GATT disciplines. This triggered a demand from the developed countries, from 1982 onwards, to initiate negotiations at the GATT on trade in services.

The saga of multilateral negotiations on intellectual property rights (IPR) is very similar to that of services negotiations. Many knowledge-based industries, particularly pharmaceuticals and films, had acquired a prominent role in the economy of many developed countries. For these countries, commercial stakes of their business entities in having stringent rules for protecting their intellectual property, particularly in developing countries, were very high. To illustrate, in the 1980s and early 1990s almost 40 per cent of the revenue of the US film industry accrued from international markets.[12] In the pharmaceutical sector, large corporate entities, such as Pfizer, were unable to leverage their patented medicines for boosting their sales in developing countries. In many countries reverse-engineering of patented pharmaceuticals to produce generic medicines was legally justified, as these countries provided patent protection to the process by which medicines were produced, and not to the products themselves. Although the generic medicines helped the poor in developing countries to buy medicines at affordable prices, this was tarred by the developed countries as being 'patent piracy'. Pfizer chairman Edmund Pratt and IBM chairman John Opel established the Intellectual Property Committee (IPC), comprising thirteen CEOs, which was at the forefront of seeking the inclusion of intellectual property in the GATT negotiating agenda.[13]

The efforts of the developed countries to expand the commercial opportunities for their economic operators resulted in the launch of GATT multilateral trade negotiations in 1986, popularly called the Uruguay Round. The negotiating agenda included a mandate on services and IPRs—the latter mainly at the behest of the IPC.[14] Whether the mandate included negotiations on standards of IPR protection, as argued by the developed countries but contested by some developing countries, with India and Brazil being at the forefront of the opposition, became a hotly contested issue. After about two and a half years of acrimonious debate, eventually the resolute resistance of India and Brazil collapsed and they fell in line to negotiate the minimum standards of IP protection. It should be noted that the IPC was active in moulding the outcome in line with their commercial interests. A 100-page document prepared by it and titled Basic framework on GATT provisions for intellectual property, contributed significantly to the final agreement.[15] Eventually, after almost seven years of protracted negotiations, the Uruguay Round was concluded and a new international organization called the World Trade Organization (WTO) came into existence in January 1995. While the rules under the GATT were largely confined to goods trade, the WTO included rules on services and IPRs. These two new areas were of economic interest primarily to the developed countries.

Doha Round of multilateral trade negotiations at the WTO continued the approach of the developed countries to seek to negotiate rules in new areas of their economic interest. What were the main issues in the Doha Round and how did the negotiations evolve?

3.4 Doha Work Programme and Thereafter: The Incomplete Negotiations

In November 2001, WTO members launched an ambitious round of multilateral trade negotiations.[16] Technically called the Doha Work Programme (frequently referred to as the Doha Round), it inter alia envisaged liberalization of trade in goods and services; substantial reductions in trade-distorting agriculture support; clarifying and improving disciplines in respect of the Anti-Dumping Agreement and the Agreement on Subsidies and Countervailing Measures; and improvements and clarifications of the Dispute Settlement Understanding. Further, it was agreed that negotiations on outstanding implementation issues would be an integral part of the Doha Work Programme. The mandate also aimed to clarify and improve WTO disciplines on fisheries subsidies. It was agreed that special and differential treatment for developing countries shall be an integral part of the negotiations, including on agriculture and industrial tariffs. On the extremely contentious issue of environment, the mandate sought to enhance the mutual supportiveness of trade and environment through negotiations on the following three specific issues: the relationship between existing WTO rules and specific trade obligations set out in multilateral environmental agreements (MEAs); procedures for regular information exchange between MEA Secretariats and the relevant WTO committees, and the criteria for the granting of observer status; and the reduction or elimination of tariff and non-tariff barriers to environmental goods and services. The negotiations were expected to be concluded not later than 1 January 2005.

Perhaps the most controversial element of the Doha Work Programme was the possibility that on four issues, collectively referred to as the Singapore Issues, negotiations would take place after the Fifth Session of the Ministerial Conference (scheduled in 2003) on the basis of a decision to be taken, by explicit consensus, at that session on modalities of negotiations. These issues were the following: relationship between trade and investment; interaction between trade and competition policy; transparency in government procurement; and trade facilitation. However, the Fifth Session of the Ministerial Conference held in Cancun in September 2003 collapsed, without taking any decision on these issues. Eventually, in July–August 2004, the General Council of the WTO decided that no work towards negotiations on three of these issues—relationship between trade and investment; interaction between trade and competition policy; and transparency in government procurement—will take place within the WTO during the Doha Round.[17] This has been discussed in detail in Chapter 7 of the book.

It was generally recognized by negotiators and trade policy analysts that the overall fate of the Doha negotiations would largely depend on the progress in Agriculture negotiations. As will be discussed in detail in Chapter 8, a coalition of developing countries, spearheaded by Brazil, India, Argentina, and South Africa—commonly referred to as the G-20—prevented the USA-EU combine from dictating terms at the negotiating table. Consequently, after 2008 the developed countries lost their zeal for concluding the Doha Round. Eventually, during the tenth ministerial conference of the WTO held in Nairobi in 2015, the WTO membership failed to endorse concluding the Doha Round on the basis of the Doha mandates. As a result, the USA got out of a tight spot at the negotiating table and freed itself 'from the strictures of Doha', an objective strongly advocated by it.[18] The limited outcomes of the Doha Round included the Trade Facilitation Agreement finalized in 2014[19] and the Agreement on Fisheries Subsidies, partially finalized during the Geneva Ministerial Conference held in 2022[20]. Two other outcomes are worth noting; first, the so-called Bali Peace Clause on public stockholding for food security purposes,[21] which has been analysed in detail in Chapter 9; and second, the decision to eliminate export subsidies in agriculture.[22] Overall, negotiations on most of the issues under the Doha Work Programme remain to be completed.

Despite the failure of the WTO Members to endorse the continuation of the Doha Round, the trend in expanding the scope and coverage of rules at the WTO to support and reflect the changing sectors of economic strengths in the developed countries continues to be evident in the developments at the WTO related to electronic commerce. After failing to secure a multilateral mandate to initiate negotiations on this issue at the Buenos Aires Ministerial Conference of the WTO held in December 2017, about seventy Members of the WTO have launched negotiations on issues related to digital trade and electronic commerce—a sector of burgeoning economic gains for the developed countries. At the time of writing, these negotiations remain to be concluded.

3.5 Influences on GATT/WTO Negotiations

While governments of the developed countries and, occasionally, a few developing countries have been influential in shaping the outcomes of multilateral trade negotiations at the GATT and the WTO, the trading system has not remained impervious to other sources of influence. In this section we briefly examine two sources of influence on these negotiations: first, corporate entities and their lobby groups; and second, the GATT and the WTO Secretariat.

As the outcomes of multilateral trade negotiations can affect the fortunes of businesses, it should not be surprising that corporate entities would evince a keen interest in GATT/WTO negotiations. However, the extent to which large corporate entities of the developed countries and their lobby groups have succeeded in influencing the negotiating agenda and the course of multilateral trade negotiations is surprising. The role of the US pharmaceutical industry in the negotiations on IPRs has already been discussed in Section 3.3. The role of the International Chamber of Commerce (ICC) in influencing multilateral trade negotiations provides another useful illustration of this trend. This lobby group, comprising prominent players of the corporate world in developed countries and in recent years a few representatives from developing countries, has remained an extremely influential voice spanning ITO negotiations in 1940s to present-day negotiations at the WTO. Established in 1919, the ICC gathered economists to advocate for its interests and became an important institutional partner for the Austrian neo-liberal economists.[23] After the draft ITO Charter enshrined the right to deviate from the orthodoxy of free trade in order to protect nascent industries against foreign competition, the ICC became active in stridently opposing the ITO even before it was born. It viewed the charter as 'a dangerous document', and characterized it as 'the first international charter of economic nationalism ever written in the history of the civilized world'.[24] The ICC's official position was that the ITO would 'not infringe enough on the sovereignty of signatories'. The 'one-country-one-vote' procedure also drew particular ire of the ICC.[25] A strong campaign against the final text of the ITO, undertaken by the ICC in partnership with the Polish-American economist, Michael Heilperin, and a few other neo-liberal economists, dealt a grievous blow to the ITO.[26]

The influence of ICC on GATT/WTO negotiations persists even today. To illustrate, while the Trade Facilitation Agreement (TFA) was being negotiated at the WTO, the supposed global income gains from it were projected by the International Chamber of Commerce to be $1 trillion.[27] With the proponents of the TFA quoting this figure ad nauseum, it almost became a magic number to goad the hesitant developing countries to expedite the conclusion of the TFA negotiations. The ICC study acquired further legitimacy when some countries, including Australia,[28] referred to it in their statements at the plenary session of the Bali Ministerial Conference of the WTO held in December 2013. However, this projection was based on many questionable assumptions, and the supposed gains from trade liberalization did not appear to have firm theoretical or empirical basis.[29] Despite these shortcomings in the study, it is a testament to the influence of ICC that it was successful in creating a narrative regarding the supposed gains from the TFA.

The second important source of influence on the GATT/WTO negotiations comes from within the system—the officials of the GATT/WTO Secretariat. To illustrate, during the 1970s and 1980s the trinity of influential GATT economist/lawyers—Jan Tumlir, Frieder Roessler, and Ernst-Ulrich Petersmann—is considered to have provided the intellectual foundation for the GATT reform process.[30] In fact Roessler, as the director of the Division of Legal Affairs at the GATT, is credited with having 'drafted the bulk of a series of historical decisions on the transition from the GATT to the WTO'.[31] The role of Arthur Dunkel, the GATT director general, in the Uruguay Round provides another example of the influence on the GATT/WTO negotiations from within the system. It is a tradition at the GATT/WTO that the director general is the chairman of Trade Negotiating Committee of multilateral trade negotiations. In this role he is expected to help countries strike compromises, resolve negotiating deadlocks, and broker deals. During the initial years of the Uruguay Round, Arthur Dunkel is supposed to have performed this responsibility with considerable objectivity.[32] However, his approach appears to have gradually changed as the negotiations entered the crucial phase of addressing seemingly intractable issues involving conflicting interests of various countries. In an effort at breaking the negotiating deadlock, he presented a comprehensive text which is popularly called the Dunkel Draft.[33] Instead of putting texts on contested issues in square brackets as should normally have been done to denote the lack of consensus on various issues, Dunkel proposed his own text. This was a significant departure from the past. He also stipulated the condition that any part of the text could be changed only if all countries agreed to it. Given the power asymmetry at the negotiating table, this stipulation considerably disadvantaged the developing countries. It would be fair to conclude that as the Dunkel Draft formed the substantial basis of the Uruguay Round agreements, by his actions Dunkel decisively influenced the end game at the negotiating table.

3.6 Struggling to Include Development Concerns in a Rich Man's Club

How have issues of interest to many developing countries been addressed at the GATT/WTO? Right from the days of the ITO negotiations to the present day at the WTO, most developing countries have struggled to push their interests and concerns regarding economic development. Why has this happened? The answer is partly provided by the following observation made in the context of certain developments during the GATT era: 'The realities of a highly asymmetric power structure and the desire not to be overly belligerent towards much more powerful trading partners' prevented 'the less economically influential states from demanding their rights'.[34] To complete the picture, the GATT was viewed as the 'property' of the industrial countries 'and they did not have to accommodate the rest of the world'; it provided 'a place where the leading countries could go off to do business by themselves'.[35]

The narrative of the GATT as an informal organization that functioned on the basis of inclusive discussion and consensus decision-making 'disguised the ways in which the existing global power structure was rigid and self-perpetuating'.[36] It appears that countries and country groups with economic and political clout have driven the agenda and substantially determined the outcomes at the GATT/WTO. In this context the internal assessment made by India of the US Suggested Charter, a US proposal made in 1946 that subsequently formed the basis of many legal provisions of the GATT rulebook, is relevant. India's contention was that the Suggested Charter sought to promote the interests of the USA and UK, while ignoring the needs of other participants[37]—an overriding and persisting concern of many developing countries even today. A former ambassador of India to the GATT puts it succinctly: almost all the time, the GATT/WTO system has been loaded with the subjects of interest to the developed countries.[38] It is, therefore, not surprising that most of the developing countries, particularly the larger economies among them, have struggled to decisively influence the outcomes at the GATT/WTO negotiating table. No doubt, there are success stories from the perspective of development concerns being addressed, but these are very few and far between.

3.7 Impact of WTO Rules on Developing Countries

The rules of the multilateral trading system can be viewed as the result of a series of political bargains among countries of differing economic and political capabilities. Each of these bargains instituted a set of rules that enhanced the economic opportunities for the developed countries, while narrowing or offering fewer opportunities for the developing countries.[39] Not only do these rules define the legal boundaries of policies that impact international and national patterns of production and consumption, but they also have a strong bearing on the development possibilities of developing countries.[40] With the rules of the multilateral trading system being expanded to cover progressively larger spheres of economic and commercial activities within, and between, countries, policy flexibility has commensurately shrunk. The rules that countries negotiate at the WTO are likely to affect the growth trajectory of a country in new and emerging areas. These rules also constrain the ability of developing countries to address the food security needs of their poor and hungry. Further, rules under the Agreement on Trade-Related Aspects of Intellectual Property Rights (TRIPS Agreement) have an impact on prices of medicines and affordable healthcare. Thus, it would be no exaggeration to say that directly or indirectly the GATT/WTO rules affect the common person within the Members of this organization.

An important question that needs to be addressed is the following: how can the same set of rules at the GATT and WTO have contrasting implications for the developed countries on the one hand, and the developing countries on the other? Following are some of the reasons for it: inclusion of provisions which benefit countries endowed with capital and technology; provisions whose advantage can be taken mostly by the developed countries; and provisions that prevent developing countries from implementing industrial policies, which were used by the developed countries during early stages of their development—the practice characterized by the Cambridge economist Ha-Joon Chang as 'kicking away the ladder'.[41] A few illustrations of the contrasting impacts of GATT/WTO rules are discussed below.

First, with a view to creating employment, many developing countries seek to attract investment in the manufacturing sector. In order to create employment upstream, they could attempt to mandate that the manufacturing plant source its inputs and raw materials domestically. However, the interest of the investor would be to have the freedom to source inputs from the cheapest source available. In this clash of interests between the economically desirable objective of the government and profit-maximizing behaviour of the investor, GATT/WTO provisions have weighed decisively in favour of the investor by prohibiting countries from mandating local sourcing of inputs.[42] These provisions also prevent countries from implementing a slew of policies to catch up with the developed countries.

Second, although some of the provisions of the WTO appear to be objective and neutral on the surface, in reality these appear to have been tailored to promote the interests of the developed countries. To illustrate, it is mainly the OECD countries which can take advantage of the provision on export credits in the Agreement on Subsidies and Countervailing Measures and provide these subsidies, which would otherwise be prohibited.[43] Third, the Agreement on Agriculture provides many examples of how the same provision confers substantial rights to the developed countries, while imposing constraints on many developing countries. Nothing illustrates this better than the provision related to a category of subsidies called Amber Box subsidies. The fundamental underpinning of the provision is that the current entitlement of a country to provide Amber Box subsidies is based on the amount of subsidy provided by it during an identified base period of 1986–1988—the higher the level of subsidy provided in the base period, the higher became the entitlement during the WTO era. As the developed countries provided a high amount of these subsidies in the base period, they acquired the right to continue to provide these subsidies in the future. On the other hand, most developing countries were fiscally prudent and did not provide these subsidies beyond a meagre amount. These countries lost the right to provide Amber Box subsidies beyond a de minimis threshold in the future.

Fourth, provisions of the TRIPS Agreement seek to protect the private rights of holders of intellectual property. As most of the holders of intellectual property, particularly in respect of patents, are from the developed countries, this agreement benefits mainly these countries. Further, on account of the commitments under this agreement, many developing countries had to bear the adverse consequences of being compelled to abandon their practice of granting patents to processes and instead had to adopt a product-patent regime. This sharply diminished the prospects of their generic pharmaceutical industries, and continues to pose a severe challenge in ensuring access to affordable medicines to the sick and poor in the developing countries.

3.8 Conclusions

It may not be incorrect to conclude that the regime of GATT/WTO, based on reciprocity, mainly benefits those who are better endowed with capital and technology. Further, subject to a few exceptions, the rules of the WTO do not sufficiently recognize that policy needs and imperatives of a developed country may be entirely different from those of a developing country. A common theme running through the evolution of the GATT/WTO over the past seventy-five years, appears to be the quest of the developed countries to negotiate binding rules in new and emerging sectors of their economic strength, such as services and intellectual property rights during the 1980s and 1990s, investment from the 1980s onwards and the digital sector from 2017 onwards. In return, the developing countries have secured some concessions which have helped them to enhance their exports to the developed countries in sectors that may not be sensitive to the latter countries. In these negotiations, while the developed countries have kept an eye on their future economic prospects, most developing countries appear to have been largely preoccupied with short-term economic interests. An important consequence of this bargain is that the multilateral trade rules at the GATT/WTO have put fetters on the ability of most developing countries to implement policies for catching up with the first-movers in the developed countries in new and emerging sectors. This long-term trend is partly a result of the strategies adopted by the developed countries in multilateral trade negotiations at the GATT/WTO—the subject of our discussion in the next two chapters.

Notes

1. Douglas A. Irwin, Petros C. Mavroidis, and Alan O. Sykes, *The Genesis of the GATT* (New York: Cambridge University Press, 2008), 5–6.
2. Irwin, Mavroidis, and Sykes, *Genesis of the GATT*, 8.
3. Amrita Narlikar, *WTO: A Very Short Introduction* (Oxford and New York: Oxford University Press, 2006).
4. For a detailed explanation of some of the reasons behind the refusal of President Truman to submit the Havana Charter for Congressional ratification see Quinn Slobodian, *Globalists—The End of Empire and the Birth of Neo-liberalism* (Cambridge, MA and London: Harvard University Press, 2018).
5. See Article II.1 of the Marrakesh Agreement Establishing the WTO.
6. Under the GATT, dumping and subsidization were recognized as the two unfair trade practices.
7. See, for example, GATT Contracting Parties, Third Session, Summary record of the twenty-second meeting. GATT/CP.3/SR.22 dated 8 June 1949. At the request of Czechoslovakia voting had to be resorted to on the question of whether or not the USA could refuse to grant export licenses on grounds of strategic significance.
8. Article XXVIII of GATT 1994 is the main provision on renegotiation of tariff concessions. In order to raise the bound rate on a product, the country has to negotiate with Members with whom the concession was initially negotiated and also with other countries which have a principal supplying interest. These negotiations require the country seeking to raise the bound rate on a product to provide compensatory concession by lowering bound rates on products of interest to these two groups of countries.

9. Bhagirath Lal Das, *The World Trade Organisation: A Guide to the Framework for International Trade* (Penang: Third World Network, 1999), 5.
10. Bhagirath Lal Das, *The WTO and Multilateral Trading System: Past, Present and Future* (London and New York: Zed Books and Penang: Third World Network, 2003), 21.
11. Data of all countries except for USA has been taken from World Development Indicators, a database maintained by the World Bank. In respect of the USA, data has been taken from WTO document WTO WT/TPR/S/16 dated 21 October 1996. United States Trade Policy Review, Report by the Secretariat Pg. 7. It should be noted that the share of services in US GDP appears to be understated, as it includes transportation, communications, wholesale and retail trade, financial services, and construction. Sectors such as tourism, entertainment, etc. appear to have been excluded.
12. Charan Devereaux, Robert Z. Lawrence, and Michael D. Watkins, *Case Studies in US Trade Negotiation Vol.1: Making the Rules* (Washington, DC: Institute for International Economics, 2006), 44.
13. Devereaux, Lawrence, and Watkins, *Making the Rules*, 55.
14. See, for example, Devereaux, Lawrence, and Watkins, *Making the Rules*, 55–76.
15. Devereaux, Lawrence, and Watkins, *Making the Rules*, 61.
16. WTO document WT/MIN(01)/DEC/1 dated 20 November, Ministerial Declaration adopted on 14 November 2001.
17. WTO document no. WT/L/579 dated 2 August 2004, Decision Adopted by the General Council on 1 August 2004 on Doha Work Programme.
18. See, for example, the statement by Michael Froman, USTR, at the plenary session of the Nairobi Ministerial Meeting of the WTO, available at https://www.wto.org/english/thewto_e/minist_e/mc10_e/mc10_planarysessions_e.htm#USA. The context for this expression is explained in the next chapter in Section 4.9.
19. WTO document WT/MIN(13)/36 dated 11 December 2013, Agreement on Trade Facilitation, Ministerial Decision of 7 December 2013.
20. WTO document WT/MIN(22)/W/22 dated 17 June 2022, Agreement on Fisheries Subsidies. Draft Ministerial Decision of 17 June 2022.
21. WTO document WT/MIN(13)/38 dated 11 December 2013, Public Stockholding for Food Security Purposes, Ministerial Decision of 7 December 2013.
22. WTO document WT/MIN(15)/45 dated 21 December 2015, Export Competition, Ministerial Decision of 19 December 2015.
23. Slobodian, *Globalists*, 34.
24. Michael A. Heilperin, 'Elephant Traps on the World Trade Charter,' *American Affairs*, (July 1950) quoted in Quinn Slobodian, *Globalists*, 130.
25. Slobodian, *Globalists*, 130.
26. Slobodian, *Globalists*.
27. International Chamber of Commerce, Payoff from the World Trade Agenda, Gary C. Hufbauer, and Jeffrey Schott, *Peterson Institute for International Economics*, 2013.

28. Statement by Hon. Andrew Robb, Minister for Trade and Investment, Australia at the Bali Ministerial Conference held during 3–6 December 2013, WTO document no. WT/MIN(13)/ST/108, dated 10 February 2014.
29. Jeronim Capaldo, Trade Hallucination: Risks of Trade Facilitation and Suggestions for Implementation. Global Development and Environment Institute, Tufts University, USA, Working Paper No. 14-02, 2014.
30. Slobodian, *Globalists.*
31. Gabrielle Marceau. 'From the GATT to the WTO: The Expanding Duties of the Legal Affairs Division in Non-panel Matters', in Gabrielle Marceau, *A History of Law and Lawyers in the GATT/WTO* (Cambridge, U.K.: Cambridge University Press, 2015), 252.
32. Interview with a former ambassador of India to the GATT, June 2021.
33. GATT document MTN.TNC/W/FA dated 20 December 1991. Draft Final Act embodying the results of the Uruguay Round of multilateral trade negotiations.
34. Rorden Wilkinson and James Scott, 'Developing Country Participation in the GATT: A Reassessment' *World Trade Review* 7, 3 (2008): 473–510.
35. Robert E. Hudec, *The GATT Legal System and World Trade Diplomacy* (Salem, MA: Butterworth Legal Publishers, 1990), 57.
36. Francine McKenzie, *GATT and Global Order in the Postwar Era* (Cambridge, U.K.: Cambridge University Press, 2020), 191.
37. UNECOSOC document no. E/PC/T/W.14 dated 21 October 1946 Government of India, Department of Commerce. Submission to the Preparatory Committee of the International Conference on Trade and Employment. Comments on US proposals for expansion of world trade and employment.
38. Das, *WTO: Past, Present and Future*, 23–24.
39. Diana Tussie and Marcela Saguier, 'The Sweep of Asymmetric Trade Negotiations; Introduction and Overview,' in Bilal Sanoussi, Philippe De Lombaerde, and Diana Tussie (eds), *Asymmetric Trade Negotiations* (London and New York: Routledge, 2011).
40. Martin Guzman and Joseph E. Stiglitz, 'Post-neoliberal Globalization: International Trade Rules for Global Prosperity,' *Oxford Review of Economic Policy*, 40 (2024): 282–306.
41. Ha-Joon Chang, *Kicking Away the Ladder: Development Strategy in Historical Perspective* (London: Anthem Press, 2002).
42. See, for example, Article III:4 of GATT 1994 and paragraph 1 (a) of Annex to the Trade-related Investment Measures agreement.
43. See Item (k) of Annex I of the Agreement on Subsidies and Countervailing Measures.

4

Strategies Used by Developed Countries Away from the Negotiating Table

4.1 Introduction

Discerning negotiating strategies is never an easy task. However, through a careful study of how negotiations evolved and by interviewing some key persons who were at the scene, it is possible to recognize coherent patterns which are suggestive of an underlying negotiating strategy. At times the strategy deduced from the events may appear to be speculative. However, if the same pattern is repeated either at different points in time, or in different areas of negotiation, it may be correct to conclude that the events were the result of an underlying strategy. It is important to appreciate that strategies are deployed not only at the negotiating table, but also away from it. A party may deploy both sets of strategies with the common objective of enhancing its leverage and bargaining strength at the negotiating table.

This chapter examines some of the strategies deployed by the developed countries away from the negotiating table during different episodes in multilateral trade negotiations spanning four decades. While most of these strategies are relevant after negotiations have formally commenced, a few of them assume salience even prior to the start of negotiations. Some of the strategies discussed in this chapter may be extremely sensitive and controversial, as these clearly encroach on the sovereignty of nations. However, instead of letting these strategies remain under a cloak of secrecy, it may be useful to cast some light on them. This would alert the WTO members countries about the strategies used by some countries to influence their behaviour at the negotiating table.

Each subsequent section in this chapter discusses one strategy and provides illustrations of its deployment across time and issues. The following

Strategies in GATT and WTO Negotiations. Abhijit Das, Oxford University Press. © Abhijit Das 2025.
DOI: 10.1093/9780198934431.003.0004

strategies are discussed in this chapter: choice of the negotiating forum, framing issues, and spinning narratives for negotiating success, influencing negotiations through research, disguising commercial interests and shooting from other's shoulders, using policy instruments to browbeat countries in trade negotiations, carrot and stick strategy, using Quislings to influence trade negotiators in developing countries, and creating a more attractive BATNA.

4.2 Choosing the Suitable Negotiating Forum

One of the important questions, particularly in the context of state-to-state negotiations, is—where to negotiate? While this might appear to be a procedural issue, in many cases the issue of the appropriate negotiating forum has been intensely contested by different parties. The choice of the negotiating forum determines the following: parties with whom to negotiate; negotiating leverage available to parties to get foot draggers onto the negotiating table; whether rules to be negotiated are binding or non-binding in nature; and whether the rules are enforceable through peer pressure, diplomatic means, or through a law-based mechanism. Why have the developed countries favoured the GATT earlier, and now the WTO, as the forum for negotiating binding rules on issues of their economic interest, even if these go beyond international trade? Box 4.1 explores some reasons for this trend.

It is important to note that in their quest for using WTO as the preferred forum for negotiations, the developed countries have engaged in an interesting strategy of forum shifting. In some instances, the developed countries have used other forums to pre-negotiate outcomes on trade-related issues, before introducing these for further negotiations at the WTO. In addition, the developed countries have started using other forums such as FTAs for pursuing negotiations on non-trade issues, and subsequently returning to the WTO with brighter prospects for success. Are there any noticeable variations in forum shifting, while using GATT/WTO as the final negotiating forum? How does forum shifting help developed countries to achieve their negotiating objectives?

Box 4.1 Why Is GATT/WTO the Preferred Forum for the Developed Countries for Negotiating Binding Rules in New and Emerging Areas?

Three sets of factors are at play for the sustained interest of the developed countries in the GATT/WTO as the preferred negotiating forum for international rule-making in new and emerging areas of economic activities. First, most of the rules at the GATT/WTO are binding in nature. In contrast, at most of the other inter-governmental organizations, such as the International Labour Organization (ILO), negotiations are undertaken more for non-binding rules and guidelines, and less for binding rules. As soft law on issues including labour and environment may not be adequate for promoting the economic interests of the developed countries, their quest for hard law makes GATT/WTO a more effective forum for negotiating binding rules.

Second, at most inter-governmental organizations the developed countries lack the leverage to persuade developing countries to take binding commitments on non-trade issues. However, at the GATT/WTO, the developed countries have secured binding commitments on issues that were considered by some developing countries to be non-trade related, such as intellectual property rights, in exchange for enhancing access of the developing countries to their markets. The lure of exporting to these markets may be difficult for many developing countries to resist, even if it requires them to agree to rules on non-trade issues that may be inimical to their interest.

Third, availability of an existing institutional mechanism for enforcing rights and obligations under an agreement on emerging issues through a binding dispute settlement system, makes GATT/WTO a doubly attractive negotiating forum for the developed countries. Even if binding rules on a non-trade issue can be negotiated at an international forum, say ILO or United Nations Environment Programme (UNEP), there would be a need to create a binding dispute resolution mechanism *de novo* at these organizations. From the perspective of the developed countries, it may not be efficient to establish binding and enforceable dispute resolutions mechanisms at multiple organizations. Further, even if the developed countries manage to establish a binding dispute resolution mechanism in respect of no-trade rules in organizations such as the ILO and UNEP, it is uncertain whether they would have the leverage to induce other countries to comply with the binding obligations. However, at the WTO, the threat of loss of market access for exports is a potent and credible threat for inducing compliance by countries that break binding rules on non-trade issues.

4.2.1 Using Outcomes at Other Forums as a Template for Negotiations at GATT/WTO

With a view to facilitating negotiations on issues of their interest at the GATT/WTO, on a few occasions the developed countries have pre-negotiated an outcome among a few countries at a forum outside the GATT/WTO, and thereafter have used the outcome as the template for further negotiation at the GATT/WTO. The specific example of WTO's Information Technology Agreement (ITA) illustrates this strategy. The template of the ITA, aimed at eliminating customs duties on information technology products, was initially discussed and negotiated among a few countries at the Asia and Pacific Economic Forum (APEC) in November 1996. Thereafter, within a month it was used to negotiate a similar agreement among 29 WTO members.[1] It has been speculated that the USA had in its mind to use APEC 'as a locus to reach agreements on specific sectors prior to the start of the new WTO negotiations'.[2] The prior background discussions and negotiations at APEC facilitated the eventual agreement at the WTO.[3] While pre-negotiating outcomes at other forums is a useful strategy adopted by the developed countries for pursuing their economic interests, a variation of this strategy—shifting to the FTA forum—is increasingly becoming common. This strategy is discussed in the next sub-section.

4.2.2 Forum Shifting: From WTO to FTAs and Thereafter Back to the WTO

In line with their evolving economic interests, the developed countries have sought to initiate negotiations on many non-trade and new issues including labour standards, environment, digital trade, and investment protection at the WTO. However, on these issues they have faced intense resistance from a large number of developing counties, many of whom view negotiations on these issues as an attempt at eroding their competitive advantage, or preventing them from implementing policies to catch up with commercially successful first movers in the developed countries. As evident from the developments at the negotiating table, during 2001–2004 the developing countries succeeded in limiting the ambitions of the developed countries in negotiating rules at the WTO on non-trade issues. In respect of labour issues, at the Doha Ministerial Conference, ministers took note of 'work under way in the International Labour Organization (ILO) on the social dimension of globalization' and reaffirmed the declaration made at the Singapore Ministerial Conference regarding internationally recognized core labour standards.[4] This fell far short of providing a negotiating mandate on this issue. In respect of investment, it was agreed that negotiations will take place after the next Ministerial Conference, which was scheduled to be held in 2003.[5] However, in 2004 it was decided that no work towards negotiations on some issues, including investment, will take place within the WTO during the Doha Round.[6] On issues related to trade and environment, while the Doha Ministerial Conference provided an ambitious negotiating mandate, the negotiations could not be concluded.[7]

In an effort at overcoming the collective opposition from many developing countries on initiating multilateral negotiations on many new issues, the developed countries have shifted attention away from the WTO, albeit temporarily, and have negotiated commitments on issues such as digital trade, labour, environment, gender, and good regulatory practices in free trade agreements (FTAs) with some developing countries.[8] In a further twist, they now seek to discuss/negotiate disciplines on these issues at the WTO, but initially with those who are willing to participate in the negotiations. To illustrate, some WTO members have launched 'dedicated discussions on how trade-related climate measures and policies can best contribute to climate and environmental goals and commitments while being consistent with WTO rules and principles'.[9] On issues related to gender, on the occasion of the WTO Ministerial Conference in Buenos Aires in December 2017, many WTO members issued the Joint Declaration on Trade and Women's Economic Empowerment, and 'agreed to collaborate on making our trade and development policies more gender-responsive'.[10] At the Buenos Aires Ministerial Conference of the WTO, 71 WTO members issued a joint statement, where they announced their intention to launch 'exploratory work' towards future WTO negotiations on trade-related aspects of electronic commerce.[11] Considerable progress appears to have been made in these negotiations, and the participating countries were hoping to conclude the agreement by 2024.[12] The most advanced of these non-multilateral initiatives relates to investment facilitation, an issue on which 124 WTO members have finalized the agreement by 29 February 2024 at the Abu Dhabi Ministerial Conference of the WTO.[13]

What lies behind this strategy of forum shifting multiple times—initially from the WTO to FTAs and subsequently from FTAs back to the WTO—and how do the developed countries stand to gain from it? There are many crucial factors behind both the limbs of this strategy. First, at the WTO, by striking coalitions, developing countries can partly counter the asymmetric power that developed countries wield at the negotiating table. This creates the possibility of some developing countries collectively impeding the negotiating objectives of the developed countries on non-trade issues at the WTO. In contrast, in an FTA negotiation between a developed and developing country, the possibility of a coalition does not exist. Consequently, the developing country has almost no option to counter the power asymmetry at the negotiating table. As a result, developing countries have a harder time securing concessions and resisting demands of the developed countries.[14] Second, in exchange for providing access to their markets at zero tariffs in FTA negotiations, the developed countries have succeeded in pushing their agenda on non-trade issues.

Gains for the developed countries from the strategy of shifting forum from FTAs and back to the WTO arise from three underlying reasons. First, the presence of provisions on issues such as labour standards, environment, gender, and digital trade chapters in FTAs provides a veneer of legitimacy to the linkage between these issues and trade. Second, after having agreed to rules on non-trade issues in their FTAs, some of the developing countries would find it difficult to oppose negotiations on these issues at the WTO. Third, as more developing countries agree to include provisions on these contentious issues in their FTAs, others would feel less inclined to persist with their opposition to these issues at the WTO. This coherent strategy of the developed countries of using

FTAs for initially finalizing agreement with one country at a time may be time consuming, but it facilitates their path to use WTO as a forum for negotiating binding rules on many non-trade issues. While some of these agreements may initially not be among the entire WTO Membership, nevertheless, these would open the doors for multilateral agreements on them at a future date.

4.3 Spinning Narratives for Negotiating Success: What You See Is Not What You Get

How issues are framed can have a profound influence on the negotiating approach of political leaders and high-level officials, who may neither have the time nor the technical expertise to understand the nitty gritty of complex issues. Often, it is not the reality at the negotiating table, but the dominant narrative around issues, which becomes the filter for perceiving developments on various issues and their likely implications for countries. The power of framing was evident during the Uruguay Round of GATT, when the US pharmaceutical sector cleverly disguised its commercial interests and instead elevated it as an ethical issue for countering 'patent piracy'.[15] This framing became pivotal in facilitating this sector to secure its negotiating objectives. How the Doha Round was launched during the Ministerial Conference in 2001 provides another example of the power and success of crafting narratives in trade negotiations. At Doha, the developing countries were strongly opposed to the launch of the multilateral trade negotiations at the WTO. In an effort to soften the resistance from the developing countries, a narrative was created that the Doha Round was meant for development. The USA and the EU were at the forefront of creating this narrative. In his plenary statement at the Doha Ministerial Conference, Pascal Lamy, the EU Trade Commissioner explicitly mentioned that development belongs 'right at the heart of the multilateral trading system'.[16] Referring to the likely contribution of the Doha Round, Robert Zoellick, the US Trade Representative, stated that it would be 'the starting point for greater development, growth, opportunity, and openness throughout the world'.[17] The fact that Zoellick mentioned 'development' before 'openness' was not lost on the developing countries. The development orientation that was promised in the negotiations played an important role in convincing the developing countries to agree to the initiation of the Doha Round.

As the Doha Round progressed, by skilfully crafting narratives at different stages of the negotiation, the developed countries succeeded in getting their version of events accepted as the truth—although the reality of the negotiating dynamics may have been entirely different. How the events unfolded in the immediate aftermath of the collapse of the Cancun Ministerial Conference in 2003 is another successful example of this strategy. Within a few minutes of the collapse of the WTO ministerial meeting at Cancun, Robert Zoellick, the USTR, quickly addressed the media and produced a masterstroke in spinning a narrative to suit the US interests. He upbraided the developing countries, who were reluctant to move ahead on Singapore Issues. He tarred them as 'won't do countries' and put the entire blame for the collapse on them. Of course, he was quick to label his allies as 'can do countries' and absolved them of any culpability for the fiasco. However, the reasons for the collapse of the meeting, and the binary of 'can do' and 'won't do' countries, appear to be at considerable variance with the spin given by Zoellick.

If we were to accept the account provided by Paul Blustein, Zoellick cannot escape blame for the failure at Cancun.[18] This was the view that prevailed even among his closest ally—the EU. According to Blustein, who cites Arancha Gonzales—Lamy's spokesperson—as his source, the internal perception within the EU delegation was that the USA had allowed the meeting to collapse on Singapore Issues so that discussion would not progress to cotton subsidies. The USA was in no position to concede even an inch on cotton, an issue on which it was on the defensive. If the negotiation had indeed shifted to cotton subsidies, it is likely that the ministerial meeting would have collapsed on this issue and the USA blamed for it. In order to prevent being blamed for its inflexible stance on cotton, Zoellick allowed the ministerial meeting to collapse on Singapore Issues.[19] Notwithstanding the reality of cotton and Zoellick's success in ducking the need to make concessions on it, his binary of 'can do' and 'won't do' countries stuck. With facts mattering less and less, his spin of the reason for the failure of Cancun Ministerial Conference has become part of the wisdom among trade negotiators, media, and mainstream academicians. A sentiment commonly articulated by many diplomats from developing countries is that bending reality to create narratives for suiting their commercial interests appears to have become par for the course for the powerful countries at the WTO.

Besides many developing countries being caricatured as 'won't do' countries, they are often accused of not having a positive agenda in multilateral negotiations. Again, the reality may be considerably different from this simplistic narrative. As will be discussed in Sections 5.5 and 5.6, the developed countries have resorted to many strategies and largely succeeded in thwarting the negotiating proposals of many developing countries. Finding their positive agenda completely blocked, it may not be unreasonable to witness the opposition of many developing countries to the demands of the developed countries. This considerably diminishes the possibility of integrative bargaining, whereby joint gains in a commercially meaningful sense can be made by the developed and developing countries.

4.4 Influencing Negotiations Through Research

Framing of issues has been a helpful strategy in promoting the interests of the developed countries in trade negotiations. However, this may not be enough to convince some countries and their stakeholders to support negotiating positions that may be inimical to their national interests. The believers and proponents need quantitative estimates to persuade the sceptics from developing countries at the negotiating table. It is here that the role of research emerging from inter-governmental organizations and reputed scholars becomes crucial.

Objective, rigorous, and empirically sound research can be a useful tool for trade negotiators for assessing the likely impacts of different options in trade negotiations. However, research becomes contentious, when it is not based on sound theoretical foundations, and yet is used with zeal to push one line in trade negotiations—as has happened on some occasions in the past. During the Uruguay Round many institutions including the World Bank and OECD made projections of welfare gains of the order of $200 billion a year, with a large share of the gains being predicted to accrue to developing countries.[20] The promise of large welfare gains appears to have been stimulus for developing countries to conclude the round.[21] These gains have not materialized. To compound the misery for a large number of countries, United Nations Development Programme's (UNDP) Human Development Report of 1997 projected that most least developed countries will be net losers from the round after full implementation of all the agreements, with Sub-Saharan Africa estimated to have lost \$1.2 billion as a result of the Uruguay Round.[22] Why did the projections made by the World Bank and OECD fail to materialize? The verdict of an eminent economist and Nobel Laureate is that the modelled scenarios did not fully reflect the actual agreements.[23]

There have been instances when international institutions have put out research that had the potential to undermine the negotiating position of some developing countries. Unfortunately, some of these studies were based on questionable assumptions. To illustrate, in 2006, the World Bank uploaded a draft paper by Maros Ivanic and Will Martin titled 'Potential Implications of Agricultural Special Products for Poverty in Low-Income Countries' on its website. This paper sought to discredit the negotiating approach of a group of developing countries at the WTO, commonly referred to as the G33, on the so-called 'Special Products' (SP) for protecting the interests of millions of small farmers. Based on an econometric model, the draft paper reached a rather alarmist conclusion. According to the draft paper, raising agricultural prices substantially through SPs 'would create large increases in poverty—sufficient in some cases to undo decades of development progress—and push the already poor deeper into poverty'. As this conclusion had adverse implications for the negotiating position of many developing countries, the G33 undertook a detailed technical analysis of the paper. In its critique, the G33 pointed out that the World Bank draft paper was fundamentally flawed in its assumptions and methodology, ignored the reality of the prevailing agrarian structures in most developing countries, and misinterpreted the proposed operation and impact of SPs.[24] The G33 conveyed the numerous technical reservations it had on the paper to the World Bank. Eventually, the draft paper was removed from the website of the World Bank. Whether the paper was merely an academic exercise, or a blatant attempt at advocacy masquerading as academic research, may never get resolved. However, the findings of a panel which evaluated World Bank research might provide some pointers (Box 4.2).

Apart from research, some of the concepts and indicators emerging from international organizations influence, or have the potential to

Box 4.2 Using Research on Globalization to Proselytize

How is it that a research paper with obvious technical flaws—such as the one on Special Products—was allowed by the World Bank to be uploaded on its website, albeit temporarily? In this context it is relevant to note some of the findings of the evaluation of World Bank research between 1998 and 2005 carried out by a panel consisting of Abhijit Banerjee (MIT), Angus Deaton (Princeton, chair), Nora Lustig (UNDP), and Kenneth Rogoff (Harvard). The panel was extremely critical of the way that the research on globalization by the World Bank was 'used to proselytize on behalf of Bank policy, often without taking a balanced view of the evidence, and without expressing appropriate scepticism. Internal research that was favourable to Bank positions was given great prominence, and unfavourable research ignored.' Thus, the views of the panel, comprising among others, two future Nobel Laureates, suggest how unbalanced research on globalization has emerged from the World Bank.

Source: Banerjee, Abhijit, Deaton Angus, Lusting Nora and Ken Rogoff. 2006. An Evaluation of World Bank Research, 1998–2005.

influence, the position of developing countries on contentious issues in trade negotiations. A good illustration of this is the Business Ready (B-READY), an international benchmarking project developed by the World Bank.[25] With many developing countries seeking to improve their performance on indicators such as the B-READY for attracting investments, their score on its constituent indicators acquires economic relevance. In respect of sustainable trade policy under B-READY, countries score points if they have ratified and implemented labour provisions and gender-specific provisions in their trade agreements.[26] Further, in respect of digital transactions, countries score points if they adhere to cross-border data flows and technological neutrality.[27] As these are issues of negotiating priorities of mostly the developed countries in their FTAs and at the WTO, the design of the B-READY benchmarking would benefit those developing countries who have aligned themselves with the negotiating priorities of the developed countries.

The examples discussed in this section should leave us in no doubt that in a subtle manner, many international institutions appear to be promoting the negotiating interests of the developed countries. This should not come as a surprise, as the developed countries have substantial influence in functioning of organizations such as the OECD and the World Bank.

4.5 Shooting from Other's Shoulders: Developed Countries Disguising Their Interests and Projecting Issues to Be in the Interest of Developing Countries

A common strategy used by the developed countries is to cleverly disguise their interests on some issues, and instead project those as being in the interest of developing countries. To illustrate, during the Uruguay Round, in order to push its own objective of negotiating stringent standards for IPR protection, the USA argued that respecting patent rights would actually benefit the developing countries by encouraging foreign and domestic investment in research and by enabling hi-tech companies to engage in technology transfer with these nations.[28] More recently, in the negotiations on fisheries subsidies under the Doha Round, an attempt was made to project certain subsidies being given by the developed countries to their fishers for fishing in African and Pacific waters as special and differential treatment in favour of the developing countries.[29]

What are the advantages of this strategy? At least three clear benefits can be identified. First, by projecting an issue as being in the interest of developing countries, developed countries escape the pressure to grant reciprocal concessions for it at the negotiating table. Second, by convincing some developing countries that an issue is beneficial to them, the developed countries seek to prevent other developing countries from establishing effective coalitions against the issue. Third, the developed countries and their allies among developing countries can try to shame the naysayers, by claiming that the latter group of countries is standing in the way of other developing countries reaping the benefits from the outcomes of negotiations on these issues. It is indeed high diplomacy, if a country manages to push its interest on an issue by not only neutralizing potential opponents by convincing them that the issue is actually in their interest, but also getting them to become demandeurs of it at the negotiating table. Not only is all warfare based on deception,[30] much of international trade negotiations also appears to be along similar lines.

4.6 Using Policy Instruments to Browbeat Countries in Trade Negotiations

While it is contestable whether the meek shall inherit the earth, what is certain is that frequently at the negotiating table it is the strong that prevail. Some developed countries have used potent policy instruments to browbeat developing countries to give up their negotiating positions, and instead support the stance of the developed countries in the GATT/WTO negotiations. It is no secret that the USA picked on Brazil and India for their active opposition to initiating negotiations on standards related to intellectual property during the initial two and a half years of negotiations under the Uruguay Round at the GATT. In an attempt at compelling the countries to change their negotiating stance on issues related to IPRs, the USA imposed 100% tariffs on $39 million worth of imports from Brazil.[31] It also started threatening India with unilateral action. These coercive actions helped the USA in advancing its objectives at the GATT negotiating table.

In a candid confession, AV Ganesan, a high-ranking Indian official who played a crucial role in the negotiations on IPRs, has identified 'the pressure exerted by the United States through its unilateral actions under Section 301 of the US Trade Act 1974 and the Special 301 provisions of the US Omnibus Trade and Competitiveness Act 1988' as an important factor in the change of India's approach to negotiations on IPRs in April 1989.[32] He also adds that 'Retaliatory action against Indian garment and other exports to the United States was looming large over India like a Damocles' sword, especially in the last few years of the Uruguay Round'.[33] In the face of the persistent threat and pressure applied by the USA, it is not surprising that within a few months of the threat of trade sanctions, Brazil and India fell in line with the wishes of the USA in the negotiations on standards of IPR protection.

4.7 Dangling the Carrot and Threatening with the Stick

While the use of the big stick has been an effective negotiating strategy deployed by the developed countries, the use of a carrot-and-stick approach by them also appears to have yielded results at the negotiating table. Typically, under this strategy the developed countries threaten to withdraw the carrot—the opportunity to export to their markets at low or zero tariffs[34]—if the concerned developing country fails to abide by their wishes in GATT/WTO negotiations. As zero-duty access into the markets of the USA and the EU has helped many developing countries to enhance their exports, the threat of its withdrawal has compelled some of these countries to align their approach at the negotiating table with that of the developed countries. The following two illustrations, spread over 25 years, will drive home the effectiveness of this strategy.

During the Uruguay Round, the USA threatened many developing countries with suspension of zero-duty access to its market under the Generalized System of Preferences (GSP) scheme, if they did not support and enact high standards of protection for IPRs.[35] In order to make the threat credible, in a few cases the USA imposed GSP penalties. This strategy appears to have been extremely effective, as the opposition from developing countries to negotiate IPRs at GATT dissipated by April 1989 and the USA and other developed countries could pursue their negotiating agenda on this issue almost unhindered.

The second example of the effective use of carrot and stick policy relates to the Trade Facilitation Agreement (TFA) finalized at the Bali Ministerial Meeting of the WTO in December 2013. Further, by July 2014, the WTO Members were mandated to agree to the protocol that would have made the TFA an integral part of the WTO family of agreements. However, many developing countries, including some African countries, had misgivings on the TFA. During May–July 2014, they showed their reluctance to agree to the protocol. In this situation of considerable uncertainty regarding the fate of the TFA, the USA stepped in. It resorted to the time-tested strategy of using the carrot and stick approach to compel the recalcitrant African countries to fall in line with its wishes on the TFA. It issued a veiled threat to stop market access benefits to the African countries under its African Growth and Opportunity Act (AGOA), if they did not support the TFA.[36] Given the high dependence of the African countries on the US market for their exports, foregoing the zero-tariff benefits under AGOA would have significantly reduced their exports. It is, therefore, not surprising that the African countries preferred to acquiesce to the TFA protocol rather than miss the opportunity to export to the USA. The redoubtable trade minister of South Africa, Rob Davies, admitted that although the African countries had concerns on the TFA, they were hesitant to get into the debate due to possible political ramifications involving AGOA.[37] The strings attached to the gift of zero-duty access to the markets of developed countries remain mostly invisible. However, as this example suggests, at crucial junctures in multilateral trade negotiations, the strings are pulled by the developed countries for decisively tilting the negotiating outcomes in their favour by persuading many developing countries to soften their opposition to the positions and interests of the developed countries.

4.8 Using Quislings to Influence Negotiating Positions of Developing Countries

A developed country does not always need to expend diplomatic capital to win over opponents among developing countries, or make side payments to them, or exercise its economic and political power to subdue them. In the context of multilateral trade negotiations, it appears that a few developed countries have mastered the art of 'cultivating' important political functionaries and key officials in developing countries and getting them to intercede on their behalf with ministers and high-level officials involved in negotiations in the developing country.[38] The crux of this strategy lies in inducing local functionaries in a developing country to influence their trade negotiators to align themselves with the positions advocated by the developed countries. Although this strategy is extremely intrusive, trade negotiators from developing countries tend to brush it under the carpet. In spite of a cloak of secrecy around this strategy, there is considerable circumstantial evidence to establish its existence. We discuss two illustrations of this strategy, which can be labelled as the Quisling strategy.[39]

T.S.R. Subramanian, who was one of the high-level Indian officials involved in the GATT Ministerial Meeting held during 24–29 November 1982, provides some candid details of this strategy. As Subramanian became India's topmost civil servant a few decades later, his narration of events at this Ministerial Meeting should be treated as credible. According to his account, at a crucial juncture in the negotiations during the 1982 GATT Ministerial Meeting in Geneva, India's Commerce Minister received a phone call from one of his ministerial colleagues, who urged him to soften India's opposition to initiate negotiation on new issues under the GATT framework.[40] At that juncture the ministerial colleague of the Commerce Minister had nothing to do with trade matters. Subramanian speculates that one of the developed countries was behind this late-night phone call. While this specific attempt failed to influence the minister and India's high-level trade diplomats, it was not for the want of trying by the developed country. The reality of the phone call is also confirmed by Bhagirath Lal Das, who was India's Ambassador to the GATT at the time of the 1982 GATT Ministerial Meeting.[41] There is considerable anecdotal evidence that this strategy was deployed repeatedly by the developed countries over the course of the subsequent decades as well, including in the illustration discussed subsequently.

The second example of the Quisling strategy relates to an important meeting on Agriculture negotiations in the Doha Round. A crucial issue under negotiation was the demand from some countries, including India, Indonesia, and Philippines, to acquire the right to impose additional duties to counter import surges and dips in prices of imported consignments of agricultural products. Commonly referred to as the Special Safeguard Mechanism (SSM), this became a highly contentious issue between the developed countries and a few developing countries on the one hand and a large number of developing countries on the other hand. Based on the recollection of a high-ranking former trade negotiator of India,[42] as given below, it is clear that a developed country had deployed the Quisling strategy in a bid to undermine India's negotiating stance on SSM.

During a crucial meeting on Agriculture negotiations in 2008, Kamal Nath, India's Commerce Minister, played hardball on the issue of SSM. In the course of this meeting in Geneva, one of India's seasoned negotiators received a text message from a very high-level government functionary in his country. The content of the message was not only surprising, but also disturbing. The message asked the following question on SSM: why is the Indian minister playing to the gallery? In the subsequent message the high-level government functionary also advised India's negotiators to soften the country's stand on SSM.

The Indian negotiator was surprised that within a few minutes of Kamal Nath talking tough on SSM in Geneva, the information had travelled to the high-level government functionary in New Delhi. On a closer scrutiny of the text message, the puzzle was solved. But it also raised an alarm. The name of a delegate from a developed country, who was present in the negotiating room, was mentioned at the end of the text message. Thus, it was evident that from the negotiating room the developed country's delegate had sent the text message to the high-level Indian functionary in New Delhi complaining about the approach of Kamal Nath. The high-level functionary had inadvertently forgotten to delete the name of the source of the message. The Indian negotiator found it disturbing that a developed country was attempting to undermine India's negotiating approach by using the influential high-level Indian functionary to intervene on its behalf. Formally, the high-level Indian functionary had little to do directly with WTO negotiations. However, he had kept a close eye on India's negotiating position on different issues. Despite remaining behind the scenes, he made his presence felt through his occasional suggestions to the negotiators. Notwithstanding his proximity to the top leadership in the country, it is to the credit of India's trade negotiators that on many occasions they could tactfully side-step his suggestions, many of which were at variance with the country's official negotiating stand. The content of the text message, along with the name of the source of the message, provides evidence that a developed country was using the high-level functionary in India as a pawn to tilt India's negotiating position in its favour.[43] This is a good illustration of the Quisling strategy in action.

4.9 Creating an Attractive BATNA

Gains in negotiations accrue to those with the most alternatives, including the availability of options outside that negotiation, often referred to bargaining power.[44] With the assurance of a better alternative to a negotiated agreement (BATNA) in its hand, a country can afford to negotiate hard. However, a BATNA may not always be readily available. In fact, countries may be required to expend considerable resources to create a BATNA. Further, it may require patience and time to create a BATNA. A glimpse of how a BATNA can be created, and its utility, is provided by the actions of the USA, which succeeded in negotiating the Trans-Pacific Partnership (TPP) Agreement and used it as a BATNA to abandon the Doha Round.

The USA, in close partnership with the EU, was at the forefront of launching the Doha Round of multilateral trade negotiations. The main objective of the USA in the Doha Round negotiations was to prise open markets for exports of its agriculture products, industrial goods, and services.[45] In addition, it sought to advance its commercial interests by using the Doha Round for negotiating binding rules on investment protection, competition and transparency in government procurement. However, as discussed in Section 3.4, the trend in the negotiations gradually started turning against the interests of the USA. In August 2004, the attempts of the USA-EU combine to negotiate binding rules on three Singapore Issues—Investment, Competition and Government Procurement—had already floundered. By the closing months of 2007 the USA found itself trapped in a double bind—unable to secure most of its interests, but at the risk of having to concede considerable ground on some issues of its defensive concern in agriculture. Continuing with the Doha Round would have meant granting concessions to the developing countries, but not securing meaningful reciprocal gains.[46]

Given this difficult situation, the USA desperately required an alternative to a negotiated outcome at the WTO, in other words an attractive BATNA that would be more closely aligned with its economic and commercial interests. With an attractive alternative outside the Doha negotiations in its pocket, it could then make credible threats to abandon the Doha Round. Its calculation is likely to have been that under such threats the countries blocking its interests at the WTO would back off. If the recalcitrant countries didn't keel over, then the USA could leave the Doha Round in a lurch and shift its energies to negotiate the alternate agreement among a few countries outside the WTO. Overall, such a BATNA appeared to be a win-win strategy for the USA. It appears to have proceeded to achieve this objective by following a two-pronged approach.

First, with a view to preventing the trend in the negotiations under the Doha Round going further against its interests, the USA dug in its heels. After December 2008, it sought to ensure that there would be no meaningful progress on most of the issues under the Doha Round. In parallel, in February 2008 the United States joined the discussions on investment and financial services under the so-called P4 umbrella, initiated by Brunei, Chile, New Zealand and Singapore in 2006.[47] The P4 gradually morphed into an agreement among twelve countries—called the Trans-Pacific Partnership Agreement. The TPP substantially reflected the US commercial and economic interest, which it was unable to secure at the WTO. Further, the TPP did not include issues on which the USA was defensive at the WTO, such as agriculture subsidies. After the TPP was finalized in October 2015, the stage was set for the USA to unleash the second prong of its strategy.[48]

Two months after the finalization of the TPP Agreement, at the tenth Ministerial Conference of the WTO, held in December 2015, the USA successfully foiled the attempt of many WTO Members to endorse concluding the Doha Round on the basis of the Doha mandates. As a result, the United States freed itself 'from the strictures of Doha', an objective strongly advocated by the USA.[49] Thus, it created a pathway for escaping from taking onerous commitments under the Doha Round, particularly in respect of farm support. With the Nairobi Ministerial Declaration[50] of the WTO having created a window for launching multilateral negotiations on issues such as investment, labour, environment etc., the provisions in the TPP could be brought back to the WTO as the template for future rule-making on these issues at the multilateral forum. The interplay between BATNA and shifting the negotiation from one forum to another can be an effective strategy for promoting the objectives at the negotiating table. However, successful deployment of this strategy requires foresight, resources, negotiating power and patience; absent any one of these components the strategy cannot succeed.

4.10 Conclusions

This chapter has examined an array of strategies deployed by the developed countries away from the negotiating table for pushing their interests in multilateral trade negotiations. At times, in pursuit of their negotiating objectives and in order to enhance the effectiveness of the strategies, the developed countries have deployed some of them in conjunction with each other. The strategies used by the developed countries to secure their negotiating objectives during the Uruguay Round of the GATT on issues related to intellectual property provides a good illustration. In order to overcome the opposition from Brazil and India to its strategy of shifting the negotiating forum on IPR issues from the WIPO to the GATT, the USA successfully used coercive strategies such as imposing high tariffs on imports from Brazil and threatening India with unilateral retaliatory tariffs on garment exports. Further, the USA created a narrative that the negotiations on IPRs were targeted against 'patent theft' and 'patent piracy'—an excellent illustration of successful framing of issues. The cumulative use of these strategies facilitated the success of the USA on IPR issues during the Uruguay Round.

What prevents most developing countries from using the strategies analysed in this chapter? In WTO negotiations, developing countries can band together and form coalitions to push their negotiating interests. On some occasions this strategy has helped them in partially overcoming power asymmetry at the negotiating table and to some extent achieving their objectives. In contrast, the power asymmetry against them gets further deepened in bilateral negotiations with the developed countries. Thus, for most developing countries, the WTO, rather than a bilateral forum, is the preferred forum for negotiating trade issues. Consequently, forum shifting may not be an effective strategy for developing countries in negotiations with the developed countries. In respect of a few other strategies, it is crucial to recognize that most developing countries are overwhelmingly dependent on the markets of the developed countries for boosting their exports. This, combined with the formidable political heft of the developed countries, rules out the possibility of the developing countries resorting to strategies such as carrot and stick policy, browbeating the developed countries in trade negotiations and using Quislings to influence trade negotiators. Further, lack of technical capacity in most developing countries reduces their chances of influencing negotiations through research. In addition, most developing countries face considerable hurdles, including relatively less access to Western news agencies, in effectively communicating their perspective and narrative on WTO negotiations to the global audience. Overall, subject to rare exceptions, it may not be practical to expect most developing countries to resort to the negotiating strategies discussed in this chapter. Most of these strategies are likely to remain the preserve of countries with political and economic clout—mainly the developed countries. At the negotiating table itself, these countries have resorted to additional strategies for securing outcomes in their favour. We discuss these strategies in the next chapter.

Notes

1. WTO document WT/MIN(96)/16, dated 13 December 1996, Ministerial Declaration on Trade in Information Technology Products.
2. Akiko Yanai, 'APEC and the WTO: Seeking Opportunities for Cooperation,' IDE APEC Study Centre Working Paper Series 99/00 No.2, Institute of Developing Economies, Chiba, 2000.
3. Yanai, 'APEC and the WTO'.
4. Ministerial Declaration adopted by the Fourth Session of the Ministerial Conference on 14 November 2001, paragraph 8 of the document no. WT/MIN(01)/DEC/1 dated 20 November 2001.
5. Ministerial Declaration adopted by the Fourth Session of the Ministerial Conference on 14 November 2001, paragraph 20 of the document no. WT/MIN(01)/DEC/1 dated 20 November 2001.
6. Decision adopted by the General Council on 1 August 2004 on Doha Work Programme, Document no. WT/L/579 dated 2 August 2004.
7. Ministerial Declaration adopted by the Fourth Session of the Ministerial Conference on 14 November 2001, paragraph 31 of the document no. WT/MIN(01)/DEC/1 dated 20 November 2001.
8. See, for example, the Agreement between the USA, Mexico and Canada (commonly referred to as the USMCA) signed on 30 November, 2018, and the Comprehensive and Progressive Agreement for Trans-Pacific Partnership (commonly referred to as the CPTT), signed on 8 March, 2018, which include detailed provisions on labour, environment, digital trade, good regulatory practices etc.; EU Vietnam Trade Agreement, signed on 30 June 2019, which includes provisions on labour, environment and human rights; and the EU-Chile Advanced Framework Agreement, signed on 13 December 2023, which includes provisions on climate change, energy, the environment, raw materials, disaster risk reduction, sustainable food systems and social issues such as labour rights, gender equality, and responsible business conduct.

9. Ministerial Statement on Trade and Environmental Sustainability, Trade and Environmental Sustainability Structured Discussions (TESSD), WTO document WT/MIN(21)/6/Rev.1 dated 3 December, 2021.
10. Joint Declaration on Trade and Women's Economic Empowerment on the Occasion of the WTO Ministerial Conference in Buenos Aires in December 2017.
11. Joint Statement on Electronic Commerce, WTO document WT/MIN(17)/60 dated 13 December, 2017.
12. See WTO website https://www.wto.org/english/thewto_e/minist_e/mc13_e/briefing_notes_e/ecommerce_e.htm. Accessed on 15 March 2024.
13. Draft Ministerial Decision on Adding the Investment Facilitation for Development Agreement to Annex IV of the WTO Agreement, WTO document WT/MIN(24)/W/25 dated 29 February 2024.
14. J.P. Singh, *Sweet Talk: Paternalism and Collective Action in North-South Trade Relations* (Stanford, CA: Stanford University Press, 2017), 23.
15. Charan Devereaux, Robert Z. Lawrence, and M.D. Watkins, 2006. *Case Studies in US Trade Negotiation Vol.1: Making the Rules* (Washington, DC: Institute for International Economics, 2006), 116.
16. Statement by Mr Pascal Lamy, Commissioner for Trade, European Communities. WTO Doha Ministerial Conference, WTO document WT/MIN(01)/ST/4 dated 10 November, 2001.
17. Statement by H.E. Mr. Robert B. Zoellick, United States Trade Representative. WTO Doha Ministerial Conference, WTO document WT/MIN(01)/ST/3 dated 10 November 2001.
18. Paul Blustein, *Misadventures of the Most Favoured Nations* (New York: Public Affairs, 2009), 155.
19. Blustein, *Misadventures of the Most Favoured Nations*, 155.
20. Susan B. Epstein, *GATT: The Uruguay Round Agreement and Developing Countries*, (Washington, DC: Foreign Affairs and National Defense Division), 1995, cited in Joseph Stiglitz and Andrew Charlton, *Free Trade For All: How Trade Can Promote Development* (Oxford and New York: Oxford University Press, 2005), 46.
21. Stiglitz and Charlton, *Free Trade For All*, 46.
22. *Human Development Report 1997* (New York and London: Oxford University Press, 1997), 82.
23. Stiglitz and Charlton, *Free Trade For All*, 46.
24. Kanaga Raja, 'G33 Criticizes World Bank Paper on Special Products', *SUNS—South North Development Monitor* no. 6170 dated 17 January 2007.
25. World Bank, Business Ready Methodology Handbook, 2023.
26. World Bank, Business Ready Methodology Handbook, 2023.
27. World Bank, Business Ready Methodology Handbook, 2023.
28. See, for example, Richard T. Rapp and Richard P. Rozek, 'Benefits and Costs of Intellectual Property Protection in Developing Countries,' *Journal of World Trade* (October 1990): 75–81.

29. Article III.3, WTO document TN/RL/W/213 dated 30 November 2007. Draft Consolidated Chair Texts of AD and SCM Agreements, Annex VIII Fisheries Subsidies.
30. Sun Tzu, *On the Art of War* trans. Lionel Giles (Atlanta, GA: Dalmatian Press, 2007), 25.
31. See Reagan, *Charging Patent Piracy, Imposes Sanctions on $39 Million of Brazilian Goods,* 5 Int'l Trade Rep. (BNA) No. 42, 1415 (26 October 1988).
32. A.V. Ganesan, 'Negotiating for India,' in *The Making of the TRIPS Agreement: Personal insights from the Uruguay Round Negotiators*, edited by Jayashree Watal and Antony Taubman (Geneva: World Trade Organization, 2015), 219.
33. Ganesan, 'Negotiating for India,' 219.
34. The two key developed members of GATT/WTO—the US and the EU—provide preferential access to their markets to the developing countries. Under various schemes, including the Generalized System of Preferences (GSP) and the Africa Growth Opportunity Act implemented by the USA, and the Cotonou Agreement implemented by the EU, these two developed members of GATT/WTO have provided duty-free access into their markets for exports from developing countries, or from groups of developing countries.
35. Susan K. Sell, 'Intellectual Property Protection and Antitrust in the Developing World: Crisis, Coercion, and Choice,' *International Organization* 49 (1995): 315–149.
36. 'Linking AGOA with TFA,' *Washington Trade Daily* 23, Number 154, 5 August 2014.
37. 'AGOA with TFA,' *WTD*, 5 August 2014.
38. T.S.R. Subramanian, *Journeys Through Babudom and Netaland: Governance in India* (New Delhi: Rupa publisher, 2004), 165.
39. The strategy of developed countries of pushing their negotiating objectives by using personnel in developing countries has been labelled 'Quisling strategy', after Vidkun Quisling. Quisling was a Norwegian politician, who collaborated with Nazi Germany during World War II. He headed the government of Norway during the country's occupation by Nazi Germany.
40. Subramanian, *Babudom and Netaland*, 170–71.
41. Personal papers of Bhagirath Lal Das, India's former ambassador to GATT, available with the author.
42. Interview with a former high-level trade negotiator of India, April 2020.
43. This episode is based on an interview with a former high-level trade negotiator of India, April 2020.
44. J.P. Singh, *Sweet Talk*, 48.
45. Statement of Robert Zoellick, USTR, during the Doha Ministerial Conference of the WTO, WTO document no. WT/MIN(01)/ST/3 dated 10 November 2001.
46. J.P. Singh, *Sweet Talk*, 48.
47. Deborah Elms, 'The Origins and Evolution of the Trans-pacific Partnership (TPP) Trade Negotiations,' Singapore: Asian Trade Centre Working Paper, 2015.

48. It may be noted that eventually, the US withdrew from the TPP Agreement.
49. See, for example, the statement by Michael Froman, USTR, at the plenary session of the Nairobi Ministerial Meeting of the WTO, available at https://www.wto.org/english/thewto_e/minist_e/mc10_e/mc10_planarysessions_e.htm#USA.
50. WTO document WT/MIN(15)/DEC dated 21 December 2015.

5
Strategies Used by Developed Countries at the Negotiating Table

5.1 Introduction

In the previous chapter, we discussed some strategies deployed by the developed countries away from the negotiating table. Developed countries have also deployed multiple strategies at the negotiating table for advancing their negotiating objectives—the focus of discussion and analysis in this chapter. It may be noted that at times the strands of strategies become so intertwined and operate in a continuum that it may not be easy to definitively classify a strategy into either of the two categories.

In this chapter we elaborate on the following strategies of developed countries at the negotiating table: keeping reluctant countries hooked to the negotiating table, exercising raw power to browbeat negotiators, sharing the negotiating load and fighting each other's battles at the negotiating table, burying issues of interest to developing countries by not engaging, spinning a spider's web to impede progress on issues of interest to developing countries, persisting with their proposals even if it takes many years to succeed, taking a giant leap through many small steps, starting soft but landing hard, salami tactics, manipulating information to secure advantage in negotiations, pressure-cooker strategy, using different dimensions of time to secure negotiating objectives, divide and prosper, and creating a facade of consensus through the use of 'clean negotiating text'.

Strategies in GATT and WTO Negotiations. Abhijit Das, Oxford University Press. © Abhijit Das 2025.
DOI: 10.1093/9780198934431.003.0005

5.2 Keeping Reluctant Parties Hooked to the Negotiating Table by Initially Granting Concessions

An important objective of the powerful players in negotiations is to prevent the foot-draggers and the weak from abandoning the negotiation and keeping them engaged. The strategy of the developed countries has been to concede ground on some issues at the initial stage of a negotiation, without insisting on a commensurate quid pro quo. This demonstrates goodwill on their part, which can be leveraged to wrest concessions at a later stage. Once the weak parties have gained some concessions initially, 'they may become desperate to see a negotiation through' and not abandon the talks.[1] The initial concessions granted to the weak parties act as baits for keeping them hooked to the negotiation.

A relevant illustration of this strategy at the WTO is evident in how the developed countries got a large number of developing countries to agree to the launch of the Doha Round of multilateral trade negotiations. As will be elaborated in Chapter 7, at the Doha Ministerial Conference in 2001 many developing countries were opposed to the launch of these negotiations, particularly in respect of the four Singapore Issues. In an effort at getting a large number of developing countries to support the launch of a new trade round, the developed countries agreed to a crucial demand of the developing countries in respect of affordable access to medicine.[2] While this issue was not directly linked with the launch of the new round, yet, this initial concession kept many developing countries hooked to the negotiating table. India, which had firmly resisted the launch of an ambitious round of trade negotiations, was mindful of losing the gains made by the developing countries on access to affordable medicine. This proved to be one of the key reasons which prevented India from walking away from the negotiating table and compelled it to eventually agree to the launch of the Doha Round.

5.3 Exercise of Raw Power

In pursuit of their negotiating objectives, developed countries have wielded raw power in a variety of forms, the principal two being the following: threatening to wield the big stick through policy changes, and in some cases carrying out the threat, to force countries to fall in line with their wishes; and browbeating ministers and negotiators who come in their way of achieving success in negotiations. In the previous chapter we have discussed in detail how the USA retaliated against some countries and compelled them to agree to negotiate standards of IPR protection in the GATT. In this section we discuss the second variant of this strategy. Reflexive response of the powerful to a situation involving a perceived threat to its negotiating objective can take various forms including the following: directly threatening and browbeating negotiators into submission; and undermining 'difficult' ministers by complaining to his prime minister/president. Trade negotiators can recount many incidents about the exercise of raw power at the GATT/WTO negotiating table by the developed countries as a negotiating strategy to tilt outcomes in their favour.

5.3.1 Browbeating Negotiators Who Come in the Way of Developed Countries

During multilateral trade negotiations, developed countries have not hesitated in browbeating negotiators from developing countries who come in their way at the negotiating table. While resort to this strategy is not frequent, it is not rare either. Nothing illustrates the use of this strategy, and also its limitations, better than the graphic description of the GATT Ministerial Meeting held on 24–29 November 1982. An important issue under negotiation in the meeting was whether GATT should commence multilateral negotiation on services, which was being pushed mainly by one developed country, but strongly opposed by a group of developing countries, led by India.

According to the recollection of Bhagirath Lal Das, who was India's ambassador to GATT during the 1982 Ministerial Meeting held in Geneva, at a crucial stage in the negotiation, a senior official from the capital of the developed country, who was in the country's delegation, stood up and said in a loud and menacing voice: 'Who in the *** delegation (name of the country withheld) is opposing the text on Services? Please tell me. We will contact his capital and have him transferred straight away.' With the seasoned and highly respected ambassador of this country not present in the meeting, others in the delegation of this developing country had to handle the dismal display of raw power. The senior-most official from this country, who was present, was somewhat mild. Clearly, he was totally stunned by the threat from the official of the developed country and was in no position to defend himself. For Das the threat was the limit of provocation. He immediately came in support of the developing country and announced in a loud voice: 'We would not like to enter into negotiation under such threats. This is not acceptable to us.' Saying this, he stood up to leave the room. The ambassador of the developed country involved in this incident immediately apologized to the official who had been threatened and calm was soon restored in the negotiating room.[3] Not many negotiators from developing countries would have mustered courage to stand up to this blatant attempt at browbeating at the negotiating table.

5.3.2 Undermining 'Difficult' Ministers by Directly Approaching the Prime Minister/President of the Country

There have been occasions when some of the developed countries did not hesitate in trying to undermine a developing country's negotiating approach by contacting the prime minister/president of the country and complaining against its trade minister. This strategy is used during crucial phases of negotiations and is mainly directed against a handful of countries, which stand in the way of the developed countries meeting their negotiating goals. It is almost a common knowledge in trade circles in New Delhi that at a crucial stage in the Doha Ministerial Conference, the prime minister of one of the developed countries spoke to the Indian prime minister, A.B. Vajpayee, and urged him to intercede with minister Maran, who was blamed for holding up a big trade deal at Doha. To the credit of the Indian prime minister, this telephone call did not work.[4]

5.4 Sharing the Load, Accommodating Each Other and Fighting Each Other's Battles

An important strategy of the two key developed country participants in GATT/WTO negotiations—the EU and the USA—is to effectively coordinate their positions and cooperate on key issues at the negotiating table. While there could be minor difference in perspectives and interests of these two members on some issues, there appears to be close synchronization and convergence in their broad approach to different aspects of multilateral trade negotiation—what issues to be included in the negotiating agenda, identifying chairs for different negotiating groups, modalities of negotiation, closing the negotiation, etc.

The strategy of close coordination and cooperation between the two largest members of the WTO was evident during the Doha Round. At a time when many developing countries were demanding steep reduction in farm support by the developed countries and trying to protect their farmers through tariffs, a joint proposal by the EU and the USA sought to achieve just the opposite outcome. Under their joint proposal, the actual reduction in domestic support by them would have been minimal. On the other hand, the tariffs of developing countries, particularly the larger among them, would have been significantly lowered. What dynamics this joint proposal unleashed will be discussed in Chapter 8.

While the close cooperation between the EU and the USA to accommodate each other's interest was clearly evident in Agriculture negotiations, the two members also fought each other's battles in certain other areas as well. To illustrate, during the Doha Ministerial Conference, Japan and some developing countries were at the forefront of the move to seek an ambitious negotiating mandate on the subject of anti-dumping. On this issue, the USA was on the back foot. Grant Aldonas, the American negotiator, was seeking to protect the US interests in the negotiation with the key proponents of disciplines on anti-dumping—Chile, Japan, and Korea. However, in some of the larger meetings on this subject, the USA chose not to be present. Instead, in these meetings it was Pascal Lamy, the EU Trade Commissioner, who appeared to be batting for the interests of the USA on anti-dumping. His frequent assertion, supposedly made in a jocular vein, was that on this issue the rest of the WTO membership was isolated against the USA. Hence, they must not press the USA too hard on this subject.[5] The final negotiating mandate that emerged protected many of the key concerns of the USA on anti-dumping.

As a payback, when the mandate on trade and environment issue was being negotiated during the Doha Ministerial Conference, it was Robert Zoellick, the USTR, who pushed ahead on behalf of the

EU—the main proponent seeking a strong negotiating mandate on this issue. However, this issue met with considerable resistance from many developing countries. Sensing the strong opposition to EU's proposal on environment, Zoellick threw a lifeline to the EU. During the crucial meeting of a handful of countries held on 13–14 November 2001, Zoellick's constant refrain was that since the EU would have to make concessions in agriculture, other countries must help the EU in securing some gains for its constituents in other areas. With the active support of the USA behind it, it is not surprising that the EU secured a strong mandate for negotiations on environment. The strategy of the USA and EU fighting each other's battles had won the day (or more appropriately the night, as the negotiations continued throughout the night of 13 November and the early hours of 14 November 2001). As part of the official Indian delegation to this Ministerial Conference, the author was privy to these developments.

Celso Amorim, Brazil's Minister of Foreign Relations and a key player in the Doha Round, provides another illustration, a rather dramatic one at that, of how the EU and the USA closely coordinate their positions and attempt to secure an advantage at the negotiating table. According to Amorim's account, during the meeting of a small group of Members comprising Brazil, the EU, India, and the USA held in Potsdam on 19–21 June 2007, Peter Mandelson, the Trade Commissioner of the EU and Susan Schwab, the USTR, started wrangling about what Amorim had said the previous night about tariff reductions on industrial goods. Amorim sensed that the shared objective of this choreographed farce was to back him into a corner and place the blame for the eventual collapse of the meeting on Brazil and India. Amorim mentions that later he found out the these two dramatis personae had met the night before in a restaurant, fittingly called Il Teatro, to 'decide upon the scene they would stage' the next day.[6]

5.5 Burying Proposals and Issues of Interest to Some Developing Countries by Not Engaging

In this section we discuss the strategy aimed at burying issues of interest to developing countries by not engaging in the negotiation. By digging in their heels and not engaging, the powerful players at the negotiating table may compel others to lower their ambition and also revise their bottom line. Further, this strategy may occasionally be used to gauge whether the proponent is merely posturing or has genuine interest in the issue. This strategy is elaborated by discussing two examples from different areas—services and agriculture.

Towards the end of the Uruguay Round, on 15 December 1993, a decision was taken at the ministerial level for undertaking negotiations for further liberalization of movement of persons across borders for delivering services. The decision was mainly aimed at providing succour to the developing countries, who felt short changed by inadequate market opening by the developed countries in this mode of supply of services—perceived to be of competitive advantage to many developing countries. It was expected that the outcome of this negotiation would result in further opening of services market by the developed countries. According to one of the key proponents of this issue, while the developed countries attended the negotiating sessions, they did not engage in any meaningful discussion. With the negotiating meetings lasting less than an hour, there appeared to be a lack of political will and good faith on the part of the developed countries to take this issue forward.[7] It is not surprising that out of sheer frustration India, Pakistan, and Philippines—the main proponents of this issue—were compelled to abandon the negotiations in an area of their interest.

An illustration from Agriculture negotiations further attests to the success of the strategy of non-engagement adhered to by the developed countries on some issues of interest to many developing countries. At the Hong Kong Ministerial Conference of the WTO, held in 2005, it was decided that the developing countries would have the right to have recourse to a Special Safeguard Mechanism (SSM) to impose additional duties in case of surge in imports of agricultural products, or dip in their prices.[8] Considerable technical work was undertaken on this issue and a detailed legal text on it was ready by December 2008.[9] Although this text had some gaps, it marked a significant progress in the negotiation on SSM. At the Nairobi Ministerial Conference held in December 2015, the need to take forward the negotiation on this issue was reiterated by the entire WTO Membership.[10] However, after this ministerial meeting, most of the developed countries refrained from engaging meaningfully on SSM.[11] Consequently, despite there being a specific mandate, even eight years down the line no progress could be made on this issue.

5.6 Impeding Progress on Issues of Interest to Developing Countries by Spinning a Spider's Web Around Them

In the previous section we discussed how the strategy of non-engagement by some developed countries has been effective in killing proposals of interest to many developing countries. In this section we discuss another strategy that has been used towards the same objective. Under this strategy, while the developed countries engage in discussions on proposals from some developing countries, they also impede progress in the negotiations by raising a large number of technical questions. No doubt, the process of dialogue can result in providing clarity on technical aspects of negotiating proposals. However, the dialogue through question and answer becomes problematic when an issue requires a political resolution, which is not forthcoming on the plea that there is inadequate technical clarity on the matter. Often, the proponents of the proposal have no option other than giving up pursuing some issues of their interests. The developed countries have used this strategy effectively to block progress on issues of particular interest to a large number of developing countries during the Doha Round.

During much of 2001, negotiations on Implementation Issues, which were issues of interest to many developing countries, occupied considerable attention of the negotiators at the WTO. As the negotiations on some of these issues unfolded, the determination of the developed countries to address them manifested in unexpected ways—impeding progress by raising technical objections. To illustrate, India made a detailed proposal for addressing the interpretation of rules on countervailing duty (CVD) investigations and their implementation by various investigating authorities.[12] In respect of one of the issues related to countervailing duty investigations, India's proposal sought to address the rampant problem of excess countervailing duties, which was hurting exports, particularly of developing countries. Despite there being considerable force in India's proposal on CVD investigations, it got mired in a technical web spun mainly by the developed countries. Almost fifty questions on the proposal were raised, mainly by the EU, the USA, and Canada. Colombia and Egypt also raised a few questions. All these were responded to by India. However, the developed countries were in no mood to agree to the proposal and refused to move ahead. Eventually no final decision could be taken on it. The strategy of spinning a spider's web around a developing country's proposal had succeeded.

Did the developed countries deliberately decide not to allow any forward movement on India's proposal on excess countervailing, or was India's proposal and responses to the questions not convincing? While during 2001 to 2017 there could have been some uncertainty on this, we now have a definite answer to this question. India's proposal on limiting countervailing duty to the amount of the subsidy eventually got validated by the judicial arm of the WTO. In the dispute *EU- Countervailing Measures on certain Polyethylene Terephthalate from Pakistan* initially the dispute panel,[13] and subsequently the Appellate Body[14] of the WTO, ruled that the relevant provisions of the ASCM did not allow investigating authorities to countervail the entire amount of the tax concession—only the concession in excess of the tax paid could be countervailed. This is precisely what India had argued in its Implementation-related proposal. This should remove any lingering doubt about the legal merits of India's proposal and the clarifications provided by it in response to the questions raised by some WTO members. The questions posed appear to have been a part of the strategy of impeding forward movement of the proposal, and less about seeking clarifications from the proponent. Many other proposals on Implementation Issues met a similar fate.

5.7 Even If You Do Not Succeed, Keep Trying

Remember the fable about King Bruce of Scotland who managed to wrest back his kingdom from the invaders after six failures? Even in trade negotiations, persistence pays. Developed countries are rarely discouraged by the lack of support for, or even stiff opposition to, their proposal—the issues are kept alive through a process of 'examination' or 'study'. Undeterred by the failures of the past, the core elements of the proposals are repackaged and put yet again on the negotiating table. In the face of such persistence by the proponents, the resistance of opponents often withers away.

The most spectacular example of success of this strategy relates to various facets of investment and protecting the interests of investors. Negotiations on this issue were initially disguised as negotiation on performance requirements—with the USA being the main proponent during the 1982 Ministerial Meeting of GATT. However, in the face of stiff resistance from many developing countries, this attempt did not succeed. But the protagonist was not deterred by this failure. It maintained pressure on the GATT Contracting Parties and eventually secured the mandate to commence negotiations on this issue at the Punta Del Este meeting in 1986, where the Uruguay Round was launched. Eventually, binding agreement on this subject became an integral part of the WTO—the TRIMS agreement. The saga of negotiation on performance requirements did not end with the TRIMS agreement. While the developed countries succeeded in prohibiting some performance requirements related to investment, they failed to secure many of their negotiating objectives. Progressively, as larger share of investments from the developed countries started flowing to the developing countries, it triggered the need to protect the interests of their investors, particularly repatriation of royalties and profits back to the home country of the investor. In this background, during the first Ministerial Conference of the WTO held in Singapore in 1996, an attempt was made to initiate negotiations on investment issues. After encountering stiff resistance from some developing countries, the proponents lowered their ambition and settled for a working group to examine the relationship between trade and investment.[15] Subsequently, at the Doha Ministerial Conference in 2001 it was agreed that negotiations for a multilateral framework on investment 'will take place after the Fifth Session of the Ministerial Conference on the basis of a decision to be taken, by explicit consensus, at that Session on modalities of negotiations'.[16]

Despite the mandate, a large number of developing countries continued to harbour strong reservations on issues related to investment. Eventually, in August 2004 this issue was dropped from the negotiating agenda of the Doha Round.[17] This issue was resurrected at the Buenos Aires Ministerial Conference of the WTO, held in December 2017, where seventy countries jointly called for 'beginning structured discussions with the aim of developing a multilateral framework on investment facilitation'.[18] Eventually, these negotiations, championed mainly by the developed countries and China, were concluded during the Abu Dhabi Ministerial Conference held in February 2024.[19] While the rules under investment facilitation are somewhat different from what the advanced economies might have envisaged in respect of investment protection, the former should be seen as creating a pathway for negotiating binding rules on the latter issue. It would be fair to conclude that issues of interest to the developed countries in the GATT/WTO negotiations seem to be more enduring than the proverbial cat with nine lives.

5.8 A Giant Leap by Taking Many Small Steps

Just as a revolution does not often happen overnight, the journey of an agreement at GATT/WTO is a story of a series of small steps. While each step may appear rather innocuous, it constitutes a firm march towards the ultimate objective of a negotiated agreement. This strategy has been manifested in different subject areas and used so repeatedly that it now constitutes a well-trodden path. The evolution of the General Agreement on Trade in Services (GATS) illustrates the success of this strategy.

As predicted by economic theory, in some developed countries the services sector started acquiring greater salience in economic activities than the manufacturing sector. By 1980 services accounted for almost 59 per cent of the GDP of the USA.[20] While the sectors of importance and competitive strengths in the developed countries were shifting towards services, the rules of international trade as contained in GATT did not cover services. From the perspective of the developed countries this gap in trade rules needed to be plugged quickly. But the problem was that most developing countries had very little commercial interest in negotiating binding rules on services, as this sector accounted for less than 45 per cent of the GDP in their economy. From the perspective of countries such as Brazil, India, Indonesia, and Malaysia, a binding agreement on services would not bring much economic and commercial benefit to their countries. Further, premature liberalization of this sector could prevent its growth in developing countries. Predictably, most of the developing countries were lukewarm, if not totally opposed, to the idea of negotiating binding rules on services at the GATT.

It was in this context of divergent economic interests between the developed and developing countries on services, that the USA made the first move at the GATT. During the annual meeting of the GATT Contracting Parties held in 1981, it persuaded other countries to convene the next meeting of the Contracting Parties at the level of Ministers in November 1982 (MM 82). During MM 82 the USTR, William Brock, made an aggressive and strong pitch for initiating negotiations on services. However, on account of firm resistance from Brazil and India, he had to lower his ambitions a few notches. Ultimately, MM 82 stopped short of providing a negotiating mandate on services. Instead, it was decided to initiate a 'work programme', which required countries to undertake national studies on services, exchange information among themselves and then consider whether a multilateral framework was necessary and appropriate. Without waiting for the conclusion of the work programme, in May 1983 the USA pushed for initiating a new round of multilateral trade negotiations, which would include new issues such as services.[21] However, this push did not see much traction from the developing countries—who, in May 1984, defiantly announced that 'Unless and until the work programme is fully implemented . . . any initiative such as a new round of negotiations would be lacking in credibility and devoid of relevance, particularly for developing countries.'[22] At the Punte del Este Ministerial Meeting of GATT, held in 1986, the USA succeeded in securing a negotiating mandate for services. Eventually, with the establishment of the WTO in 1995, the General Agreement on Trade in Services (GATS) became a part of the multilateral trading system. Thus, what appeared in the GATT agenda as a part of the work programme in 1982, eventually became the subject matter of a full-fledged agreement in 1995. 'Once the process of "study" or "examination" starts, "negotiation" and "agreement" generally follow, sooner or later.'[23]

5.9 Starting Soft, Landing Hard

A strategy that has been resorted to by the developed countries effectively is to initially advocate a moderate position on an issue, but gradually harden their stance as the negotiation progresses. How, and why, does this strategy work? Is there any concrete illustration of this strategy?

By refraining from taking a hard line on an issue of their interest at the outset of a negotiation, the developed countries succeed in whittling down opposition to their proposal. Thereafter, in the negotiations with the opponents, who would merely be a handful of countries, the proponent hardens its stand. Through stratagems such as exercising raw power, issue linkage, or by making side payments, the proponent gets its way on an option that is more stringent than its initial soft position. With the small group of opponents no longer opposing even the hard option, the larger group of countries quickly acquiesces to the demands of the proponent. The key to success of this strategy is that it is easier to deploy the stratagems against a small group of countries, as compared to a larger group, and reap the negotiating benefits. It would take an exceptionally courageous country from the larger group, which had initially not opposed the soft option, to protest later against the hard option.

How the EU succeeded in having its way on issues related to trade and environment during the Doha Ministerial Conference provides a good illustration of this strategy. This requires some elaboration. When Murasoli Maran, India's beleaguered trade minister, slowly made his way to the Presidential Suite 11 at around 6 p.m. on 13 November 2001, for a do-or-die meeting of about two dozen WTO members, issues related to trade and environment were far from his mind. The negotiating text issued earlier in the day by the Chairman of the Ministerial Conference had protected his interest on the subject.[24] It excluded negotiation on the controversial issue of trade and environment—being pushed by the EU with considerable zeal. Maran was more pre-occupied with the four Singapore Issues and how to continue his dogged opposition to the initiation of negotiations on them. However, when he and other ministers walked out of the Presidential Suite during the early hours of the morning on the next day, rubbing their eyes and barely awake after a marathon and gruelling ten-hour meeting, they had almost agreed to a text that mandated negotiations on issues related to trade and environment. How did this come about?

In respect of trade and environment, the Draft Ministerial Text prepared by the Chairman of the Ministerial Conference and circulated to the WTO Members earlier in the day[25] provided for negotiations on two issues—reduction, or elimination, of tariffs and non-tariff barriers on environmental goods and services; and procedures for regular information exchange between secretariats of Multilateral Environment Agreements (MEAs) and the relevant WTO committees. Crucially, the Draft Ministerial Text had a non-negotiating component—WTO's Committee on Trade and Environment (CTE) to give particular attention to the relationship between the MEAs and the multilateral trading system and make recommendation on future action, including the desirability of negotiations on it. As the text did not provide a negotiating mandate for MEAs and their relationship with the relevant WTO agreements, it did not evoke strong opposition from most developing countries, including India. However, when the discussions among a limited group of about two dozen countries commenced at 6 p.m. on 13 November 2001, the EU and the USA confronted the small group with a text that provided for negotiations on the relationship between specific trade obligations set out in MEAs and the existing WTO rules. Maran and ministers from other developing countries in the small group were unable to prevent this hard text from galloping ahead. Eventually, the hard text was included in the final Doha Ministerial Declaration.[26]

If the hard text had been included in the Draft Ministerial Text prepared earlier in the day and circulated to the entire Membership, it is likely to have encountered stiff resistance from many developing countries. It would have been dead on arrival. By starting with a soft text, the EU managed to contain the opposition to its goal of securing a negotiating mandate for the relationship between MEAs and WTO obligations. Thereafter, its task was limited to hectoring and browbeating the handful of opponents in the small group meeting into submission.[27] The strategy of starting soft, but landing hard, proved to be handy and effective in pushing EU's negotiating objective on this subject.

5.10 Manipulating Information to Secure Advantage

Access to right information at the appropriate time is crucial in most situations that involve decision-making. In negotiations at the WTO involving more than a hundred countries, manipulation of information by some developed countries has been used as a strategy for pursuing negotiating gains. In this section we discuss two illustrations of this strategy.

Coalitions among developing countries are fragile, particularly during ministerial conferences. Spreading misinformation as a strategy to splinter coalitions appears to have been resorted to in some ministerial meetings. An effective use of this strategy was witnessed during the Doha Ministerial Conference. India was leading the charge against initiating negotiations on the four Singapore Issues. In the initial days of this meeting, the African countries were supporting India and it appeared that the Singapore Issues were in for a rough ride. A multi-pronged strategy for creating a schism between India and the African countries, including by spreading misinformation, seems to have been set in motion.

In a meeting of the African countries, a prominent African minister, known for his closeness to the developed countries, said that the group should rethink its opposition to the Singapore Issues as India had struck a deal with the USA and the EU behind their back. However, the ambassador of another African country had already got wind of this rumour and in an attempt at pre-empting the misinformation from spreading, had requested the Indian ambassador, S. Narayanan, to be available near the venue of Africa Group meeting. This African ambassador said: 'We must not believe in these rumours. India's ambassador is available nearby. Let us call him and get the facts.' However, the prominent minister came out with this unforgettable ludicrous statement: 'India's ambassador does not know that his country's position has changed. There is no point in calling him here.'[28] Thereafter, the support of African countries for India's position on the Singapore Issues became lukewarm. Spreading misinformation had worked rather well. Although the prominent minister had become a conduit for spreading the misinformation, the developed countries, who were the main proponents of the four Singapore Issues, were the beneficiaries.

This strategy was deployed again, this time during the Cancun Ministerial Conference in 2003. At this ministerial meeting the opposition to the Singapore Issues had become more widespread than what had been witnessed at Doha. With almost 100 countries opposing the Singapore Issues, the time had come to create fissures among the developing countries. A rumour started swirling that a prominent member of the coalition was in the process of defecting. Arun Jaitley, India's

Commerce Minister, became wise to the mischief afoot. In order to dispel any notion of cracks appearing in the group against the Singapore Issues, a press conference was quickly organized. The minister under suspicion was given a prominent role in responding to queries from the media. This sent a strong message of cohesion within the coalition. Prompt action prevented damage that could have arisen from rumour-mongering and spreading misinformation.[29]

5.11 Pressure-Cooker Strategy

We have discussed some strategies that require developed countries to either indulge in power play or make side payments in order to stamp their will on the developing countries, which resist their overtures. Are there strategies that are deployed to achieve the same objective, but without expending any capital—diplomatic or monetary? A particularly effective and low-cost weapon in the arsenal of developed countries can be termed as the pressure-cooker strategy. What is this strategy and how does it work?

As the name suggests, this strategy is used for applying intense pressure on developing countries to change their approach to key issues at the negotiating table. The important point to note is that the pressure applied is neither political nor financial, but intellectual. The general contour of this strategy is to organize a meeting and pit the minister or high-level negotiator from a 'difficult' country against a group of seemingly neutral experts, but who, in reality, have been hand-picked to espouse the objectives of the developed countries. With all the other speakers singing the same tune, it becomes extremely challenging for the contrarian voice to escape this intellectual contest without mental scars. More often than not, the 'difficult' country falls in line rather than go against the tide. In a rare publicly available account, T.S.R. Subramanium narrates how India's trade minister, who was subjected to this strategy, could articulate his opposition to initiating negotiations on services only in muted terms and his implied acquiescence was announced as full support for the US position.[30]

A minor variation of this strategy was visible in small group meetings organized on different negotiating topics during 2014–2015 for deciding the work programme on different issues under the Doha Round after the Bali Ministerial Conference. If we were to closely examine the composition of different groups, it would become obvious that in some of the groups a developing country with a particular negotiating position was arrayed against most others having an opposite negotiating position.[31] The attempt clearly was to intellectually isolate the contrarian voice, which may thereafter be compelled to rethink its negotiating stance.

5.12 Effective Use of Time in Its Different Dimensions

Many negotiators will aver to the role of time as an important variable in determining the outcome of negotiations. This variable has been used effectively in different strategies by the developed countries for meeting their negotiating objectives. During ministerial conferences of the WTO, long meetings, at times lasting almost twelve hours, have become a norm. As observed by the author, developed countries are able to rotate their officials in these meetings. On the other hand, most developing countries rarely have more than one or two well-informed top-level government officials. Consequently, the same officials have to continue to participate in the marathon negotiating sessions. With weary and fatigued negotiators from developing countries contesting against almost fresh and alert negotiators from the developed countries, the outcome of the marathon negotiating sessions is usually a foregone conclusion. This strategy can help break the resistance of opponents of the developed countries on different issues. We have already seen how at the Doha Ministerial Conference developing countries conceded considerable ground on trade and environment linkage during the ten-hour meeting held on 13–14 November 2001.

Another shrewd use of time as a strategy is to convene at extremely short notice a one-to-one meeting between a developing country and the Director General of WTO, or with a developed country, at odd hours, either at the dead of night or during the early hours of the morning. A sleep-deprived minister staggering into crucial meetings is not an unusual sight during ministerial conferences. It requires a minister with amazing stamina to protect her country's interest effectively during such meetings.

Perhaps the most effective use of time as a negotiating strategy gets manifested during the last few hours of WTO ministerial conferences. Key decisions in WTO negotiations are normally taken by small groups of countries. Most developing countries are generally not aware of the developments within these small-group meetings. However, after the final outcome of the ministerial conference—usually in the form of a draft ministerial declaration—has been circulated to all the Members, adequate time is rarely made available to countries for examining its implications. Even if the delegation of a developing country includes a lawyer—a luxury which most developing countries do not have—a couple of hours may be woefully inadequate to understand the implications of a draft ministerial declaration and its related documents. These documents are dense with legalese and technicalities, whose meaning is comprehensible to only those who have been closely involved in negotiating the text. With the deadline of the ministerial meeting looming and little prospects of postponing their departure, most developing countries silently acquiesce to an outcome whose implications they may not fully understand. By confronting the developing countries with an outcome literally at the last moment, the developed countries have managed to extract 'consent'. Despite protests after the meeting, this process has been repeated at various ministerial conferences, including at Nairobi (2015).[32] It would thus appear that this pattern has become a part of the strategy of the developed countries to push their negotiating interests in these important meetings.

5.13 Salami Tactics for Overcoming Opposition at the Negotiating Table

How do developed countries respond when they encounter extremely stiff opposition from a handful of countries at the negotiating table? In some situations in the past, they opted to tackle the problematic countries separately, preferably one by one—and not collectively—at the negotiating table. How does this strategy help? By dealing with each country separately and using the big stick, the developed countries can effectively ratchet up pressure on the recalcitrant countries. This strategy also creates an opportunity for information asymmetry, which can be exploited to convey to one recalcitrant party that the other opponents have backed down. Fearing isolation, each country falls in line with the negotiating objective of the developed country. This would not be possible, if the opponents were to be persuaded collectively.

During the past decade, salami tactics has unfolded in another guise to whittle down the opposition at the WTO to the negotiating objectives of the developed countries on non-trade issues, such as labour, environment, and investment. We have already had a glimpse of this aspect of salami tactics while discussing issues related to the negotiating forum. Instead of confronting the opponents of contentious issues collectively at the WTO, the USA and the EU have chosen to engage with some developing countries individually through FTA negotiations. By getting one developing country at a time to agree to rules on non-trade issue in the FTAs, the USA and the EU are gradually getting more developing countries to cross over to their side. This strikes at the root of the opposition to negotiating non-trade issues at the WTO. No doubt this tactics requires patience, but it can be extremely potent in helping the USA and the EU to push their interests on non-trade issues at the WTO.

5.14 Divide and Prosper

One of the sources of power at the negotiating table, particularly for developing countries, is to form coalitions and coordinate negotiating positions with other countries. The strategic response of the developed countries is rather predictable—divide and prosper; weaken the coalitions that stand in their way and secure their negotiating objectives. This strategy works best in conjunction with certain other strategies—use of carrot and stick, making side payments, salami tactics, using bilateralism to systematically break the unity of developing countries, and spreading misinformation. In our discussion of these complementary strategies, we have already got a glimpse of the divide and prosper strategy. Chapter 8 provides details of how this strategy was used by the developed countries in an attempt at splitting the G-20 coalition in Agriculture negotiations.

Another manifestation of this strategy is to divide developing countries into different categories and require varying level of obligations from them, while proposing the most stringent obligations on those developing countries who have the potential to provide competition to the developed countries. With most of the groups of developing countries focusing on their narrow national interests and being comfortable with the level of obligations sought to be imposed on them, the incentive for these countries to create coalitions, or join coalitions created by the more advanced developing economies, would decline. A good illustration of this strategy can be found in the WTO negotiations aimed at disciplining subsidies that contribute to over-capacity and over-fishing. The most recent version of the negotiating text available in April 2024 divides the developing countries into the following five categories: least-developed countries, developing countries whose share of the annual global volume of marine capture production does not exceed 0.8 per cent, countries who have graduated from the LDC category, developing countries who are amongst the ten largest providers of fisheries subsidies, and the residual developing countries not falling into any of the four categories.[33] While developing countries in the first two categories are not proposed to be subjected to prohibition on subsidies that contribute to over-fishing and over-capacity, countries in the other three categories are proposed to be subjected to the prohibition after a transition period and for fishing in different geographical areas. Most of the developing countries, as well as the LDCs, are included in the first two categories, which will not face the pinch of the new rules on fisheries subsidies. With the national interests of most of the developing countries in respect of fisheries subsidies likely to be already protected through various exceptions, it is not surprising that about a dozen developing countries, who would be required to take the most onerous commitments, were unable to create an effective coalition in these negotiations. It is relevant to note that this group includes countries such as Argentina, India, Indonesia, Mexico, Peru, and Philippines—some of whom could seek to pose competitive challenge to the economic prospects of the developed countries in the marine sector. By isolating these countries from the other developing countries, the strategy of divide and prosper appears to have succeeded in these negotiations.

5.15 Strategy of a Clean Negotiating Text: Creating a Facade of Consensus

Individuals chairing meetings relating to negotiations at the GATT/WTO play a crucial role in creating consensus and helping countries to reach compromises on knotty issues. How a chair conducts meetings, prioritizes issues, summarizes discussions, perceives support or lack of it for some proposals and reflects them in the negotiating text become critical in determining the outcome of negotiations. It is reasonable to expect that the chairpersons of negotiating bodies at the GATT/WTO would remain even-handed and balanced in the discharge of their responsibilities. No doubt chairpersons have been mandated by the Trade Negotiating Committee to 'reflect consensus, or where this is not possible, different positions on issues'.[34] However, there have been occasions when negotiating texts prepared by some chairpersons of the meeting resulted in pushing the negotiating interest of one or more developed countries. This creates a suspicion that chairs have not always been independent in their functioning, and on some occasions may have come under the influence of some powerful players at the negotiating table. The possibility of this being a negotiating strategy cannot be ruled out.

One way in which a chair can promote the negotiating interests of a few countries is by preparing a clean text that reflects the views of those countries, while largely ignoring other perspectives on that issue. In fact, the initiation of the Doha Round can be construed to be based on this strategy. It is a norm that the draft text for the ministerial declaration is initially negotiated by the diplomats in Geneva. The chairman of WTO's General Council has the responsibility to prepare the draft ministerial declaration and generate consensus by finding the common ground even among divergent positions. Thereafter, the text is transmitted to the chairman of the Ministerial Conference for further negotiations during the ministerial conference. The normal practice is to put square brackets around issues and proposals on which there is no consensus. Absence of square bracket indicates that there is consensus on that part of the text.

During the preparatory process in Geneva for the Doha Ministerial Conference, it became amply evident that deep divergence among WTO Members existed on many issues. This has been described in detail in

Chapter 7. The appropriate course of action would have been to reflect the different alternatives in the draft ministerial text. However, the chairman of the General Council chose not to follow this option. He ignored the different viewpoints among the WTO Members and on his own responsibility, transmitted a clean text dated 27 October 2001 without any square brackets to the Qatari Trade Minister, who was to be the chairman of the ministerial conference.[35] How did the clean text strategy disadvantage the opponents and promote the interests of proponents of the relevant issues?

Although the draft ministerial text was transmitted to the chairman of the ministerial conference at the responsibility of GC chairman, it became the basis for further negotiation at Doha. As this clean text articulated the perspective of the proponents of the four Singapore Issues, other countries had to wage an uphill struggle to make themselves heard, even if they initially had the numbers behind them. On the other hand, the proponents did not have to expend much negotiating resources, as their views were fully captured in the negotiating text. This asymmetry decisively tilted the negotiating landscape against the opponents of the Singapore Issues and prepared the ground for the eventual outcome as there was very little time and opportunity to accommodate alternate views.[36] Instead of the differences being resolved through negotiations among Members, at the stroke of a pen the chairman appears to have bulldozed his views. This was effective in pushing the interests of the developed countries—the main proponents of the Singapore Issues.

It is relevant to discuss another brazen attempt by the chairman of a negotiating group in the Doha Round to tilt the negotiating text in favour of the USA on an extremely controversial issue in anti-dumping, popularly called zeroing. Without going into technical complexities, dumping calculations based on zeroing inflate the anti-dumping duty. This adversely affects the exporter subject to anti-dumping duty. In many disputes, the Appellate Body of the WTO has ruled against the practice of zeroing. While most of the WTO Members have accepted the verdict against zeroing, the USA is yet to reconcile itself to the strictures against this practice in its domestic anti-dumping investigations. In the course of negotiations on Anti-Dumping Agreement during the Doha Round, one of the proposals explicitly sought to prohibit zeroing. This had the backing of most of the countries at the negotiating table. Of course, the USA opposed this proposal. To the horror of the countries, the negotiating text[37] prepared by the chairman of the negotiating group indicated that there was a consensus to permit zeroing, although this stand was favoured by just one country—the USA. This text of the chairman was met with angry protests from other members at the negotiating table. Although the chairman eventually made amends, his credibility had taken a hit.[38]

5.16 Conclusions

In this chapter, we have discussed the strategies deployed by the developed countries at the negotiating table of the GATT/WTO. It is interesting to observe that at the core of most of the strategies used in multilateral trade negotiations are the four weapons frequently mentioned in ancient Indian statecraft—saam (to convince and conciliate with reasons); daam (to placate with gifts); dand (to threaten with punishment); and bhed (divide and conquer).[39] In conjunction with the strategies away from the negotiating table examined in the preceding chapter, the developed countries have succeeded in repeatedly outwitting the developing countries at the GATT/WTO. This further raises the odds stacked against the developing countries at the negotiating table.

Can the developing countries be expected to deploy the strategies examined in this chapter? Some of these strategies are based on economic and political power at the negotiating table being skewed significantly in favour of the developed countries. It is, thus, unreasonable to expect most developing countries to resort to strategies such as browbeating others at the negotiating table, divide and prosper, salami tactics, starting soft and landing hard, and pressure-cooker strategy. Further, most developing countries do not have the technical capacity to either share each other's load or spin a spider's web around the proposals of the developed countries. In addition, if a developing country refuses to engage in the proposals made by a developed country, the former is likely to be ignored at the negotiating table. While on some occasions a few developing countries have successfully resorted to this strategy, these are very few and far between. Inadequate technical capacity and insufficient institutional memory also constrain most developing countries from persisting with their proposals for many years, despite facing constant opposition at the negotiating table. It is only in respect of the basic issue related to human survival—food security—that many developing countries have demonstrated the patience to persist with their negotiating objectives over decades. Finally, developing countries do not have the agency to use the strategy of a clean negotiating text.

Before we proceed to the next chapter to discuss the challenges that confront developing countries in multilateral trade negotiations, an important clarification is in order. The discussion of strategies deployed by the developed countries is in no way meant to pass a judgement on them. Negotiations are about securing national interests through various means. These countries have the resources, economic and political clout, better alternatives, instruments, and the ability to use various strategies to promote their interests at the negotiating table. As some developing countries become economically more powerful, we should not be surprised if they also start resorting to similar strategies.

Notes

1. Peter Drahos, 'When the Weak Bargain with the Strong: Negotiations in the WTO', *International Negotiation* 8, 1 (2003): 79–109.
2. Declaration on the TRIPS Agreement and Public Health adopted on 14 November 2001 by the Doha Ministerial Conference, WTO document WT/MIN(01)/DEC/2 dated 20 November 2001.
3. Based on personal papers of Bhagirath Lal Das, available with the author.
4. This episode is based on interview with a former Indian negotiator.
5. The author was a participant in some of these meetings.
6. Celso Amorim, *Acting Globally, Memoirs of Brazil's Assertive Foreign Policy* trans. Michael Marsden (Maryland, MD: Hamilton Books, 2017), 254–255.
7. Mohan Kumar, *India's Moment* (Gurugram: HarperCollins Publishers, 2023).
8. Paragraph 7 of the Hong Kong Ministerial Declaration adopted on 18 December 2005, WTO document WT/MIN(05)/DEC dated 22 December 2005.
9. Paragraphs 132–146 of the Revised Draft Modalities for Agriculture, WTO document TN/AG/W/4/Rev.4 dated 6 December 2008.
10. Special Safeguard Mechanism for Developing Country Members, Ministerial Decision of 19 December 2015, WTO document WT/MIN(15)/43 dated 21 December 2015.
11. Interview with an Indian government official involved in Agriculture negotiations, May 2020. The author was a witness to some of the meetings of the Special

Sessions of the Committee on Agriculture, where the discussion on SSM barely lasted a few minutes.

12. Implementation-related issues referred to the Committee at the request of the chairman of the General Council on 31 July 2001, WTO document G/SCM/W/462 dated 3 September 2001.
13. Report of the WTO panel in the dispute *EU—Countervailing Measures on Certain Polyethylene Terephthalate from Pakistan*, WTO document WT/DS486/R dated 6 July 2017.
14. Report of the WTO Appellate Body in the dispute *EU—Countervailing Measures on Certain Polyethylene Terephthalate from Pakistan*. WTO document WT/DS486/AB/R dated 16 May 2018.
15. Paragraph 20 of the Singapore Ministerial Declaration, adopted on 13 December 1996, WTO Document WT/MIN(96)/DEC dated 18 December 1996.
16. Paragraph 20 of the Doha Ministerial Declaration adopted on 14 November 2001, WTO document WT/MIN(01)/DEC/1 dated 20 November 2001.
17. Doha Work Programme Decision Adopted by the General Council on 1 August 2004, WTO document WT/L/579 dated 2 August, 2004.
18. Paragraph 4 of the Joint Ministerial Statement on Investment Facilitation for development, WTO document WT/MIN(17)/59 dated 13 December 2017.
19. Draft Ministerial Decision on Adding the Investment Facilitation for Development Agreement to Annex IV of the WTO Agreement, WTO document WT/MIN(24)/W/25 dated 29 February 2024.
20. United States Trade Policy Review, page 7 of the Report by the Secretariat, WTO document WTO WT/TPR/S/16, 1996. It should be noted that the share of services in US GDP appears to be understated, as it includes transportation, communications, wholesale and retail trade, financial services, and construction. Sectors such as tourism, entertainment, etc. appear to have been excluded.
21. Shrirang P. Shukla, 'From GATT to WTO and Beyond,' WIDER Working Papers (1986–2000) 2000/195. Helsinki: UNU-WIDER, 2000.
22. John Croome, *Reshaping the World Trading System: A History of the Uruguay Round* (The Hague: Kluwer Law International, 1996), 22.
23. Bhagirath Lal Das, *The WTO and the Multilateral Trading System: Past, Present and Future* (London and New York: Zed Books and Penang: Third World Network, 2003), 146.
24. WTO document JOB(01)/140/Rev.2 dated 13 November 2001.
25. Paragraph 32(ii), WTO document JOB(01)/140/Rev.2 dated 13 November 2001.
26. Paragraph 31(i) of the Ministerial Declaration adopted on 14 November 2001, WTO document WT/MIN(01)/DEC/1, dated 20 November 2001.
27. See, for example, K.M. Chandrasekhar, *As Good as My Word: A Memoir* (Gurugram: HarperCollins Publishers, 2022), 75. Chandrasekhar participated in the Doha Ministerial conference and was subsequently India's ambassador to the WTO. Recounting the developments in this small group meeting, he recalls hearing Maran shouting 'You are trying to ambush me'.

28. Based on an interview with S. Narayanan, former ambassador of India to the WTO, March 2023.
29. The author witnessed this episode first-hand. It was further confirmed in a newspaper article by Arun Jaitley's daughter Sonali Jaitley. 'Not just my father, he was India's son', writes Sonali Jaitley. 23 August 2020. Hindustan Times.
30. T.S.R. Subramanian, *Journeys Through Babudom and Netaland: Governance in India* (New Delhi: Rupa publisher, 2004), 166.
31. Based on an interview with a former Indian trade negotiator, October 2020.
32. It is relevant to note that within a few minutes after the formal conclusion of the Nairobi Ministerial Conference in December 2015, India's ambassador to the WTO wrote a letter of protest to the DG WTO.
33. Additional Provisions on Fisheries Subsidies. Draft Text, WTO document TN/RL/W/278 dated 12 April 2024.
34. WTO document TN/C/1 dated 4 February 2002.
35. WTO document JOB(01)/140/Rev.1 dated 27 October 2001.
36. Bhagirath Lal Das, *The WTO and the Multilateral Trading System: Past, Present and Future* (London and New York: Zed Books and Penang: Third World Network, 2003), 178.
37. Paragraph 2.4.3 of the text of the Anti-dumping Agreement, WTO document TN/RL/W/213 dated 30 November 2007.
38. Based on an interview with a former trade negotiator from a developing country, January 2020.
39. L.N. Rangarajan (edited, rearranged, translated and introduced), *Kautilya The Arthashastra* (Gurugram: Penguin Books, 1992), 572.

6

Odds in GATT and WTO Negotiations Stacked Against Developing Countries

6.1 Introduction

During the days of the GATT, developing countries confronted an array of challenges at the negotiating table. Even at the WTO, for most of the developing countries, the situation has not changed in any substantial manner. Many of them have adopted either of the two strategies—remaining silent and aloof; or taking a rigid line in supporting or opposing a proposal, but eventually failing to achieve their negotiating objectives. The relative lack of success of developing countries in decisively influencing the outcomes of GATT/WTO negotiations can be traced to the external environment characterized by asymmetry in political and economic power within which international trade negotiations are undertaken; as well as internal factors related to institutional and human resource deficiencies. In this chapter we discuss the following four themes: first, the constraints faced by developing countries in multilateral trade negotiations arising from external factors and internal deficiencies; second, strategic response of developing countries at the negotiating table; third, the response of developing countries after making vital concessions at the negotiating table; and fourth, a serious attempt at the institutional level aimed at analysing the weaknesses of India during the Uruguay Round of multilateral trade negotiations.

6.2 Constraints Faced by Most Developing Countries Arising from the External Environment

In the context of trade negotiation it has been noted that the global distribution of power has situated the developing world in a 'definitional

Strategies in GATT and WTO Negotiations. Abhijit Das, Oxford University Press. © Abhijit Das 2025.
DOI: 10.1093/9780198934431.003.0006

inferiority'.[1] We discuss the following two factors which appear to have contributed to this situation: vulnerabilities arising from relatively smaller markets in developing countries as compared to the developed countries; and institutional bias towards addressing the concerns of developed countries.

6.2.1 Vulnerability Arising from Overwhelming Dependence on Markets of Developed Countries

An important source of power asymmetry at the multilateral negotiating table can be traced to the significant disparity in the size of markets between the developed countries on the one hand, and most developing countries on the other. As most developing countries have small domestic markets, their economic development is critically dependent on exports. With the developed countries providing some of the largest markets for exports, it is not surprising that developing countries are overwhelmingly dependent on the USA and the EU for enhancing their economic prospects through trade. To illustrate, in the year 2000, the EU and the USA accounted for almost 48 per cent of exports of the Least-Developed Countries (LDCs). Owing to the rise of China, this figure declined to 38 per cent in 2015. On the other hand, a relatively small proportion of the exports of the developed countries are destined for developing country markets. During 2000, less than 1 per cent of total exports of the EU and the USA had the LDCs as their destination. By 2015, this had increased marginally. This asymmetry in pattern of exports has telling consequences for multilateral trade negotiations.

History of multilateral trade negotiation vividly demonstrates how developed countries have used access to their market as a powerful bargaining chip in trade negotiations to compel export-dependent smaller countries to offer larger concessions than they would otherwise have been willing to offer. This merits some elaboration through specific illustrations—textiles and agriculture. From 1960s onwards the USA and other developed countries restricted exports of textiles and clothing products from developing countries by imposing quota limits. These GATT-inconsistent textile quotas severely dented the export prospects of many countries—Brazil, Hong Kong, India, Indonesia, Korea, Pakistan, etc.—for whom the textile sector was one of the most important constituents of industrialization after the Second World War. With their export prospects progressively diminishing, during the Uruguay Round of GATT, these developing countries made it an important priority to bargain elimination of the textile quotas by the developed countries. As a quid pro quo, the developing countries had to swallow a bitter pill by having to endorse the Agreement on Trade-Related Aspects of Intellectual Property Rights (TRIPS Agreement) and General Agreement on Trade in Services (GATS) finalized during the Uruguay Round. These agreements were perceived to be against the interests of most developing countries.

Agriculture provides another illustration of how the developing countries find themselves almost perpetually trapped in asymmetric outcomes. In 1955, the GATT Contracting Parties decided to grant a Waiver to the USA in order to enable it to impose quantitative restrictions on imports of agricultural products,[2] otherwise not permitted under provisions of Article XI:1 of GATT. The decision of the GATT Contracting Parties was mainly influenced by the threat from the USA that it would leave the GATT, if it was not granted the Waiver. While the Waiver was supposed to be 'temporary' in nature, the USA benefitted from the exception from the generally applicable GATT provisions for almost 40 years. This created a precedent for some developed countries to short-circuit the GATT rules for not only providing very high subsidies to their farmers, but also restricting imports from other countries. During the Uruguay Round, an attempt was made to get rid of these exceptions and bring some discipline in the area of agriculture.

The new agreement negotiated during the Uruguay Round, the Agreement on Agriculture, ostensibly got rid of the past distortive and GATT-inconsistent practices. However, the agreement was riddled with many provisions that are imbalanced and loaded against the developing countries.[3] Many of these provisions appear to be objective and neutral, but have vastly different implications for the developed and most developing countries. A few of these provisions are discussed in detail in Chapters 8 and 9. During the Doha Round two coalitions of developing countries, popularly referred to as the G-20 and the G-33, made strenuous efforts to redress some of the imbalances. If we analyse the progress in these negotiations, the strategy of the developed countries to create new asymmetries in the rules on agriculture trade becomes evident. A close examination of the negotiating text issued in December 2008 shows how the developed countries had successfully negotiated carve-outs and exceptions for diluting the rules that would have been otherwise applicable to them.[4] These carve-outs and exceptions would have created new imbalances and additional sources of asymmetry in the eventual agreement, if the Doha Round had been concluded.

Overall, most developing countries find themselves trapped in a cycle of asymmetric agreements. Each bargain struck for promoting their interest in one area was accompanied with changes in existing rules, or even rules in new areas, which were stacked against most of them. In order to redress past imbalances, in future the developing countries would be required to make further concessions at the negotiating table. By cleverly leveraging the dependence of developing countries on their markets for exports and negotiating agreements with asymmetric provisions, the developed countries always retain bargaining chips for squeezing concessions from the developing countries in future negotiations—almost a self-perpetuating advantage.

6.2.2 Institutional Bias Towards the Developed Countries

In general, 'the global system remains biased towards addressing the imperatives of rich and powerful countries'.[5] This observation finds specific resonance in the architecture and framework of rules of the multilateral trading system of the GATT/WTO, as well as the functioning of its secretariat. In this sub-section we briefly discuss both these sources of institutional bias towards the developed countries. It may be noted that the institutional bias may have arisen on account of the skewed nature of power dynamics during much of the negotiations at the GATT/WTO.

It is well accepted that 'the main features of the GATT/WTO have been shaped according to the pattern of the laws and practices of the major developed countries, particularly the US'.[6] In this context, it is relevant to recall the following observation of Kenneth Dam, the eminent scholar of trade and trade policy: the GATT was a 'direct expression of US views on the appropriate form of concerted action in the commercial policy area'.[7] Some of the key principles of the GATT were based on similar concepts contained in the bilateral agreements contracted by the USA in 1930s and 1940s, which were designed to protect the economic interests of the USA. This provided a clear advantage to the USA and other developed countries right from the initial days of the GATT. The slant in the rules in favour of the developed countries became more pronounced with the transition from the GATT to the WTO. To illustrate, many provisions contained in the Agreement on Agriculture are tailored to favour the developed countries. This aspect is discussed in detail in Chapters 8 and 9.

The bias that emerged in the multilateral trading system had not gone unnoticed by the developing countries even during the negotiations that resulted in the establishment of the GATT. This is amply clear from the following extract from a submission by the Government of India to the Preparatory Committee of the International Conference on Trade and Employment in 1946 providing comments on the American Proposals, which represented an important step in the evolution of rules contained in the GATT: Emanating from a country like the United States and accepted in principle by the United Kingdom, these proposals obviously reflect the needs and attitudes of advanced industrial countries and do not take sufficient note of the special difficulties and problems of undeveloped countries like India.[8]

Apart from the bias inherent in the rules of the multilateral trading system in favour of the developed countries, on certain occasions the conduct of even the senior officials of the GATT/WTO Secretariat appears to suggest that the multilateral trading system is more responsive to the interests of the USA and other developed countries. To illustrate, an excellent history of 50 years of protectionism by the developed countries in the textiles sector provides shocking details of the role of the executive secretary of the GATT during 1959–1960 in facilitating the creation of the edifice of textile quotas—an objective avidly pursued by the USA.[9] While this episode took place during the GATT era, even under the WTO regime, on some occasions the approach of the Director General (DG) of WTO does not appear to have been balanced, as he gave prominence to selected issues. To illustrate, during 2017–2020 the DG made statements that provided support, often tacit but at times even explicit, to the group of countries, led mainly by the developed countries, who were negotiating on issues such as electronic commerce.[10] As these negotiations were being undertaken without any multilateral mandate from the WTO members, these became extremely contentious. The WTO membership appeared to be split between those who were in favour of these negotiations and others who opposed them. In these circumstances, the DG would have been expected to remain neutral on these issues, without taking sides.

6.3 Internal Constraints in Effective Participation at the Negotiating Table

Apart from the external constraints discussed in the previous section, internal factors hobble many developing countries in effectively participating in multilateral trade negotiations. These constraints arise from their limited resources and insufficient capacity to follow the technical complexities of trade negotiations. In this section we discuss the following internal constraints: inadequate human resource and technical capacity; lack of capacity to initiate negotiations on issues of their interest; institutional deficiencies; lack of adequate internal coordination; inadequate understanding of technical issues and preparation at the political level; and dependence on foreign institutions for research support and advice.

6.3.1 Inadequate Human Resource and Technical Capacity to Analyse Trade Issues and Participate in Multilateral Trade Negotiations

Effective participation in negotiations requires a country to have an adequate number of negotiators in Geneva, commensurate with its interests in different areas. Some developing countries do not even have a presence in Geneva, where the WTO is located. Even if some countries have a local diplomatic presence in Geneva, their missions are often served by a skeletal staff. Further, a handful of staff has to service multiple intergovernmental organizations in Geneva—ILO, UNCTAD, UNHCR, WHO, WIPO, WTO, etc. Very few developing countries have a dedicated set of officials dealing exclusively with WTO issues. This prevents many of them from even participating in WTO meetings, particularly if negotiations on different issues are held simultaneously. Further, not many developing countries have negotiators who can match the technical expertise of their counterparts from the developed countries. The demands on human resources of developing countries become more onerous during ministerial meetings. These constraints can be appreciated by studying India's participation during the Uruguay Round.

The team of negotiators which negotiated on India's behalf during the Uruguay Round of negotiations was just too small in size, compared to the task at hand. At no point during the entire negotiation did the combined team of officials in New Delhi and Geneva exceed even seven negotiators. In addition, India's negotiating team included neither a trade lawyer nor a practicing economist. The possibility of engaging an economist with quantitative skills was not even envisaged. The team comprised mainly career civil servants and diplomats, many of whom had little exposure to GATT and international trade negotiations prior to the Uruguay Round. No doubt, the stellar qualities of many of the officials in India's negotiating team prevented a complete rout at the negotiating table. However, personal brilliance cannot be an adequate substitute for strong institutional capacity to provide negotiators with inputs required for engaging effectively in multilateral trade negotiations. India's inadequate capacity during the Uruguay Round contrasts sharply with the resources deployed by the developed countries. If anecdotal evidence is to be believed, the delegation of one of the developed countries included an expert whose main role was to assess the implications of legal provisions mandating certain calculations to be based on simple average, trade weighted average or the so-called Olympian average in the negotiations on agriculture.[11] No wonder, the USA and the EU were able to protect their interests, particularly in agriculture, during the Uruguay Round.

In recent years some developing countries have enhanced their technical capacity for participating in the negotiations. Despite this positive development, the constraint of insufficient technical capacity to examine issues related to international trade negotiations persists in most developing countries. However, it is also a reality that many developing countries appear to have failed in effectively utilizing the expertise on economic and legal issues available domestically to support their efforts in GATT/WTO negotiations.

6.3.2 Inadequate Technical Capacity in Developing Countries to Initiate Negotiations on Issues of their Interest

The difference in technical capacity between the developed and developing countries to engage in multilateral negotiation becomes extremely glaring when we examine the record of these countries in pushing issues of their interest onto the trade negotiating agenda. The developed countries have repeatedly demonstrated their institutional capacity to finalize multilateral agreements on issues that went beyond merchandise trade, such as services and protection of intellectual property rights. They are also doggedly pursuing other non-trade related issues, such as electronic commerce, for negotiating binding rules. In respect of each of these issues, the developed countries initially identified the impediments hampering their commercial gains in the markets of developing countries, created a link between these hurdles and international trade and turned them into negotiating proposals. Of course, in many instances, the link with international trade was at best extremely tenuous.

In contrast to the success of the developed countries in securing agreements on issues of their interest, in the entire history of GATT/WTO, it is difficult to identify more than a handful of issues that were initially not in the rule-book, but subsequently became a matter of multilateral trade negotiations primarily at the behest of developing countries and resulted in binding commitments. Most developing countries appear to lack the technical capacity to select issues of their interest and articulate them as negotiating propositions. No doubt, in respect of some issues on which multilateral agreements were finalized, such as trade facilitation, some developing countries were among the proponents. However, most of these developing countries were merely following the lead of the developed world. This underscores the wide gulf in institutional and technical capacity between the developed and developing countries to use the multilateral platform to convert issues of their interest into binding agreements.

6.3.3 Institutional Deficiencies in Developing Countries

As if technical challenges faced by individual negotiators were not enough, developing countries also face considerable institutional challenges. In order to be effective and successful at the negotiating table, countries must have institutional mechanisms for deciding their negotiating priorities, negotiating approach, bottom line on different issues, evaluating the outcome of negotiations, code of conduct for the negotiators and enforcing their accountability. If a systematic examination were to be undertaken, it is quite likely that most developing countries would fall short on these aspects. It is instructive to discuss some symptoms of institutional deficiencies in developing countries.

It is not usual to observe that in many developing countries, negotiating positions suddenly take a U-turn with a change in the negotiator—a clear sign of institutional weakness. How India was unable to sustain its two-year long dogged opposition to negotiating IPR standards during the Uruguay Round after the departure of SP Shukla, its Ambassador to the GATT, and before his successor could join, is a telling pointer in this direction. Another sign of institutional weakness in many developing countries is the lack of robust mechanism for holding trade negotiators accountable for their performance at the negotiating table. Nothing illustrates this better than the actions of a senior official from a developing country. In an important area of negotiation, he refused to utilize the negotiating chips which his negotiators had assiduously created over the years.[12] Far from facing serious consequences for his actions, the senior official had a rather smooth climb on the slippery bureaucratic ladder—an ominous sign of institutional weakness. Perhaps he could indulge in such reckless behaviour, as he was confident of his misdemeanours remaining undetected by the rickety accountability mechanism in his country.

Linked with the lack of accountability of negotiators is another institutional shortcoming in developing countries—the basic requirement of creating documents and preserving records about trade negotiations. A litmus test of institutional strength should be whether, a few years after the conclusion of a negotiation, internal documents are available in a country that would help an enquirer discern why it took a particular negotiating position on an issue. It is not certain how many countries would pass this test even in respect of the Doha Round. Insufficient attention to this vital requirement results in negotiating incompetence and facilitates inept and unscrupulous negotiators to escape bureaucratic retribution for their actions at the negotiating table. Further, it deprives developing countries from benefiting from the wisdom that might be gleaned from past negotiations.

6.3.4 Lack of Internal Coordination

In the context of international trade negotiations, divergence in interests between different departments of the government on some issues is not unusual. Most, if not all, countries have internal mechanisms for resolving such conflict of interest among different parts of the government. What is important is that once the negotiating position on an issue has been decided, the entire government should speak in one voice in official statements and publicly available documents issued by the government. What are the pitfalls, if internal difference in opinion among different departments of the government is publicly aired? First, public airing of divergent views on key negotiating issues can create confusion in the minds of other countries at the negotiating table. They may not be fully able to understand the negotiating position and the actual interest of the country concerned. Second, once other countries become aware that there is no national consensus on an issue, they may seek to undermine the negotiating position of the country by quoting the views of the departments that contradict the official negotiating position of the country. Third, the negotiator of the country may feel somewhat uncertain about what negotiating position to espouse, given the divergent views emerging from different parts of the government. Fourth, some sections among the domestic stakeholders in the country may not have certainty on whether the government would negotiate in their interest.

6.3.5 Inadequate Understanding of Issues and Insufficient Preparation at the Political Level

At crucial junctures in trade negotiations, the top negotiator is called upon to take quick decisions. As political personalities cannot be expected to read endless reams of paper, in order to get a grasp on the issues, they rely mainly on background preparation and extensive briefing by their officials. What separates a top negotiator in a ministerial meeting—often a political personality—is the preparation made for understanding inherently complex issues. Detailed briefing of ministers by their officials lies at the heart of the preparation for ministerial meetings. The efforts of even the most competent officials can come to a naught if their minister has not found the time for getting adequately briefed on issues of crucial interest to the country. Developments at the Nairobi Ministerial Conference of the WTO provide some useful illustrations of the constraints imposed on many developing countries on account of inadequate technical preparation by their political masters.

First, at the Nairobi meeting, the commerce minister of one of the larger developing countries, and a key player at the negotiating table, was completely taken aback by the draft negotiating text on eliminating export subsidies in agriculture. During the negotiation, the minister is supposed to have admitted not being adequately briefed on this issue.[13] Second, developments within the negotiating team of another developing country at the Nairobi Ministerial Conference had a more devastating impact. Some developing countries, popularly called the G-33 coalition, were at the forefront of seeking a permanent solution to the problem of public stockholding of food grains for food security purposes. However, at the Nairobi meeting, one of the key proponents of this issue abruptly changed its stance. The trade minister of this country appeared to have totally abandoned the issue of food security. In the speech delivered at the plenary session of the meeting, the minister did not refer to this issue—not even indirectly. Apparently, he carried the intellectual baggage of free trade too far and refused to listen to even a single word of briefing from his officials in support of food security. The rest of his country's delegation was shell-shocked and had a hard time coming to terms with his attitude to food security. The only redeeming feature for the country was that it came back to the path of supporting food security—an issue of considerable national importance to it—after the Nairobi Ministerial Conference.[14]

In contrast to the preceding examples, the thoroughness with which the developed countries, particularly the United States Trade Representative and EU's Trade Commissioner, participate in WTO's ministerial meetings is worth emulating. They come to the ministerial meetings fully prepared with technical details and legal options. On some occasions in the past, ministers from a few developing countries were able to match the developed countries. While these instances are rare, Celso Amorim of Brazil and Arun Jaitley of India were extremely effective at the Cancun Ministerial Conference in 2003. This was mainly on account of their grasp of the technical nuances of the issues under negotiation. Amorim, who was reputed to have a 'forensic grasp of his brief', was candid in admitting that he would have been a layman were it not for the constant briefings by his officials.[15] But more often than not, the participation of ministers of developing countries in ministerial meetings is marked by reading prepared statements and not being able to engage meaningfully in the negotiations. While the qualities demanded of a minister during ministerial meetings are rather stringent, civil servants can perhaps do little in choosing the minister with suitable qualities for representing them during ministerial meetings. An interesting exception to this reality is mentioned in Box 6.1.

Box 6.1 Putting the Right Minister at the Negotiating Table

At the Punta del Este ministerial meeting of the GATT, which launched the Uruguay Round of Multilateral Trade Negotiations in 1986, the Indian delegation was led by Vishwanath Pratap Singh, the Finance Minister of the country. As international trade negotiations come within the domain of the Commerce Ministry in India, the presence of V.P. Singh as the leader of the delegation, and not the country's Commerce Minister, might be considered to be unusual. Thereby hangs a tale.

During his short stints in the Commerce Ministry, initially as a junior minister during 1976–1977 and subsequently as the senior minister in 1983–1984, V.P. Singh had created a strong impression on some of the civil servants who were closely involved in GATT negotiations. Not only did he understand the nuances of negotiations, but also revelled in its pressure-cooker atmosphere.

Prior to the Punta ministerial meeting, SP Shukla, India's ambassador to the GATT, was summoned to New Delhi to brief the

Commerce Minister and other ministers about the forthcoming meeting. Although the Commerce Minister was a highly regarded politician, he was new to the Ministry of Commerce and was not familiar with the nuances of a complex continuum of negotiations preceding the ministerial. Further, he was burdened with the dual charge of the Ministry of External Affairs.

During an informal luncheon meeting with a high official in a crucial position in the government, Ambassador Shukla discussed the difficult path ahead for the country at the forthcoming Punta meeting. Both of them simultaneously said 'wish V.P. Singh could lead the delegation'. They left it at that.

When the Indian delegation departed for Uruguay, a few days after this luncheon, there was not even a hint that V.P. Singh would lead it. En route to Punta, the delegation spent a night in Buenos Aires. Next morning, word reached the delegation that the Commerce Minister had to leave for some 'urgent' meeting at the UN in New York and would not be coming to Punta. In his absence, V.P. Singh was nominated by the government as the leader of India's delegation to the Punta ministerial meeting. Evidently, the unseen hand and influence of the high official had worked the government machinery to put the right minister at the negotiating table.

Source: Interview with S.P. Shukla, India's former ambassador to the GATT, March 2021.

6.3.6 Dependence on Foreign Institutions for Research Support and Advice

As multilateral trade negotiations become more complex, developing countries need research support for analysing the implications of different options at the negotiating table on various issues and drafting negotiating proposals. However, the reality is that most developing countries lack advanced institutions for undertaking high-quality, sophisticated and rigorous research, which is required for assessing the economic impacts of various negotiating proposals. Often, they have to rely on inter-governmental organizations and other international organizations for research inputs. However, as discussed in Section 4.4, research emerging from some international organizations may not be objective and could even be tilted against the negotiating objectives of many developing countries. This points to the perils of developing countries engaging international organizations for undertaking research to support their efforts at the negotiating table. In the absence of domestic expertise on multilateral trade issues, some of the developing countries have sought the assistance of foreign experts. However, it remains uncertain whether foreign experts provide objective advice that is in the best interest of the host developing country, or they push the negotiating objectives of their home country. In multilateral trade negotiations, developing countries need to be aware of the risks of engaging experts from the developed countries as their advisors.

6.3.7 Limited, or No, Capacity to Offer Side Deals

An important strategy often deployed by the developed countries is to offer side deals to some developing countries in order to get them on their side. However, offering side deals could involve providing preferential market access to exports from developing countries at lower tariffs, providing direct financial assistance for trade-related capacity building, providing lines of credits for exports, etc. Given the huge asymmetry in financial muscle between the developed countries on the one hand and most developing countries on the other hand, it is not surprising that developing countries have been unable to offer effective side deals to other developing countries.

6.4 Response of Developing Countries at the Negotiating Table

Faced with the handicaps mentioned in the previous section, it is not surprising that developing countries have been repeatedly outmanoeuvred at the negotiating table. Most of them have no choice but to remain aloof and silent in the negotiations, while accepting the final outcome with helplessness. At times a few of them vociferously take a strong stand on a few issues. But lacking a Plan B, often their stiff resistance is followed by complete collapse and consequently they defer to the negotiating objectives of the developed countries. Another behavioural pattern evident at the negotiating table is developing countries granting concessions without extracting any reciprocal gains. Finally, on a few occasions, some developing countries create coalitions and engage collectively at the negotiating table. In this section we examine these types of responses of developing countries, with specific illustrations.

6.4.1 Remaining Aloof, Silent and then Resigned to the Final Outcome

It is well documented how most developing countries have generally remained almost mute spectators to the events unfolding at the negotiating table of GATT/WTO. In the process, they are compelled to silently accept the outcome of negotiations.[16] This response of most developing countries has been especially evident in some of the ministerial meetings of the GATT/WTO, as discussed below.

At the Punta del Este Ministerial Meeting of the GATT in 1986, developed countries pushed aggressively for initiating negotiations on new issues—services and intellectual property rights. Brazil and India took a tough stand and strongly opposed these issues. Personal papers of B.L. Das, an official of UNCTAD at that time, capture the mood and response of most other developing countries to the new issues. Although Das was not physically present in the negotiating room at this crucial meeting, he was watching the developments from outside, though from close quarters through intense interactions with ambassadors of many developing countries. This is what he has recorded: 'Other developing countries were generally silent in the meetings, though they were often fuming in the lounge against these proposals (on new issues). When I asked them why were they not speaking out openly in the negotiating rooms, they would indicate that it was a losing game and they did not feel encouraged to be involved in it. Thus, most of them had assumed a rather passive attitude, more because of a sense of defeat than out of conviction.'[17] Perhaps the experience of how concerns articulated by them in the past had been brushed aside by the powerful countries made many developing countries diffident at the negotiating table.

What transpired at the Punta meeting was not an isolated episode. The response of most developing countries has continued to remain along familiar lines—silence in the negotiating room and resigned to the eventual outcome. Be it the Doha Ministerial Meeting, which launched the Doha Round, or the Nairobi Ministerial Meeting, which failed to endorse with consensus continuing with the Doha Round, most developing countries had little say in the outcome. No doubt many of them were annoyed at being excluded from the negotiations, but few of them formally protested. When confronted with the outcomes that were negotiated by a small group of countries, it is extremely rare to see a developing country having the will and courage to stand up and oppose such outcomes. Subject to a few rare exceptions, even on those occasions when some developing countries participated actively in the negotiations, they were not able to exert a decisive influence on the final outcomes.

6.4.2 Stiff Resistance Followed by Complete Collapse

Another common response of many developing countries in multilateral trade negotiations has been to strongly oppose certain issues. However, after coming under intense pressure from developed countries, complete collapse of the developing countries has been fairly common in GATT/WTO history. On many issues, resisting the proposals of developed countries was not merely the opening gambit, but was also the only response of developing countries. No calibrated response, consisting of different alternatives, appears to have been formulated by them. In the face of unrelenting and sustained pressure from the developed countries, developing countries have ended up conceding everything, without gaining almost anything in return. Let us understand this response at the negotiating table by considering how the mandate on intellectual property rights (IPR) evolved during the Uruguay Round.

When the Uruguay Round was launched, the mandate on IPRs specified that 'the negotiations shall aim to clarify GATT provisions and elaborate as appropriate new rules and disciplines. Negotiations shall aim to develop a multilateral framework of principles, rules, and disciplines dealing with international trade in counterfeit goods, taking into account work already undertaken in the GATT.'[18] It was difficult for India and

Brazil to accept the proposition that the mandate included negotiating standards for protecting IPRs. However, no sooner had the negotiations started than the USA and Japan started pushing for negotiating IPR standards. For two years India and Brazil firmly opposed expanding/re-interpreting the mandate on IPR. However, in April 1989, India made a vital concession by agreeing to include IPR standards in the Uruguay Round negotiations. There was no quid pro quo in the form of reciprocal concession from the major developed countries. Thus, apart from firmly opposing the negotiation on IPR standards, India had no other option in its pocket. The climb down from tough talking to meekly agreeing to negotiate IPR standards was rather precipitous. When the crunch time came, the country was compelled to give up its initial negotiating position and totally accept what it had been actively opposing for two years—a middle ground does not appear to have been contemplated.

6.4.3 Granting Concessions without Securing Commensurate Gains

Another response of many developing countries in multilateral trade negotiation is to make concessions at different stages of negotiations without securing reciprocal benefits. Why do developing countries get trapped in this behaviour? On a few occasions they may provide non-reciprocal concessions for securing 'goodwill' at the negotiating table. It is also likely that these countries may not have fully grasped the implications of their responses to complex issues at the negotiating table, as illustrated in the decision on the moratorium on customs duties on electronic commerce.[19] At the Geneva Ministerial Conference of the WTO held in 1998, the developing countries were confronted with a proposal that appeared to be rather harmless.[20] The proposal, mooted by the USA, sought to prohibit countries from imposing customs duties on electronic transmissions. At a time when the use of Internet had not yet become widely prevalent and popularity of online retail was still a few years down the line, most countries were not imposing customs duties on electronic transmissions. Perhaps the developing countries assessed that the practice of not imposing customs duties on electronic transmissions prevailing in 1998 would not have significant commercial implications.

Thus, the developing countries accepted the proposal without any detailed examination of its likely consequences in the future. Many of them may not even have imagined that they were granting a non-reciprocal concession to a handful of developed countries.

While the 1998 decision imposing moratorium on customs duties on electronic transmissions was applicable on a temporary basis,[21] it has almost inevitably been extended at subsequent ministerial conferences of the WTO. Within a decade of the original decision, considerable volume of commercial transactions was being undertaken online. This is when many developing countries started feeling the pinch of the temporary moratorium. If the moratorium had not been in place, some developing countries could have raised tax revenue by imposing customs duties on goods delivered through electronic transmissions. As most of these products originated in the developed countries and developing countries were mainly consumers of these products, the latter had handed a huge concession to the former. How skewed this concession has been in favour of the developed countries can be gauged from the fact that out of the total revenue loss suffered by all countries on account of the moratorium, more than 95 per cent of it was incurred by the developing countries.[22] Failure to envisage how online technology would evolve and the Internet would become a powerful business tool within a few years after 1998, resulted in almost one-sided concession by the developing countries. Despite intense efforts of some developing countries—India in December 2019[23] and also Indonesia, Pakistan, South Africa, and Sri Lanka at the crunch time during the 12th Ministerial Conference of the WTO held in Geneva in 2022—the temporary moratorium continues to enjoy a long life.

6.4.4 Failure to Pursue Issues of Interest

In multilateral trade negotiation it is not infrequent to find that some developing countries enthusiastically make proposals for pushing their interest. However, on encountering stiff resistance and strategic disengagement from the developed countries, their efforts often fizzle out. We have already discussed how the developing countries gave up on most of the Implementation Issues during the Doha Round after encountering a spider's web of technical questions around these proposals. Even earlier, developing countries were compelled to abandon negotiations on movement of personnel under the GATS, as the developed countries failed to show political will to engage in these negotiations.[24] Rarely have the developing countries shown patience, strategic nous and dogged determination to persist with their proposals, despite the roadblocks created by other countries in negotiations.

6.4.5 Forming Coalitions to Negotiate Collectively

On some occasions, some developing countries have formed coalitions and sought to negotiate collectively. The term 'coalition' refers to cooperation and coordination among groups of countries in which the members are cognizant of their collective existence.[25] Formation of coalitions can be viewed as the natural response of the weak at the negotiating table in order to either confront or extract concessions from the strong.[26] It has been surmised that coalitions are more effective for the weak when there is a diffusion of power than when power is concentrated among a few parties at the negotiating table.[27] Benefits of coalitions in WTO negotiations include the following: pooling of technical resources by the coalition partners; enhancing the bargaining power of the constituents due to their collective economic clout; sharing the research load; weight of numbers enhances the legitimacy of the negotiating submissions and demands of the constituents; and insurance against counter-action by the powerful at the negotiating table.[28] If a coalition acquires credibility and traction, it may become difficult for the powerful to ignore it. In this context the coalition led by Brazil and India on some agriculture issues—popularly referred to as G-20 during the Doha Round of multilateral trade negotiations at the WTO—proved to be a game changer. This is discussed in detail in Chapter 8. Creating, nurturing and sustaining coalitions may be a separate negotiation in itself. Other coalitions of developing countries with varying degrees of success include coalitions against textile quotas and related issues during the Uruguay Round and the 'Like-Minded Group' on 'Implementation Issues' during the Doha Round. The latter coalition sought to address three broad problems which arose from the implementation of the Uruguay Round Agreements: non-realization of anticipated benefits from these agreements, agreements with provisions which were viewed as being asymmetric and imbalanced and many special and differential treatment provisions not imposing any specific obligation on the developed countries.

Lest the reader gets an impression that only the weak seek to strike coalitions for steering negotiation in their favour, it is useful to bear in mind that in GATT/WTO negotiations, the two strongest players at the negotiating table—the USA and the EU—have worked in tandem to protect each other's core interests. It may not be an idle speculation that an informal, if not formal, coalition between these two players has been instrumental in perpetuating their dominance in negotiating multilateral trade rules. A few specific episodes of the informal coalition have been discussed in Section 5.4.

6.5 Response of Developing Countries after Making Vital Concessions in Negotiations

Given the odds stacked against most of the developing countries at the negotiating table, it is not surprising that the course of negotiations and the end results are rarely in their favour. However, it is a reality that at crucial junctures in multilateral trade negotiations, as well as at the conclusion of the negotiations, fear of domestic backlash prevents developing countries from publicly admitting their failure, even if they have conceded considerable negotiating ground without securing commensurate gains. Often, lack of accountability mechanisms within the government, and inadequate technical expertise on trade issues outside it, forecloses the possibility of any meaningful scrutiny of the positive spin given by developing country negotiators to their concessions at the negotiating table. This prevents honest introspection and appropriate course correction for enhancing negotiating competence. How have some developing countries sought to justify to their constituencies unreciprocated concessions in negotiations? In this section we examine some typical behaviour patterns of developing countries after making concessions in international trade negotiations.

6.5.1 Focus on the Supposed Gains, Ignore the Concessions

After granting substantial concessions, without securing commensurate gains, a common response of developing countries is to focus on the minuscule gains. Further, curtailing the initial ambitions of the developed countries at the negotiating table is also depicted as a negotiating gain. It is also not unusual for many developing countries to remain silent on the concessions made by them. India's official response to the outcome of the Doha Ministerial Conference demonstrates these three characteristics.

Prior to the Doha Ministerial Conference, India was firmly opposed to any negotiation on the four Singapore Issues as well as on non-issues such as labour and environment. Further, India had sought resolution of Implementation Issues, prior to agreeing to initiation of a new round of multilateral trade negotiations. What was the government's official assessment of the outcome? In response to a question in the parliament,[29] the government focused on some of the Implementation Issues that had been resolved at the Doha Ministerial Conference. In passing, it also mentioned that the outstanding Implementation Issues would be addressed as part of the Doha Round. Thus, what the government stated on the floor of the parliament was factually correct; what remained unstated was that most of the commercially meaningful Implementation Issues could not be resolved by the ministerial conference, although there was a commitment to pursue these issues further in negotiations. On the issue of environment, the reply of the government mentioned that the meeting 'decided to initiate negotiations only on few items of agenda of Committee on Trade and Environment (CTE) while the remaining items have been referred to the study process until the Fifth Ministerial Conference'. Thus, the government took credit for limiting the negotiating ambition of the EU on this issue, but remained silent on the concessions made. On Singapore Issues, the government focused on postponing the negotiations to the next ministerial meeting.

6.5.2 Downplay the Significance of the Concessions

Another common response of some large developing countries after granting substantial concessions at the negotiating table is to downplay their significance, if not totally deny having made the concessions. As mentioned earlier, for more than two years India, along with Brazil and a few other developing countries, strongly resisted negotiating standards of IPR protection in the Uruguay Round. This issue remained extremely contentious as late as the mid-term review of the negotiations held in Montreal during 5–9 December 1988. However, during the meeting of high-level officials held in Geneva during 5–8 April 1989, India reversed its stand and agreed to negotiate 'the provision of adequate standards and principles concerning the availability, scope and use of trade-related intellectual property rights'.[30]

Reacting to media reports that India had watered down its stand on IPR issues, the official press release of the government categorically denied it. Interestingly, the press release remained totally silent on reversal of India's stand by agreeing to negotiate IPR standards after resisting it for over two years. Instead, it focused on how 'India's primary effort has been to ensure that discussions under GATT on trade-related aspects of intellectual property in the Uruguay Round conceded at Punta del Este do not in any way prejudice the interests of the developing countries'.[31] This was a bit disingenuous, to say the least. As already discussed in Section 4.6, twenty-six years after this episode, AV Ganesan, a high ranking official, who was a member of the Indian delegation that participated in the mid-term review meeting in Montreal in December 1988 and the meeting in Geneva in April 1989, candidly admitted that India had indeed changed its negotiating stand in the latter meeting. Although the government's media release in April 1989 downplayed the significance of the concessions by categorically denying that it had even been made, this was far from the reality at the negotiating table.

6.5.3 Create a Narrative that the Concession Was in the Country's Interest

Despite its stiff opposition to negotiating IPR standards at the GATT, India sought to rationalize its concession in April 1989 from another perspective. A narrative was sought to be created that negotiating IPR standards was in fact in the interest of the country. Leading the charge in this regard were two prominent business advocacy groups in

India—Confederation of Engineering Industry (CEI) and the Federation of Indian Chambers of Commerce (FICC). CEI president was of the view that 'negotiations would lead to solutions' on patents, which would have a bearing on the future of the consulting industry in India.[32] The FICC secretary went a step further and emphasized that 'better patent protection would encourage foreign investment and technology transfer that India needs.'[33] Whether the two business advocacy groups were articulating well-considered views based on the interests of the country remains unclear. It is relevant to note that the argument about the link between strong patent protection and foreign investment continues to be used by the global pharmaceutical industry to deter India and other developing countries from using flexibilities under the TRIPS Agreement, such as compulsory licensing, which might have an adverse impact on windfall profits of big pharma.

6.5.4 Divert Attention to Other Issues

There is no denying the fact that countries seek to strike trade deals with a view to enhancing their export prospects or attracting foreign investment. However, after failing to secure any meaningful concession, some countries seek to divert attention from the core interests to other sources of supposed benefits. This approach was adopted by Colombia's chief trade negotiator to justify one-sided concessions to the USA in Colombia—US FTA. He stated that the main benefits of the FTA would not be from trade, but from the changes in domestic regime that would be required to be undertaken by Colombia.[34] This confession appears to be an attempt at justifying and rationalizing many one-sided concessions wrested from Colombia by the USA in its FTA negotiations. In this section we have discussed attempts by governments to justify and defend before their domestic constituencies almost one-sided concessions granted to the developed countries. If these governments actually start believing these narratives, the possibility of learning lessons from their failures at the negotiating table diminishes. What is required is soul searching, in order that corrective action can be taken in the future. Do we have examples of such soul searching and what were the consequences?

6.6 Soul Searching

Most governments may be loath to publicly admit and deliberate upon the reasons for their failure at the negotiating table. However, it is not uncommon for them to examine the reasons for failure—but away from the public gaze. If this exercise is undertaken with sincerity, thoroughness, and honesty, lessons from past mistakes can be identified and perhaps also implemented in future negotiations. In this section, in the context of the concessions made by India during the Uruguay Round, we discuss two attempts at soul searching by the Indian government. The first episode relates to the abrupt change in India's negotiating position on negotiating IPR standards in April 1989, and the second is concerned with the overall outcome of the Uruguay Round.

6.6.1 Half-hearted Attempt at Soul Searching After Granting Concessions on IPR Standards

Some aspects of the episode regarding India's abrupt concessions on negotiating IPR standards during the Uruguay Round have been discussed in this chapter. While in public the government sought to downplay the concessions as being merely procedural, internally there appears to have been some concern at the domestic backlash against India's U-turn on this issue. This became evident when the country's Commerce Minister, Dinesh Singh, visited Geneva within a few months after the IPR climb-down by India. During this visit, he sought a joint meeting on this issue with three high-level Indian officials who had been closely involved in GATT negotiations earlier, and at that juncture were posted in various international organizations in Geneva. Each of the three officials was not only knowledgeable about GATT negotiations and its nuances, but also had impeccable credentials as senior civil servants. All of them eventually rose to become permanent secretaries to the government. Thus, their analysis of India's concessions on IPR standards should be viewed as being objective and credible.

Dinesh Singh initiated the conversation by mentioning that there had been some criticism in India about the country's recent move in the GATT negotiations regarding IPR issues. He admitted that he had come to Geneva to ascertain what the facts were and to understand the implications of the change in India's negotiating approach. He sought the views of the three of them on the line that India had taken in the IPR negotiations. One of the officials was forthright in emphasizing that India had made a major concession in agreeing to negotiate IPR standards, a basic issue which it had been opposing for a long time. His view was that it had damaged India's interest and that it could be justified only if there had been some quid pro quo through a secret deal by which the USA had made some vital commitments to India, perhaps in some critical and sensitive area. The minister denied any secret deal with the USA and clarified that the IPR issue stood on its own. Thereafter, in a very strong statement, another official lamented that India had caved in totally under the US pressure and it had been a very wrong move. Finally, the third official was blunt in saying that India had surrendered totally before the USA as never before. This surrender was very damaging for India. He went on to give details of how India had been resisting the pressures in the past, both in Geneva and Delhi, and now it had all been lost. He used some very strong language about the people who had been involved in this surrender.[35]

The Minister did not respond to the views and comments of the three officials. If the minister had been looking for some support for the change in India's position, it was not forthcoming from the three officials. Eventually, nothing appears to have emerged from this sharp conversation. Perhaps the heat of the negotiation, with multiple pulls and pressures from various directions, and the lack of a strong accountability mechanism within the government, prevented an honest introspection and course correction. In contrast, the soul searching done by a parliamentary committee, a few years after the conclusion of the Uruguay Round, resulted in important changes in how India would negotiate trade agreements in future.

6.6.2 Addressing the Weaknesses in Negotiations Head On: Ashok Mitra Committee

In India's system of parliamentary scrutiny of the government, specific committees are periodically constituted to examine in-depth specific aspects of functioning of different ministries and departments. The Department-related Parliamentary Standing Committee on Commerce that was constituted on 5 June 1998, was chaired by Ashok Mitra, an erudite and well-respected parliamentarian. The committee was greatly concerned over the evolving relationship of India with the WTO. It invited leading economists, scientists, former diplomats associated with the Uruguay Round negotiations and senior functionaries of the government for intense discussions focusing on three aspects: how had India engaged in negotiations during the Uruguay Round, what could be the implications of some of the obligations arising from the WTO agreements and making recommendations for enhancing effectiveness of India's commercial diplomacy. Although the committee had forty-two members, one of the five parliamentarians nominated to the Core Group on India's relationship vis-à-vis the WTO was Murasoli Maran, a future Commerce Minister who would play a crucial role at the Doha Ministerial Conference.

Based on its interactions with a galaxy of persons with profound insights into the working of the GATT/WTO and possessing expertise in international trade, the committee opined that 'there is no denying the fact that the manner in which our flanks have been exposed in the arena of international negotiations in the recent period is a source of considerable concern.'[36] The committee sought to draw lessons from India's weaknesses during the Uruguay Round, and cast a harsh light on internal shortcomings and external vulnerabilities.

Turning its gaze inwards, the committee observed that the implications of the Uruguay Round agreements were not the subject of 'any extensive or intensive public discussion.'[37] It was the committee's view that other departments or ministries of the government are only dimly aware of how the Ministry of Commerce functions in organizing its WTO-related work.[38] It found 'the imperative necessity to introduce transparency in our government's acts and activities vis-à-vis the WTO. Until now, such transparency has been sadly lacking.'[39] In brief, the key recommendations of the committee included the following: greater transparency and consultations with experts within and outside the government; coalition building with other developing countries; and if need be, taking a tough line with the developed countries in order to protect national interest. Maran's subsequent action, as detailed in Chapter 7, demonstrated that he practiced as a minister, what he had preached as a member of this influential parliamentary committee. The comprehensive review by the committee had a profound impact on many aspects of India's engagement in international trade negotiations. The government implemented most of the recommendations of the committee, thereby bringing some fundamental changes in India's participation in multilateral trade negotiations.

6.7 Conclusions

As discussed in this chapter, most developing countries face multiple constraints at the negotiating table, which arise from the external environment and internal factors. By having fewer alternatives, most developing countries find themselves in a weak bargaining position at the negotiating table.[40] Many developing countries are also trapped in a vicious circle whereby in order to mitigate some of the asymmetric outcomes and measures of questionable legality implemented by the developed countries in the past, they are compelled to agree to asymmetric outcomes in new agreements.

In spite of the constraints hobbling most developing countries at the negotiating table, there have been episodes in multilateral trade negotiations where a group of developing countries succeeded in achieving some of their negotiating objectives. No doubt, these instances have been few and far between. Nevertheless, these success stories mark a significant departure from the usual response of resignation and helplessness from developing countries and their inability in securing most of their negotiating objectives. The episodes also provide valuable insights for understanding what strategies have worked for the developing countries.

The next three chapters of the book discuss how some developing countries helped shape the course of negotiations in three areas—Singapore Issues, agriculture, and food security. These three episodes have been chosen to highlight the strategies deployed at different stages of negotiations—agenda setting, negotiating dance, and end game. The negotiation histories of the three striking episodes at a granular level show how decisions were made and what difference strategies made to the final outcomes. They add value to the known knowledge about how the use of multiple strategies and tactics provides agency to many developing countries for influencing negotiating outcomes in their favour.

Notes

1. William Zartman, *The Politics of Trade Negotiations between Africa and the European Economic Community: The Weak Confront the Strong* (Princeton: Princeton University Press, 1971).
2. United States request for Waiver in connection with Section 22 of the Agriculture Adjustment Act, GATT Document L/315, dated 28 January 1995.
3. See, for example, Bhagirath Lal Das, *The WTO Agreements: Deficiencies, Imbalances and Required Changes* (London and New York: Zed Books and Penang: Third World Network, 1998), 62–66.
4. Rajan S. Ratna, Abhijit Das, and Sachin K. Sharma, 'Doha Development Agenda for Developed Nations: Carve Outs in Recent Agriculture Negotiations', New Delhi: Centre for WTO Studies Discussion Paper No.8, 2011.
5. Susan Joekes and Rohinton Medhora, *Trade Policies in Developing Countries: What Role for Capacity Building and Research?* (Ottawa: IDRC, 2001), 5.
6. Bhagirath Lal Das, *The WTO and the Multilateral Trading System: Past, Present and Future* (London and New York: Zed Books and Penang: Third World Network, 2003), 19–20.
7. Kenneth Dam, *The GATT—Law and International Economic Organization* (Chicago and London: University of Chicago Press, 1970), 12.
8. United Nations Economic and Social Council document no. E/PC/T/W.14 dated 21 October 1946 Government of India comments on US proposals for expansion of world trade and employment. Preparatory Committee of the International Conference on Trade and Employment, p. 58.
9. Sanjoy Bagchi, *International Trade Policy in Textiles: Fifty Years of Protectionism* (Geneva: International Textiles and Clothing Bureau, 2001), 16–29.
10. The following statement of Roberto Azevedo, the DG WTO, at the meeting on Joint Statement on Electronic Commerce at Davos on 24 January 2020, is relevant (available on https://www.wto.org/english/news_e/spra_e/spra300_e.htm): 'Substantive deliverables on e-commerce—if not full agreements, then concrete negotiating texts or partial agreements—would show the world that this process is serious about articulating shared rules of the game for digital trade. Softer outcomes in Nur-Sultan, such as a general stocktaking or a roadmap, would be a missed opportunity. I hope you will send a strong message to your negotiators to fully engage in the coming months. I will support you in any way I can.'
11. Agreement on Agriculture includes provisions such as paragraph 8(a) of Annex 2 which mandates calculation based on 'a three-year average based on the

preceding five-year period, excluding the highest and the lowest entry'. This provides an illustration of the concept of Olympian average.

12. Interview with a trade negotiator from a developing country, June 2023.
13. Interview with an official of the concerned country, September 2020.
14. Interview with an official of the G33 coalition, June 2020.
15. Amorim, *Acting Globally*, 336.
16. Bhagirath Lal Das, 'South Needs to Change Strategies in WTO,' *SUNS- South North Development Monitor*, 9 December 1998.
17. Based on personal papers of Bhagirath Lal Das, a former official of UNCTAD, available with the author.
18. Ministerial Declaration on the Uruguay Round, GATT document MIN.DEC dated 20 September 1986.
19. Declaration on global electronic commerce adopted on 20 May 1998, WTO document WT/MIN(98)/DEC/2.
20. Global Electronic Commerce, Proposal by the United States, WTO document WT/GC/W/78 dated 9 February 1998.
21. Declaration on global electronic commerce—adopted on 20 May 1998, WTO document WT/MIN(98)/DEC/2.
22. Rashmi Banga and Richard Kozul-Wright, 'Moratorium on Electronic Transmission: Fiscal Implication and Way Forward,' UNCTAD Research Paper no. 47, 2020.
23. Interview with J.S. Deepak, a former Ambassador of India to the WTO, February 2021.
24. Mohan Kumar, *India's Moment* (Gurugram: HarperCollins Publishers, 2023), xiii.
25. Amrita Narlikar, *International Trade and Developing Countries: Bargaining Coalitions in the GATT & WTO* (London: Routledge, 2003).
26. Zartman, *The Politics of Trade Negotiations.*
27. J.P. Singh, 'Weak Powers and Globalism: The Impact of Plurality on Weak-Strong Negotiations in the International Economy,' *International Negotiation* 5 (2000): 449–84.
28. Narlikar, *Bargaining Coalitions*, 14–16.
29. Government of India, Ministry of Commerce and Industry, Rajya Sabha Unstarred question number 177, answered on 20 November 2001, titled Reaction to WTO draft declaration.
30. Mid-term Review, Multilateral Trade Negotiations Uruguay Round, Trade Negotiating Committee, GATT document MTN.TNC/11 dated 21 April 1989.
31. No bending on patent issue. 9 April 1989. Press Information Bureau, Government of India. Available on the following link: https://archive.pib.gov.in/archive/ArchiveSecondPhase/COMMERCE/1989-JAN-DEC-COMMERCE/PDF/COM-1989-04-09_062.pdf
32. Karthik Nachiappan, *Does India Negotiate?* (Oxford and New Delhi: Oxford University Press, 2019), 169.

33. Karthik Nachiappan, *Does India Negotiate?* (Oxford and New Delhi: Oxford University Press, 2019), 169.
34. Luis J. Garay, Philippe De Lombaerde, and F. Barberi, 'Negotiating the Colombia-US FTA: A Colombian Perspective,' in *Asymmetric Trade Negotiations* edited by Bilal Sanoussi, Philippe De Lombaerde, and Diana Tussie (London and New York: Routledge Taylor and Francis Group, 2011).
35. Based on the personal papers of Bhagirath Lal Das, India's former Ambassador to GATT, available with the author.
36. Paragraph 10, Department-related Parliamentary Standing Committee on Commerce, Thirty fifth report on India and WTO, Rajya Sabha Secretariat, December 1998.
37. Paragraph 7, Department-related Parliamentary Standing Committee on Commerce, Thirty fifth report on India and WTO, Rajya Sabha Secretariat, December 1998.
38. Paragraph 12, Department-related Parliamentary Standing Committee on Commerce, Thirty fifth report on India and WTO, Rajya Sabha Secretariat, December 1998.
39. Paragraph 12, Department-related Parliamentary Standing Committee on Commerce, Thirty fifth report on India and WTO, Rajya Sabha Secretariat, December 1998.
40. J.P. Singh, *Sweet Talk: Paternalism and Collective Action in North-South Trade Relations* (Stanford, CA: Stanford University Press, 2017), 50.

7

Overcoming Odds at the Negotiating Table

Removing Three Singapore Issues from the Negotiating Agenda

7.1 Introduction

Much of the drama surrounding the launch of the Doha Round of multilateral trade negotiations in 2001 centred around whether the negotiating agenda should include four contentious issues, commonly referred to as the Singapore Issues. These are the following: relationship between trade and investment ('Investment'); interaction between trade and competition policy ('Competition'); transparency in government procurement ('Government Procurement'); and trade facilitation. With the developed countries pitching the launch of the Doha Round as an antidote to the tragic events of 9 September 2001, the deck was stacked against a large number of developing countries. After many twists and turns, eventually, in August 2004, the General Council of the WTO decided that three of the four Singapore Issues 'will not form part of the Work Programme set out in that Declaration and therefore no work towards negotiations on any of these issues will take place within the WTO during the Doha Round'.[1] How India, which was left almost alone in opposing negotiations on Singapore Issues at Doha, and even without holding many cards, managed to turn the table two and a half years down the line, provides many interesting insights into negotiating strategy. As India played a critical leadership role in these issues, the strategies deployed by it to

Strategies in GATT and WTO Negotiations. Abhijit Das, Oxford University Press. © Abhijit Das 2025.
DOI: 10.1093/9780198934431.003.0007

remove three Singapore Issues from the negotiating agenda are at the core of this chapter.

The subsequent four sections describe the chequered history of the four Singapore Issues at the GATT/WTO. While examining these issues in depth, each section provides an outline of the commercial interests behind the push for negotiating binding rules. It also identifies some reasons underpinning the opposition of many developing countries to initiate negotiations on these issues. Any analysis of Singapore Issues and the developments at the Doha Ministerial Conference would be incomplete without understanding the role played by Murasoli Maran, India's Commerce Minister. Section 7.6 keeps Maran at the centre of the discussion and attempts to answer an important question—what were the key influences that shaped Maran's world view on WTO? The next five sections provide an insider's account of the developments on Singapore Issues during 2001–2004. Section 7.7 goes into some detail of the last meeting of WTO's General Council held in the pre-Doha phase in October–November 2001. Deliberations in this stormy meeting provide a unique example of the chairman of a negotiating forum ignoring and overriding the views and concerns of many parties, thereby tilting the negotiations against the interests of a large number of developing countries. Section 7.8 discusses the developments at the Doha Ministerial Conference and in particular it describes what went on behind the last-minute drama before the Doha Work Programme (popularly called the Doha Round) was launched. Section 7.9 provides details of how India regrouped after the retreat at Doha and galvanized other developing countries to come together to oppose the Singapore Issues. Section 7.10 describes the negotiating dynamics during the Cancun Ministerial Conference in 2003 and examines some of the reasons behind the collapse of this meeting. Section 7.11 briefly provides information on the meeting of WTO's General Council held in July–August 2004 when three Singapore Issues were removed from the negotiating table. Section 7.12 attempts to capture the essence of negotiating strategies deployed by India and a few other developing countries in getting three of the four Singapore Issues off the negotiating table. Section 7.13 draws some important lessons from this episode from the perspective of negotiating strategy.

7.2 Trade and Investment: The Phoenix Rises and then Falls, Repeatedly

Among the four Singapore Issues, Investment was perhaps the most controversial and problematic from the perspective of many developing countries. What commercial interests underpin the persistent attempts of the developed countries at negotiating binding rules on investment at GATT/WTO? What attempts were made at the GATT/WTO to initiate negotiations on this issue? Why were developing countries opposed to negotiating binding rules on this issue?

Developing countries are on the radar of foreign investors primarily for the reason that markets in developed countries are almost saturated, while those in larger developing countries are expanding. Thus, by investing in manufacturing facilities and services entities in developing countries to meet the local demand and also export from there, foreign investors stand to make huge profits. The basic objective of the developed countries in seeking binding rules on investment is to ensure that their investors have the freedom to enter developing countries and invest in sectors of their choice without being constrained in their operations and remittance of profits by actions of the host government, thereby maximizing their profits.

Starting from 1982, developed countries have made multiple attempts at negotiating binding multilateral rules on investment. During the Uruguay Round, the proponents sought to negotiate comprehensive disciplines on liberalization of investment and protecting the rights of foreign investors in host countries. Not satisfied with the outcome of the Uruguay Round—the Agreement on Trade-Related Investment Measures (TRIMS Agreement), which was confined mainly to reasserting the existing GATT obligations—within two years of coming into existence of the WTO, in 1996, the developed countries made another attempt at initiating negotiations on investment. Although they failed to secure a mandate to initiate negotiations, yet the WTO Members decided that a Working Group in the WTO would study the relationship between trade and investment.[2] At the Doha Ministerial Conference in 2001 it was agreed that negotiations on this issue would take place on the modalities of negotiations to be decided at the next ministerial conference to be held in 2003.[3] Eventually, in August 2004, the General Council decided that

Investment would no longer be part of the negotiating agenda during the Doha Round. Despite repeated setbacks, negotiating rules on investment has remained an important priority mainly for the developed countries over the past four decades and recently China.

Although developing countries are often extremely keen to attract foreign investment, why have many of them shown little, or no, keenness to push for an agreement on investment at the WTO? At the heart of this paradox lies the divergence in interests of the foreign investor and the host country receiving the foreign investment. Provisions in investment agreements can put fetters on the ability of the host government to pursue economic and social objectives, as the foreign investor can sue the host government if the actions of the government are perceived to diminish the investor's prospect for profits. Most developing countries want to retain the right to regulate foreign investors for pursuing desirable socio-economic objectives, without being constrained by multilateral rules on investment or facing retaliatory action by the foreign investors.

7.3 Trade and Competition Policy: Seeking to Eliminate Competition from Developing Countries

Although the legal text of GATT did not address issues related to trade and competition comprehensively, these issues did not remain totally ignored either. The Havana Charter provided a comprehensive framework for international cooperation in respect of anti-competitive practices of public and private enterprises. The GATT itself contained certain provisions seeking to discipline activities of state trading enterprises. Further, in 1960, the GATT Contracting Parties agreed to a Decision on Arrangements for Consultations on Restrictive Business Practices, which recognized that restrictive business practices may hamper the expansion of world trade and economic development of individual countries.[4] However, it did not attempt to create binding rules to deal with such practices. The General Agreement on Trade in Services (GATS) contains certain specific provisions on competition policy.[5] As was the case with Investment, some of the developed WTO Members, particularly the EU, pushed strongly for initiating multilateral negotiation on Competition. From 1996 to 2004 this issue followed a course similar to Investment.

Apart from seeking to address anti-competitive problems, the developed countries used this issue to argue that foreign firms should have effective equality of opportunity as domestic firms in the domestic market. Their aim was to prohibit enjoyment of any special privileges by domestic firms, particularly in developing countries. This would have constrained the growth of domestic firms in developing countries, but facilitated the prosperity of foreign firms. It is also interesting to note that at the WTO, the developed countries, particularly the USA, were reluctant to discuss some of the core anti-competitive practices that hurt developing countries and their firms, especially hardcore export cartels. Thus, negotiating multilateral rules on competition appeared to be a convenient smokescreen for reducing competition from firms based in developing countries.

What is the approach of many developing countries to this issue? Unlike negotiating a multilateral agreement on investment, which is perceived by many developing countries to be adverse to their interests, their approach to Competition is more nuanced and less negative. It is interesting to note that during the Ministerial Meeting held in Marrakesh during 12–15 April 1994 for formally concluding the Uruguay Round, India's Minister of Commerce, Pranab Mukherjee, stated the following: 'there are certain significant issues of trade policy which could not get discussed in the Uruguay Round, and any future work programme of the WTO should try to address them first. These are matters relating to restrictive business practices and other aspects of competition policy.'[6] In fact, many developing countries made constructive proposals on Competition under the Working Group during 2001–2003. Despite their active participation, they continued to remain hesitant in agreeing to negotiations on this issue. Eventually, Competition was taken off the negotiating table in 2004.

7.4 Transparency in Government Procurement: Mirage of the Pot of Gold at the End of the Rainbow

Article III of GATT 1994 prohibits countries from playing favourites between domestically manufactured goods and imported products. This obligation to accord non-discriminatory treatment to imported goods and domestic products is commonly referred to as national treatment. An important exception to this obligation is the flexibility provided to countries to bend in favour of their domestic products in respect of purchases made by governments for their own use. This allows governments to shut out foreign products from being supplied in governmental purchases.[7]

As with Investment and Competition, at the Singapore Ministerial Conference of the WTO held in 1996, a working group was established to conduct a study on transparency in government procurement practices.[8] The attempt at negotiating binding rules on government procurement, supposedly confined to transparency requirements, was aimed at getting rid of the exception to national treatment and extending the scope of non-discriminatory treatment even to government procurement. However, on account of stiff resistance from developing countries, this issue was removed from the negotiating agenda of the Doha Round in August 2004. Why is this issue important for the developed countries? Why did the developing countries resist inclusion of this issue in the negotiating agenda at the WTO?

Most developed countries were already receiving non-discriminatory market access in each other's government procurement markets. The main objective of the developed countries in seeking negotiations on this issue was to secure a share in the purchases made by governments, particularly in larger developing countries. How lucrative this market is can be gauged from the fact that in some years the value of procurement by countries such as India, Brazil, and Argentina, was substantially higher than even the value of their merchandise imports. While India's imports of goods during 2001—the year when Doha Round was launched—was around $51 billion, the size of government procurement market in the country was estimated to be around $64 billion.[9] Clearly, negotiations on this issue were an attempt by the developed countries to secure binding rules which would provide huge commercial opportunities to their economic operators in government procurement markets that had remained excluded from the non-discriminatory obligation under the GATT/WTO rules.

During the Doha Round, negotiations on this issue were supposedly to be limited to transparency aspects of the purchase procedures, without requiring access to government purchases. However, developing countries were apprehensive that once negotiations commenced, the veneer of confining it to transparency would be soon cast aside and developed countries would seek to negotiate market access in government procurement. This perception informed the response of developing countries on this issue. Further, some of the developing countries sought to utilize government procurement as an instrument to provide a boost to their domestic producers, as was done by the developed countries in the past.[10] As developing countries were nowhere near the levels of economic development of the developed countries, naturally they were reluctant to give up this policy instrument which could be effective in giving a fillip to their economy. It is, therefore, not surprising that developing countries strongly opposed negotiations on transparency in government procurement.

A special mention needs to be made of the carrot dangled by developed countries in order to attract developing countries to the negotiating table on this issue. A narrative was created that purchases by governments in developed countries provide immense opportunities to developing countries to enhance their exports. In fact, the reality was entirely different. Most of the purchases made by the governments in developed countries was from their domestic sources; only a miniscule amount was procured from foreign sources. A detailed examination of the notification on government procurement purchases by the EU for the year 2006 is extremely revealing: for every Euro 100 of government procurement by the EU, less than half a Euro was sourced from suppliers outside the EU.[11] Clearly, the pot of gold awaiting developing countries at the end of a rainbow called government procurement is likely to be merely a mirage.

7.5 Trade Facilitation: The Issue that Remained on the Negotiating Agenda

The Singapore Ministerial Declaration directed the Council for Trade in Goods to 'undertake exploratory and analytical work . . . on the simplification of trade procedures in order to assess the scope for WTO rules in this area.'[12]

Negotiating binding rules on the fourth Singapore Issue, Trade Facilitation, popularly viewed as cutting the bureaucratic red tape in import–export procedures, elicited three specific concerns from many developing countries. First, those developing countries with weak export capability were reluctant to agree to legally binding obligations on trade facilitation, as they apprehended that these rules would result in an increase in their imports without corresponding higher exports. This could have an adverse effect on their trade balance. Second, many countries were worried about the cost of implementing the obligations related to trade facilitation. Most developing countries, particularly the poorer ones among them, were concerned at the possibility of having to divert public spending from desirable areas of development priority such as healthcare, education, and poverty eradication, in order to meet the new obligations on trade facilitation, which might emerge from the eventual agreement. Third, the eventual agreement was not seen as having the potential to enhance the export prospects of developing countries. It is also likely that some of the opposition to this issue arose as the four Singapore Issues were viewed as a single package. After the Singapore Issues started getting unbundled during the Cancun Ministerial Meeting in 2003, resistance to negotiation on Trade Facilitation diminished. Finally, when the decision time came in August 2004, this was the only Singapore Issue which remained on the negotiating table. After intense negotiation for almost a decade, and at times encountering seemingly intractable roadblocks, eventually the Trade Facilitation Agreement was finalized in November 2014.

Having discussed the four Singapore Issues, let us get to know the man who sought to keep the four Singapore Issues off the negotiating agenda of the WTO—India's Commerce Minister, Murasoli Maran.

7.6 Minister Murasoli Maran: Attributes and Influences

As outlined above, most developing countries had little commercial gain to garner from binding rules on the Singapore Issues; instead, they had much to lose. Any discussion of strategies for removing the three Singapore Issues from the negotiating agenda is almost inextricably linked with India, whose two towering Commerce Ministers with contrasting personalities, Murasoli Maran and Arun Jaitley, left an indelible mark on India's engagement at the WTO and altered the course of the

Doha Round. What were some of the traits of Maran? What can explain his views on WTO and international trade negotiations?

Before turning to politics, Maran had acquired considerable renown for writing screenplays for films in Tamil—one of the prominent languages in India. However, if being articulate and persuasive are the hallmarks of a successful negotiator, Maran seemed to fall short on these requirements. At the negotiating table, he was a man of few words; just how few, Bob Zoellick, the USTR, Pascal Lamy, the EC Trade Commissioner, and Mike Moore, the Director-General of the WTO, might have wondered during the long meetings at the Doha Ministerial Conference. Further, he did not possess a deep technical knowledge of the different elements of each Singapore Issue. He was not someone who discussed options and strategies with his negotiating team. In turn, most of his senior officials were somewhat hesitant in giving him suggestions, as he viewed even a hint of difference of opinion with him as a sign of compromise with his objectives. Thus, Maran did not fit the mould of a successful negotiator, as envisaged in academic literature. Yet, Maran was eventually successful in meeting his negotiating objectives, which definitely was not a matter of chance. Perhaps the clue to Maran's success lies in his world view of the WTO, and his ability to anticipate problems and prepare contingency plans for them in advance. Moreover, when the crunch time came during the final few hours of the Doha Ministerial Conference, he demonstrated the wisdom to accept the frank advice offered by India's ambassador to the WTO.

Maran's long stint of 36 years as a member of India's parliament had sharpened his political instincts and engrained a sense of what is politically possible and how to achieve it. Being a minister under three prime ministers had exposed him to the underlying currents and influences that go into decision-making at the highest level of the government. Before becoming the Commerce Minister in 1999, he was an active member of the Department-related Parliamentary Standing Committee on Commerce chaired by Ashok Mitra. In Section 6.6.2, we have discussed the deliberations and recommendations of this committee.

It is relevant to recall some of the observations of the Ashok Mitra Committee, which might have influenced Maran's perception of the WTO. The committee lamented that 'it is a bit of a myth that international trade blesses those who demonstrate economic efficiency. On the contrary, the global network of trade is dominated by monopoly elements who impose their iniquitous rules on those who are relatively weakly placed.'[13] Turning to the issue of protecting and promoting national interests at the WTO, the following observation of the committee appears to have anticipated, or perhaps shaped, what Maran was to do at Doha: 'If our mind is cluttered by apprehension about how the economically powerful nations would react to our show of intransigence, we were unlikely to progress very far.'[14] A few years later, as he faced the combined might and wrath of the USA and the EU on the Singapore Issues, Maran would have derived inspiration from this observation of the committee.

Whether, or not, to initiate negotiations on the four Singapore Issues was a crucial question on the agenda of the Doha Ministerial Conference held in November 2001. How did the negotiation on this crucial question evolve during the preparatory process in Geneva and subsequently at the Doha Ministerial Conference?

7.7 Ambassadors in Action at the WTO: Fractious Meeting of the General Council on 31 October–1 November 2001

During much of 2001, one of the main questions before the WTO membership was whether to continue the work programme on the Singapore Issues as mandated by the WTO in 1996, or to agree to initiate negotiations on them. Bridging the gap between the two contrasting approaches was a tough challenge for the negotiators, who were intensively involved in drafting the outcome document, commonly referred to as the Doha Ministerial Declaration, that would be adopted by the Doha Ministerial Conference. During the preparatory process held in Geneva during July–October 2001, negotiations on the draft ministerial text on the Singapore issues proved to be extremely divisive. This exercise was led by Stuart Harbinson, the Chairman of WTO's General Council (GC). The initial version of the text circulated on 26 September 2001 provided different options, some of which reflected, at least partially, the views of a large number of developing countries opposing initiation of negotiations on the four issues.[15] These countries had clearly and forcefully articulated their unwillingness to initiate negotiation on these issues. Instead, they sought continuation of the 1996 work programme.

Despite the intense efforts of the Chairman of the GC, repeated attempts at finding common ground among the different positions were going nowhere. Finally, the GC Chairman took the step of formulating a clean text that neither proposed different options on the Singapore Issues nor did it reflect the divergence in positions among the WTO Members.[16] This text was circulated to the WTO Members on 27 October 2001 and subsequently discussed during the meeting of the GC held on 31 October and 1 November 2001. In respect of two Singapore Issues—transparency in government procurement and trade facilitation—the text stated 'we agree to negotiations'. Thus, the Harbinson Text explicitly provided for launching negotiations on these two issues at the Doha Ministerial Conference. In respect of the other two Singapore Issues—Investment and Competition—the text was more subtle. On both these issues, the text stated that 'At the Fifth Session, a decision will be taken on modalities of negotiations in this area'. The opponents of Singapore Issues interpreted this to mean that investment and competition would already be on the negotiating agenda. All that would remain after the Doha Ministerial Conference would for WTO members to take a decision on which modality to adopt for taking the negotiations further.

In his remarks during the meeting of the GC held on 31 October and 1 November 2001, on the agenda item 'Preparation for the fourth Ministerial Conference', Harbinson, as the Chairman of GC, stated that he and the DG (WTO) 'did not plan to revise these texts further'.[17] Instead, they 'intended to transmit them to ministers on their own responsibility', for consideration at the Doha Ministerial Conference.[18] Thus, the WTO Members had no opportunity to influence this text. Given this background, it is not surprising that the meeting of the GC was acrimonious.

As indicated by the statements made at the GC meeting, a large number of developing countries were extremely critical of the GC Chair for completely ignoring their positions, priorities, or proposals on the Singapore Issues. In particular, the draft text on Investment and Competition issues attracted the considerable ire of many countries. These countries had seen through the ruse of the Chairman's text, which implied that members agree for negotiations on these two issues, and only the modalities of the negotiations would be decided at the Fifth Ministerial Conference to be held in 2003. Barbados, Egypt, Honduras, India, Indonesia, Kenya, Pakistan, Sri Lanka, Zambia, Zimbabwe, and many other developing countries, one after another, denounced the Harbinson Text in rather strong terms.[19] These countries, in turn, were at the receiving end of Morocco—a developing country that was a proponent of negotiations on these two issues. While Morocco 'sympathized with the situation of many countries who had serious concerns over this issue', it urged that 'Members should try to de-dramatize this issue'.[20] However, this, not so gentle an admonition, failed to prevent countries from voicing their stiff opposition to the text on the Singapore Issues. The GC meeting demonstrated how the tussle between the proponents and opponents of negotiations on the Singapore Issues had turned into a negotiation between the opponents and the GC Chairman. Eventually, through the strategy of using a clean text mandating negotiations, and not reflecting the alternate perspective, round 1 went to the proponents.

7.8 Resistance and Retreat at Doha During 9–14 November 2001

After the draft ministerial text was transmitted to Youssef Hussain Kamal, the Qatari Finance, Economy and Trade Minister and Chairman of the Doha Ministerial Conference, by the GC Chairman, action shifted to the Doha Ministerial Conference. A narrative was created by the developed countries that in the aftermath of the attack on the Twin Towers on 11 September 2001, successful conclusion of the Doha Ministerial Conference would contribute to world peace. Politics, never far from trade even in normal times, was sought to be used to pursue economic ends at the Ministerial Conference.

In initial parleys prior to commencement of the Ministerial Conference, Maran repeatedly made known his resolve to oppose the Singapore Issues being included in the negotiating agenda of the WTO. In his plenary statement, Maran emphasized that developing countries did not have the capacity to deal with these issues, which impinged strongly on domestic policies that were well removed from trade. Further, he raised a legal question whether the 'Marrakesh remit for WTO which talks only of multilateral trade relations permit these other issues to be covered?'[21] India's firm stand emboldened a few developing countries to persist with their opposition to these issues. On 11 November, even the WTO spokesperson, Keith Rockwell, was compelled to admit that 'India is opposed to the inclusion of investment in WTO and they are not alone in opposing it.'[22] Many developing countries complained that they were being pushed into signing up to a deal by the threat that failure would destroy the WTO and damage the world economy. Some delegates told development lobby groups that the 'European Union and the US are threatening the most recalcitrant developing countries with losing access to western markets under established trade deals if they continue to oppose new talks.'[23]

As the Ministerial Conference progressed, the opposition to launching negotiations on the Singapore Issues started gradually withering away. It is relevant to go back to the negotiating text and examine where matters stood on 13 November regarding securing a negotiating mandate on Singapore Issues. In respect of transparency in government procurement and trade facilitation, the draft text continued to mandate launching of negotiations by the Doha Ministerial Conference.[24] This was in line with what the GC Chairman had proposed. However, on Investment and Competition, the text had inched closer to what Maran may have desired. While the text of the GC Chairman had mandated a decision on modalities of the negotiations by the next ministerial conference (to be held in 2003), the revised text on the table was more explicit in postponing the decision on initiating negotiations on these two issues. On both the issues the text contained the following: 'we agree that at the Fifth Session of the Ministerial Conference a decision will be taken on whether to launch negotiations.'

By the evening of 13 November it was clear that not more than half a dozen countries were with India in opposing negotiations on Singapore Issues. But Maran was not yet done. He continued his resolute resistance to the launch of negotiations on these issues. Unable to dent Maran's defence, the time had come for the developed countries to resort to an old strategy—bypass the minister and reach out directly to the head of the government. Phone lines were worked and the leader of a prominent developed country contacted Prime Minister Vajpayee, complaining how India was holding up a substantial global trade deal. The Indian prime minister is supposed to have responded by saying that he was not aware of the details of the negotiations being held in Doha and mentioned that Maran, the minister on spot at Doha, was well versed with the negotiating issues. Further, he expressed full confidence in Maran.[25] The much-apprehended phone call had failed to produce results for the developed world. As will be discussed later in this chapter, Maran's foresight in anticipating that such a gambit would be attempted and his pre-emptive moves to counter it had worked.

With a view to resolving the contentious issues related to agriculture, environment, and Singapore Issues, on the evening of 13 November Youssef Kamal convened a meeting of around twenty countries. In this meeting Maran was the main target of Bob Zoellick (USTR) and Pascal Lamy (EC Trade Commissioner) on the negotiating mandate on Singapore Issues. They repeatedly asked Maran why he continued to oppose the inclusion of Singapore Issues in the Doha negotiating agenda. Maran, probably being cognizant of his limitations in articulation, refused to give any detailed response. He stated that India's position on the Singapore Issues had been explained previously on a number of occasions.[26] This charade of exchanges between India, EU, and the USA went on for quite some time. The man of few words, whose preferred medium of expression was the world of silver screen, had driven the hard-boiled negotiators from the developed countries up the wall. By the time the marathon meeting ended in the early hours of 14 November, most of the countries in the meeting were agreeable to having a common text on the four Singapore Issues mandating a decision on modalities of the negotiations by the next Ministerial Conference. This was perhaps based on a suggestion by Malaysia, which had concerns on Government Procurement. Maran, despite being physically exhausted, continued to stick to his guns. Was this reckless brinkmanship or a shrewd negotiator, confident of his clout, at work? Developments in the next few hours would provide a clue to this conundrum.

Within a few hours of the marathon meeting, on 14 November Youssef Kamal and WTO Director General Mike Moore, sought a meeting with Maran at 10 a.m.[27] Maran requested India's Ambassador to the WTO, S. Narayanan, a highly respected diplomat in Geneva's trade circle, to accompany him to this meeting. Ambassador Narayanan, by temperament a calm person, was getting increasingly anxious about the consequences for India of blocking the final deal. En route to the meeting, he explained to Maran that it would be the developing countries who would be extremely critical of India, if it continued to block the Doha Declaration. In particular, Narayanan informed Maran that some African countries had started venting their disappointment at missing out on the deal on access to affordable medicine,[28] if India continued to oppose negotiations on Singapore Issues. Further, the African, Caribbean and Pacific (ACP) countries would be unhappy for being denied tariff preference in the EU, if the Doha Ministerial Conference failed. He concluded that while the agreement gradually emerging on Singapore Issues might not fully protect India's interest, Maran had fought enough to extract the best possible deal for the country and it was time to leave the battle to be fought another day. Maran listened to Narayanan with rapt attention. He realized that the strategy of resisting to extract better terms had run its course, and it was time to compromise.[29]

During the meeting held at 10 a.m., Youssef Kamal and WTO Director Mike Moore impressed upon Maran the need for successfully concluding the Ministerial Conference. They also pointed out to him that India was the only country left opposing the text on Singapore Issues. Maran, true to his personality, remained taciturn and largely silent during the meeting. He let Narayanan do much of the talking. Narayanan explained that the text implied that negotiations on Singapore Issues would commence automatically at the next Ministerial Conference and the members would merely be required to choose between different modalities for negotiations—including opt-in and opt-out approach and plurilateral approach. All those present in the meeting were keen to avoid yet another failure after the fiasco at the Seattle Ministerial Conference held in 1999. Eventually, it was decided that Youssef Kamal, as the Chairman of the Ministerial Conference, would read out a statement addressing India's concerns. Officials of the WTO Secretariat swung into action, drafted the Chairman's statement providing his understanding of the text on Singapore Issues and showed it to Maran, who was agreeable to it.[30]

The Chairman's Statement provided the clarification that at the fifth session of the Ministerial Conference 'a decision would indeed need to be taken by explicit consensus, before negotiations on trade and investment and trade and competition policy, transparency in government procurement, and trade facilitation could proceed. In my view, this would also give each member the right to take a position on modalities that would prevent negotiations from proceeding after the Fifth Session of the Ministerial Conference until that member is prepared to join in an explicit consensus.'[31]

Hurriedly, the final plenary of the Ministerial Conference was convened on the evening of 14 November and amidst applause all around, the Doha Round of Multilateral Trade negotiations was launched. After having stretched the patience of ministers from many countries and pushed the launch of the Doha Round of the multilateral trade negotiations to the edge of a cliff, India opted for a strategic retreat. Was this resistance to Singapore Issues India's last high, before it would dissipate into meek acquiescence, as had happened during the Uruguay Round—TRIPS being a prominent case in point? As subsequent events would show, India's strategic retreat at Doha did not turn into a rout. How did the country manage to regroup forces during 2002–2004 and turn the table?

7.9 Regrouping to Fight Back after Retreat at Doha

After the Doha Ministerial Conference, a question in the minds of many officials in India's Department of Commerce was how to engage constructively on the four Singapore Issues and convince other countries of the risks of negotiating binding rules on them. India adopted a two-pronged approach. First, undertaking research and using it to highlight the downside for most developing countries of binding rules at the WTO; and second, reaching out to other countries, with the objective of creating a strong coalition against these issues.

7.9.1 Using Research to Clarify and Buttress Opposition to Initiating Negotiations on Singapore Issues: 2002–2003

At Doha, Maran had repeatedly emphasized that India, as well as many developing countries, did not fully understand the implications of negotiating binding rules on Singapore Issues. Something had to be done about it. No sooner was the negotiating team back from Doha than it got into the act and put together a blueprint for preparing technically sound proposals for consideration of the WTO Membership highlighting the adverse consequences of binding multilateral rules on these issues. V.S. Seshadri, who was the joint secretary in charge of Singapore Issues, went about this task in a methodical and meticulous manner. He engaged some of the leading trade economists in the country to prepare in-depth papers, particularly on two issues—Investment and Competition. But he also took care to ensure that the submissions to the WTO were presented in a manner that would be comprehensible to non-economists.

During 2002–2003 India made detailed submissions on the following aspects of Investment: development provisions (WT/WGTI/W/148, 7 October 2002), non-discrimination (WT/WGTI/W/149, 7 October 2002), modalities for pre-establishment commitments based on a GATS-type positive list approach (WT/WGTI/W/149, 7 October 2002) and investors' and home government's obligations (WT/WGTI/W/152, 19 November 2002). While the first three submissions mentioned above were made solely by India, the last submission was made jointly by China, Cuba, India, Kenya, Pakistan, and Zimbabwe. These were the only submissions made by countries opposing negotiations on Singapore Issues. The remaining forty-three submissions were made by the proponents of the negotiations. Thus, the role played by India's submissions in raising awareness about the adverse consequences for developing countries of binding rules on Investment cannot be overemphasized. An interesting line adopted by Seshadri in the WTO discussions was to highlight how binding rules on some of these issues would prevent developing countries from using policy measures that had been used by the developed countries in the past for their economic development—classic examples of 'kicking away the ladder', a concept made popular by the Cambridge Economist Ha-Joon Chang.

7.9.2 Cementing Opposition to Initiating Negotiations on Singapore Issues: 2002–2003

India rounded off its efforts aimed at cementing opposition against negotiations on Investment by organizing an international conference in New Delhi on trade, investment, and development. Held during 18–20

May 2003, the meeting was organized in partnership with UNCTAD. It brought together Geneva-based delegates and capital-based officials from fifteen developing countries. Most participants returned from this meeting convinced that binding rules on investment would not be in their interest.[32] India's efforts in organizing this meeting had paid off. This energized many developing countries to oppose negotiations on Singapore Issues. This would subsequently facilitate the creation of a broad-based coalition at the Fifth Ministerial Conference of the WTO, which was held in Cancun in September 2003.

7.10 Battleground Cancun

The Doha mandate required that at the Fifth Ministerial Conference, the WTO Members take a decision on modalities of negotiations on the four Singapore Issues. This decision was required to be taken by explicit consensus.[33] Further, the Chairman's Statement at the closing session of the Doha Ministerial Conference had clarified that each member would have the right to take a position on modalities, that would prevent the negotiations from proceeding after the Fifth Ministerial Conference. Thus, the Fifth Ministerial Conference, which was scheduled to be held in Cancun, Mexico, during 10–14 September 2003, was set to determine the fate of the Singapore Issues. The Cancun Ministerial Conference was preceded by a series of informal meetings at the ministerial level of some WTO members during November 2002 to July 2003, and eventually culminated in intense diplomatic activity in Geneva.

As part of the preparatory process for the Cancun Ministerial Conference, WTO Members convened in a formal meeting of the General Council on 25–30 August 2003. During this meeting, the main task before the trade negotiators was to consider the text of ministerial declaration to be transmitted to Mexican Minister Derbez, the chairman of the Ministerial Conference, for being negotiated by the ministers at the meeting. Unlike the surcharged atmosphere of a similar GC meeting held in 2001 prior to the Doha Ministerial Conference, the ambiance in 2003 was less tension laden. In sharp contrast to the approach adopted in the Harbinson Text in 2001, which had ignored the divergent positions of countries, the text prepared by Carlos Pérez del Castillo, the ambassador of Uruguay and the Chairman of GC, did not unabashedly ignore the differences in positions of countries on various issues.

Adopting an inclusive approach, the Castillo Text contained different options on the contentious issues, thereby giving a fair picture of the contemporary developments at the negotiating table.[34] On Singapore Issues, the Castillo Text provided two options. The first option endorsed the launch of negotiations, and on each issue the relevant Annex on modalities was referred to. The second option reflected the position of many developing countries that the situation did not provide a basis for commencement of negotiations and that clarification process should continue. Thus, in the absence of consensus on Singapore Issues, the Castillo Text provided options to the ministers for promoting discussions at the Cancun Ministerial Conference. The battleground thereafter shifted from Geneva to Cancun.

During 10–14 September 2003 Cancun, the popular tourist resort in Mexico, with its gentle aquamarine sea and sandy white beach, hosted the Fifth Ministerial Conference of the WTO. In deference to the prevailing hot and humid weather conditions, the delegates had been advised to shun formal suits in favour of more comfortable clothes—an exception that would otherwise have been unthinkable in the context of protocol-driven international diplomacy. This was not the only departure from the past. As the developments at the Ministerial Conference would demonstrate, the developed countries failed spectacularly in pushing their negotiating agenda. The dynamics of negotiations and balance of negotiating strength appeared to have changed. This would not only have a profound impact on the future contours of the Doha Round, but also influence the fate of the WTO itself. How did the negotiations on Singapore Issues evolve at Cancun? How did the opponents of these issues make their voices heard? What led to the collapse of this crucial meeting?

7.10.1 Opposition to Negotiations on Singapore Issues Gathers Momentum

When the ministers convened at Cancun for the Fifth Ministerial Conference, they started deliberating on the Castillo Text as the basis for the final ministerial declaration. During the deliberations, which were chaired by Luis Ernesto Derbez, Mexico's Secretary for External Relations, a large number of developing countries made it amply clear that the time was not ripe for negotiating binding rules on Singapore Issues. These countries wanted the study process on these issues to continue. To illustrate, the Caribbean countries were emphatic that 'The Singapore Issues have far-reaching implications for national economies, including the constriction of policy space, the irreversibility of negotiation outcomes and implementation costs. It is imperative that the process of clarification of these issues should continue before contemplating negotiations on these subjects.'[35] The African Union, LDCs, and ACP countries were of the view that further clarification be sought on certain issues in the Doha mandate. They reaffirmed that negotiations on the modalities should not start until there is 'explicit consensus.'[36]

How 'explicit consensus' was gathering steam became obvious on the evening of 12 September, when Arun Jaitley, India's Commerce Minister, had a brief meeting with Pierre S. Pettigrew, Minister of International Trade for Canada and the facilitator for Singapore Issues, at the Cancun Ministerial Conference. Pettigrew told Jaitley: 'I am in a problem. Will you bail me out?' Jaitley, always ready with a quick repartee, retorted: 'You do not have a problem. Your job is the easiest, because Doha mandates an explicit consensus and obviously there is no explicit consensus. All you have to say is I am here, sitting right in front of you and saying no.'[37]

While different country groups were making their opposition known in no uncertain terms, a larger coalition representing about fifty countries was created at Cancun. In a joint communiqué to Pierre Pettigrew, the coalition noted that 'there is no explicit consensus on the modalities for negotiations as per the Doha Mandate.' It was 'of the firm view that there is no option to pursue other than the continuation of the clarification process.'[38] While the message of the coalition against Singapore Issues was loud and clear, it did not seem to make an impact on Chairman Derbez. In the revised Draft Cancun Ministerial Text of 13 September 2003, despite the lack of explicit consensus, it was proposed to launch negotiations on trade facilitation and transparency in government procurement. In respect of the other two Singapore Issues—Investment and Competition—the text provided for continuing the clarification process.[39] Later in the day, when this text was discussed in the meeting of

Heads of Delegation, an overwhelmingly large number of developing countries sharply criticized the provisions on Singapore Issues. If a count of the countries opposing Singapore Issues had been taken, it could well have crossed a hundred. 'One' country's opposition at Doha had swelled to a 'hundred' at Cancun.

In the face of stiff resistance from a large number of countries, how would the developed countries have tackled this situation in the past? Perhaps striking side deals and breaking coalitions would have been an imaginable strategy, as had been resorted to at Doha. However, it is important to mention that at the Cancun Ministerial Conference, the developed countries had either run out of carrots for side deals, or were confident of having their way without deploying this stratagem. On one issue a game-changing possibility existed, but its domestic compulsions appear to have prevented the USA from making any serious effort at negotiating a side deal. Before discussing what this issue was, it is relevant to discuss how the ghost of explicit consensus, conjured by Maran at Doha, would come to haunt Cancun.

7.10.2 Minted at Doha, 'Explicit Consensus' Gains Currency in Cancun

Maran's dogged resistance at Doha and the final clarification by Chairman Kamal inspired some development-oriented civil society organizations (CSO) to adopt explicit consensus as their rallying cry against Singapore Issues. These organizations adopted an innovative method for communicating their message. They distributed T-shirts with 'Explicit Consensus' written on both sides. However, what became a blockbuster item was a unique ribbon to be worn around the neck—a lanyard—for holding the official conference badge. 'Explicit Consensus' in different languages was written all along the lanyard. This worked like magic. In no time many delegates could be seen picking the lanyards from CSO desks and using them to hang their conference entry badges. The reaction of the organizers of the conference was quite unexpected. Delegates who showed the official entry badge, but were also wearing these lanyards, were not allowed entry into the main conference venue.[40] The justification given for the action was that the lanyards were confusing the security guards in performing their duty. What remained unanswered was whether security guards had to examine the badges or the lanyards to which the badges were attached. However, what did get answered in the minds of many delegates, particularly from the smaller developing countries, was that each of them had the ability to stop negotiations on Singapore Issues. Maran's legacy of 'explicit consensus', minted at Doha, may not have been endearing for some countries, but for many others it had an enduring power.

While these interesting developments were taking place outside the main conference centre, at the negotiating table itself another issue was unleashing turbulence at the ministerial conference—the unsympathetic response of the USA to the problem of cotton subsidies.

7.10.3 Developments on Cotton Subsidies: Harvesting Poverty

Historically, the USA has provided extremely high subsidies to its cotton farmers. In 2001, subsidies targeted specifically to US cotton farmers were as high as 74 per cent of the value of cotton production in that year.[41] This figure would go up a few notches if we were to add the subsidies under other schemes that were available to all agricultural products. High cotton subsidies depressed world prices and devastated the economies of some African countries, which are overwhelmingly dependent on cotton for their development. These included Benin, Burkina Faso, Chad, and Mali. The pathetic plight of cotton farmers in these countries was brought to light in a briefing paper by Oxfam.[42] This stirred almost passionate action by some WTO Members and there was a concerted demand from many countries that the USA should give a commitment to reduce its cotton subsidies. At Cancun, this demand reached a crescendo.

Instead of attempting to address the core issue of cotton subsidies being raised by the African countries, the response of the USA was to look for solutions that did not even touch the fringe of the problem. Right from the time when this issue was raised in Geneva, the US response was that resources must be found to assist these countries in diversifying their economies. At the Cancun Ministerial Conference, the USA showed no flexibility to even contemplate any subsidy cuts. Thus, it lost an opportunity of cutting a deal on cotton, which could thereafter have been used as a bait for keeping all countries engaged at the negotiating table on other issues. This response is not surprising as cotton farmers in the USA are typically rich and also constitute a powerful political lobby. At the conference venue rumblings started being heard against what was perceived by many countries as the unsympathetic attitude of the USA to the genuine problems of some of the poorest WTO members. This would have had the unintended consequence of hardening the resolve of many developing countries to become strident in their opposition to the Singapore Issues. The developing countries were in for a surprise, when they entered the Green Room meeting convened by Chairman Derbez on 14 September.

7.10.4 Sequencing Issues for Discussion: Chronicle of Collapse of the Meeting Foretold

Normally, it is the prerogative of the chairman of the meeting to decide the sequence of issues to be taken up on the negotiating agenda. Often, this is a matter bereft of any controversy. However, during the meeting with a handful of countries held on 14 September, Chairman Derbez decided to start with one of the most divisive issues, the four Singapore Issues, and left other issues for subsequent discussion. Seeing that the coalition of developing countries had remained steadfast in its opposition to negotiations on the Singapore Issues, Pascal Lamy, the Trade Commissioner of the EU, did something that few could have imagined. He offered to remove two Singapore Issues from the negotiating agenda. According to K.M. Chandrasekhar, who was India's Ambassador to the WTO at the time of the Cancun Ministerial Conference, Chairman Derbez identified Investment and Competition for being dropped from the negotiating agenda.[43] However, after witnessing the wrangling among the countries on which two issues should be removed, Derbez adjourned the meeting to allow countries to consult among themselves.

During the recess, the talk outside the negotiating room was that Investment and Competition should be taken out of the negotiating agenda. However, most of the African countries were of the view that they did not have the capacity to implement agreements on Trade

Facilitation and Government Procurement. This group was not in favour of unbundling the Singapore Issues. The ACP Group held a similar position. When the meeting reconvened in the afternoon of 14 September, the African Group made it clear that they wanted all the four issues removed from the negotiating agenda. However, South Korea and a few other countries were emphatic that they would not agree to the removal of even one Singapore Issue.[44] Citing these irreconcilable positions, Chairman Derbez quickly closed the Ministerial Conference without any outcome. Most of the countries in the meeting were shocked by the turn of events. As the ministers started trickling out of the meeting, the delegates of countries who had opposed dropping even a single Singapore Issue off the negotiating agenda appeared apprehensive that they would be blamed for collapse of the Cancun Ministerial Conference. They need not have worried. Within a few minutes of the conclusion of the meeting, Bob Zoellick played his masterstroke in blame shifting. As has been described in detail in Section 4.3, he lay the entire blame for the collapse of the meeting on the developing countries for opposing negotiations on Singapore Issues, while playing down his own role in not engaging meaningfully on the issue of cotton subsidies. With some hidden hands having pulled the plug on the Ministerial Conference at Cancun, did it spell doom for the Doha Round? How did the negotiations get revived within a few months?

7.11 Finally Getting Three Singapore Issues off the Negotiating Table: General Council Meeting During 31 July–1 August 2004

Despite the salubrious climes of Cancun, the Fifth Ministerial Conference had created a chill between the USA on the one hand and some developing countries on the other. However, within a few months of the collapse of the Cancun Ministerial Conference, Zoellick showed considerable leadership in writing letters to the WTO Members and reignited the process of cleaning the mess created at Cancun. A meeting of WTO's General Council was convened at the end July 2004 to take stock and provide guidance for further negotiations. After having revealed its bottom line at Cancun, the EU found it almost impossible to retract its offer of removing two Singapore Issues. Consequently, during this GC meeting, not two, but three, Singapore Issues were taken off the table. Only Trade Facilitation remained on the negotiating agenda of the Doha Round. Maran, who had been reviled by an EU spokesperson as a 'madman' blocking the consensus at the Doha Ministerial Conference,[45] would have felt vindicated at the turn of events and may even have smiled from his heavenly perch.

7.12 Strategies Deployed by India to Remove Three Singapore Issues from the Negotiating Agenda

As discussed in the previous sections of this chapter, the strong push for including the four Singapore Issues in the negotiating agenda of the Doha Round of multilateral trade negotiation triggered an equally determined resistance from some developing countries. In respect of Investment, the opposition witnessed during the Doha Round was, to some extent, a spill-over of past tensions on this issue. The developing countries were worried that binding rules on these issues at the WTO would deprive them of the elbow room to pursue development-oriented policies. Further, they saw little gains for their economies from these issues. They had to confront formidable odds at the negotiating table. Arrayed against them were the two most powerful Members of the WTO—USA and the EU. In addition, other developed countries and a few advanced developing countries had joined forces with the powerful duo. Given the huge asymmetry in economic and political clout of the proponents and opponents of Singapore Issues, in hindsight, it appears nothing short of a miracle that the opponents prevailed. This was not a matter of chance. The outcome was a result of clear strategies used by the key countries opposing the launch of negotiation on these issues. This section discusses the strategies deployed by India and other developing countries who were seeking to get the Singapore Issues off the negotiating agenda of the Doha Round.

7.12.1 Planning and Preparing

In order to engage effectively in negotiations, one of the main prerequisites is detailed planning and preparation. This is not a one-time activity, but a continuous process throughout the negotiations. Intrinsic to this is the necessity to constantly review the strategy and make suitable course corrections. In the context of the intense tussle on inclusion of Singapore Issues in the negotiating agenda, the following aspects related to planning and preparation merit some discussion: understanding the key issues; deciding as a threshold issue whether to oppose inclusion of Singapore Issues in the negotiating agenda or to engage with the hope of shaping the negotiations in line with national interest; managing domestic constituencies; and finding resource for undertaking research. These aspects are discussed below.

7.12.1.1 Maran educating himself on key issues

A negotiator should have adequate technical knowledge of the issues on the table and their implications on his country. In addition, the negotiator should have a reasonable understanding of the interests and strategies of other key players in the negotiations. Maran went about educating himself about the Singapore Issues, particularly Investment, in a systematic manner. He personally undertook a detailed study of the various papers prepared by the United Nations Commission on Trans-National Corporations. In addition, he read with considerable interest and appreciation the writings of Bhagirath Das, India's former ambassador to GATT, and of Martin Khor, the intrepid and knowledgeable expert in the civil society community. On one occasion, he invited Das for a detailed discussion on the substance of these issues and the strategy to be followed at the Doha Ministerial Conference.[46] Apart from deepening his understanding of the technical aspects of Singapore Issues, this meeting served another purpose: to convince his own officials of the correctness of his approach.

If Maran had educated himself with the details of Singapore Issues, why did he choose to stonewall instead of engaging with Lamy and Zoellick in the small group meeting on 13–14 November? Perhaps Maran was shrewd to realize that inclusion of Singapore Issues in the negotiating agenda was not contingent on legal arguments and economic implications, but was more dependent on global political dynamics. Further, he would have been modest enough to realize that in oratory skills he was no match to either of these two formidable personalities. Hence, stonewalling would have appeared to be a better option, rather than engaging in lengthy legal and economic arguments.

7.12.1.2 Opposing issues at the threshold, instead of agreeing to negotiations and hoping to shape the agenda

A party which spots issues in the negotiating agenda that may be inimical to its interests, finds itself in the following quandary: should it stay out of the negotiations and hope that in its absence the negotiations will flounder; or should it join the negotiations and aspire to mould the eventual outcome according to its interests and concerns. Neither of the two options is free from risks. By staying out of the negotiations, a party may still be compelled to accept the final outcome, if the negotiations on issues against its interests are a part of the larger multilateral negotiations encompassing other issues. Further, the country might not have adequate economic and political heft to stall the negotiations by its absence from the negotiating table. In the context of multilateral trade negotiations, the USA can do this, and perhaps even the EU and now China. But most of the other countries might not be in a position to prevent negotiations from moving ahead, despite their absence at the negotiating table.

On the other hand, joining the negotiations with the hope of influencing the final outcome comes with its own share of risks. First, by joining the negotiations, a country might impart momentum to the negotiating process. This is particularly relevant for larger developing countries, if they are likely to be the main source of concessions at the negotiating table. Second, the ability of a country to influence the course and content of negotiations depends on many factors: economic and legal arguments, backing of coalitions and political and economic clout of the party concerned. Thus, no developing country can enter a negotiation with the self-belief that it would be able to decisively stamp its imprint on the final outcome.

Given the risks involved in both courses of action—opposing inclusion of damaging issues in the agenda and staying out of negotiation; or joining the negotiation in the hope of influencing the agenda—Maran was confronted with a thorny dilemma. His deliberation with India's former trade negotiators and other experts in the Ashok Mitra Parliamentary Committee, would have left him in no doubt that India and other developing countries would face an uphill battle in defending their interests, if they acquiesced to negotiations on Singapore Issues. Therefore, as a threshold decision, he chose the path of opposing inclusion of these issues in the negotiating agenda. By exercising this option, he would also have been cognizant of being in a position to secure the best terms possible for protecting the interests of his country, and those of other nations, who might want to align with him. On the other hand, if he were to remain silent and not oppose these issues, he would have been left with almost no leverage to defend his country's interests. Hence, the decision to oppose Singapore Issues had considerable merit from the perspective of negotiating strategy.

7.12.1.3 Managing domestic constituencies

It has been emphasized in different chapters that negotiations at an international forum are almost always accompanied by negotiations with different groups at home with divergent economic interests. Building a domestic consensus around a negotiating issue in itself does not guarantee that the country will be able to adhere to the negotiating line endorsed by its stakeholders. For a negotiator to be able to pursue her line, she must strategize for making sure that her decisions are not altered by her political superiors.

In the specific context of international trade negotiations, the calculus can get extremely complicated, if opponents of a country on an issue also happen to be allies on geopolitical issues. In such a situation the country may be compelled to make its priorities in international trade subservient to the larger objective of maintaining good political relations with other countries. Given this challenge, how Maran managed to keep the Indian prime minister on his side on Singapore Issues, is a master lesson in strategy.

During October 2001, Maran met leaders of different political parties, including leaders belonging to parties opposed to the government. He also met leaders of various trade unions. While the obvious agenda of these meetings was to inform the political leaders and trade unions about the risks in initiating negotiations on the Singapore Issues and secure their endorsement of the government's stand on various WTO issues,[47] at another level Maran was achieving something more. He was building a formidable political constituency in favour of his tough line on these issues. A few weeks before the Doha Ministerial Conference, he led a delegation of leaders of parties across India's varied political spectrum to meet Prime Minister Vajpayee. In this meeting Maran remained almost silent, and let other leaders bat for him. They virtually extracted a promise from Vajpayee that he would back Maran if leaders from any developed country were to approach him to request Maran to tone down his opposition to the Singapore Issues.[48] While Maran was battling it out at Doha, leaders of some developed countries sought to undermine him by opening a back channel to Vajpayee. When the much-apprehended phone call from the leader of a developed country came to the Indian prime minister, he kept his word and continued to support Maran. The pre-emptive deft moves made by Maran a few weeks before the Doha Ministerial Conference paid off.

7.12.1.4 Using experts for undertaking research to underpin submissions

At Doha, Maran witnessed how within a few days after having spoken against the Singapore Issues at the plenary session of the Ministerial Conference, country after country fell in line with the wishes of the developed countries. However, it was also on account of many developing countries not having a good understanding of the technical complexities of Singapore Issues and their likely impact on them. In order to plug this yawning gap, within a short time after returning from Doha, Maran and his officials decided to tap expertise outside the government. They roped in knowledgeable trade economists to undertake research for underpinning India's submissions, particularly on Investment. In order to put this on a sustained footing, the officials managed to ear-mark financial resources for the research. Overall, the decision not to rely solely on expertise within the government but to commission research from academics was to play a vital role in shaping the discourse against initiating negotiations on Singapore Issues.

7.12.2 Shaping the Agenda

In the meetings leading to the Doha Ministerial Conference, the proponents of negotiations on Singapore Issues had attempted to create a narrative that binding rules on these issues would be in the interests of developing countries. In the interregnum between Doha Ministerial

Conference in 2001 and Cancun Ministerial Conference in 2003, India made detailed submissions to the working groups that had been created to study each of the four Singapore Issues. Through these submissions, India sought to formulate an alternate narrative from the development perspective. The submissions, particularly those on Investment, highlighted the risks for developing countries from negotiating binding rules. These submissions openly challenged the narrative created by the developed countries on gains from binding rules on Singapore Issues.

Another initiative taken by India, the workshop on Investment organized by it in May 2003, proved to be crucial in shaping the agenda. It offered a unique opportunity to many developing countries to explore ideas in an amiable environment and to realize that many of them had similar concerns regarding the adverse impact of binding rules on Investment. Further, the timing of the workshop was almost perfect. As it was held not too close to the Cancun Ministerial Conference, the participating countries got adequate time to cross the bureaucratic layers within their government in order to decide their national position on this issue. On the other hand, it was not held too far in advance of the ministerial meeting for the impact of the workshop to wear off in the intervening period. This was influential in creating a narrative against this issue.

While India was forcefully seeking to shape the narrative on Singapore Issues, it recognized that many of its arguments might be too technical for high-level policymakers and ministers to grasp quickly. This could limit the impact of its efforts aimed at creating an alternate narrative. To overcome this problem, India's ambassador to WTO, K.M. Chandrasekhar, got crisp and easy to understand two-page documents prepared on each Singapore Issue for wide dissemination among developing countries, media, and civil society organizations. These documents captured the essence of the arguments against Singapore Issues and clearly explained how the ability of governments to make and implement policies for national development could be substantially curtailed by binding rules at the WTO. These two-pagers became quite popular not only among the delegates, but also among the media, which used the information in their articles. This simple strategy proved to be effective in communicating many developing countries' version of the narrative on Singapore Issues.

7.12.3 Framing Issues

This case study on Singapore Issues provides a fascinating account of how effective framing of issues can play a crucial role in determining outcomes at the negotiating table. While there was no attempt at framing issues at the Doha Ministerial Conference by the opponents, however, the picture had changed quite dramatically by the Cancun Ministerial Conference. How was the issue framed at Cancun? How did this come about? Was it a part of a coherent strategy or merely coincidental?

During the Doha Ministerial Conference, some developing countries spoke against initiating negotiations on Singapore Issues. They gave many reasons for their opposition—agenda of the WTO was already overloaded, Singapore Issues were non-trade related, binding rules on these issues would not be in the interests of developing countries, etc. None of these reasons was presented in a manner that could have encapsulated the core of the opposition in a few words. Perhaps there was no realization of the need to do so. However, the final text of the Ministerial Declaration—'we agree that negotiations will take place after the Fifth Session of the Ministerial Conference on the basis of a decision to be taken, by explicit consensus, at that Session on modalities of negotiations'—provided the material for framing of the issue after Doha.

The words 'explicit consensus' focused on the process of negotiations on Singapore Issues and drew attention to the ability of even a single country to stop negotiations from proceeding. Use of 'explicit consensus' had started gaining currency in discussions in Geneva after the Doha Ministerial Conference. Subsequently, in their plenary statement at the Cancun Ministerial Conference, many ministers referred to it. What might have imparted a heightened meaning to 'explicit consensus' was the frustration among a large number of developing countries at the exclusionary manner in which the Harbinson Text was bulldozed prior to Doha Ministerial Conference despite their strong reservation and the perception of non-transparent decision making at the Doha Ministerial Conference. It is, thus, possible that the opponents of the negotiations may have felt empowered by the imagery evoked by 'explicit consensus'. What proved to be the tipping point was the use of 'explicit consensus' by civil society groups to lend a sharper edge to their campaign against the negotiations on Singapore Issues. This is likely to have contributed to mobilizing opinion among developing countries' delegates against these issues.

With more and more countries talking about 'explicit consensus', the negotiators had finally found the vocabulary to suitably frame their opposition to Singapore Issues in a catchy and popular manner. Preventing delegates from entering the venue of Cancun Ministerial Conference if they used lanyards with 'explicit consensus' written in different languages for hanging the official badge, as described earlier, further demonstrated that the two words had struck the right note.

7.12.4 Building and Sustaining a Coalition

Doha and Cancun saw contrasting responses to coalitions of some developing countries. The coalition, forged prior to Doha, could not survive even one day at the Doha Ministerial Conference. In contrast, the coalition against Singapore Issues at Cancun was created almost impromptu and proved to be more enduring and effective. What explains the contrasting outcomes? What strategies were deployed to retain the cohesion of the coalition at Cancun? This sub-section is based on the first-hand experience and observations of the author, who was part of the official Indian delegation to both these Ministerial Conferences.

The Like Minded Group (LMG), led by India and comprising other developing countries, including Cuba, Dominican Republic, Egypt, El Salvador, Honduras, Indonesia, Malaysia, Sri Lanka, and Uganda, was active in Geneva during 2000–2001 in articulating the interests of a large number of developing countries. The LMG raised many issues, including more than a hundred issues collectively called Implementation Issues. In addition, the LMG was also opposed to launching negotiation on Singapore Issues. At the Doha Ministerial Conference, the Indian delegation was totally preoccupied in defending its position against the combined onslaught of the USA and the EU, and it could not engage effectively with other LMG members. In India's absence, no other country made any attempt to rally the LMG together and coordinate their positions. Unable to grapple with the carrot-and-stick policy of the developed countries, in no time the LMG just withered away.

In contrast, at the Cancun Ministerial Conference the coalition against Singapore Issues was almost completely focused on these issues. Its energies were not frittered away on other issues. Unlike the LMG, the coalition at Cancun was not critically tethered to India's leadership and its fortunes at the negotiating table. Instead, the leadership of the coalition was assumed by a few other developing countries, particularly Malaysia. This ensured that the coalition would continue to function effectively, even when some of its leaders were engaged in negotiations on other issues. At Cancun, each day, most of the members of the coalition would meet to discuss developments of the day and to coordinate their positions. This prevented rumours and misinformation from being spread, and cemented the coalition by creating trust among its constituents. In addition, the core group of countries in the leadership role remained regularly in touch with each other for doing the thinking and planning the strategy. The understanding among the coalition partners was quite remarkable. When ministers and ambassadors of some of their countries were preoccupied in other meetings, their senior officials confidently interacted with ministers of other partners, without any apprehension of ruffling protocol-related feathers. Further, when the rumour of defection by an important member surfaced, prompt action by Jaitley quelled the potential desertion. This incident has been described in Section 5.10.

Another strategy used by the core group of leaders of the coalition was to focus on areas of agreement and avoid divisive issues. It was no secret that some of the countries in the coalition may not have been unhappy with just two issues—Investment and Competition—being dropped from the negotiating agenda. However, for Malaysia, it was mainly transparency in government procurement which appeared to be a red line. For some other countries, all the four issues were absolutely no go. If the coalition had pondered over unbundling the four issues and dropping just one or two of them, it would have splintered in no time. The leaders wisely played down arguments against internal trade-off among the four issues and channelled the sensitivities of different countries on individual issues as an effective shield against all the four issues as a whole.

The developing countries coalition at Cancun showed considerable shrewdness in constantly engaging with non-government organizations and regularly briefing them about developments at the negotiating table.

This helped prevent misinformation from being spread. In turn, the NGOs wrote influential articles in the media supporting the coalition. This helped create a narrative in favour of the coalition. The coalition also reached out to other developing countries and explained the reasons for opposing Singapore Issues. Sensing the strong current, many countries outside the coalition decided to go with the flow and oppose these issues. Undoubtedly, this strengthened the hand of the coalition.

7.12.5 Engaging at the Negotiating Table

So far, in this section, we have mainly discussed strategies outside the negotiating table. We now turn to strategies deployed at the negotiating table to remove three of the four Singapore Issues from the negotiating agenda. We focus on the core strategy used by Maran at Doha—resisting firmly and eventually yielding after extracting the best possible deal under the prevailing circumstances. This also provides insights into the larger question facing trade negotiators—when to compromise and cut a deal? Finally, Maran's strategy also underscores an important point—not all battles can be won and some battles have to be left to be fought another day.

A crucial decision point for any negotiator is—when to resist and when to yield? Yielding too early may result in the country foregoing the possibility of a better deal at a later stage in the negotiations. Further, by yielding, the negotiator might impart momentum to the negotiations that might eventually be inimical to its interest. On the other hand, if the negotiator continues to resist without yielding, she runs the risk of either being completely sidelined and ignored in the negotiation, or being made the scapegoat for its failure. It requires a shrewd negotiator, endowed with wisdom and assisted by experienced hands, to choose the suitable time to give up resistance and finally yield. How the text on the four Singapore Issues evolved during the negotiating process, initially at Geneva and thereafter at Doha, provides insights into the strategic thinking of negotiators confronting the resist-yield dilemma.

At Doha, on Singapore Issues Maran held few aces in his hand. He was actually negotiating against tremendous odds. First, the asymmetry in economic and political power between India and the USA-EU combine was extremely daunting. Further, Maran would have been cognizant that his resistance on Singapore Issues risked damaging political relations with these countries, albeit temporarily. Second, countries opposing Singapore Issues were few, and as the Ministerial Conference progressed the number steadily declined. Third, the developed countries had created commercially meaningful opportunities for striking side deals—tariff preferences for ACP countries—and inducing many developing countries to stop opposing the negotiations on Singapore Issues. Fourth, with the US positioning launch of a new multilateral trade round as a counter to global terrorism, it would have been politically difficult for Maran to stand up to the developed countries. Fifth, the danger of his intransigence on Singapore Issues sinking the TRIPS Decision on Access to Affordable Medicine kept Maran hooked to the negotiating table.

Given the constraints mentioned above, it is unlikely that Maran would have persisted with his opposition to the bitter end. This is apparent from the following statement of a senior Indian official to the media: 'At no stage was India considering not being part of a multilateral negotiation. So, we did all the damage control we needed to, annexed major gains on an overwhelming majority of issues, and didn't use the veto. After all, a veto would have nullified gains made by the Africa, Pacific and Caribbean group, as indeed, the entire group of Least Developed Countries as well.'[49] This suggests that India used the strategy of doggedly resisting negotiations on Singapore Issues in order to extract concessions and eventually yielded when the limit of this strategy was reached.

But how does one decide that the limit of the strategy has been reached? This can be answered by comparing Chairman Kamal's negotiating text circulated on 13 November 2001 and the deliberations in the small group held later in the day. The former text retained the provisions mandating launching of negotiations on trade facilitation and transparency in government procurement. But it explicitly postponed the decision on initiating negotiations on Investment and Competition to the fifth ministerial conference more. However, during the Green Room meeting held during 13–14 November, many countries appeared agreeable to a similar text in respect of all the four issues: decision to be taken in respect of modalities of negotiations at the next Ministerial Conference of the WTO. This could be considered to be a bit of a setback for Maran. From his perspective diminishing returns at the negotiating table had set in. Thus, any further resistance is likely to have reduced his gains on Investment and Competition. The time for yielding and cutting a deal had arrived.

However, even while yielding, Maran succeeded in extracting something important through the Chairman's Statement—the negotiations could be stopped if any country was not in a position to move ahead. Maran's dogged resistance should be viewed as part of a strategy to extract the best terms for India. His yielding should also be viewed from another perspective—the need to constantly review strategy. Negotiations are a dynamic process in which positions evolve. As other countries had moved, India was left with no option at the end, other than yielding and fighting the battle another day.

7.13 Conclusions

Normally, which issues are to be included in the negotiating agenda is a threshold matter to be settled at an early stage in the negotiating process. However, as this chapter vividly demonstrates, this threshold question itself can become extremely contentious and could encompass all the four stages of negotiation in deciding just the scope of the agenda. What are some of the lessons from the perspective of negotiating strategy, which emerge from the episode of Singapore Issues?

First, the importance of anticipating problems and exploring possible solutions in advance can prove to be an effective strategy during the planning and preparation phase. Second, the importance of a trade negotiator being familiar with the issues involved in the negotiation and their likely impact on her country cannot be overemphasized. Third, on many occasions a negotiator has to decide whether to oppose an issue or remain silent. Linked with this is one of the central dilemmas confronting a negotiator—when to resist and when to yield. The ability to take the correct decision on this question can really test the mettle of even battle-hardened negotiators. Fourth, the importance of managing domestic constituencies, so that the position of the negotiator is not undermined by other countries acquires considerable importance. This is particularly true when attempts are made by some parties to bypass the negotiator and instead deal directly with her superiors. If such a situation is apprehended, the negotiator must take advance action for ensuring that her negotiating position is fully backed by the superiors. Fifth, the role of research by credible experts in creating a narrative in favour of a country, or breaking the momentum of negotiations, is clearly evident from the impact of India's submissions on Investment. Linked with this is the desirability of a country reaching out to other parties at an opportune moment and persuading them about the correctness of its approach at the negotiating table—as was done by India through the workshop jointly organized with UNCTAD in May 2003. Sixth, the impact of suitably framing an issue is brought out quite clearly in the context of Singapore Issues at the Cancun Ministerial Conference. Seventh, how the heft of a party can be enhanced through coalitions is demonstrated in this chapter.

In addition to lessons on strategies deployed by India and other developing countries, this episode provides another important lesson. The chair of a negotiating group can wield tremendous power. The actions of the chair can substantially tilt the negotiations in favour of one set of parties, thereby putting at a severe disadvantage another set of parties at the negotiating table. Further, by deciding which issues to take up earlier in a negotiation, the chair's actions can directly or inadvertently protect the interests of some parties. Thus, parties at the negotiating table must set clear rules of conduct for the chair. This will ensure transparency and predictability in negotiations and to a certain extent enhance the possibility of even-handed actions by the chair.

Notes

1. Doha Work Programme, Decision adopted by the General Council on 1 August 2004, WTO document WT/L/579 dated 2 August 2004.
2. Singapore Ministerial Declaration adopted on 13 December 1996, WTO document WT/MIN(96)/DEC dated 18 December 1996.
3. Ministerial Declaration adopted on 14 November 2001, WTO document WT/MIN(01)/DEC/1 dated 20 November 2001.
4. GATT document Basic Instruments and Selected Documents 9S/28, of 18 November 1960.
5. Article VIII of GATS seeks to ensure that any monopoly supplier of services in the territory of a member does not act in a manner inconsistent with the general obligation of MFN treatment.

6. GATT document MTN.TNC/MIN(94)/ST/38 dated 13 April 1994.
7. A small group of WTO Members, who are signatories to the plurilateral Government Procurement Agreement (GPA), have voluntarily given up recourse to this exception. In respect of government procurement of goods and services, these countries provide non-discriminatory treatment to other signatories, but not to non-signatory countries.
8. Singapore Ministerial Declaration adopted on 13 December 1996, WTO document WT/MIN(96)/DEC dated 18 December 1996.
9. There is no commonly accepted estimate of the value of government procurement in different countries. Certain studies have estimated the size to be 13 per cent of the GDP of a country.
10. See, for example, Mariana Mazzucato, *The Entrepreneurial State: Debunking Public vs Private Sector Myths* (Penguin, 2018). The book discusses in detail how the US government has used government procurement as an effective policy instrument for boosting its domestic players in sectors of new and emerging technologies.
11. The calculation by the author is based on EU's notification of Government Procurement Statistics for 2006 to the WTO.
12. Singapore Ministerial Declaration adopted on 13 December 1996, WTO document WT/MIN(96)/DEC dated 18 December 1996.
13. Paragraph 46 of 35th Report on India and WTO. 1998. Department-related Parliamentary Standing Committee on Commerce, Parliament of India.
14. Paragraph 46 of 35th Report on India and WTO.
15. WTO document JOB(01)/140 dated 26 September 2001.
16. WTO document JOB(01)/140/Rev.1 dated 27 October 2001.
17. Paragraph 68 of the Minutes of the meeting of the General Council held on 31 October and 1 November 2001, WTO document WT/GC/M/71 dated 13 December 2001.
18. Paragraph 68 of the Minutes of the meeting of the General Council held on 31 October and 1 November 2001, WTO document WT/GC/M/71 dated 13 December 2001.
19. Minutes of the meeting of the General Council held on 31 October and 1 November 2001, WTO document WT/GC/M/71 dated 13 December 2001.
20. Paragraph 148 of the Minutes of the meeting of the General Council held on 31 October and 1 November 2001, WTO document WT/GC/M/71 dated 13 December 2001.
21. Statement by the Honourable Murasoli Maran, Minister of Commerce and Industry, India, at the Plenary Session of WTO Ministerial Conference at Doha, WTO document WT/MIN(01)/ST/10 dated 10 November 2001.
22. Rohit Bansal, 'India Not Isolated, Admits WTO', *Financial Express*, 12 November 2001.

23. Charlotte Denny, 'Developed World Accused of Bully-Boy Tactics at WTO,' *The Guardian*, 12 November 2001.
24. WTO document JOB(01)/140/Rev.2 dated 13 November 2001.
25. Interview with a former Indian trade negotiator, February 2023.
26. Interview with a former Indian trade negotiator, February 2023.
27. Interview with S. Narayanan, who was India's Ambassador to the WTO at the time of the Doha Ministerial Conference, May 2023.
28. Declaration on the TRIPS Agreement and Public Health adopted by the Doha Ministerial Conference on 14 November 2001, WTO document WT/MIN(01)/DEC/2 dated 20 November 2001.
29. This paragraph is based on an interview with S. Narayanan, who was India's Ambassador to the WTO at the time of the Doha Ministerial Conference, May 2023.
30. This paragraph is based on an interview with S. Narayanan, who was India's Ambassador to the WTO at the time of the Doha Ministerial Conference, May 2023.
31. Available on the following website and accessed on 23 May 2023: https://www.wto.org/english/thewto_e/minist_e/min01_e/min01_chair_speaking_e.htm
32. India & the WTO, May 2003. Vol. 5. No. 5. New Delhi: A Monthly Newsletter of the Ministry of Commerce and Industry.
33. It may be noted that 'explicit consensus' was mentioned earlier in the context of the four Singapore Issues in the 1996 Singapore Ministerial Declaration of the WTO.
34. WTO document JOB(03)/150/Rev.1 dated 24 August 2003.
35. Caribbean Declaration on the Fifth Ministerial Conference of the WTO, Communication from Jamaica, WTO document no. WT/MIN(03)/6 dated 29 August 2003.
36. Position of the African Union, Least-Developed Countries, Caribbean and Pacific Countries on the new (Singapore) Issues, WTO document WT/MIN(03)/W/19 dated 12 September 2003.
37. Keynote address of Arun Jaitley at FICCI-UNCTAD Seminar on Reflections on post-Cancun Agenda—the way ahead, organized in New Delhi on 22 October 2003. India and The WTO, Vol. 5 No. 10–11, October–November 2003. New Delhi: A Monthly Newsletter of the Ministry of Commerce and Industry.
38. Joint Communiqué to H.E. Mr. Pierre S. Pettigrew, Minister of International Trade for Canada & the facilitator for Singapore Issues, at the Cancun Ministerial Conference dated 12 September 2003. India & the WTO, September 2003.
39. WTO document JOB(03)/150/Rev.2 dated 13 September 2003.
40. The author was witness to many delegates being stopped from entering the main conference venue for wearing the ribbon with 'Explicit Consensus' written on it.
41. Calculations based on Domestic Support notification of the USA to the WTO.

42. 'Cultivating Poverty: The Impact of US Cotton Subsidies on Africa', Oxfam Briefing Paper no. 30, 2002.
43. K.M. Chandrasekhar, *As Good as My Word: A Memoir* (Gurugram: HarperCollins Publishers, 2022), 104.
44. Chandrasekhar, *As Good as My Word*, 104.
45. Chandrasekhar, *As Good as My Word*, 104.
46. Personal papers of Bhagirath Lal Das, India's former ambassador to GATT, available with the author.
47. Press Information Bureau. 2001. Maran holds consultations with political parties ahead of Ministerial. 19 October.
48. Based on an interview with a former Ambassador of India to the GATT, who got a first-hand account from one of the leaders of a political party, who was present in the meeting with Vajpayee, April 2021.
49. Rohit Bansal, 'India Inc Gives Maran 10/10 on Doha Performance', *Financial Express*, 16 November 2001.

8

Davids Join Hands to Take on Goliath in the Battle on Agriculture

8.1 Introduction

Despite it being 15 August, a day celebrated with considerable joy and festivity by Indians as their country's Independence Day, the sombre look on the face of K.M. Chandrasekhar, India's ambassador to the WTO, could not be missed. Felipe de Seixas Correa, the ambassador of Brazil, who was walking beside him, also appeared rather pensive. They had just come out of a closed-door meeting of a handful of countries (commonly referred to as a Green Room meeting in GATT/WTO parlance), where it became evident that the negotiating effort of many developing countries over the past one and a half years was at the risk of being rendered meaningless. Power asymmetry at the WTO negotiating table was at work, once again. Given their economic might and political clout, the European Union and the United States are formidable players at the WTO negotiating table. When they join hands, the combine becomes an almost unstoppable force—a reality that was evident in the Green Room meeting. A negotiating proposal in agriculture, jointly submitted by the EU and the USA a few days earlier, was on the verge of becoming the basis for future negotiations, with concerns of most developing countries counting for nothing.

Something had to be done, and done quickly, if the objective of the USA and the EU of not conceding even an inch to the developing countries and instead rewriting the new rules for agriculture subsidies and trade to their advantage was to be thwarted. This was not an easy task, as the two prominent developing countries, Brazil and India, who could lead a coalition of developing countries, had conflicting interests on some key issues in Agriculture negotiations under the Doha Round. However, in the face of the unfolding crisis and with resentment flaring

Strategies in GATT and WTO Negotiations. Abhijit Das, Oxford University Press. © Abhijit Das 2025.
DOI: 10.1093/9780198934431.003.0008

against the USA-EU proposal, Seixas Correa made a bold suggestion to Chandrasekhar. He proposed that the two countries join hands in opposing the combined might of the EU and the USA in the Agriculture negotiations.[1]

Initially, Chandrasekhar was a bit unsure about the viability of a partnership between the two developing countries with divergent interests. For Brazil, an export powerhouse in agriculture, India, with hundreds of millions of middle-class consumers, appeared to be an extremely lucrative market for its farm exports. On the other hand, India's main objective in the Agriculture negotiations was to protect its farmers from imports by retaining the right to impose high tariffs. Despite this fundamental fault line, Chandrasekhar preferred to focus on the positives in Seixas Correa's suggestion. What would have encouraged Ambassador Chandrasekhar to go along with Brazil was the reassurance by Correa that Brazil would effectively protect the interests of India's farmers and that they would fight the battle together.[2] Then and there, without any further thought and even without consulting their capitals, the two ambassadors decided that their senior diplomats with expertise in agriculture—Rajesh Aggarwal from India and Flavio Damico from Brazil—would work together and prepare a counter-proposal. The instruction to the two trusted diplomats was straightforward—remain closeted, work together, and emerge from the room only after the counter-proposal was finalized.[3] Little would the two ambassadors have realized that they had triggered a process that would not only successfully challenge the power equations entrenched in multilateral trade negotiations for over five and a half decades, but also provide a blueprint for genuine reforms in agriculture. What started as defiance by those sought to be marginalized, would soon acquire centre-stage. Henceforth, the narrative at the negotiating table would be dominated by the perspective of some developing countries and not the USA-EU combine.

When the EU and the USA made the joint negotiating submission in the Agriculture negotiations, it appeared that the developing countries would be compelled to march in lockstep with the collective wishes of the USA-EU combine. However, from September 2003 onwards and for almost five years, a coalition of developing countries, commonly referred to as the G-20, prevented the USA and the EU from rewriting the rules of the game in the mould of their narrow interest while marginalizing the interest of most developing countries. Yet, in the end game, the G-20 could not prevail and the negotiations remained deadlocked without any definitive conclusion. Nevertheless, the formation of the G-20 and its role is extremely unique in the history of multilateral trade negotiations and eminently suitable for a detailed examination—the subject matter of this chapter.

The second section of this chapter provides a historical perspective of agriculture during the GATT days and discusses some technical details of the Agreement on Agriculture (AOA) negotiated during the Uruguay Round of multilateral trade negotiations under the GATT. Section 8.3 introduces the mandate for the Agriculture negotiations as contained in the Doha Ministerial Declaration and analyses the heterogeneity of interests of key groups of countries at the negotiating table. Section 8.4 goes into some depth and examines the submission made by the USA-EU combine in August 2003, the key event which triggered the creation of the G-20. Section 8.5 seeks to capture the special circumstances which led to the creation of the G-20 and how it earned its spurs with a landmark negotiating proposal on 20 August 2003. Section 8.6 discusses the key elements of this negotiating submission. Section 8.7 charts the rise to prominence of the coalition at the negotiating table. Section 8.8 analyses the overall role of the G-20 in the Agriculture negotiations, and identifies specific issues on which it had a decisive influence. Based on the discussions in the preceding sections, Section 8.9 identifies the specific strategies deployed by the G-20 which helped establish its influence in the bargaining exercise. Section 8.10 discusses the role of power and information in the success of the G-20, and derives important conclusions from this chapter.

8.2 Agriculture from GATT to WTO: A Blighted Harvest for Many Developing Countries

The manner in which the issue of agriculture has been addressed at the GATT/WTO, has remained a matter of considerable disappointment and frustration for many developing countries. Be it during the GATT era, or under the WTO regime, they have had to grapple with the protectionist approach of the developed countries towards this sector; but at the same time being compelled to remain on the back foot to protect farm livelihoods in their own countries against the attempts of the developed countries to pry open their markets. In this section we discuss how agriculture remained highly protected under the GATT, whose rules and special dispensations were tailored to accommodate the protectionist concerns of the developed countries.[4] When attempts were made to reform the rules on agriculture in the multilateral trading system, what emerged was an agreement—Agreement on Agriculture (AOA)—whose provisions were cleverly crafted to enable the developed countries to continue to distort global markets through subsidies, while putting fetters on developing countries to support their farmers. The asymmetries and imbalances in the AOA are analysed in the second part of this section. The unfairness in the AOA, from the perspective of a large number of developing countries, helps in explaining the reaction of Brazil and India when the USA-EU combine sought to rewire the rules of the AOA during the Doha Round.

8.2.1 Agriculture Remained Highly Protected During the GATT Era

In the GATT era, the disciplines on agriculture were softer compared to the disciplines on industrial products. The USA found it difficult to comply with even these soft disciplines. Within a decade of coming into existence of the GATT, it sought and subsequently obtained a waiver in 1955 in order to address the surplus of many farm products.[5] As a result of this waiver, the United States was free to impose quantitative restrictions on imports of agricultural products for almost 40 years, not otherwise permitted under provisions of Article XI:1 of GATT 1994.

With the USA showing the way, some other GATT members (technically called contracting parties) followed suit and succeeded in protecting their farm policies from legal challenges, either through waivers (Belgium and Luxembourg), or through special clauses in the terms of their accession to the GATT (Switzerland). Public policy instruments in most developed countries included price and supply management tools, quantitative restrictions and high tariffs on imports. For some agricultural products (e.g., rice in Japan) market access for imports was almost non-existent. The European Community (EC) extensively used a system of variable levies, whereby lower the price of the imported consignment of agriculture products, higher would be the import duty. This ensured that the price of the imported agriculture product was not lower than the price prevailing in the EC market. Consequently, for many decades the EC farmers were kept shielded from the competitive forces of the world market.[6]

Given the protectionist intent of the developed countries towards their agriculture sector, it is not surprising that merely feeble attempts were made to liberalize agriculture trade during the initial rounds of GATT negotiations. This gave the developed countries considerable leeway in using protectionist trade policy instruments to almost insulate their domestic agriculture markets from import competition. However, at the end of the Tokyo Round of multilateral trade negotiations in 1979, there was a sense of discomfort among many developed countries about their protectionist policies in agriculture and the need was felt to improve multilateral rules in this area. This provided the impetus for agriculture negotiations during the Uruguay Round. However, as discussed in the subsequent sub-section, the outcome of these negotiations skewed the rules against the interests of many developing countries.

8.2.2 Agreement on Agriculture: Supposedly Moving Towards a Fair and Market-Oriented Trading System

An important outcome of the Uruguay Round of Multilateral Trade Negotiations was the Agreement on Agriculture, which introduced disciplines under three pillars—Market Access, Domestic Support, and Export Competition. The mandate of the Uruguay Round provided a basis for initiating a process of reform of agriculture trade. While a handful of countries with interest in exporting agricultural products, commonly referred to as the Cairns Group, were active in the initial stage of the negotiations, the final agreement included many commitments based on the bilateral understanding between the EU and the USA, commonly referred to as the Blair House accord of November 1992.

The overall objective of the Agriculture negotiations during the Uruguay Round was to move towards a fair and market-oriented trading system in agriculture. While the provisions contained in the AOA marked an important step in this direction, the final agreement failed to rein in the billions of dollars of farm subsidies provided by the developed countries. In a candid admission, a former US Agriculture Secretary—Dan Glickman—stated that farming has become 'largely an income transfer program.'[7] While farmers in developing countries wait for the harvest from their farms, most farmers in the developed countries appear to gain more from the harvest of government cheques. In a graphic account of the overwhelming dependence of farmers in the USA on government subsidies, a commentator mentions the following: 'Good crops or bad, high yields or low, it hardly matters, the cheques roll in from the federal government. Upwards of half of the farmers who receive some form of federal assistance, would go out of business, if the government were to suddenly stop providing the financial handouts.'[8]

It has now been recognized that the AOA is riddled with asymmetries and imbalances that adversely affect the interests of most developing countries.[9] Most of the asymmetries have arisen from the structure of the obligations contained in the AOA. Generally speaking, the entitlements for maintaining high tariffs, ceilings on providing domestic support and export subsidies were determined on the basis of past levels during historical base periods, as specified in the AOA and its related documents.[10] Thus, countries that were providing huge domestic support and export subsidies in the past, acquired the right to continue to do so in future as well; while those countries that were more disciplined and provided no subsidies, or low levels of support in the base period, lost the right to provide high domestic support and export subsidies. Further, countries that were blocking imports through a plethora of non-tariff barriers acquired the right to use a policy instrument called Special Safeguards (SSG) to counter import surges and import price dips.[11] Those countries that were not resorting to non-tariff barriers were punished, as they were forbidden from using this policy instrument. The message emerging from the AOA cannot be missed—reward the protectionist countries, but punish those who had a more open trade regime for agriculture products.

Among the three pillars under the AOA, the Domestic Support pillar is the most skewed against the interests of many developing countries. The starkest imbalance under this pillar pertains to domestic support measures which were considered to distort trade or have an impact on production. These measures are popularly called Amber Box subsidies. Government schemes in which the amount of subsidy depends on current factors—prices of farm produce, quantity of production, area of land cultivated, etc.—fall in the Amber Box. For most developing countries, the rules of the AOA dictate that subsidies provided under schemes that are targeted to specific agricultural products cannot exceed 10 per cent of the value of production of the concerned product. Further, subsidies, which are not product specific, but available to all agricultural products, can be provided up to 10 per cent of total value of agriculture production. On the other hand, the developed countries and a few developing countries, such as Argentina and Brazil, benefit from a more generous dispensation on Amber Box subsidies. Each of these countries has a country-specific monetary entitlement—popularly called an AMS limit—which is the maximum amount of subsidy that can be provided under the Amber Box. AMS limit for the USA is $19.1 billion, while that for the EU is €67 billion.

How are the countries with an AMS limit at an advantage compared to developing countries with no AMS entitlement? The maximum amount of subsidy that a developing country with no AMS entitlement can target to each product cannot exceed 10 per cent of the value of production of the concerned product. On the other hand, countries with AMS entitlements can concentrate their product-specific subsidies on a handful of products. This has resulted in a very high level of subsidization as compared to the value of production of a product. Further, the developed countries have complete freedom to choose the products in which to concentrate their subsidies. Some of the products in which subsidies in the USA in some years exceeded 50% of the value of production include the following: Rice (82%); Canola (61%); Sugar (66%); Cotton (74%); Mohair (141%); and Wool (215%).[12] In the EU some of the products with subsidies exceeding 50% of the value of production include the following: Butter (71%); Skimmed Milk Powder (67%); Apples (68%); Cucumber (86%); Lemon (60%); Pear for Processing (82%); Tinned Pineapple (108%); Tomatoes for Processing (61%); Rice (66%); Olive Oil (76%); White Sugar (120%); and Tobacco (146%).[13]

After the AOA started getting implemented and its provisions were closely scrutinized, the asymmetries and imbalances in this agreement came to the fore.[14] The Doha Round provided an opportunity to set right some of the skewed rules of the AOA. What was the mandate for Agriculture negotiations in the Doha Round, and how did the negotiations proceed in the initial phase until August 2003?

8.3 Agriculture in the Doha Round: From Mandate to Pre-Cancun Phase

With the long-term objective of substantial progressive reductions in support and protection in agriculture, the AOA provided a built-in agenda for initiating further negotiations by 1999. Pursuant to this, even before the launch of the Doha Round, some of the WTO members made proposals for modifying the AOA. However, serious negotiations commenced after the launch of the Doha Round in November 2001. In this section, we briefly discuss the mandate for Agriculture negotiations in the Doha Round, how the interests of different countries were stacked, developments outside the negotiating table, initial skirmishes between the USA and the EU and subsequently their mutual accommodation.

8.3.1 Doha Mandate for Agriculture Negotiations

The Doha Ministerial Declaration provided the broad mandate for the aim, scope, and direction of negotiations on agriculture. These include the following: substantial improvements in market access; substantial reductions in trade-distorting domestic support; and reductions of, with a view to phasing out, all forms of export subsidies. The mandate also provided for special and differential treatment being an integral part of all elements of the negotiations, so as to be operationally effective and to enable developing countries to effectively take account of their development needs, including food security and rural development.[15] Thus, the mandate constituted a sound base for making demands on the major developed countries for commitments in the areas of domestic support and export subsidies. Further, the development needs of the developing countries, especially for food security and rural development, was formally recognized for negotiating new rules.

8.3.2 Agriculture Negotiations: Heterogeneity of Interests

How were the interests of various countries in agriculture aligned? During the Uruguay Round a group of countries with strong export interest formed an influential coalition, popularly referred to as the Cairns Group. The prominent and active countries of this group included Australia, Argentina, and Brazil. Most members of the Cairns Group, particularly these three prominent countries, had a vibrant domestic agriculture sector, characterized by large mechanized farms but few farmers. Despite their strengths, they were unable to export substantially either to the developed countries on account of subsidies provided by the latter group of countries; or to other larger developing countries, on account of their high import tariffs. In line with their perceived competitive advantage, the main negotiating objective of the Cairns Group was liberalization of agriculture trade through reduction of tariffs and subsidies. During the Uruguay Round, the US and the EC were at the focus of the negotiating efforts of the Cairns Group. This group continued to remain active during the initial years of the Doha Round. However, unlike the Uruguay Round, during the initial months of the Doha Round some members of the Cairns Group were not hesitant in demanding that the developing countries reduce their tariffs on agricultural products.

Some developed countries, such as the EU, Japan, Switzerland and Norway, had mainly defensive interest in agriculture, on account of high domestic support, high tariffs, or use of export subsidies. Although the USA was the largest subsidizer in agriculture, its interests were a bit different from these four WTO Members. It sought reduction in domestic support by the EU and had an aggressive interest in promoting exports of its agri-business by pushing for reduction in tariffs in both developed and developing countries. It was also a proponent of eliminating export subsidies. Notwithstanding the minor differences in the negotiating interests of the USA and these four developed country members of the WTO, the fact remains that without direct government intervention, agriculture may not be economically sustainable in these countries.

Finally, in many developing countries a large share of their population depended on agriculture for its survival. Unlike the USA and the EU, where agriculture is mainly commercial, in many developing countries such as Ghana, India, Indonesia, Nigeria, Philippines, Tanzania, and

Turkey, farming is mainly for sustenance and a matter of survival. Most of what is harvested is used by the farmers in these countries for their own consumption. Extremely small farm size, non-mechanized farming, and intensive agricultural practices are the main features of this sector in these countries. Their main interest in Agriculture negotiations was to protect their teeming millions of farmers from the risk of low-priced and subsidized imports from the developed countries. At the negotiating table they were interested in seeking cuts in farm support provided by the developed countries, and sought to retain their right to impose high tariffs on agriculture imports. After its accession to the WTO, China's interests appeared to be similar to those of this group of developing countries. However, during the initial years of the negotiations, it was mostly silent at the negotiating table. Thus, it was difficult to guess what position it would advocate in the negotiations. Interests of some of the smaller developing countries, particularly in the group of African, Caribbean, and Pacific countries, were quite similar to those of India, Indonesia, and Philippines.

It is relevant to mention that despite the insignificant share of agriculture in GDP and employment in the USA and the EU, this sector continues to be treated by them as being special and sensitive. While the USA and the EU aggressively seek to protect their agriculture on the ground of it being politically sensitive, these countries are not prepared to treat agriculture in many developing countries also to be sensitive. Although the USA-EU combine is lukewarm in applying the principles and practices of free trade to their agriculture sector, they expect the developing countries to adhere to these principles.[16]

8.3.3 Developments Outside the Negotiating Table

Certain developments outside the negotiating table raised serious doubts about the commitment of the USA and the EU to cut farm support. Within six months of launch of the Doha Round, in May 2002 the president of the United States approved the new American Farm Act (Farm Security and Rural Investment Act of 2002), which substantially increased domestic subsidies for agricultural products, notably for cotton, wheat, corn, soy beans, rice, and sorghum. An expert commented ironically: 'at the WTO

Ministerial in Doha, Qatar, in November 2001, the United States reconfirmed its anti-subsidy position. But, only six months later, it gave a generous 80% increase in support for its farm sector, in an act that would make even the Europeans blush.'[17] In June 2003, when the EU reformed its Common Agricultural Policy (CAP), it appears to have ignored the Doha Mandate. The reformed CAP maintained export subsidies at a high level. EU's lack of ambition to modify the CAP to fit the 'development agenda of Doha' was one of the most notable and commented upon characteristics.[18]

8.3.4 Agriculture Negotiations: Initial Skirmishes Between USA and EU

The initial days of agriculture negotiations saw sharp exchanges between the USA and the EU. On tariffs, the USA sought the adoption of a formula that would harmonize tariffs at low levels in different countries—higher the existing tariff on a product, higher would be the reduction; if the existing tariffs were low, they would face lower cuts. Its approach to reduction in domestic support was also along similar lines. Higher the domestic support, higher the reduction. As the EU had the highest entitlement for granting Amber Box support, it would have taken a big hit. On market access, the EU had sensitivities in reducing tariffs in about 50–60 products. Thus, it advocated a linear cut approach—on each product the tariff being reduced by a fixed percentage. On export subsidies, the USA sought their elimination. As the largest provider of these subsidies, the EU would have had to make a large sacrifice.

Despite negotiating for more than one year, the divergence in the positions of the USA and the EU prevented any meaningful forward movement. In an attempt at imparting momentum to the negotiations, Stuart Harbinson, the Chairman of the Special Session of Committee on Agriculture, the body where Agriculture negotiations were being held, presented to the Members draft modalities paper dated 17 February 2003. However, it failed to provide a middle ground between the USA and the EU. This posed a threat to the success of the next Ministerial Conference of the WTO, which was scheduled to be held in Cancun, Mexico, in September 2003.

8.4 US-EU Joint Proposal on Agriculture: Mutual Accommodation but Marginalising Interests of Others

The fault lines between the two developed members persisted in the mini-ministerial conferences organized at Sharm El- Sheikh in June 2003 and Montreal in July 2003. The main reason for the stalemate in Agriculture negotiations was the inability of the EU to reach a consensus among its member states on reforming its CAP. At the end of the Sharm El-Sheikh meeting, the US Trade Representative Robert Zoellick said that, 'while we've been discussing ways to move the negotiations forward, it's become clear that whether we move ahead or get stuck very much depends on the European Union'.[19] During the subsequent mini ministerial meeting held at Montreal during 28–30 July 2003, many countries urged the USA and the EU to find a compromise, in order to enable the Agriculture negotiations to move ahead. In these meetings it also became increasingly clear that Australia, as the main player in the Cairns Group, was not inclined to take a tough stand against the combined interests of the USA and the EU.[20] This diminished the role of the Cairns Group as an effective counter-point to the developed countries in these negotiations. In a bid to reconcile their differences the USA and EU came out with a joint paper,[21] which accommodated their mutual interests, but ignored the concerns of a large number of developing countries. It is relevant to discuss the technical details of this submission, and its implications, in respect of the three pillars of Agriculture negotiations.

Some of the key elements in the Domestic Support pillar as contained in the joint proposal were the following: reduce the most trade-distorting domestic support measures; expand the Blue Box[22] by adding some new criteria; and reduce de minimis[23] for developed and developing countries. Four aspects of the proposal on domestic support did not go unnoticed by the developing countries. First, by focusing on the most trade-distorting domestic support, the joint proposal did not seek a comprehensive reform of farm support of the developed countries; second, expanding the Blue Box, used mainly by the developed countries, would go against the basic mandate of 'substantial reduction in trade-distorting domestic support' and provide additional flexibility to the USA to accommodate its counter-cyclical subsidy payments[24]; third, as the reduction in de minimis was envisaged for all WTO Members, it would further constrict the policy options of many developing countries to support their farmers, which was already fairly constraining under the existing rules; and fourth, by remaining silent on the Green Box,[25] the joint proposal excluded the tens of billions of dollars of domestic support provided by the developed countries under this predominant category from any new disciplines. The proposal, particularly in respect of the Blue Box, would have enhanced the flexibility of the USA to provide subsidies to its farmers.

The USA-EU joint submission came at a time when the high farm subsidies in the developed countries were getting exposed at different forums in innovative ways. To illustrate, UNDP's Human Development Report (2003) mentioned that 'OECD per capita subsidies for cows and cotton bolls are considerably higher than OECD per capita aid for Sub-Saharan Africa'.[26] The report drove the point home forcefully by providing some telling statistics. According to the report, in the year 2000 the EU provided an annual subsidy of $913 per cow; but the EU's annual aid to Sub-Saharan Africa was a measly amount of $8 per African person. The corresponding figures for Japan were even less flattering. It provided $2700 annual subsidy for each cow and a paltry amount of annual aid of $1.47 per African person. The subsidy of $10.7 million per day provided by the USA to its cotton farmers, and $3.1 million per day as US aid to Sub-Saharan Africa, was no less shocking. The report also noted that the OECD agriculture subsidies amounting to $311 billion in 2001, not only dwarfed their $52 billion aid to all countries, but also exceeded the combined GDP of Sub-Saharan Africa at $301 billion.[27]

In the Market Access pillar, the Doha Declaration mandated 'substantial improvement in market access'. However, what the USA-EU joint paper proposed would have allowed the EU to get away without any substantial reduction in the 50–60 products which had high tariffs. On the other hand, developing countries, which had high tariffs on 100 or more products, would have been required to make very steep cuts. At the core of the differential impact of the same set of tariff cuts lay the difference in tariff structures between the developed members, particularly the EU, and a large number of developing countries. Overall, the proposals under the Market Access pillar were tailored to help the EU to keep its markets closed for its sensitive products, but would have prised open the agriculture markets in developing countries.

With regard to export subsidies, the ambition in the USA-EU joint paper was more limited than even the Doha mandate. It sought elimination of export subsidies on a limited number of products, while allowing Members to continue with these subsidies on other products. This would have provided considerable elbow room to the EU—the most prominent user of this policy instrument—to continue with its export subsidies.

With insufficient political traction in the Cairns Group to resolutely respond with a counter-proposal to effectively address subsidies and protection in accordance with the Doha Mandate on Agriculture and fulfil its development dimension,[28] the two heavyweight members might have expected an easy pass for their joint submission. However, as discussed in the next section, they were in for a rude surprise.

8.5 Responding to a Crisis Situation: The G-20 Is Created and Emerges on the Negotiating Stage

When the USA-EU joint proposal was discussed by the WTO Members on 14 August 2003, it became the subject of intense criticism. Some countries, particularly those with export interest in this sector, viewed the joint proposal as an attempt to lower the ambition of the negotiation by pandering to the sensitivities of the domestic agriculture lobbies in the EU and the USA. Other developing countries perceived it as an ambitious attempt at opening their agriculture markets.[29] As Brazil's Foreign Relations Minister, Celso Amorim was to comment later, 'the deal between Brussels and Washington constitutes a step backwards, which, if accepted by the rest of the countries would result in an unjustifiable sacrifice of the objectives of the Round, including its fundamental theme'.[30] Another view was that the USA and EU 'were not making any new concessions to the developing countries, but were presenting a decidedly anti-development posture'.[31] However, the predominant sentiment among a large number of developing country negotiators in Geneva was that the history of the USA and the EU writing many of the provisions of the Agreement on Agriculture during the Uruguay Round was being repeated with the developing countries being rendered anxious bystanders.

While making a presentation on the joint proposal, Mogens Peter Carl of the EU and Allen Johnson of the USA repeatedly mentioned that the proposals were not final decisions, and could be further negotiated with other members. However, this failed to carry conviction among most developing countries. The perception that the USA and the EU wanted the outcome of their mutual accommodation to be treated as a fait accompli in the negotiations got further reinforced during the small group Green Room meeting held on 15 August 2003. During the meeting it hit Brazil and India that the USA-EU proposal was on the verge of becoming the basis of future negotiations. Argentina, too, was in no mood to let the USA-EU escape from making meaningful cuts to their farm subsidies, since the only negotiating venue to eliminate all forms of export subsidies and substantially reduce domestic support is the WTO, as regional trade agreements cannot address subsidies. If this opportunity was lost at the WTO, heavy subsidization in agriculture would remain for decades until a next Round.[32]

The first section of this chapter has described how the ambassadors of Brazil and India decided to join hands and instructed their trusted diplomats with expertise in agriculture issues to prepare a counter-proposal. Let us take forward the story from there.[33]

After a hurried lunch, Aggarwal and Damico set to work. They spent an hour studying the USA-EU proposal again and deciding their strategy. They came to two conclusions. First, instead of trying to reconcile their mutual differences and balancing their competing interests, the duo decided to adopt an inclusive approach based on their common interests. Second, in order to highlight how their proposal would be different from the USA-EU joint paper, Aggarwal and Damico decided to adopt the overall structure and language of this joint submission. Within this overall framework, in order to provide a counter-narrative, they would attempt to tweak the technical details contained in the USA-EU joint paper. This approach would help countries quickly grasp the difference in technical details between the two proposals. By dinner time, the first draft of the counter-proposal was ready and conveyed to their respective ambassadors.[34]

Early next morning, on 16 August, Ambassadors Seixas Correa and Chandrasekhar discussed the draft counter-proposal with Ambassador

Alfredo Chiaradia of Argentina and Gabriel Taboada (delegate for Agriculture of the Permanent Mission of Argentina to the WTO). Argentina was broadly in agreement with the draft.[35] The three ambassadors in the field took the political risk on their shoulders and became the founders of what would subsequently be known as the G-20 coalition. The strong support provided by their respective technical teams was an important factor in the success of this initiative.

Further, Brazil and India took another important step. After a brief confabulation, the ambassadors of these two countries decided to approach China for its support.[36] In the afternoon they met Ambassador Sun Zhenyu of China, who made one suggestion about addressing particular concerns of recently acceded Members and immediately gave his personal approval.[37] He transmitted the proposal to his capital. With the support of four developing countries behind the counter-proposal, these countries moved with confidence in canvassing support from other developing countries. In parallel, they sought clearance from their capitals for the joint proposal. By the time the counter-proposal was formally submitted to the WTO, sixteen countries—Argentina, Brazil, Bolivia, China, Chile, Colombia, Costa Rica, Ecuador, Guatemala, India, Mexico, Paraguay, Peru, Philippines, South Africa, and Thailand—had signed on to it. The coalition labelled itself as the G-20, as the counter-proposal was submitted to the WTO on 20 August 2003.[38] It changed the negotiating dynamics overnight. What were the main elements of the G-20 proposal?

8.6 Key Elements of the G-20 Submission

While the G-20 submission retained the overall structure of the USA-EU joint paper, it contained important technical details that were substantially different from the latter. The key elements contained in the G-20 submission in respect of the three pillars are discussed below.

In the Domestic Support pillar, unlike the USA-EU joint proposal, which was at best a modest attempt at reducing domestic support of the developed countries, the G-20 sought a more comprehensive and ambitious reform of farm support of the developed countries. In pursuance of this objective, the G-20 proposed reduction in all forms of trade-distorting domestic support measures. This was to be done separately for each category of trade-distorting domestic support, as well as for the cumulative amount provided under all the categories taken together. An additional dimension was that the G-20 proposal required reduction in domestic support on a product-specific basis. This was aimed at restricting the flexibility available mainly to the developed countries to concentrate domestic support in a few products, while staying within their overall AMS limit.

Apart from the proposals on the Amber Box, the G-20 also made specific suggestions on other categories of domestic support. It sought the elimination of the Blue Box, a category of subsidy that was supposed to be production-limiting, but had become a loophole for providing almost unlimited subsidy to farmers in the EU. Direct payments under the Green Box had become yet another mechanism for the developed countries to provide subsidies to their farmers without any monetary ceiling. The G-20 suggested capping/reducing these liberal handouts provided by the developed countries. Finally, the G-20 proposed cutting the de minimis support provided by the developed countries. In pursuance of the development objective of the Doha Round, the G-20 proposed expanding the flexibility for developing countries to provide support to their farmers.

In the Market Access pillar, the G-20 proposal would have prevented the EU from protecting some of its products behind tariff walls, thereby providing access into its market for imports of these products. Further, the G-20 proposed discontinuing the Agricultural Special Safeguards[39] for the developed countries. For developing countries, the G-20 proposal sought lower tariff reductions, longer implementation periods, and establishment of the so-called Special Products (SP), which would take cuts lower than what may otherwise be required under an agreed formula. An important suggestion of the G-20 was establishing a Special Safeguard Mechanism (SSM) for developing countries.

The G-20 proposals on export competition were more stringent than the USA-EU joint paper. The G-20 sought complete elimination of export subsidies on all products. The G-20 also sought extension of the special and differential treatment provision that would allow developing countries to continue to grant export subsidies for reimbursing costs of marketing and transportation for export shipments.

What was the political significance of the G-20 submission and what was the response to it, particularly from the developed countries?

8.7 Establishment of G-20 Becomes a Watershed, Acquires Legitimacy, and Changes the Narrative in Agriculture Negotiations

The G-20 was an attempt by many developing countries to have a greater say in the negotiations. They were no longer prepared to remain mute props, while letting the main dramatis personae—the USA and the EU—script the final agreement. It was also an attempt at changing the focus of the negotiations. In contrast to most previous attempts by the developing countries to articulate a common position, in which they essentially had a defensive position, through the G-20 developing nations were able to 'advance a constructive agenda based on forward-looking proposals'.[40] In the words of Brazilian Foreign Minister, Amorim, the G-20 countries had 'rebelled against a proposed agreement that would not address the main issues concerning agriculture reform and its impact on international trade'.[41]

However, the G-20 was viewed by some countries as sheer obstruction or dangerous deviation from the pre-established path.[42] In particular, Peter Carl, the EU negotiator, attacked the G-20 submission at a Heads of Delegation meeting convened on 20–21 August 2003 at the WTO. Resorting to angry and unusually non-diplomatic tones, Carl accused the sponsors of being 'needlessly confrontational' and introducing a North-South confrontation into the WTO.[43] He chided the proponents for aiming at the stars in the hope of getting to the moon.[44] This immediately elicited a quick-witted repartee from Brazil's Ambassador, Felipe de Seixas Correa, who said that 'it was not the moon that the co-sponsors wanted, but down-to-earth markets in Europe and elsewhere for their products through reforms to the unfair agricultural system'.[45]

While the initial anger and frustration of the EU and USA at the G-20 proposal was hidden from no one, they started working stealthily behind the scenes to split the nascent coalition. Within a few days of the G-20 proposal, the EU invited India's key diplomats for a lavish luncheon meeting at a plush venue in Geneva. At this meeting, fine dining was merely incidental. The main item on the menu was to inveigle India to abandon the coalition. The EU's bait was that it would protect India's defensive interest within the USA-EU framework by the use of suitable numbers in the tariff reduction formula. The EU also darkly hinted that

India would be a loser in the coalition, given its conflicting interests with Brazil. While the Indian diplomats relished the meal, they refused to bite the negotiating bait.[46] Perhaps they no longer had any faith in the EU's promises. Even after the Cancun Ministerial Conference, Geneva-based EU diplomats persisted in their efforts at persuading India to abandon the G-20. Again, they met with little success.[47]

While the EU was attempting to wean away India from the G-20, the USA was also active in the shadows. It tried to persuade the G-20 members having interest in exporting agriculture products that they would gain more by working closely with other members of the Cairns Group than with the G-20. It is the perspective of some negotiators of G-20 and academics that under sustained pressure from the USA, a few countries quit the G-20.[48] This perspective is not without substance. It is perhaps too much of a coincidence that some of the countries which left the G-20 were also the countries with whom the USA subsequently signed free trade agreements.

Despite the initial scepticism of some Members, particularly the prominent developed countries, the G-20 could not be ignored at the negotiating table. Its primary source of legitimacy arose from the fact that it represented more than 60 per cent of the world population. It was some of the concepts contained in the coalition's counter-paper of 20 August 2003 and its subsequent technical proposals, and not the proposals contained in the USA-EU joint paper, that became the basis of further negotiations during 2003–2008. This proved to be a watershed in Agriculture negotiations at the WTO. But the influence which G-20 acquired in the negotiations did not come about automatically, or even overnight. It was the outcome of an incremental process, guided mainly by the founding countries, particularly Celso Amorim of Brazil and Arun Jaitley of India. Apart from the initial efforts leading to the creation of this coalition in Geneva in August 2003, other important landmarks include the following meetings: WTO Ministerial Conference at Cancun in September 2003; and a series of meetings of the G-20 in Brasilia (December 2003), New Delhi (March 2005), Dalian (July 2005), and Bhurban (September 2005).

During the Cancun Ministerial Conference of the WTO held in September 2003, the G-20 sought a meeting with Robert Zoellick, the US Trade Representative. After considerable hesitation, perhaps stemming from a deep resistance to grant the coalition a formal recognition,

Zoellick reluctantly agreed to meet the G-20 on 10 September 2003. According to an Indian negotiator, Zoellick's body language was extremely tense throughout the interaction. Having heard the demands of Amorim and Jaitley with increasing annoyance, Zoellick responded in an irritated tone. He is reported to have said the following: 'Yes, by giving very high domestic support, the US is a sinner. But what is the G-20 willing to pay, so that the US can atone for its sins?' Zoellick, being a shrewd negotiator, was preparing the ground for extracting the maximum value for the concessions that the USA would have to make in cutting farm support. Hearing Zoellick's remarks, Jaitley supposedly said in a hushed tone, audible only to some listeners near him, 'This is like a child who first kills his parents and thereafter seeks mercy on the plea that he is an orphan.' Although Zoellick left the meeting in a sour mood, the G-20 had achieved its primary objective of being taken seriously as a negotiating group.[49]

The political credibility of G-20 as a negotiating block acquired further heft in a meeting at Brasilia hosted by Brazil on 11–12 December 2003. This meeting was organized at a time when there was some uncertainty regarding the survival of G-20. As part of bilateral side deals with the USA, by October 2003 some countries, such as Colombia, Costa Rica, Ecuador, El Salvador, Guatemala and Peru, had abandoned the G-20. These developments may have compelled some observers to wonder whether the enthusiastic welcome accorded to the G-20 was already wearing off, barely two months after its establishment. With the very existence of the coalition at stake, the foremost objective of the Brasilia meeting was to reaffirm the unity of the group.[50] Further, at this meeting, the G-20 'engaged in a constructive dialogue' with the WTO Director General Supachai Panitchpakdi on 'how to move forward the negotiations in the light of the discussions in Geneva.' The G-20 also had 'a positive and open dialogue with Trade Commissioner Pascal Lamy, of the EU, on the respective positions on agriculture with a view to consider new possible approaches to make progress in the negotiations.'[51] The presence of Supachai and Lamy in this meeting clearly signalled that this conglomeration of developing countries had become a potent force to be reckoned with at the negotiating table.

Getting a formal recognition as a negotiating block was not sufficient for the G-20 to be taken as a serious player at the negotiating table. What enhanced the G-20's credibility was its ability to counter the developed countries with its own technically sound negotiating proposals, with progressively increasing details. Kamal Nath, India's Commerce Minister, provided another important reason for the credibility of the coalition. Addressing the media in Geneva in October 2005, he highlighted that the composition of the G-20 was not of a common interest, but one of diverse interests. These diverse interests had come together with the unity of purpose which gave it credibility.[52] Further, the G-20 succeeded in being viewed as an inclusive platform, as it championed issues of particular interest to many developing countries even if they were outside its fold. To illustrate, the G-20 was at the forefront of seeking expeditious reduction in subsidies granted to cotton, an issue of immense economic significance for many African countries. G-20 was also supportive of food security concerns of India, Indonesia, and Philippines. Having seen how the G-20 was created and how it garnered credibility and influence, it is relevant to understand how exactly this changed the narrative in Agriculture negotiations.

8.8 Influence of the G-20 in the Agriculture Negotiations

The approach of USA-EU on the one hand, and the G-20 on the other hand, represented contrasting visions on how the Agriculture negotiations should proceed. Where would the balance in the negotiations eventually tilt? On this question would hinge the overall fate of the Doha Round. The USA-EU joint paper sought to protect and promote their interests by proposing insignificant reduction in their farm subsidies and offering limited additional market access. On the other hand, this proposal was extremely ambitious in seeking to pry open the agriculture markets in developing countries. In contrast, the G-20 approach was at the other end of the spectrum—seeking steep cuts in farm subsidies of the developed countries, seeking meaningful market access for exports in the developed countries, but protecting the livelihood and food security of farmers in many developing countries.

In light of the divergent perspectives of the USA-EU combine and the G-20, it is relevant to examine whether the G-20 was effective in influencing the trajectory of the negotiations on agriculture. If we examine the last substantive version of the draft modalities text prepared by the chairman of the Committee on Agriculture (Special Session)[53] (commonly referred to as the December 2008 Modalities Text or Rev.4 Text) and compare its contents with the submissions of G-20, it would be amply clear that the coalition significantly influenced the course of negotiations on most of the crucial issues. No wonder that Tim Groser, New Zealand's Ambassador to the WTO, remarked that the G-20 was 'a masterpiece of economic diplomacy'.[54]

In the Domestic Support pillar, G-20 was at the forefront of demanding reduction in the total trade-distorting support, as well as in its components—AMS and de minimis support. This was reflected in the December 2008 Modalities Text which provided for reduction of the so-called Overall Trade Distorting Support (OTDS)[55] as well as its three components—AMS[56], de minimis,[57] and Blue Box support.[58] If the provisions of this modalities text had been implemented, the developed countries would have had to make significant cuts in their ceiling to provide trade-distorting agriculture subsidies.[59] While these reductions would have been undertaken for all agricultural products taken together, the G-20 also succeeded in garnering consensus on imposing monetary ceilings on AMS[60] and Blue Box support[61] which could be provided to each product.

The efforts of the G-20 were aimed not only at seeking reductions in farm support provided by the developed countries, but also negotiating hard for the right of the developing countries to retain existing flexibilities, and also acquire additional rights, to support their farmers. The December 2008 Modalities Text exempted most of the developing countries from any reduction in de minimis support. Furthermore, in respect of the contentious issue of public stockholding for food security purposes, it was the proposal of the G-20 which found acceptance among the entire WTO membership.[62]

In the Market Access pillar, the G-20 was extremely influential in creating consensus on the formula for cutting bound tariffs on agricultural products. In this journey, an important contribution of the G-20 was to clearly demonstrate how the Blended Formula proposed by the USA-EU[63] was a fundamentally flawed approach to agricultural market access. In a short, but piercing submission, the G-20 clearly showed how the Blended Formula would 'fail to deliver substantial improvements in market access', especially for products protected by tariff peaks.[64] It also demonstrated how this formula would create 'inequitable results' on the different tariff structures of the developed and developing countries.

In the game of thrust and parry at the negotiating table, the blow dealt by the G-20 to the Blended Formula proved to be decisive and this approach to tariff cuts became a mere footnote in the history of the Doha Round. Henceforth, it would be the tiered formula for tariff reduction, championed by the G-20, that would occupy centre stage in the negotiations.[65] Further, as advocated by the G-20, the total average tariff cut by the developed countries was required to be above a minimum specified threshold. As stated in the December 2008 Modalities Text, the developed countries would have been required to undertake an average tariff cut of at least 54 percent.[66] Further, in line with the initial submission of the G-20, the Modalities Text specified that the bound rate for developed countries on an agriculture product would be capped at 100 per cent[67]. However, the developed countries succeeded in securing certain exceptions to this provision. On the defensive front, partly in deference to defensive concerns of India, Indonesia, and a few other developing countries, the G-20 pushed for exclusion of certain percentage of products from tariff reduction by the developing countries. This, too, found a specific mention in the December 2008 Modalities Text.[68]

In respect of the Export Competition pillar, the G-20 succeeded in its endeavour at seeking elimination of export subsidies.[69] This was an outcome of persistent efforts by Brazil and India in cornering the EU—the main provider of export subsidies. It is relevant to mention that eventually at the Nairobi Ministerial Conference of the WTO held in 2015, the entire WTO membership agreed to the elimination of export subsidies. However, by that time the G-20 had receded into dormancy. G-20 also succeeded in protecting the flexibility available to developing countries to continue to provide export subsidies for reimbursing costs related to marketing and transportation of their exports for five years after the elimination of export subsidies.[70]

As an overall assessment, it would be accurate to mention that the G-20 emerged as an influential voice at the negotiating table. It wrested the initiative from the developed countries and prevented the USA-EU combine from writing the new rules of agriculture trade in the mould of their mutual interest. While the G-20 changed the course of the Agriculture negotiations during the Doha Round, it is a reality that it lacked the political heft to decisively conclude the negotiations. After having pushed the USA-EU combine into a corner, the G-20 was unable to deliver the final knockout punch. After failing to strike a deal in July 2008, the developed countries lost interest in pushing the Doha Round to a successful conclusion and refused to engage constructively. With the wind having been taken out of the sails of the Doha Round, the raison d'être for G-20 no longer existed after 2008.

8.9 Strategies Used by G-20

The role and influence of G-20 in multilateral trade negotiations is complex and unique from several perspectives. No doubt coalitions of developing countries had been influential on certain occasions in the past, particularly in the area of textiles and intellectual property rights during the Uruguay Round of the GATT. The G-20 phenomenon was something different and it stands out in sharp contrast to the previous experience and the marginal influence of developing country coalitions in multilateral trade negotiations at the GATT/WTO.

Never before in the history of the multilateral trading system had a group of developing countries succeeded in limiting, if not checkmating, the interests of the USA and the EU for five long years. Unlike some of the coalitions in the past, the G-20 was influential in the core area of the negotiations, around which hinged the overall progress of the multilateral negotiations. The coalition proved to be long-lasting, with the core members remaining committed to its basic objective of seeking reduction in farm subsidies of the developed countries. They could see through the divisive tactics of the developed countries and most of them did not fall in the trap of making side deals bilaterally with either the USA or the EU. In contrast, in the past the coalition of developing countries quickly withered away as soon as the constituent countries came under political and economic pressure applied by some of the developed countries.

In a significant departure from some of the earlier coalitions of developing countries, G-20 was not merely an initiative to criticize the proposals of USA-EU. It became a vehicle for providing practical alternatives for solving some of the knotty problems at the negotiating table. Its submissions went beyond the rhetoric of development and were recognized for their complex and technical details. It is also relevant to note that while some of the developing country coalitions of the past comprised countries with considerable convergence of interest on the core issues around which the coalition was built, yet again the G-20 was different. Although the core issue of seeking reductions in agriculture support provided by the developed countries was the unifying element within the G-20, the coalition also had to tread a fine line between market-seeking ambitions of Argentina and Brazil on the one hand, and defensive interests of India and Indonesia on the other. This would have made the task of managing the G-20 coalition challenging for its leaders. Despite this challenge, many consider G-20 to be the catalyst for power shifts during the Doha Round.[71] In short, the G-20 represents the collective ability of a handful of countries to contribute substantially and meaningfully to the key issues at the negotiating table. Given the unique characteristics of the G-20 coalition and its achievements, the strategies deployed by the group merit a detailed discussion.

8.9.1 Planning and Preparing

Planning and preparing is an exercise that a party is expected to be deeply involved in, throughout the course of negotiations. The first and foremost priority for the G-20 was to plan and prepare for creating an effective coalition and sustaining it, an objective in which Brazil and India invested considerable resources. Strategies underlying this objective have been discussed earlier. In addition, as part of planning and preparing, the G-20 had to set up mechanisms for equipping the coalition with technical knowledge and analysis. Further, given the fact that on some issues related to Agriculture negotiations Brazil and India were at the opposite ends of the spectrum, both the countries had to manage their domestic constituencies to support the coalition. While both these aspects are examined below, it is relevant to note that planning and preparation was also facilitated by regular meetings of a core group of ambassadors in Geneva.

8.9.1.1 Equipping Negotiators with Technical Knowledge and Analysis

During the Doha Round, Agriculture negotiations involved a plethora of issues which were complex from multiple perspectives. First, in order to engage effectively at the negotiating table, the constituent countries needed to understand the legal implications of the existing provisions of the AOA, as well as of the proposals on the negotiating table. As many of the concepts and provisions in this agreement were rooted in the historical context of the Uruguay Round, a plain reading of them would have confounded even a seasoned trade negotiator. Second, the coalition also needed to gain an understanding of how the negotiating proposals would get translated into reduction of tariffs and subsidies, and the likely obligations which would arise for different WTO members. Third, it was essential for the coalition to have systematic information on the tariff structures of different countries, amounts of subsidies in different categories under the agreement and existing agriculture subsidy schemes being implemented by the developed countries. Fourth, it was in the interest of the coalition to have an in-depth understanding of how the existing rules of the AOA are biased in favour of the developed countries and thereafter make an assessment of whether the proposals of developed countries would further skew the rules against the developing countries. What mechanisms were in place for grappling with these challenges and responding with technically sound and mandate-oriented proposals?

The G-20 appears to have been twice-blessed in confronting the daunting challenges posed by the technical complexities in Agriculture negotiations. First, some of the negotiators of Brazil and India were old hands with many years of experience in handling WTO matters. To illustrate, on matters of comprehending political sensitivities of different countries, as well as having a deep understanding of the technical details of the complicated issues at the negotiating table, few ministers could match Celso Amorim, the Brazilian minister. Further, the Brazilian Ambassador to the WTO, Luiz Felipe de Seixas Correa was acknowledged for his strategic acumen as well as technical expertise. Complementing Felipe from Brasilia was Clodoaldo Hugueney, Itamarty's Undersecretary for Economic Affairs, who was known for his mastery of both the big picture and minute details of various issues in the Agriculture negotiations. Clodoaldo, whose passions included listening to Indian classical music, had the ability to impress his audience with carefully crafted words laced with numbers, legal arguments, and humour.

On the Indian side, the two Commerce Ministers during the crucial years of 2003–2008 were effective in their own way. Arun Jaitley, who played a pivotal role in the creation of the G-20, was a renowned lawyer who needed just one briefing from his officials in order to grasp the technical details of WTO issues. It should come as no surprise that at the Cancun Ministerial Conference, Jaitley's brilliance was evident in how he got the better of Lamy and Zoellick in interpreting the mandate on agriculture export subsidies. This was a result of detailed preparation over many briefings in New Delhi and at Cancun. His stewardship of the negotiating team made life less difficult for his officials. He was always happy to give the credit to Dipak Chatterjee, India's Commerce Secretary, and K.M. Chandrasekhar, India's ambassador to the WTO, for keeping the G-20 together at Cancun Ministerial Conference.

Kamal Nath, Jaitley's successor, had the uncanny ability of extricating himself, even if pushed into a corner by the USA and the EU. He made his mark through pithy statements at the negotiating table, which encapsulated the key demands and concerns of India and the G-20. In his endeavour to get the USA to agree to deep cuts in trade-distorting subsidies, he would often rile Zoellick with the following request: 'Bob, give me a dollar, just one dollar, of your subsidy.'[72] Implicit in this simple statement was that the USA should agree to a ceiling which would require it to cut slack and effectively reduce its subsidies, instead of negotiating a ceiling which would provide enough headroom to the USA to actually enhance the subsidies granted to its agriculture from the prevailing levels. On another occasion, he is reported to have quipped: 'Bob, next time when we meet, please bring a picture of a US farmer. I have only seen US agribusiness, but never a US farmer.'[73] Again, the simple statement hid a sharp punch, as most of the subsidies in the USA were provided to agribusiness. In addition to Jaitley, Nath, and Chandrasekhar, mention must be made of two outstanding Indian negotiators for their contribution to the G-20—Rajesh Aggarwal and Vandana Aggarwal. Their mastery of the technical details relating to the AOA and the Agriculture negotiations, as well as a good sense of what was achievable at the negotiating table, was an asset not only for India but also for the G-20 coalition.

While a team of brilliant negotiators is an advantage, there can be no substitute for institutions for providing backend analysis and support for the negotiator. In India, even prior to the formation of G-20, the Department of Commerce had already tied up with some academic institutions and think-tanks for undertaking research to support the government in Agriculture negotiations. Subsequently, this group was expanded. In this regard, the following three institutions stood out for their technical analysis and incisive examination of the negotiating issues in respect of agriculture: Indian Institute of Foreign Trade, National Council for Applied Economic Research, and the UNCTAD India Programme. In Brazil, the Institudo de Estudos do Comercio e Negociacoes Internacionais played an important role in providing relevant research for the negotiators. These institutions supported the planning efforts of the coalition. Overall, the presence of a core group of knowledgeable and experienced negotiators, in conjunction with investment in technical work by reputed institutions, provided the G-20 with the power of expertise as well as the power of persuasive capacity within the coalition as well as at the negotiating table.

8.9.1.2 Managing Domestic Constituencies

Another key component of planning for negotiations relates to managing the internal dynamics among stakeholders with different and at times even divergent interests. G-20 provides a good illustration of Putnam's metaphor of international negotiations being a two-level game requiring parallel domestic negotiations among different stakeholders within a country. This was particularly evident in Brazil and India. Traditionally, Brazil's approach to multilateral trade negotiations was guided by the export interests of its agri-business. This was reflected in the country's active participation in the Cairns Group. Pushed by its agri-business, Brazil had positioned itself as an important player in seeking substantive reform of the AOA. Given its strong export interest, how did the Brazilian government manage its domestic constituency and align itself with India—a country with substantial defensive interest in agriculture? What was the internal dynamics within Brazil, which enabled Amorim to observe the following: 'Between Cairns and India, we will stick with India'?[74] In short, how did the Brazilian government convince its agri-business about changing its position from aggressively seeking access for its exports and instead bringing it closer to India?

A number of developments facilitated the resolution of sharp internal differences among the stakeholders in Brazil.[75] First, as mentioned earlier, despite the strong nudge from Brazil, the Cairns Group, particularly Australia, appeared to be unwilling to take a strong line against the agriculture subsidies of the USA-EU combine. Thus, it appeared unlikely that Brazil's ambitions for its agri-exports would be fulfilled by hanging on to the coat-tails of the Cairns Group. Second, the USA-EU joint proposal of 13 August 2003 made it abundantly clear that Brazil would need to change its export-centric approach, if it were to strive for substantive reforms in the AOA. There was also a risk that the joint proposal could render Brazil irrelevant within the Cairns Group. Third, an internal study by the Brazilian government concluded that the country's export interest would not be affected, even if India's proposals about limited market opening by developing countries were to be agreed to at the negotiating table. Finally, the new government under President Lula sought greater prominence on the global stage through partnership with other developing countries. These developments appear to have convinced a section of the private sector that the regressive USA-EU joint proposal could be countered only by moderating the country's market access ambitions and striking effective coalitions with some developing countries.[76]

Compared to Brazil, managing domestic constituencies proved to be less difficult in India. An important reason for this was that unlike Brazil there was no strong divergence in interests among different segments of stakeholders in India. There was almost no prominent stakeholder group representing export interest, which could challenge the defensive interest of most of the farmers' organizations. However, delivering the coalition was not without its birth pangs.

While the counter-proposal was rolling along smoothly in Geneva, when it was sent to New Delhi for the government's formal approval, it almost came unstuck.[77] Arun Jaitley, India's Commerce Minister, quickly grasped the strategic significance of the emerging coalition and provided unstinted backing to the counter-proposal. However, one of his influential ministerial colleagues had a tactical problem in aligning with Brazil. The old argument that Brazil's intention was to secure market access for its agriculture exports in India appeared to have blind-sided Jaitley's senior ministerial colleague. He was perhaps under the influence of some of his officials, who were unable to see the larger gains from the coalition, and instead chose to focus on the conflict in the positions of the two countries. Sensing the risk of the fragile coalition falling apart if India did not back the counter-proposal, Jaitley used his immense skills as a brilliant lawyer to bring the recalcitrant minister to his corner. After Jaitley's firm and decisive intervention, India formally blessed the counter-proposal and remained the bedrock of support for the G-20.

8.9.2 Shaping the Agenda

G-20 demonstrated the ability of a coalition of developing countries to become a key player in shaping the agenda of Agriculture negotiations. It was successful in providing a counter-narrative to the USA-EU joint proposal for reforming the AOA. What enabled the G-20 to participate so effectively in multilateral rulemaking on agriculture and being taken seriously?

Two strategies can be ascribed to the success of G-20 in shaping the agenda. First, in its negotiating proposals the G-20 eschewed the developed versus developing rhetoric and instead chose to make mandate-oriented negotiating proposals backed by substantive research. Nevertheless, the G-20 also insisted on special and differential treatment provisions in favour of developing countries. In terms of technical details, the G-20's proposals could match those of the developed countries. Further, G-20 used its research to bring out the shortcomings in the proposals by the USA-EU combine. This helped the coalition in legitimizing its negotiating approach and provided substance to its bargaining.[78] Research generated by G-20 also exposed how some of the proposals by USA-EU would enable the two developed members of the WTO to escape from making any meaningful concessions, while requiring the developing countries to make onerous commitments for opening their agriculture markets. In short, the G-20 used the power of its technical expertise for becoming persuasive at the negotiating table and influencing the negotiating agenda.

The second strategy used by the G-20 for influencing the agenda was effective communication. The coalition demonstrated the ability to articulate its agenda in a manner that was comprehensible to many countries. Despite the negotiating issues being dense with legal and technical details, the G-20 wrote its proposals in a manner which helped the negotiators to clearly distinguish these from the approach of the USA-EU combine. Nothing highlighted this more than the first submission of the G-20 made on 20 August 2003, in which the coalition retained the structure of the USA-EU joint proposal, but had a substantially different content. This strategy enabled the negotiators to quickly compare the two proposals and comprehend how the visions for agriculture reform in these two proposals were like chalk and cheese. G-20 also used media releases to effectively convey its message to the negotiators outside the coalition. By succeeding in getting its message across to other countries, the G-20 positioned itself to influence the agenda. This strategy was also effective in getting many developing countries outside its fold to support its negotiating approach.

8.9.3 Framing Issues and Creating a Favourable Narrative

There is considerable academic literature to suggest that how a problem is framed, or the way a question is posed, can influence how the issue is perceived by others at the negotiating table. This can crucially influence the course of negotiations. How did the G-20 frame the negotiating issues for pushing its overall negotiating objectives and interests?

Given the diversity of interests among the coalition partners, the G-20 had to find a delicate balance. If the G-20 had framed the negotiating issues in terms of opening markets for exports, this would have made India extremely uncomfortable. On the other hand, if the issues were posed in terms of reducing developed countries' agriculture subsidies, this would have considerably narrowed the scope of G-20's comprehensive vision for agriculture reform.[79]

Cognizant of the constraints in suitably framing the negotiating issues, the G-20 adopted a novel track. It framed its negotiating position as a quest for equitable agriculture reform. This not only skirted contentious perspectives, but also provided other advantages. The mention of 'agriculture reform' was sufficiently broad to cover the entire gamut of issues championed by the G-20. 'Equitable' reinforced the notion that the AOA negotiated during the Uruguay Round was skewed in favour of the developed countries and that the asymmetry required to be corrected during the Doha Round by concluding a more balanced agreement. It would also have provided assurance to India that its defensive interests would not be compromised. In conjunction with demanding equitable agriculture reform, the coalition also leveraged the claim of the Doha Round to be a 'development round' as a critical argument against the proposals of the USA and the EU.[80] By suitably framing its overall negotiating approach, the G-20 was able to strike the right chord with most developing countries and get its perspective across to them.

8.9.4 Building and Sustaining a Coalition

For nearly five years, the G-20 was successful in overcoming the asymmetry in economic and political power with respect to the USA-EU combine, and negotiating on almost equal footing with the developed countries. It derived its strength from bargaining based on coalition. However, creating a coalition, as well as nurturing and sustaining it, is a mini-negotiation in itself involving cooperation in a competitive setting. This is beset with multiple challenges. The leaders of the coalition are usually confronted with many issues, including the following: which parties to seek out for coalition building, how to resolve internal conflicts among the coalition partners, how to retain the cohesion of the coalition and foster mutual trust among its partners, and how to provide a distinct identity to it. Unlike most previous attempts at the GATT/WTO, the G-20 did not fall apart like leaves in wintry weather. Despite the attempts of the USA and the EU to nip at its heels, the coalition remained largely intact and also effective. What strategies helped the G-20 in retaining its cohesion to stamp its imprint in the Agriculture negotiations?

8.9.4.1 Political Commitment and Leadership Role

Although the G-20 was formally born in Geneva during August 2003, the political origin of the coalition goes back to the Brasilia Declaration signed by Brazil, India, and South Africa in June 2003. In respect of WTO issues the declaration included the following: 'They stressed the need to fully carry out the Doha Development Program and emphasized how important it is that the results of the current round of trade negotiations provide especially for the reversal of protectionist policies and trade-distorting practices, by improving the rules of the multilateral trade system. They reiterated their expectation that negotiations will gain new political impetus and that it will be possible to overcome deadlocks on issues of fundamental interest to developing countries, before the Fifth Ministerial Conference in Cancun.'[81] This fostered a climate of political trust between these three countries, who provided the nucleus of the coalition. Brazil demonstrated its complete political commitment to the G-20 by hosting the first high-level meeting of the coalition in Brasilia in December 2003. This meeting came at a time when defections by a few developing countries threatened to rip asunder the nascent coalition. Subsequently, India hosted a G-20 summit in March 2005. However, political commitment is an essential, but not sufficient, ingredient for creating an effective coalition. It must have a leader, who not only assumes the responsibility of sustaining the coalition, but is also prepared to make sacrifices.

Brazil had the strategic nous to realize that for the coalition to have any chance of success, it would have to moderate its interest in seeking markets for its agriculture exports. Seeing the advantage of having India and Indonesia within the fold of the coalition induced Brazil to sacrifice some of its export interests. Celso Amorim, in particular, showed skill and wisdom in adapting Brazil's approach according to the needs and compulsions of its coalition partners, thereby adding political, economic, and technical heft to the coalition.

8.9.4.2 Choice of Coalition Partners

The strength and credibility of the G-20 arose from the reality that it not only represented more than 60 per cent of the world population, but also lay in the fact that countries with some conflicting interests had joined hands under its banner for seeking an equitable reform of the AOA. While the political nucleus of the coalition was provided by Argentina, Brazil, India, and South Africa, these countries reached out to a few other countries with a request to join the coalition. In particular, it was a masterstroke by Filipe Correa of Brazil and K.M. Chandrasekhar of India to persuade China to partner with them. At that time China had been a WTO member for less than two years and had not yet become an economic and political behemoth. Although Ambassador Sun of China struck an impressive presence, yet he rarely articulated strong views on any issue at the negotiating table. After the largest developing country according to GDP became one of the founding members of the coalition, many other developing countries would have felt encouraged to join its fold.

8.9.4.3 Enhancing Mutual Trust Among Coalition Partners and Containing Defection

Given the conflict in interests among some of the key coalition partners, how did the G-20 remain effective at the negotiating table for five years? In particular, despite Brazil and India having divergent interests on some issues in agriculture, a high level of trust developed between the two countries at all levels. Witnessing these two countries working in harmony inspired confidence and trust in other members of the coalition. It was this sense of mutual trust which helped some of its members to realize that their interests were better protected by being inside the coalition, rather than by opting out of it. Thus, some of the G-20 countries showed immense wisdom in not getting lured into the traps laid by the developed countries to split the coalition. This helped minimize defections from the coalition. When a few defections did happen in October 2003, within two months Brazil took decisive action by organizing a meeting of the G-20 ministers in Brasilia in December 2003. The meeting signalled to the outside world that the coalition not only continued to remain in existence, but was also vibrant with its core remaining intact. It also provided an occasion for removing any misunderstanding among the constituent countries, which could have created fissures in the future. Overall, the Brasilia meeting served the useful purpose of consolidating the coalition at a difficult time.

8.9.4.4 Internal Coordination

An important reason for keeping the G-20 relevant and on top of issues was how internal coordination was organized. For this purpose, the leaders of the coalition established certain formal and informal mechanisms. A core group, comprising ambassadors Alfredo Chiaradia of Argentina, Luiz Felipe de Seixas Correa of Brazil, K.M. Chandrasekhar of India, Sun of China, and Faizel Ismail of South Africa, would meet frequently to take stock and strategize. Acknowledging the immense competence of Seixas Correa on technical, tactical, and political fronts, the other four ambassadors would usually defer to his views during these meetings.[82] Regular interaction between capital-based officials provided another opportunity for internal coordination. Finally, coordination between the ministers of the G-20 countries was facilitated through a series of minister-level meetings organized by some of the constituent countries.

How did the coalition arrive at common positions on different issues? On many issues the G-20 adopted an inclusive strategy. Instead of seeking to reconcile differences among members, the attempt was to focus on points of convergence. Often technical research was useful in helping build consensus within the group. However, this strategy fell short on some issues and the coalition was compelled to bridge the gap between differing positions among its members. On this delicate aspect, a two-step approach emerged within G-20. Each issue would initially be discussed between Brazil and India. After these two countries had arrived at a common position, it would thereafter be discussed with rest of the coalition. On some issues, in order to arrive at a common position, concessions were made by all. Even if a few countries were not fully satisfied with a common position on some issues, they preferred to go along with Brazil and India. They recognized the political reality that after Brazil and India had come to an understanding on an issue, nothing further would be gained in seeking to negotiate with either side.[83]

Another important aspect of coordination within the coalition was external communication. Rules in this regard were clear. Coalition partners would speak in one voice and there was no airing of differences in public. This strategy helped in retaining the unity of the coalition and generally dissuaded some countries, which were outside the coalition, from taking advantage of internal differences among members for breaking the coalition.

How did internal coordination within the G-20 get articulated at the negotiating table? Whenever an issue was discussed in the negotiations, many G-20 members would speak in support of the common position.

In informal negotiations in different formats such as G-4 (comprising Brazil, EU, India, and USA); and Five Interested Parties (Australia, Brazil, EU, India, and USA), in order to respect the common position of G-20, Brazil and India adopted a practical approach. On issues of domestic support, export subsidies, and tariff reduction Brazil would take the lead and India would support it. On issues of defensive concern, such as excluding some products from cuts mandated by the tariff reduction formula, India would lead the charge and Brazil would not contradict it.

8.9.4.5 Expanding the Influence of the Coalition: Outreach to Other Countries and NGOs

One of the strategies adopted by the G-20 was to accommodate and take up issues of interest to some developing countries outside its fold. To illustrate, the group forcefully took up the issue of reduction of cotton subsidies granted by the USA. This was an issue of immense economic salience for some of the African countries whose economies were overwhelmingly dependent on this commodity. Further, at some of its meetings, such as the Ministerial meeting of the G-20 held in New Delhi on 18–19 March 2005, coordinators of the Africa Group, ACP Countries, CARICOM, G-33, and LDCs participated on equal footing with members of the G-20. This helped the coalition in expanding its circle of influence and secured the support of other countries outside the group for its agenda. Further, before submitting some of its key proposals, such as the proposal on the main elements on market access for a framework in May 2004, the G-20 consulted some of its allies outside the coalition.[84] Sustaining the coalition and expanding its reach by accommodating interests of as many partners as possible, appears to have been the strategic mantra of G-20.

A crucial partnership with an important country group appears to have been forged by accident, or to put it more accurately, during a car ride which narrowly escaped accidents. Amorim graphically describes sharing a car with Dipak Patel, the Trade Minister of Zambia and the coordinator of LDCs, and bonding over a ride 'that set our pulse racing' on account of the high speed of the car and the driver's disregard for basic traffic rules.[85] The acquaintance between the two in the car ride in New Delhi soon got translated into an enduring mutual support at the negotiating table.

G-20 did not limit its outreach and partnership to governments of countries outside its fold. In pursuit of its negotiating objectives, the G-20 recognized the importance of partnership with civil society organizations. Amorim candidly admits that Oxfam, an influential international civil society organization, was 'an important ally' and its good reputation assisted in 'legitimizing our campaign against agriculture subsidies of the rich'.[86]

8.9.4.6 Providing a Formal Identity to the Coalition

In order to create a sense of identity among the G-20 members, at the ministerial meeting in New Delhi in 2005, a distinct logo was designed and adopted by the coalition. In addition, a dedicated website was created for articulating the coalition's viewpoint on agriculture negotiation. These steps communicated the message that G-20 was different from other coalitions.

8.9.5 Engaging at the Negotiating Table

As the G-20 came into existence after the agenda for the Agriculture negotiations had been decided, its efforts were directed towards focusing attention on specific aspects of the agenda. This required the G-20 to engage intensely in an iterative process of offers and counter-offers. It did not shy away from taking the bull by the horn, amply evident in its formation. Nor was the G-20 hesitant in making compromises and accepting less than what it had initially aspired for, for example in its approach to elimination of the Blue Box. What are some of the strategies which the G-20 deployed while engaging at the negotiating table?

8.9.5.1 Making a Credible Counter-Offer and Preventing Negotiations from Becoming Anchored Around the USA-EU Joint Proposal

Within a week of the USA-EU joint proposal, the G-20 had made its counter-proposal. Swift response was as important as the content of the counter-proposal to prevent two dangers. First, the founders of G-20 realized the danger of getting trapped into bargaining on terms dictated by the USA-EU framework, which was perceived by many developing countries to be loaded against their interest. Second, in the absence of the counter-proposal, there was a risk of some developing countries supporting the USA-EU proposal. Some of the key G-20 negotiators have explicitly stated that they had complete clarity in their first move: make sure that USA-EU submission does not become the basis for further negotiations.[87] The counter-proposal ensured that an alternate framework for negotiations, backed by many developing countries, was firmly on the table. Therein lies the significance of the first submission of the G-20. The coalition demonstrated its strategic sense in seizing the moment and creating a momentum at the negotiating table in a direction different from what the USA-EU had envisaged.

8.9.5.2 Engaging Constructively with Options and Not Merely Opposing

The G-20 showed strategic nous in not only creating an alternate template for Agriculture negotiations, but also in remaining nimble footed by proposing constructive options for many negotiating issues. Seeking reduction in domestic support of the USA and EU was the core element of the G-20's agenda. One option before it would have been to merely oppose the proposal of USA-EU on this issue and demand more ambitious tariff and subsidy cuts by the developed countries. However, in the absence of any viable alternate proposal, even the most dogged resistance would have withered away and the USA-EU approach would have eventually prevailed. Instead, the G-20 chose to engage with the USA-EU combine and made technically sound and mandate-specific proposals on the issue. This helped in advancing the negotiations and carried the G-20 agenda forward. Brazil's Amorim explicitly acknowledged this at a media meet in Geneva on 11 October 2005, where he stated that if things were moving at the negotiating table after Cancun Ministerial Conference, it was largely due to the efforts of the G-20. According to him, the G-20 kept coming up with proposals and new ideas to move the negotiations forward.[88] Hence, from the strategic perspective, engagement was the right choice for G-20.

8.9.5.3 Seeking to Corner the USA and the EU: Game of Shifting Alliances

Before the formation of the G-20, the USA had supported the EU on market access and the EU backed the USA on domestic support. However, as Agriculture negotiations progressed, this mutual accommodation of each other's interests appears to have weakened. The EU seemed inclined towards seeking reduction in trade-distorting domestic support of the USA. On the other hand, the USA sought commitments from the EU for enhanced market access for exports of agriculture products. Given this dynamic between the two developed countries, how did the G-20 position itself? Ambassador Chiaradia of Argentina provides a partial answer to this question. According to him, the task of the G-20 was to move the USA and the EU beyond their bottom lines.[89] How did the two main leaders of the G-20, Brazil and India, seek to do this? In informal negotiating meetings of G-4 (comprising Brazil, EU, India, and USA), India and Brazil would engage in a game of shifting alliances to corner the USA and the EU on their respective defensive points. According to Amorim, when domestic support would be discussed, Brazil and India would align with the EU in trying to secure concessions from the USA. On the other hand, when market access, including tariff cuts would be discussed, Brazil would align with the USA in seeking ambitious commitments from the EU.[90]

8.9.5.4 Strategic Choices in the G-20 Pitching Its Bid on Negotiating Issues

An important strategic decision for parties at the negotiating table is—where to pitch its bid? The G-20, too, had to grapple with this difficult question, particularly in respect of reduction in domestic support and cuts in bound tariffs. Where did the G-20 pitch the numbers for cuts in domestic support? If it had proposed modest cuts in trade-distorting support of the USA and EU, the outcome of negotiations would have gone against the professed objective of 'real cuts in applied level of domestic support'. On the other hand, if the G-20 had proposed subsidy cuts at unrealistically high levels, this would have been dismissed by the USA and EU as being politically 'undoable'; thereby providing them an excuse for not engaging with the G-20 proposal.

On the issue of domestic support, the G-20's objectives were very clear. The coalition was looking for appropriate numbers that would result in real cuts in the level of support actually provided by the developed countries. Amorim put this objective rather lucidly in a media interaction in Geneva on 11 October 2005, where he said that 'The man or woman in the street will look at these numbers, (and) they want to see whether the overall distorting support actually diminished'.[91] As succinctly observed by Kamal Nath, the G-20 proposals were not extreme, and much of the starting point of Agriculture negotiations began with the G-20 submissions.[92] The quest for proposing the 'doable' appears to have been informed with the reality of seeking real cuts in domestic support.

On agriculture market access, the G-20 truly walked the middle path between the extreme positions of the EU's protectionist orientation and the market access seeking approach of the USA, which professed liberalization but with exceptions for protecting its interest. Speaking in an informal meeting of the Committee of Agriculture (Special Session) on 21 October 2005, many G-20 members argued that the group's proposal on market access was a result of a difficult compromise within the group. The proposal was 'the result of intensive negotiations among a diverse group of developing countries with exporting and importing interests, and represents the benchmark for an ambitious outcome that safeguards the legitimate concerns of poor farmers in the developing countries'.[93] This proved to be the magic formula, as eventually the proposal on tariff reduction by the G-20 provided the middle ground around which compromise among WTO members was reached.[94] Whether the G-20 was shrewd enough to guess the zone of possible agreement and tailored its initial proposal suitably, or the convergence around its proposal was fortuitous, cannot be definitively resolved. However, as the Doha Round could not be concluded, the compromise remained only on paper and it could not be translated into action.

8.9.6 Leveraging Issue Linkage

Agriculture negotiations during the Doha Round provide some fascinating illustrations of how countries use issue linkage to advance their interest at the negotiating table. On multiple occasions during 2005, the EU was on the back foot for failing to provide credible offers in the Market Access pillar. The EU's oft-repeated justification for its low ambition proposal was that unless there was progress in other areas of negotiations, particularly on services and industrial tariffs, it would be unable to make concessions in Agriculture negotiations. The G-20 was not lacking in resorting to issue linkage. As a justification for its reluctance to cut agriculture tariffs, Kamal Nath, India's Commerce Minister would often repeat 'artificial prices caused by continued subsidies cannot seek real market access'. On another occasion he mentioned that tariff reduction is not the only pre-condition for market access. 'For real market access to accrue, it is also necessary that export subsidies, domestic support, and non-tariff barriers are eliminated.'[95] Clearly, he linked reduction in agriculture tariffs by some developing countries with reduction in domestic subsidies and export subsidies by the developed countries.

While negotiators seek to create linkages between different issues to derive leverage at the negotiating table, at times their efforts may also be directed towards preventing others from using this strategy against them. K.M. Chandrasekhar, India's ambassador to the WTO during 2002–2004, recognized the risk of a link being established between the public health issue on the one hand and agriculture issues on the other hand at the Cancun Ministerial Conference. He was apprehensive that if the former issue was left to be resolved at Cancun, the beneficiaries of the issue may take a less strident position on other issues, including those relevant for the G-20.[96] His constructive role in resolution of the public health issue prior to the Cancun Ministerial Conference was effective in preventing an issue linkage, which might have diluted the effectiveness of the G-20 at this meeting.

8.10 Conclusions

Agriculture occupied the central position during the heyday of the Doha Round of multilateral trade negotiations. On this issue, high stakes were involved for both developed and developing countries. Retaining the right to subsidize their agriculture and agri-business but seeking to prise open the markets of developing countries was the main aim of the USA-EU combine. On the other hand, many developing countries sought to convince the developed countries to cut their farm subsidies, while seeking to protect their own farmers from subsidized imports from other countries. Some developing countries were more interested in securing market access—in both developed and developing countries—for their farm exports. To make an already complex situation more complicated, these negotiations involved a plethora of issues whose technical details were comprehensible to only a handful of negotiators and trade policy experts. It was in this turbulent cauldron that the G-20 made its mark through its swift action for creating a coalition to respond effectively to the challenges posed by the EU-USA combine. The G-20's first negotiating submission should be viewed as an attempt to prevent the negotiation from getting fixated around the USA-EU proposal, which would have locked in countries to negotiate on terms decided by the developed duo. It appears almost inconceivable that Argentina, Brazil, and India could have succeeded in exerting the influence on the Agriculture negotiations to the extent that the G-20 did, if they had acted separately and outside the context of the coalition. The G-20 helped channel the discontent among many developing countries unleashed by the USA-EU proposal. Therein lies the rationale for coalitions and lessons for the future.

The influence of the G-20 in Agriculture negotiations is an excellent illustration of the truism that strength lies in numbers. When the coalition came into existence, the negotiating agenda was almost decided and countries were in the phase of 'negotiating dance'. The coalition provided the power of relevant technical expertise, power of persuasive capacity and enhanced the political heft of its constituent countries. The coalition provided resources for research, analysing proposals made by other countries and preparing joint responses in the onerous task of engaging constructively in these negotiations. Sharing the load among the coalition partners was another benefit for the G-20 members. Further, the coalition provided a shield to its key members from being politically and economically targeted by the developed countries. Having ticked two of the three boxes relevant for success at the negotiating table—power and information—the coalition succeeded in enhancing the overall bargaining strength of its constituent countries at the negotiating table.

Diversity of interest of its constituent members could have diffused the negotiating efforts of the G-20 and pulled it in different directions. Further, conflict of interest among some of the coalition partners in respect of some core issues could have paralysed it into inaction, thereby impeding the G-20 from making meaningful negotiating proposals. However, the strong leadership provided by Brazil and high level of trust between Argentina, Brazil, and India, transformed the diversity into a source of strength for the G-20. Considerable credit for scripting this game-changing episode should go to the ministers and officials of these three countries who, despite some difference in their national interests, saw the larger picture and decided to join hands.

Notes

1. K.M. Chandrasekhar, *As Good as My Word: A Memoir* (Gurugram: HarperCollins Publishers, 2022), 90.
2. Based on an interview with Rajesh Aggarwal, a former Indian trade negotiator on agriculture issues, September 2018.
3. Based on an interview with Rajesh Aggarwal, a former Indian trade negotiator on agriculture issues, September 2018.
4. See, for example, Petros C. Mavroidis, George A. Berman, and Mark Wu, *The Law of the World Trade Organization (WTO) Documents, Cases and Analysis* (West, 2010), 381–382.
5. United States request for waiver in connection with Section 22 of the Agriculture Adjustment Act, GATT Document L/315 dated 28 January 1995.
6. See, for example, Mavroidis, Bermann and Wu, *Law of WTO*, 382.
7. Timothy Egan, 'Failing Farmers Learn to Profit from Federal Aid', *New York Times*, 24 December 2000, quoted in *The WTO and the Multilateral Trading System: Past Present and Future* by Bhagirath L. Das (Penang: Third World Network, 2003), 82.
8. Egan, 'Failing Farmers Learn to Profit from Federal Aid'.
9. Bhagirath L. Das, *The WTO Agreements: Deficiencies, Imbalances and Required Changes* (London and New York: Zed Books and Penang: and Third World Network, 1998), 62–66.
10. See Modalities for the Establishment of Specific Binding Commitments Under the Reform Programme, Note by the Chairman of the Market Access Group, GATT document MTN.GNG/MA/W/24 dated 20 December 1993.
11. See Article 5 of the Agreement on Agriculture. Canada (10%), EU (31%), Japan, (10%), Norway (49%), Switzerland (59%), and USA (10%) were the prominent developed Members who could invoke SSG on a large number of agriculture products for shielding them from import competition. Figures in brackets indicate the percentage of agricultural products on which these Members could invoke SSG. On the other hand, as most of the developing countries did not maintain non-tariff barriers, they did not acquire the right to invoke SSG.
12. Calculations based on Domestic Support notifications of the USA to WTO's Committee on Agriculture.
13. Calculations based on Domestic Support notifications of the EU to WTO's Committee on Agriculture.
14. See, for example, Das, *WTO Agreements Deficiencies*, 62–66.

15. Paragraph 13 of the Ministerial declaration adopted on 14 November 2001, WTO document WT/MIN(01)/DEC/1 dated 20 November 2001.
16. Das, *WTO Past, Present and Future*, 50–51.
17. Anuradha Mittal, 'Giving Away the Farm: The 2002 Farm Bill', Backgrounder, Oakland, *Food First*, 8, no. 3 (Summer 2002).
18. Adriano Soares, Campolina de Oliveira, 'G-20: Origin, Meaning, and Implications for Brazilian Trade Policy', Rio de Janeiro: CPDA/UFRRJ, Masters Thesis, 2004, 137.
19. WTO Members Fail to Make Progress at Mini-Ministerial, 25 June 2003. *Bridges* 7, no. 23.
20. Pedro da Motta Veiga, 'Brazil and the G-20 Group of Developing Countries'. Available on https://www.wto.org/english/res_e/booksp_e/casestudies_e/case7_e.htm. Last accessed 23 May 2020.
21. JOB (03)/157 (restricted), circulated on 13 August 2003.
22. Blue Box refers to direct payments provided under production-limiting programmes in accordance with Article 6.5 of the AOA.
23. See Article 6.4 of the AOA. For developed countries product-specific domestic support which would otherwise be required to be included in a Member's calculation of its Current AMS where such support does not exceed 5 per cent of that Member's total value of production of a basic agricultural product during the relevant year. For these countries non-product-specific domestic support which would otherwise be required to be included in a Member's calculation of its Current AMS where such support does not exceed 5 per cent of the value of that Member's total agricultural production. The corresponding figure for the de minimis percentage for developing countries is 10 per cent.
24. Subsidies under counter-cyclical payments fall when domestic price of the relevant agriculture product rises and vice versa.
25. Green Box refers to domestic support provided in accordance with provisions of Annex 2 of the AOA. WTO Members are permitted to provide domestic support under Green Box without any financial ceiling, provided the schemes are in accordance with the provisions of Annex 2 of the AOA.
26. 'Millennium Development Goals: A Compact Among Nations to End Human Poverty', Human Development Report, 2003, 155.
27. UNDP MDG Report, 156.
28. Interview with Gabriel Taboada, former delegate for Agriculture of the Permanent Mission of Argentina to the WTO, March 2023.
29. Based on interview of a former Indian negotiator, August 2019.
30. Celso Amorim, 'The Lesson of Cancun', *Politica Externa* 12, no. 3 (December 2003/January/February 2004): 27–36 quoted in 'The G-20: Its Origin, Evolution, Meaning and Prospects' by Nelson Delgado and Adriano Soares, *Global Issues Papers* 25. Heinrich Boll Stiftung, 2005.
31. Nelson Delgado and Adriano Soares, 'The G-20: Its Origin, Evolution, Meaning and Prospects', *Global Issues Papers* 25. Heinrich Boll Stiftung, 2005.

32. Interview with Gabriel Taboada, former delegate for Agriculture of the Permanent Mission of Argentina to the WTO, March 2023.
33. How the initial draft of the G20 counter-proposal was developed is based on interviews with Rajesh Aggarwal, former Agricultural Counsellor of India to the WTO (September 2018) and Gabriel Taboada, delegate for Agriculture of the Permanent Mission of Argentina to the WTO (March 2023). It is also corroborated by Chandrasekhar, *As Good as My Word*, 90–91.
34. This paragraph is based on interview with Rajesh Aggarwal, former Agricultural Counsellor of India to the WTO.
35. Interview with Gabriel Taboada, former delegate for Agriculture of the Permanent Mission of Argentina to the WTO, March 2023.
36. Based on interview with Rajesh Aggarwal, former Agricultural Counsellor of India to the WTO, September 2018. It is also corroborated by Chandrasekhar, *As Good as My Word*, 90–91.
37. Based on interview with Rajesh Aggarwal, former Agricultural Counsellor of India to the WTO, September 2018. It is also corroborated by Chandrasekhar, *As Good as My Word*, 90–91.
38. WTO document JOB(03)/162 dated 20 August 2003.
39. Under provisions of Article 5 of the Agreement on Agriculture, the developed countries and a few developing countries have the flexibility to impose Special Safeguard duties to counter surge in imports and dips in import prices of agricultural products. These duties are over and above the customs duties.
40. Celso Amorim, 'Brazilian Foreign Policy under President Lula (2003–2010): An Overview'. Available on http://www.scielo.br/scielo.php?script=sci_arttext&pid=S0034-73292010000300013 (last visited 15 February 2020).
41. Amorim, 'Brazilian Foreign Policy under President Lula'.
42. Amorim, 'Brazilian Foreign Policy under President Lula'.
43. Martin Khor, '"G-17" Get Broad Developing Country Support, Attacked by EC', *SUNS- South North Development Monitor* 5402, 22 August 2003.
44. Khor, '"G-17" Get Broad Developing Country Support'.
45. Khor, '"G-17" Get Broad Developing Country Support'.
46. This episode is based on an interview with a former Indian trade negotiator, August 2019.
47. Based on an interview with a former Indian trade negotiator, August 2019.
48. Delgado and Soares, 'The G-20: Evolution'.
49. Details of the meeting mentioned in this paragraph are based on interview with a former Indian trade negotiator, August 2019.
50. Delgado and Soares, 'The G-20: Evolution'.
51. G-20 Ministerial Communique December 19 2003 at 5 a.m., available with the author.
52. Kanaga Raja, 'G20 to Present its Own Figures in Agriculture Talks', *SUNS- South North Development Monitor* 5893, 13 October 2005.

53. WTO document TN/AG/W/4/Rev.4 dated 6 December 2008.
54. Celso Amorim, *Acting Globally, Memoirs of Brazil's Assertive Foreign Policy* trans. Michael Marsden (Maryland, MD: Hamilton Books, 2017), 256.
55. WTO document TN/AG/W/4/Rev.4 dated 6 December 2008, paragraph 3 page 4.
56. WTO document TN/AG/W/4/Rev.4 dated 6 December 2008, paragraph 13 page 6.
57. WTO document TN/AG/W/4/Rev.4 dated 6 December 2008, paragraph 30 page 8.
58. WTO document TN/AG/W/4/Rev.4 dated 6 December 2008, paragraph 38 page 10.
59. US would have cut its OTDS from $48.2 billion to $14.5 billion and the EU from €110 billion to €22 billion. Turning to the reduction in separate components of the OTDS, the sharpest cut would have happened in AMS. The USA would have reduced its AMS from $19 billion to $7.6 billion, while the EU's AMS would have come down from €67 billion to €20 billion.
60. WTO document TN/AG/W/4/Rev.4 dated 6 December 2008, paragraphs 22–23, page 7.
61. WTO document TN/AG/W/4/Rev.4 dated 6 December 2008, paragraph 40, page 11.
62. WTO document TN/AG/W/4/Rev.4 dated 6 December 2008, Annex B, Page 38.
63. The Blended Formula for tariff cuts proposed in the USA-EU joint paper would have required countries to group their agriculture products into three categories, with each category being subject to different types of tariff cuts. A limited number of tariff lines would have been subject to average cuts, with each such product taking at least a minimum specified cut. The average cut would have allowed the EU to fully secure its defensive interest of retaining relatively high tariffs on 50–60 products. The second category of products would have been subject to extremely steep cuts through the so-called Swiss Formula. After securing its interest of retaining high tariffs in 50–60 odd products, the EU would have been comfortable in taking steep cuts through the Swiss Formula on a large number of products, which were already at a low level. On the other hand, a large number of products of developing countries would have been subject to extremely steep tariff cuts through the Swiss Formula. Finally, in respect of the residual category of products, Members would have been required to allow imports duty free. With low tariffs already on a large number of products, the EU would have not found it difficult to meet this requirement. On the other hand, developing countries would have had to make deep concessions, were they to bring tariffs down to zero even on a handful of products.
64. Communication from the G-20, WTO document TN/AG/GEN/9 dated 7 May 2004.
65. WTO document TN/AG/W/4/Rev.4 dated 6 December 2008, paragraph 61, page 14.
66. WTO document TN/AG/W/4/Rev.4 dated 6 December 2008, paragraph 62, page 14.
67. WTO document TN/AG/W/4/Rev.4 dated 6 December 2008, paragraph 76, page 16.

68. WTO document TN/AG/W/4/Rev.4 dated 6 December 2008, paragraph 129, page 23.
69. WTO document TN/AG/W/4/Rev.4 dated 6 December 2008, paragraph 162, page 29.
70. WTO document TN/AG/W/4/Rev.4 dated 6 December 2008, paragraph 164, page 29.
71. See, for example, Kristen Hopewell, 'Different Paths to Power: The Rise of Brazil, India and China at the WTO', *Review of International Political Economy* 22(6) (2015): 1128–1158.
72. Based on interview with a former Indian negotiator, August 2019.
73. Based on interview with a former Indian negotiator, August 2019.
74. Delgado and Soares, 'The G-20: Evolution.'
75. Delgado and Soares, 'The G-20: Evolution.'
76. Information contained in this paragraph is based on Delgado and Soares, 'The G-20: Evolution.'
77. This episode is based on an interview with a former Indian negotiator, August 2019.
78. Amrita Narlikar and Diana Tussie, 'Multiple Access Points: Knowledge Creation for the Group of Twenty', in *The Politics of Trade: The Role of Research in Trade Policy and Negotiation*, ed. Diana Tussie (Dordrecht, Leiden and Boston: Republic of Letters Publishing BV, 2009).
79. Based on interview with Rajesh Aggarwal, former Agricultural Counsellor of India to the WTO, September 2018.
80. Narlikar and Tussie, 'Knowledge Generation for the Group of Twenty', in *The Politics of Trade* edited by Diana Tussie, 213–238.
81. Paragraph 14 of India-Brazil-South Africa Dialogue Forum, Brasilia Declaration, 6 June 2003.
82. Based on interview with Rajesh Aggarwal, former Agricultural Counsellor of India to the WTO, September 2018.
83. Based on interview with Rajesh Aggarwal, former Agricultural Counsellor of India to the WTO, September 2018.
84. Based on interview with Rajesh Aggarwal, former Agricultural Counsellor of India to the WTO, September 2018.
85. Amorim, *Acting Globally*, 268.
86. Amorim, *Acting Globally*, 270.
87. Interviews with Rajesh Aggarwal, former Agricultural Counsellor of India to the WTO (September 2018) and Gabriel Taboada, former delegate for Agriculture of the Permanent Mission of Argentina to the WTO, March 2023.
88. Kanaga Raja, 'G20 to Present Its Own Figures in Agriculture Talks', *SUNS- South North Development Monitor* No. 5893, 13 October 2005.
89. Raja, 'G20 to Present Its Own Figures.'
90. Amorim, *Acting Globally*, 276.
91. Raja, 'G20 to Present Its Own Figures.'

92. Raja, 'G20 to Present Its Own Figures'.
93. Kanaga Raja, 'Agreement Needed by 31 October or No Hong Kong Deal', *SUNS-South North Development Monitor* 5901, 25 October 2005.
94. WTO document TN/AG/W/4/Rev.4 dated 6 December 2008.
95. Raja, 'Agreement by 31 October'.
96. Chandrasekhar, *As Good as My Word*, 84–85.

9

Securing Rules to Fight Hunger and Poverty

9.1 Introduction

Summer nights in New Delhi in June are usually hot and humid. For J.S. Deepak, Additional Secretary in India's Department of Commerce, this summer night in the last week of June 2014 felt more oppressive than usual. While walking towards the office of Nirmala Sitharaman, India's Commerce Minister, at 11 p.m., he was experiencing mixed emotions—eagerness and anticipation, but tinged with considerable apprehension. As he would confess later, he almost felt like a schoolboy awaiting his results.[1] A seasoned and clear-headed civil servant, he was rarely assailed with self-doubt in the discharge of his official responsibilities. He was known to be extremely persuasive, and able to marshal different strands of information with impeccable logic to establish his point of view. Yet, that night he was not so sure. An internal note of the department, endorsed by him, had formally suggested to Sitharaman that India should do the unthinkable at the WTO—block the process of inclusion of the Trade Facilitation Agreement (TFA) into the WTO family of agreements.

Deepak was aware that implementing the suggestion contained in the internal note would open India to intense criticism at the WTO. India would be accused of going back on what it had agreed to in respect of the Trade Facilitation Agreement at the Bali Ministerial Conference of the WTO six months ago. He was also definite that this was the only option available to India for getting the WTO Members to fulfil their side of the bargain on another issue decided at Bali—the commitment to negotiate a permanent solution to the problem of public stockholding for food security purposes. Would he be able to convince the Commerce Minister to take an unprecedented decision that could rock the already unsteady ship of the Doha Round of WTO negotiations? More importantly, would

Strategies in GATT and WTO Negotiations. Abhijit Das, Oxford University Press. © Abhijit Das 2025.
DOI: 10.1093/9780198934431.003.0009

he be able to impress upon her that this bold move might also provide the last opportunity for India to obtain satisfaction on the issue of food security? He was reminded of the role played by India's system of procurement of food stocks in making the country self-sufficient in food grains and enabling the poor to purchase food grains at affordable prices. The country had come a long way from the 'ship-to-mouth' existence in the 1960s, when it was substantially dependent on generous food aid provided by the USA for feeding India's poor and the hungry.

Earlier in the day, Deepak had already had a brief 10-minute meeting with the Commerce Minister, during which she did not appear to be enthusiastic about the proposal contained in the departmental note.[2] However, she agreed to discuss it in detail at 11 p.m. In the intervening twelve hours, Deepak had alerted the office of the Indian Prime Minister about his proposed course of action.[3] With the clock ticking in the minister's office, it was well past midnight. But there was no sign of the minister. She was busy with her additional work related to the Ministry of Finance. Deepak was acutely aware that he had less than thirty-six hours to secure endorsement of the department's proposal from the higher echelons of the political leadership in the country and send instructions to India's ambassador to the WTO withholding the country's assent to go ahead with the Trade Facilitation Agreement. It was, thus, crucial to get the minister's approval within the next few hours. He was mentally prepared for a long night. What he was not prepared for was to wait another day for her endorsement. By then it would be too late.

Eventually, by 1 a.m. the Commerce Minister finished her work at the Finance Ministry and arrived at her office in the Department of Commerce. Despite having a long and tiring day in office, she gave Deepak a patient hearing. Within an hour the minister agreed with the departmental proposal.[4] Perhaps a gentle hint from a seasoned trade negotiator, who now held an extremely influential position in the government, might have helped in making her mind up. This tough decision would trigger intense criticism in the international media, as well as within India. Nevertheless, it set in motion a chain of events that would culminate in India meeting some of its negotiating objectives on the issue of public stockholding for food security purposes. This chapter narrates the events leading to the meeting between the minister and Deepak, and the aftermath of the decision taken by the minister.

While the preceding two chapters of this book have focused on the earlier stages of the negotiating process, this chapter discusses strategies deployed by India at the last stage of the negotiations. The main themes of the chapter are two-fold: role of issue-linkage in negotiations and analysing strategies behind India's brinkmanship at the negotiating table. While civil servants are usually perceived to be mere cogs in the government machinery, this chapter describes the stellar role played by three officials in steering the negotiations in a direction which enabled India to achieve many of its objectives on the issue of food security. Section 9.2 briefly discusses the problem of food security and describes the policy responses in some countries. Section 9.3 discusses the disciplines contained in the Agreement on Agriculture and examines how its rules constrain governments in many developing countries in implementing policies targeted at feeding their poor. Section 9.4 provides details of how the negotiation on the issue of food security progressed in the Doha Round until 2013.

As the negotiations on public stockholding for food security purposes and the trade facilitation became intertwined, Section 9.5 briefly describes the fundamental aspects of the negotiations on trade facilitation. Section 9.6 discusses developments at the negotiating table on both these issues during a few months prior to the Bali Ministerial Conference held in December 2013. Section 9.7 discusses the developments related to food security in Geneva during October–November 2013 and the influential role of some civil society organizations in goading India to negotiate harder on this issue at the Bali Ministerial Conference. How did the negotiations on food security and trade facilitation evolve at the Bali Ministerial Conference? Was India able to achieve its negotiating objectives on the former issue? We examine these questions in Section 9.8. Section 9.9 briefly describes the differential pace at which the negotiations on the two issues progressed in the post-Bali phase up to July 2014. Section 9.10 recounts the tumultuous events related to food security during August–November 2014, which eventually culminated in the decisions on the two issues being taken by WTO's General Council in November 2014. Section 9.11 identifies the key strategies used by India in securing its negotiating objectives on the issue of public stockholding for food security purposes. Section 9.12 provides the main conclusions from this chapter.

9.2 Food Security: Problem and Policy Responses

> There are people in the world so hungry, that God cannot appear to them except in the form of bread.[5]

With vast swathes of population living in hunger and being undernourished, for decades many developing countries have been confronting the problem of food security. This issue has attracted the attention of many multilateral organizations, including the United Nations, Food and Agriculture Organization, and the WTO. What exactly is meant by food security? What are the challenges in addressing food security? Where do most of the people living in a state of hunger and undernourishment reside? What have been some of the policy responses to address this problem?

Food security is defined by Food and Agriculture Organization (FAO) when all people, at all times, have physical and economic access to sufficient, safe, and nutritious food that meets their dietary needs and food preferences for an active and healthy life. Being able to purchase food is said to be as important as countries' ability to produce their own food. However, in countries classified by FAO as having 'widespread lack of access', the majority of the population is considered to be unable to procure food for themselves due to their low-income levels. Apart from low purchasing power among the poor to buy food, other factors that hinder food security include the following: inadequate domestic food stocks, stagnant domestic agriculture and volatility in food prices in the international markets. Further, food consumption accounts for a large share of expenditure out of the total household income in developing countries. Therefore, even small changes in food prices can have major socio-economic effects in these countries. In light of this, it becomes an important responsibility of governments in developing countries to ensure that sudden and sharp volatility in prices of food stocks are contained and the purchasing power of the poor enhanced to buy food at an affordable price. It is important to appreciate that most of the undernourished people in the world reside in developing countries. Developed countries in Northern America and Europe have a meagre share of the world's undernourished people.

Ensuring food security remains one of the most daunting challenges confronting countries in the world. The difference in the nature of agriculture in the developed countries and most of the developing countries has been mirrored in their policy responses to address food security. In the developed countries, such as the USA, the share of agriculture in total employment and national income is substantially lower as compared to other sectors of the economy. Further, given the high level of subsidies provided to agriculture, enhancing the purchasing power of farmers may not be relevant for ensuring food security. Instead, the USA focuses on providing direct food aid in the form of food stamps to the poor and needy. The food stamps can be redeemed by the beneficiaries at designated stores. This is one category of policy response for bringing food on to the table of the poor and hungry in the USA and some other developed countries. However, the budgetary cost of this option is rather high, as can be discerned from the fact that during 2000 the USA spent $32 billion on the direct domestic food,[6] which increased to $194 billion by 2021.[7] Thus, only governments with deep pockets can provide direct food aid.

In contrast to the situation in the developed countries, in most developing countries, including India and Indonesia, agriculture continues to provide a high share of employment in the economy. The farming community in these countries constitutes an economically weak and exceptionally vulnerable section of the population, which is unable to procure food for itself due to low level of income. Thus, increasing the purchasing power of the rural population can be an effective policy instrument for ensuring food security. In pursuance of this objective, governments in many developing countries have been purchasing food stuff from farmers at prices announced by them in advance of the harvest, commonly referred to as administered prices. This serves two objectives. First, government acquisition of food stuff at administered prices provides certainty to farmers of sale at an assured price level. This prevents distress sale by small farmers, insulates them from price fluctuations, and stabilizes their income. Consequently, small farmers acquire the purchasing power to buy food, particularly during the lean season. Second, food stocks acquired by the government are subsequently released to the poor and the hungry at subsidized prices; thereby ensuring supply at affordable prices. Thus, procurement of food stocks by the government at administered prices and their distribution at subsidized prices are two complementary policy instruments used by many developing countries to ensure food security. It also relieves cash-strapped governments in developing countries from the financial burden of providing huge subsidies for direct food aid, as is prevalent in the USA. A report by the UN Special Rapporteur on the Right to Food has recognized that public procurement policies to support local producers can make an important contribution to the realization of the right to food.[8] Developing countries which implement these policies include Egypt, India, Indonesia, Jordan, Kenya, Pakistan, Tunisia, Turkey, Zambia, and Zimbabwe.[9]

In this section we have discussed some of the constraints faced by developing countries in addressing the challenges related to food security. A more recent impediment in the efforts of countries to eliminate hunger relates to certain commitments of countries at the WTO. This aspect is discussed in detail in the next section.

9.3 Food Security and Asymmetric WTO Rules: Yielding Insecurity

There is an inherent asymmetry in WTO's Agreement on Agriculture (AOA) regarding policy instruments to address the problem of food security. Rules of the AOA allow countries to provide unlimited amount of direct food aid to sections of the population in need.[10] The scheme of food stamps provided by the USA is a good illustration of utilization of this provision of the AOA. On the other hand, as most developing countries face severe resource crunch, they are unable to use this provision. Instead, many of them implement a policy of acquiring and holding stocks of food products at administered prices and subsequently releasing it at a price lower than market price to the target population in need. However, the subsidy on account of acquiring food stocks from farmers at administered prices cannot exceed a ceiling prescribed by the AOA. Once a country is close to breaching the ceiling, it will have to either lower the acquisition price or reduce the quantity of food stocks to be purchased, in order to stay within the mandated ceiling. Both these options would adversely affect the food security of small farmers from whom the government purchases food stocks. Rules regarding public stockholding programmes under the AOA have been discussed in Box 9.1.

Box 9.1 Food Security Boxed

Under the rules of AOA, subsidies which meet the criteria of having minimal or no effects on production or international trade are classified in the so-called Green Box. WTO members have the flexibility to provide subsidies without any ceiling through schemes that comply with the requirements of the Green Box.

Paragraph 3 of Annex II of the AOA specifies the following two conditions for public stockholding schemes for food security purposes to fall in the Green Box: first, the purchases of food by the government should be made at prevailing market prices; and second, sales from food security stocks shall be at prices not lower than the prevailing domestic market price. In many developing countries, including Egypt, India, Indonesia, Pakistan, and Zambia, the government purchases food stocks from farmers at administered prices determined by the government in advance of the harvest. As these prices tend to be higher than the prevailing domestic market prices, government food stock procurement schemes do not fit into the Green Box. Instead, these schemes fall within the Amber Box with a ceiling on the value of the subsidy.

Under the rules of AOA, for most developing countries the total amount of subsidies under various schemes that can be given specifically to a particular product cannot exceed 10 per cent of the value of production of that agricultural product.[a] To illustrate, if the total value of production of rice in a developing country is $900 million, the government cannot provide subsidies targeted exclusively at rice beyond $90 million. If the country procures rice at administered prices, the subsidy under this scheme will be treated as subsidy specific to rice and cannot exceed this ceiling.[b] But the real complexity arises in how the amount of the subsidy is calculated for schemes of public stockholding for food security purposes. Herein lies the root of much of the problem encountered by many developing countries. Under the AOA, the subsidy amount in a particular year involves a comparison between the administered price at which the food stock is procured by the government in that year and the external reference price (ERP), which is based on the historical trade data for the specific product during the base period of 1986–1988 for the concerned developing country.

The point to note about the subsidy calculation is that higher the acquisition at administered price, higher will be the amount of the subsidy. Similarly, higher the quantity of the food stock that is procured, higher will be the amount of the subsidy. Thus, the amount of subsidy that a large number of developing countries can provide for addressing food security challenges through schemes involving procurement by governments at administered price is circumscribed by the disciplines of the AOA. This puts fetters on them in pursuing the overall objective of ensuring food security.

Source: Broadly based on the relevant provisions of the Agreement on Agriculture.[a] See Article 6 of the Agreement on Agriculture.[b] See note 5 of the Agreement on Agriculture.

Some developing countries realized the problems in AOA rules regarding public stockholding programmes implemented by them and sought to get them addressed during the Doha Round. What specific proposals were made in the negotiations and how did these progress?

9.4 Doha Round and Food Security: One Step Forward and Two Steps Backward

The focus of the discussion in this chapter is on the endgame in the negotiations on public stockholding for food security purposes, spanning almost two years during 2013–2014. However, in order to provide the context for the endgame, it is relevant to understand what happened at earlier stages of the negotiations. An overview of how the negotiations on this issue evolved until 2008 is provided in this section.

Even before the launch of the Doha Round, many developing countries were acutely aware of how the rules of the AOA could constrain them from fully addressing the problem of food security. During the negotiations that were already built into the agreement,[11] some proposals were made on the issue of food security. To illustrate, in one of its submissions, India proposed a 'Food Security Box' for developing countries and identified specific measures for promoting food security.[12] An important suggestion in this regard was that the subsidy that might arise from government procurement of food stocks from low-income and resource-poor farmers would not fall in the Amber Box and hence not subject to the 10 per cent ceiling. This approach would be a recurrent theme for India and many other developing countries during the Doha Round.

When the Doha Round was launched in November 2001, the Doha Declaration specifically provided that 'special and differential treatment for developing countries shall be an integral part of all elements of the negotiations . . . and shall be embodied in the Schedules of concessions and commitments and as appropriate in the rules and disciplines to be negotiated, so as to be operationally effective and to enable developing countries to effectively take account of their development needs, including food security and rural development'.[13] This was reiterated in the July 2004 Framework: 'Having regard to their rural development, food security and/or livelihood security needs, special and differential treatment for developing countries will be an integral part of all elements of the negotiation.'[14] Thus, the issue of food security was firmly on the agenda of Doha Round. How was this issue taken forward in the negotiations?

In the initial years of the negotiations, a proposal by the African Group sought to exclude public stockholding programmes of developing countries from being included in the subsidy calculations under the Amber Box. This would have provided considerable policy flexibility to developing countries for implementing food security programmes based on acquisition of food stocks by governments at administered prices.[15] Subsequently during 2002–2008 the negotiation on this issue was marked by uncertainty and occasional U-turns. This is evident in the various consolidated negotiating texts prepared by the chairperson of the Committee on Agriculture Special Sessions—the formal negotiating body for Agriculture negotiations—during 2003–2008. Eventually, the last version of the consolidated negotiating text retained the provision for treating procurement of food stocks for public stockholding outside the Amber Box, provided that the acquisition of stocks was done with the objective of supporting low-income or resource-poor producers.[16] It is relevant to note that this provision was not within square brackets, thereby implying that the entire WTO membership was agreeable to it. It is understood that sometime during 2008, at the technical level India and the USA had agreed to even doing away with the requirement of acquisition of stocks 'with the objective of supporting low-income or resource-poor producers'. However, this meeting of minds could not be replicated at the political level.[17]

After 2008, there was no substantive progress at the negotiating table on most of the Doha Round issues. The issue of public stockholdings for food security purposes re-emerged at the negotiating table in 2012. Its subsequent journey is inextricably linked with another issue—trade facilitation. In the next section we briefly discuss the negotiations on trade facilitation.

9.5 Trade Facilitation Negotiation: The Other Half of the Food Security Equation

Trade Facilitation was one of the four Singapore Issues, which was pushed by the developed countries and a few developing countries for negotiating binding rules during the Doha Round at the WTO. As discussed in Chapter 7, while three Singapore Issues were eventually removed from the negotiating agenda of the Doha Round by the so-called July Framework in 2004, trade facilitation as an issue remained on the negotiating table. Although negotiators were struggling to make progress on most of the other issues in the Doha Round, to some extent trade facilitation appeared to buck this trend. Nevertheless, even negotiations on trade facilitation faced considerable headwinds. What were these negotiations about and what misgivings did many developing countries have about these negotiations?

Trade facilitation negotiations sought the simplification, harmonization, and standardization of border procedures involved in import and export of goods. Reducing transaction costs related to border clearance of goods was another objective of the negotiations. Many developing countries had two apprehensions about the negotiations: first, concerns on the likely cost of implementing the obligations related to trade facilitation; and second, trade facilitation being viewed by them as being an instrument for facilitating imports by them, rather than their exports getting a boost in the markets of the developed countries.

While the intensity of negotiations on most Doha Round issues ebbed after 2008, the negotiations on trade facilitation moved ahead. There was a perception among some developing countries that the agreement on this issue would be finalized and with that the Doha Round would be declared to have been completed.[18] A few developing countries were deeply disappointed and concerned at this turn of events. They were of the view that restricting the substantial result of the Doha Round to an agreement on trade facilitation would represent an imbalanced outcome of the negotiations that was ostensibly for development. These countries decided that along with an agreement on trade facilitation, there must be a conclusive outcome on at least one substantive issue of interest to them. It was in this context that in 2012 a handful of developing countries, spearheaded by India's Ambassador to WTO, Jayant Dasgupta, decided to revive the issue of public stockholding for food security purposes.[19] This approach had the strong backing of Rajeev Kher, the Additional Secretary in India's Department of Commerce with responsibilities related to WTO issues. This was the first step in creating a linkage between the two issues—trade facilitation and public stockholding for food security. How did the linkage influence the trajectory of negotiations on these two issues?

9.6 Food Security and Trade Facilitation: Linked Initially, But Separated Subsequently

Having decided to revive the issue of public stockholding and food security, the G-33 coalition of developing countries[20] spearheaded by Indonesia, Philippines, and India, made a detailed negotiating submission,[21] proposing certain amendments to the Agreement on Agriculture. While this submission also included proposals on other issues related to Agriculture negotiations, in respect of food security it suggested the following specific amendment to the Agreement on Agriculture: 'acquisition of stocks of foodstuffs by developing country Members with the objective of supporting low-income or resource-poor producers shall not be required to be accounted for in the AMS'. This might appear to be old wine in a new bottle, but at that juncture the objective of the G-33 was not to propose a new negotiating text. Its immediate objective was to bring the issue of food security back to the negotiating table and also signal to the WTO members that progress on trade facilitation would have to go hand in hand with forward movement on food security.

While food security staged a comeback on the negotiating table in 2012, what was happening on the trade facilitation front? As discussed earlier, many developing countries had strong reservations about taking legally binding commitments on various aspects of trade facilitation. They adopted an approach whereby many of the obligations would become less onerous and, in some instances, rendered non-mandatory. This created a logjam at the negotiating table, as the proponents of the negotiations were keen on an agreement with binding commitments. It is not surprising that during the early months of 2013, there was divergence of views among the WTO members on more than a hundred specific points in the negotiating text. India was one of the countries at the forefront of resisting the efforts of proponents for a legally binding agreement. India also started highlighting the need for an overall balance between the negotiations on the two issues.[22]

Did the linkage between progress in trade facilitation and food security secure any specific gains for India and other developing countries on the latter issue at the negotiating table? While it is difficult to arrive at a definitive answer to this question, nevertheless, some developed countries started showing more receptivity towards India's concern on food security. To illustrate, in discussion with Ambassador Dasgupta during April–May 2013, Jean-Luc Demarty, the EU's Director General of Trade and an erstwhile negotiator on agriculture, conveyed his opposition to any amendment to the AOA. However, the EU indicated its willingness to work for the so-called peace clause which would provide some assurance to India that other WTO members would not bring legal challenges to its public stockholding programmes, even if the amount of the subsidy attributable to these programmes exceeded the prescribed limit.[23] This was perhaps the first constructive suggestion from a developed member of the WTO on the issue of food security, after it staged a comeback at the negotiating table in 2012. It is uncertain, and perhaps doubtful, whether this issue would have got any meaningful traction if its linkage with trade facilitation had not been adroitly created by a handful of developing countries.

Some WTO members viewed with concern India's opposition to trade facilitation as a negotiating ploy to secure progress on the issue of food security.[24] For these countries, a linkage between food security and trade facilitation could spell doom for the latter issue at the negotiating table.

The nexus, so assiduously created by India and a few other developing countries, needed to be broken, if the trade facilitation negotiation was to progress. Towards this end, a narrative was created painting India as the villain of the piece—not for the first time and certainly not for the last. India's supposed obstructionist role in the trade facilitation negotiations soon became the talk of the town. This narrative started gathering traction, not only in Geneva, but also in top political circles in New Delhi. In order to appreciate what happened next, it is relevant to digress a bit into geo-political dynamics of those days.

The developments on food security at the WTO were taking place in an environment where India had started becoming diplomatically close to a prominent developed country. India's strong stand on food security was viewed as having the potential to create friction points in the broader context of this deepening bilateral relationship. This elicited the following informal advice to India's trade negotiators and other high officials in the Department of Commerce: 'don't annoy big brother; keep big brother in good humour; and don't indulge in any brinkmanship on food security'.[25] No doubt the issue of food security was important for India, but evidently it was being made subservient to India's larger geo-political interests.

In this atmosphere, two far-sighted and wise persons stood out for being steadfast in championing the cause of food security at the WTO. First, Jayant Dasgupta, India's ambassador to the WTO, clearly conveyed to his government that during the meetings in Geneva he would push the envelope on food security to the maximum extent possible. Thereafter, it would be up to the political leadership in the Indian government to decide the approach on this issue at the Bali Ministerial Conference. Second, Rajeev Kher, the Additional Secretary in the Department of Commerce with responsibilities related to WTO issues, played a sterling role in putting the issue of food security above geo-political and diplomatic considerations. He showed courage by repeatedly emphasizing the importance of this issue in high-level meetings in New Delhi. He alerted the political leadership in no uncertain terms of the likely adverse fallout if India failed to secure its negotiating objectives on this issue. As would be discussed in the next section, he was to play an important role in formulating India's final negotiating mandate on this issue for the Bali Ministerial Conference.

Given the geo-political imperatives mentioned above, India appears to have started going a bit soft on its opposition to trade facilitation. Henceforth, India started talking more about internal balance in the outcome of trade facilitation negotiation, while continuing to highlight the importance of the issue of food security.[26] In internal discussions within the government, the possible gains for the country from an agreement on trade facilitation, supposedly from improvements in India's system for customs clearance, started acquiring prominence.[27] Lost in the geo-political calculus and the new found love for trade facilitation was the bargaining chip that had been cleverly minted in Geneva for securing gains on the issue of food security. The link between food security and trade facilitation had started to fray.

Dismayed at this turn of events, a former secretary of the Department of Commerce privately cautioned the government authorities against delinking the issue of public stockholding from trade facilitation.[28] A former ambassador of India to the WTO likened the situation with going to battle after surrendering arms and with hands tied.[29] However, the wise counsel of these former officials, who had been previously involved in WTO negotiations, failed to make an impression on the key decision-makers in the government. On the eve of the Bali Ministerial Conference held in December 2013, the downward spiral in India's strategic thinking on WTO negotiations, triggered by geo-political compulsions and being portrayed in a negative light on trade facilitation, would eventually push the country to the brink on the issue of food security. Had it not been for the active and timely intervention by some civil society organizations, India would have been compelled to agree to a solution that would have provided protection for its public stockholding programmes for merely four years and not thereafter. We turn to these developments in the next section.

9.7 India Almost Buckles Before Bali, But Bucked Up by the Civil Society at the Last Stage

The build-up to the Bali Ministerial Conference held in December 2013 provides a fascinating glimpse of how internal dynamics within a country can influence its position at the negotiating table. Having weakened the nexus between food security and trade facilitation, it was not surprising that India found itself pushed into a corner on the former issue.

The developed countries were in no mood to concede more than the bare minimum necessary on food security, in order to prevent India from walking away from the negotiations on trade facilitation. India was being offered a face-saving solution, which was largely meaningless. The zone of possible agreement appeared to have shrunk considerably and the Indian negotiators in Geneva were left with few bargaining chips in their pocket for extracting a satisfactory deal on public stockholding for food security purposes. It should, therefore, not come as a surprise that in the weeks preceding the Bali Ministerial Conference, India was unable to negotiate a deal that would have substantially protected its interest on food security. This section initially describes developments at the negotiating table during October–November 2013. Thereafter, we discuss how quick action by some civil society organizations in India compelled the government to take a tougher stand on the issue of food security.

9.7.1 Neither Peace nor Security in the Peace Clause Option: Losing the Plot

In the previous section we saw that in mid-2013 the EU signalled its receptivity to a peace clause for insulating public stockholding schemes from legal challenges under the WTO's Dispute Settlement Mechanism. The G-33 made a final attempt at seeking a more ambitious resolution of this issue in its favour prior to the Bali Ministerial Conference. It made a proposal in October 2013, reiterating its earlier suggestion to amend the AOA for keeping subsidies attributable to procurement of food stocks outside the Amber Box.[30] Recognizing that the amendment to the AOA could take some time, the G-33 proposed that at the Bali Ministerial Conference, the WTO members should take a supplementary decision to address the issue of food security. It proposed three alternatives in this direction. First, calculation of subsidies should be based on the trade data of recent years, instead of 1986–1988; second, developing countries should have the flexibility to make adjustments for inflation while calculating the amount of subsidy attributable to procurement of food stocks by governments at acquisition prices; and third, the WTO members would exercise restraint in initiating disputes on account of subsidies that might be attributable to procurement of food stocks (the so-called peace clause option).

The reaction of the developed countries to the G-33 proposal was along expected lines. There appeared to be no appetite to discuss any option other than the peace clause. With India having already signalled that it would no longer link progress on food security with trade facilitation, perhaps the developed countries had no incentive to accommodate India's interest on food security beyond the bare minimum. In fact, during his visit to New Delhi in early October 2013, Roberto Azevedo, who had recently been appointed as the Director General of the WTO, cautioned India not to expect the duration of the peace clause to be more than one year.[31]

In the weeks preceding the Bali Ministerial Conference, scheduled to be held during 3–7 December, 2013, intense negotiations were undertaken in Geneva. The focus of these negotiations was two-fold: first, the duration of the peace clause; and second, the conditions to be complied with by the developing country for resorting to the peace clause. After days of intense and tough bargaining, eventually a provisional deal appears to have been hammered out by the ambassadors and delegates in Geneva. The deal essentially provided for the WTO members to refrain from challenging public stockholding programmes of developing countries undertaken for food security purposes. The duration of the peace clause was four years. Thereafter, the WTO membership would have been required to take a decision on continuing the peace clause.[32] The implication of the deal was clear—after four years India and other developing countries would be required to expend more diplomatic capital and grant more concessions for securing an extension of the peace clause. The deal was subject to formal approval by the governments. It was kept under wraps and not brought into the public domain.

The peace clause provisionally agreed in Geneva in November 2013 bore almost no resemblance to the solution to the problem of food security, as sought by the G-33 earlier. While the G-33 had proposed a peace clause as an option in its submission in October 2013, this was premised on the assumption that the WTO members would work towards an amendment of the Agreement on Agriculture for keeping subsidies on account of government procurement of food stocks outside the calculations of the Amber Box. In the provisional deal struck in Geneva, there was no reference to working towards such an amendment.

Having made its interest on the issue of food security subservient to larger geo-political considerations and delinking the negotiations on food security from trade facilitation, payback time for India had arrived. After having battled hard for about two years, India appeared to have buckled in the last few days prior to the Bali Ministerial Conference. What were the consequences of this development in India? How was the situation retrieved?

9.7.2 Civil Society Makes Trouble, of the Right Kind

The deal on public stockholding, struck in Geneva prior to the Bali Ministerial Conference, mandated that the peace clause would be applicable for four years. Thereafter, the WTO membership would have been required to take a decision on continuing its application. However, there was an apprehension that one prominent developed country was against even the four-year period. It was prepared to agree to the peace clause for two to three years, but not beyond that. Thus, the deal provided no certainty that the public food stockholding schemes of developing countries would not be subject to legal challenges on the expiry of the four-year period. India appears to have reluctantly acquiesced to the provisional deal in Geneva. Even the officials in India's Department of Commerce were resigned to the peace clause that would insulate the public procurement scheme from legal challenges only for a short duration, not exceeding four years.

As the deal was not made public, initially it did not trigger any large-scale negative response. However, with just a few days left for the Bali Ministerial Conference, details about the deal reached some civil society organizations (CSO) in India active in the area of international trade. After that, all hell broke loose. There was a general uproar among these organizations and farmers' groups. They felt extremely let down by the deal on public stockholding for food security purposes.[33] Given the four-year duration of the peace clause, they were apprehensive that when India would need it the most, which would be a few years later, there would be no certainty that it would still be under implementation.[34] Despite not being fully aware of the technical details about WTO issues, these organizations came to the right conclusion that the limited duration of the peace clause would put a huge question mark on India's scheme of procurement of food stocks, including for rice and wheat, once the subsidy exceeded the 10 per cent ceiling.

In almost no time, some of the CSOs in India got their act together. They reached out to prominent politicians and farmers' leaders in India. What they achieved in a very short time proved to be extremely influential. First, the political heads of some of the provinces in India, where rice and wheat are procured in substantial quantities for building public stockholding, wrote strong letters to India's prime minister urging a review of India's acquiescence to a four-year peace clause.[35] Second, Basudeb Acharia, who was the Chairman of the Committee on Agriculture in India's lower house of parliament, drew the attention of the prime minister to the huge adverse impact of the provisional deal and demanded his 'immediate intervention to reject the Peace Clause'.[36] Third, Shanta Kumar, a highly respected parliamentarian and Chairman of the Parliamentary Standing Committee on Commerce, addressed a letter to the prime minister urging him not to accept the 'current formulation of peace clause and give instructions to our Ambassador to oppose the peace clause'.[37] Fourth, many farmers' leaders repeatedly wrote to the prime minister along similar lines.[38] The efforts of CSO activists working in the area of right to food resulted in a prominent political quarter conveying a clear message to the government that the peace clause with a limited duration of four years was not in India's interest. Instead, the government was firmly urged to negotiate for a longer period of application of the peace clause.[39]

On account of the pressure created by these developments, the political leadership in India was left with no choice other than striving for a longer period of validity of the peace clause at the Bali Ministerial Conference. Timely intervention by the civil society organizations had prevented the country from completely buckling under the pressure of a major developed country and accepting a decision that might not have remained in force when most required. At this juncture, Rajeev Kher, who was now the Special Secretary in India's Department of Commerce, played a crucial role in channelizing the strong sentiment among stakeholders in India against a short-duration peace clause, and secured the mandate for negotiating a peace clause going beyond four years. How did India battle it out on this issue at the Bali Ministerial Conference? What hurdles did it face and what was achieved?

9.8 Bali Ministerial Conference: Making an Interim Peace

Bali, the tourist hub of Indonesia, is renowned for its colourful and attractive hand-crafted wooden masks. Unlike a Balinese mask, which takes many hours of painstaking carving and painting, when trade ministers, ambassadors, and delegates assembled in Bali for the Ministerial Conference of the WTO, the general perception was that not many negotiating hours would be spent in chiselling the deal on food security. Most WTO members assumed that India would go along with the food security deal hammered out in Geneva just a few days ago. In parallel, the last few glitches in the agreement on trade facilitation could be ironed out after some intense negotiation. Thus, the Bali Ministerial Conference was anticipated to be historic for concluding these two deals. In this section we discuss how the events related to these two issues unfolded at the Bali Ministerial Conference, which was held during 3–7 December 2013.

9.8.1 India Wages a Single-Handed Battle

In informal meetings in Bali, held prior to the commencement of the WTO Ministerial Conference, India let it be widely known that it was not satisfied with the peace clause having a life of merely four years. As many countries which were implementing public stockholding programmes would have benefited from a longer duration peace clause, India had expected that it would not be the lone voice on this issue. Indonesia, its most important ally on the issue, was unable to take a strong line in support of India. Being the host of the ministerial meeting, perhaps Indonesia was more anxious about ensuring a successful outcome of the meeting, than securing its negotiating objectives in the area of food security.[40] Further, the G-33 coalition, which was the main proponent of food security, appeared to have receded into a shell.

In bilateral meetings organized at India's initiative, while many developing countries expressed their support for the issue of food security, they did not come out openly in India's favour.[41] Some developing countries, which were purchasing food stocks at government mandated prices for building public stocks, appeared to have left it to India to fight the battle.[42] At this juncture a statement from some developing countries calling for a peace clause with a longer period of application would have lent some political weight to India. However, this was not forthcoming. An impression went around that India was fighting for itself, and not on behalf of a large number of countries. Some might even have been misled into believing that India was merely posturing for satisfying its domestic constituencies. The thundering statement at the plenary of the Bali Ministerial Conference delivered by Anand Sharma, India's Commerce Minister, was unable to dispel this notion.

Quick to sense the undercurrents, the USA, which was the main country opposing India's demand for a longer duration of the peace clause, was extremely reluctant to engage directly with India on this issue. It was left to Roberto Azevedo, the Director General of the WTO, to find a solution that would be acceptable to all parties. However, the initial parleys between Sharma and Azevedo, often held at inconvenient hours at night, did not result in any forward movement on India's demands on the peace clause. With neither India nor the USA showing any signs of climbing down, the ministerial meeting was heading for a collapse. The stage was set for blaming India for plunging the WTO into yet another crisis. However, three crucial developments retrieved the situation from the brink.

South Centre, an inter-governmental organization based in Geneva, had been active in supporting developing countries to engage effectively in the Doha Round. Martin Khor, its Executive Director, had the unique ability of identifying common ground and forging solidarity among many developing countries. At the Bali Ministerial Conference, his abilities in this direction came to fore. He realized that a peace clause with a longer duration was in the interest of many developing countries, besides India. He also grasped that this was not achievable, unless India received the backing of some other developing countries. With the larger objective of facilitating developing countries to secure the desired peace clause, he organized a lunch during early days of the Bali Ministerial Conference.[43] This provided an opportunity to more than a dozen developing countries to exchange notes on their public stockholding programmes. The message went home loud and clear—it was in their interest to speak out openly in favour of a peace clause with a longer duration. Indirectly, the luncheon meeting demonstrated the political backing of some developing countries for India's negotiating position, which had so far not been explicit. The narrative that India was fighting the battle on food security solely for its gains, and the issue was of little interest to many developing countries, had been deflated.

In a parallel development, Rob Davies, the South African Trade Minister, felt troubled by the possibility that while the intransigence of the developed countries in finding a solution to the food security problem could precipitate the collapse of the Ministerial Conference, the blame would be quickly put on India's shoulders. As a country, South Africa had little to gain from the peace clause. However, Davies was cognizant that many African countries stood to benefit from the type of peace clause for which India was fighting. Further, he was aware that many African countries stood to gain very little from the Trade Facilitation Agreement. He met Azevedo and conveyed two clear messages. First, it was not just India, but many other developing countries that would benefit from a peace clause with a longer duration. Second, it would be completely wrong to blame India for the deadlock at the negotiating table. As he crisply and colourfully put it, 'it would be inappropriate to hang India out to dry'.[44] A country which did not stand to benefit from the peace clause had batted strongly for India and other developing countries.

To buttress India's position further, in a press conference held on 5 December 2013, Anand Sharma, India's Commerce Minister, made a strong pitch for a peace clause with a longer duration. It left no one in any doubt that India was serious on this issue and was not merely posturing for domestic political gains.[45] This enhanced the credibility of its negotiating stance. The tide was slowing turning, but what did it bring in its wake?

9.8.2 Bali Peace Clause: Sowing Seeds of Future Unrest and Insecurity

In the face of India's firm stand of not accepting a peace clause limited to a four-year duration, and with signals from some countries that they were with India on the issue of food security, frantic attempts were made by DG Azevedo and Gita Wirjawan, Chairman of the Bali Ministerial Conference, to seek a compromise. Kher proposed an unambiguous language which would have made it clear that the duration of the peace clause would be until a permanent solution was agreed and adopted by WTO members.[46] After repeated rounds of discussions, it was obvious that the USA was not willing to agree to an unambiguous language regarding the duration of the peace clause.[47] Thereafter, the choice before India was stark—continue to stick to its guns and run the risk of the peace clause sinking completely, or live with some ambiguity. Confronted with the resist versus yield dilemma, eventually India agreed to the following text[48] which was a bit ambiguous, but could have been interpreted to give it comfort:

1. Members agree to put in place an interim mechanism as set out below, and to negotiate on an agreement for a permanent solution, for the issue of public stockholding for food security purposes for adoption by the 11th Ministerial Conference.
2. In the interim, until a permanent solution is found, and provided that the conditions set out below are met, Members shall refrain from challenging through the WTO Dispute Settlement Mechanism, compliance of a developing Member with its obligations under Articles 6.3 and 7.2 (b) of the Agreement on Agriculture (AOA) in relation to support provided for traditional staple food crops in pursuance of public stockholding programmes for food security purposes existing as of the date of this Decision, that are consistent with the criteria of paragraph 3, footnote 5, and footnote 5&6 of Annex 2 to the AOA when the developing Member complies with the terms of this Decision.

The Ministerial Decision on Public Stockholding for Food Security Purposes, popularly referred to as the Bali Peace Clause, committed the WTO members to negotiate a permanent solution to the problem of food security. The commitment required the permanent solution to be adopted within four years by the XI Ministerial Conference of the WTO. It ensured that there would not be a hard end to the peace clause after four years; the possibility of its extension beyond four years existed. In addition, an interim mechanism was agreed, which would insulate public stockholding programmes of developing countries from legal challenges under the WTO. This was subject to the food security programmes complying with various conditions which were contained in the Bali Peace Clause.

There was some legal uncertainty on whether the interim mechanism would continue to remain in force beyond the XI Ministerial Conference, if no permanent solution was found by that time. The Bali Decision could be interpreted as implying that the 'interim' referred to the period between the date of the Decision and the XI Ministerial Conference. Under this interpretation, the Bali Peace Clause would lapse after XI Ministerial Conference, if no permanent solution to the problem was found by then. In contrast, India held the view that 'interim' referred to the time between the Bali Decision and when a permanent solution was found. Notwithstanding the ambiguity, India declared victory and the WTO members congratulated themselves for having saved the Ministerial Conference from yet another collapse. At that juncture, few could have imagined that this issue would become stormy within seven months. However, this is a matter to be discussed in the next section. But before coming to that, it is relevant to briefly outline what was achieved on trade facilitation at the Bali Ministerial Conference.

9.8.3 Finalizing the Trade Facilitation Agreement

While India was battling it out to secure a peace clause going beyond four years, most of the other WTO members were engaged in providing the finishing touches to the Agreement on Trade Facilitation. The sticky parts, which could not be addressed during the negotiations in Geneva, were miraculously treated as having been resolved at Bali, objections of many developing countries notwithstanding. The ministers concluded the negotiations on the Agreement on Trade Facilitation (TFA) and established a Preparatory Committee on Trade Facilitation (the 'Preparatory Committee') under the General Council to perform such functions as may be necessary to ensure the expeditious entry into force of the Agreement. Further, the Preparatory Committee was tasked to draw up a Protocol of Amendment (the 'Protocol') to include the Trade

Facilitation Agreement in the WTO family of agreements. The General Council was mandated to meet no later than 31 July 2014 to adopt the Protocol drawn up by the Preparatory Committee.[49] The circumstances under which this deadline could not be adhered to by the WTO members is described in the next section.

9.9 India Blocks the TFA Protocol and Rocks the WTO: Breaking Ranks

How did the negotiations on the TFA Protocol and a permanent solution for food security progress in the post-Bali phase? Did WTO members comply with the promises made on these two issues at Bali? In this section we initially describe the contrasting pace of progress of the TFA Protocol and the food security issue. This provides the background for discussing the internal process in India prior to taking the decision of not supporting the TFA Protocol and the backlash against the country triggered by this decision.

9.9.1 TFA Protocol Races Ahead, Food Security Barely Off the Start Line

Within no time after the Christmas break in 2013, the proponents of the TFA urged the WTO members to 'roll up their sleeves and get into the trenches' for completing the formalities related to the Protocol for making the TFA a legal text of the WTO. In parallel, work was expected to be undertaken for arriving at a permanent solution to the problem of food security. However, deliberations at the WTO during January–June 2014 clearly showed that while the Protocol for the TFA was galloping, there was almost no engagement on the issue of food security. By the first week of May, WTO members had concluded the legal review of the TFA. India and a few other countries started apprehending that the commitment of the USA and other prominent players to work towards a permanent solution was weakening.[50]

India was left in little doubt that the USA had almost no intention of engaging constructively on this issue, after the latter made a submission proposing elements of a work programme, which would provide the basis for making recommendations regarding a permanent solution.[51] Short of questioning the Bali Peace Clause, through the submission, the USA articulated that public stockholding was only one tool used to address food security. The US view was that disciplines regarding public stockholding were already addressed in the AOA. This was a pointer that it was not willing to negotiate new rules on this issue. It also proposed the following: developing a set of best practices for food security policies, including public stockholding; identifying policies that promote trade liberalization and food security as broadly as possible for all Members; and establishing an exhaustive list of notification and monitoring procedures. The suspicion that the USA was resorting to the time-tested strategy of impeding progress on an issue of interest to developing countries by spinning a spider's web around it might not have been without some basis.

India's anxiety was heightened by another development. Some influential scholars on WTO issues scrutinized the Bali Peace Clause and raised questions regarding its legal validity.[52] Some others came to the conclusion that it would not remain operative after the XI Ministerial Conference of the WTO. In other words, its validity was limited to four years. Thus, India found itself buffeted from all sides—no progress on a permanent solution and doubts about the legal status and duration of the Bali Peace Clause. With the meeting of the General Council for giving finishing touches to the TFA Protocol already scheduled to be held in the first week of July 2014, yet again India found itself pushed into a corner and unable to take the negotiations on public stockholdings forward in line with its interest. While prior to the Bali Ministerial Conference it was the CSOs that had jolted the government into taking a firm stand, in June 2014 the momentum to carry forward India's agenda on public stockholding emerged from within the government.

9.9.2 Linkage Between TFA and Public Stockholding Explicitly Established

Within a couple of months after the Bali Ministerial Conference, J.S. Deepak took charge of India's WTO negotiation, as the Additional Secretary in India's Department of Commerce. He quickly reviewed the developments after Bali Ministerial Conference and was left with no illusion about the fate of the negotiations for a permanent solution, if the TFA Protocol was approved by the General Council. He came to the conclusion that the key to making progress on food security lay in preventing the TFA Protocol from being approved by the General Council[53]—the textbook issue-linkage.

Circumstances for implementing this audacious strategy appeared propitious. In May 2014, a new government, with a strong nationalist sentiment as its calling card, had been voted into power in India. It was reasonable to assume that the government may not be disinclined to take tough decisions, if it portrayed India as a strong nation willing to stand up for its interests on the global stage.[54] Another element in the decision matrix was that by forcefully taking up the issue of public stockholding and food security, the government would be 'able to buttress its credentials with the farmers—an important political compulsion at that time'.[55] In addition, the Principal Secretary to Prime Minister Modi, Nripendra Misra, had been closely involved in WTO negotiations about a decade ago. He could be relied upon to explain to the prime minister the rationale and necessity of blocking the TFA Protocol in order to protect India's scheme of public stockholding from legal challenges at the WTO.[56] Further, the growing political closeness between India and a prominent developed country that had compelled India to tone down its position on the food security issue during May–November 2013, was no longer a constraining factor.[57] Finally, Deepak had a reputation of not shrinking from taking calculated risks and altering the status quo. All these diverse strands coalesced into Deepak endorsing an internal note on what India should do on the issue of food security at the WTO. He strongly argued for India not supporting the TFA Protocol.

On receiving the note, Rajeev Kher, a veteran of many trade negotiations and who had by that time become India's Commerce Secretary, perceived the merits in Deepak's arguments, as well as the risks latent in his approach. He suggested that Deepak reflect on the risky strategy for another twenty-four hours. Within twenty-four hours, Deepak was back with the file and Kher readily endorsed his proposal for consideration of India's Commerce Minister.[58] What transpired between Deepak and the Commerce Minister has already been described in the opening paragraphs of this chapter. Not only did the minister approve the proposal for consideration of the prime minister's office, but also strengthened the statement that would be delivered by India blocking further progress on the TFA during the meeting of the Preparatory Committee on Trade Facilitation (PCTF) to be held in the first week of July.

In a strongly worded statement during the meeting of the PCTF held on 2 July, India mentioned that the pace of implementation of the Bali Decisions had been 'skewed heavily in favour of Trade Facilitation and virtually all other Decisions have been relegated to the background. This is unacceptable.' Providing a historical perspective, India further stated that in 'round after round, developing countries have been called upon to concede more and more, with little being offered in return. But hope springs eternal and it was with that which has spurred developing countries to set the past aside and continue to negotiate in good faith.' Delivering a hard punch, India stated: 'We are deeply concerned that the Ministerial Decision on Public stockholding for Food Security Purposes is getting sidelined. In this, and in other areas, instead of engaging in meaningful discussions, certain members have been attempting to divert attention to the policies and programmes of selected developing country members. The issues raised are in no way relevant to the core mandate that we have been provided in the Bali Decisions. . . . My delegation has expressed concern about the uneven pace of work at previous meetings of the PCTF but despite that the imbalance in progress has persisted for months. . . . Till we have an assurance that members will engage in negotiations in good faith for finding a permanent solution on public stockholding and other deliverables, especially those for the LDCs, India will find it difficult to join the consensus on the Protocol of Amendment.'[59] Through its statement India had explicitly linked inclusion of the TFA as a legal agreement of the WTO with progress on the issue of public stockholding.

In the subsequent meeting of the General Council held on 25 July, India reiterated its position of not supporting the TFA Protocol until its concerns on food security were addressed. The US response was equally hard hitting. Michael Punke, the US ambassador to the WTO minced no words and said that 'a small number of WTO members are indicating that they no longer stand by their commitments to implement the TFA . . . Today, we are extremely discouraged that a small handful of members in this organization are ready to walk away from their commitments at

Bali, to kill the Bali agreement, to kill the power of that good faith and goodwill we all shared, to flip the lights in this building back to dark.'[60] In parallel, Roberto Azevedo, the Director General of the WTO, gave a call to minister Sitharaman, perhaps to gauge the seriousness and resolve of India to pursue its approach to oppose the TFA Protocol. India's mission to the WTO conveyed to Azevedo that India's statement of 2 July was a well-considered decision of the government.[61]

In a last-ditch effort at salvaging the situation, towards the end of July Azevedo convened an informal meeting of the WTO's Trade Negotiating Committee. Perhaps he was under an impression that India might not stand firm, and if it were to be offered a face-saving option, it might back down. He suggested that India's concerns on food security could be addressed through a Chair's statement, which would include the following operative sentence: 'I would like to place on record that it is understood that, notwithstanding the objective of adopting a permanent solution on the issue of public stockholding for food security purposes by the 11th Ministerial Conference, the interim mechanism set out in WTO/MIN(13)/38 is to remain valid, subject to the terms of that Decision, until such time as a permanent solution is found.'[62] India found the proposal completely inadequate for addressing its concerns and rejected it without any hesitation.[63]

The 31 July deadline for adoption of the TFA Protocol passed without the impasse being broken. Predictably, India's approach elicited disbelief and dismay among many WTO members. Some countries, perhaps more out of optimism, hoped that eventually India would climb down as it had done on many occasions in the past. However, this was not to be, until its concerns of public stockholding were addressed. Before coming to that story, it is relevant to briefly recount the reaction in India to the TFA-food security logjam.

9.9.3 India Excoriated, but Stands Firm

As expected, India's decision to block the adoption of the TFA Protocol, raised a storm and triggered considerable adverse response. Yet, few could have apprehended the strong condemnation of India's action, at the international level as well as domestic. Some leading Indian industrialists belonging to a prominent business advocacy group, reached out to the government and urged a rethink of India's stand of opposing the TFA Protocol.[64] Whether this view was a result of an internal analysis by industry advocacy group of the likely impact on India of the TFA, or whether it was based on the narrative of 'US $1 trillion gains'[65] from the agreement, spun by the developed countries and widely publicized in many newspaper articles, may not be known. As the industry advocacy group is often perceived as an influential voice, its views on the TFA could not be completely ignored by the government. Further, India's decision of opposing the adoption of the TFA Protocol attracted considerable media attention, mostly critical of the government. Many of the screaming headlines lambasted the government for blocking a supposed $1 trillion trade deal.

Another alarming development was that a few influential personalities who were perceived to have the ear of the government were almost unsparing in their criticism of the government's decision not to support the TFA Protocol. To illustrate, a strident criticism of India's stand on TFA-food security imbroglio came from Surjit Bhalla, an economist. In two articles published in a leading newspaper, Bhalla expressed the opinion that by blocking the TFA at the WTO, India had made itself a laughing stock in the eyes of the world community.[66] Further, in these articles he castigated India's stand as being unprincipled. Had Bhalla been any other economist, his views may not have carried much weight with the government. However, his was an influential voice, which can be fathomed from the responsibilities that were subsequently entrusted to him. He was a member of the government's Economic Advisory Council. During 2018–19, he chaired the High-Level Advisory Group constituted by India's Commerce Minister for advising the government on India's future engagement in international trade. In 2019, Bhalla was appointed India's Executive Director at the International Monetary Fund. Despite the fact that Bhalla's harsh indictment of India's stand on the TFA appeared to have been based on flawed arguments and contained certain technical errors,[67] his views would have been listened to with considerable attention by the government.

Another prominent critic of the government's stand on the TFA was T.N. Srinivasan, a highly respected US-based economist of Indian origin. He had impeccable credentials and decades of active academic career in various universities in the USA in the area of policymaking and international trade. In a talk delivered on 2 September 2014 at a prominent think-tank in New Delhi, he lampooned the government for opposing the TFA. Further, his criticism of India's public food stockholding programme appeared to be based on an incomplete understanding of the relevant WTO provisions.[68] Some prominent agriculture economists, who were present in the meeting, pointed out the flaws in his reasoning and opinion. Perhaps keeping his age and past achievements in mind, they were rather polite to him. An anchor of a popular television show on economic issues witnessed the sad spectacle. She wondered loudly why Srinivasan had not pulled down the curtains on his public meetings for his own good.[69] Like Bhalla, Srinivasan too had the potential of influencing some high-level functionaries in the government.

The illustrations discussed above highlight how, despite using flawed reasoning riddled with technical errors, influential personalities could have swayed the government to change its approach. However, even in the face of mounting criticism and censure, the government held firm on its stand on the TFA Protocol. Its main concern was not the TFA, but the adverse impact on farmers, if the country was compelled to make changes to its scheme of procuring food stuff at administered prices. Now that India had succeeded in its primary objective of preventing adoption of the TFA Protocol, what plan did it have to secure its ends on the issue of food security? How was the issue finally resolved?

9.10 From Bali Peace Clause to a Perpetual Peace Clause: Rewriting the Script

After India rattled the WTO with its brinkmanship, the question foremost on the minds of many negotiators was whether India and the USA would find ways of getting off the brink or would they let matters drift and fall off the brink. In this section we discuss India's attempts at breaking the deadlock triggered by its approach on TFA, while seeking to take forward its agenda on food security. We focus on the following three crucial moves made by India, which eventually helped it to break the deadlock and also secure some of its negotiating objectives: explaining its position to some developing countries and soliciting their support on food security; leveraging the meeting between the leaders of India and USA to bring the issue of food security on the bilateral agenda; and taking the lead in bilateral negotiations with the USA in Geneva which eventually resolved the crisis. It needs to be mentioned that a small team of officials in the Department of Commerce comprising Rajeev Kher, Commerce Secretary, J.S. Deepak, Additional Secretary and Anu Mathai, Director, played an extremely crucial role in strategizing and securing India's negotiating objectives on this issue.

9.10.1 India Reaches Out to Other Countries

The issue of public stockholding for food security purposes was perceived by most WTO members to be an issue of interest mainly to India. India had not done much legwork in coordinating with other developing countries before pulling the plug on the TFA Protocol. In the wake of the deadlock in July 2014, India reached out to about a dozen developing countries,[70] which were implementing schemes similar to that of India, and sought their support. India also explained to them the reasons behind it blocking the TFA Protocol. This move was aimed at creating partnerships for pushing forward the agenda on food security. Unlike some occasions in the past, in August 2014 India's overture on this issue received a positive response from many countries. This strengthened India's hand and provided it some assurance that it was not fighting a lone battle. But more importantly, it was also aimed at helping some countries realize that not only were they in the same boat as India, but some of them were also in breach of the subsidy limit mandated by the AOA. This helped inject a sense of urgency for making progress on the issue of food security.

9.10.2 Engaging with the USA at the Highest Political Level

During internal discussions within the Indian government, it became clear that the issue of public stockholding was becoming an irritant in India–USA bilateral relations. India's Ministry of External Affairs was extremely keen that the Department of Commerce should utilize the bilateral summit between Prime Minister Modi of India and President Obama of the USA, scheduled to be held in September 2014, to resolve this issue. On its part, the Department of Commerce provided detailed briefing to key members of Prime Minister Modi's delegation so that India could push its stand on public stockholding and seek accommodation with the USA.[71]

India's preparatory actions yielded results. This was reflected in the following sentence in USA-India Joint Statement issued after the meeting between the two leaders: 'The leaders discussed their concerns about the current impasse in the World Trade Organization and its effect on the multilateral trading system, and directed their officials to consult urgently along with other WTO members on the next steps.'[72] After the leaders' bilateral summit, India's Ministry of External Affairs conveyed a clear message to the Department of Commerce: the USA would be willing to engage with India constructively on the issue of food security; do not let the problem fester; and negotiate quickly and wrap up the deal, before any complication arises in bilateral relations.[73]

9.10.3 Getting Off the Brink

Having opened a window through the leaders' bilateral summit, the onus was now on India to take forward the negotiations on the public stockholding issue. In pursuance of this, it was decided that India's officials would meet their US counterparts in Geneva. A delegation headed by J.S. Deepak carried out these negotiations in Geneva in October 2014. The USA, which was resistant to directly negotiating with India on this issue at Bali, and had lambasted it for flipping off the lights at the WTO, had suddenly become amiable in Geneva. Perhaps a direction from President Obama had done the trick.

Within forty-five minutes of the meeting between the two countries, a breakthrough was achieved. The USA agreed that the language of the Bali Peace Clause would be modified to clarify that its duration would extend beyond four years, if a permanent solution was not adopted by the XI Ministerial Conference. India also tried to dilute some of the conditions attached to the Bali Peace Clause. However, it did not succeed on this point. Nevertheless, securing certainty in the duration of the Bali Peace Clause, an issue that the USA had refused at Bali, was a big gain for

India. When news of this development was conveyed to the Commerce Secretary Kher, his instruction to the delegation in Geneva was clear—as long as you have succeeded on the duration of the Peace Clause, clinch the deal.[74]

What now remained to be done was to craft a suitable text for making the Bali Peace Clause permanent, until a permanent solution to the issue of public stockholding was adopted. This required a series of discussions with the USA and frequent exchange of drafts between the two countries. On this aspect, India's Ambassador to the WTO, Anjali Prasad, played a crucial role.[75] Eventually, on 27 November 2014, the General Council of the WTO adopted the decision on public stockholding for food security purposes,[76] with the following crucial paragraph:

> If a permanent solution for the issue of public stockholding for food security purposes is not agreed and adopted by the 11th Ministerial Conference, the mechanism referred to in paragraph 1 of the Bali Decision, as set out in paragraph 1 of this Decision, shall continue to be in place until a permanent solution is agreed and adopted.

Having secured its negotiating objective on the issue of food security, India had no reason to continue to oppose the TFA Protocol. Consequently, in the same meeting in which the decision on public stockholding was adopted, the General Council also adopted the TFA Protocol. Thus ended a remarkable episode in the history of multilateral trade negotiations. This was definitely an event for the ages and also worthy of analysis from the perspective of negotiating strategy.

9.11 Strategies Deployed by India

For almost one year, the USA had refused to constructively discuss the issue of food security with India. Yet, the USA conceded to India's core demand on this issue, within forty-five minutes of the meeting in Geneva in October 2014. Given the substantial asymmetry in political clout and economic prowess between the USA and India, this is definitely a unique instance of a relatively weaker party managing to change the behaviour of a stronger negotiating partner. India's success at the negotiating table on public stockholding issue highlights the power of taking calculated risks.

This episode also provides a salutary lesson—how a country can lose its way at the negotiating table by resorting to wrong strategies and tactics. What strategies did India pursue to achieve its negotiating objectives on the issue of food security? This question is at the centre of the discussion in this section.

9.11.1 Planning and Preparing

After witnessing the contrasting speed at which negotiations on trade facilitation and food security progressed in the post-Bali phase, the first and foremost priority for India was to plan and prepare for brinkmanship. What encouraged India's negotiators in this direction? What preparations were made and how did India manage its domestic constituencies?

9.11.1.1 Equipping negotiators with technical knowledge and analysis

The first step in planning and preparing for any negotiation is to constitute a team with all relevant technical competencies to assist and participate in it. In India, the tradition had generally been that government officials, mainly from the Department of Commerce and India's Permanent Mission to the WTO, would participate in WTO negotiations. There was some reluctance to involve non-government persons directly in the negotiations, or even in the preparatory work. This began to change in 2013. During the negotiations on public stockholding for food security purposes, the Department of Commerce directly involved an economist[77] at the Centre for WTO Studies, and a private lawyer[78] with expertise on WTO issues. The pivotal role played by the economist is described at relevant places in this section. The legal expert was available almost round the clock for drafting proposals and scrutinizing texts received from the USA, throughout the period of July–November 2014. Matching resources with requirements proved to be crucial during the post-Bali phase of negotiations on this issue. Both these non-government experts equipped India's negotiators with technical details and legal options, thereby enhancing the effectiveness of India's negotiating effort.

9.11.1.2 Knowing the needs of countries at the negotiating table

An important element in preparing for any negotiation is to understand the needs of others at the negotiating table, as well as one's own needs. A negotiator who makes a reasonable guess about what someone's needs are, stands a greater chance of success. During March–June 2014, India's negotiators made two assessments about the needs of countries at the negotiating table. These were crucial in underpinning the country's strategy of opposing the TFA Protocol for securing its negotiating objectives on food security.

First, India made an assessment of its own needs regarding the compliance of its scheme of public stockholding in future years with the obligations under the Agreement on Agriculture.[79] Based on a detailed and comprehensive number crunching by the economist at the Centre for WTO Studies, India's negotiators grasped that the country would need immunity from legal challenges to its scheme of public stockholding not immediately, but after four to five years. Given the ambiguity in the Bali Peace Clause, there was a danger that the USA might not countenance to India invoking the Peace Clause when the country would need it. Thus, the ambiguity regarding the duration of the Bali Peace Clause needed to be clarified.

The choice before India's negotiators was whether to obtain clarity on the Bali Peace Clause in 2014 itself, or to postpone the fight closer to the date when India would be at the risk of exceeding the WTO-mandated subsidy limit. The risk in postponing the battle to a later date was two-fold. There was no certainty that at a later date the USA would come to the negotiating table on this issue. Further, even if the USA were to agree to negotiate with India on it a few years down the line, the former would be in a position to drive an extremely hard bargain. With the breach of WTO subsidy limit round the corner, India would have been almost desperate to protect its public stockholding scheme from legal challenges. India's vulnerability on this issue would have provided the USA and some other countries an opportunity to extract disproportionately large concessions from it. Thus, the internal assessment of India's own needs pointed to the strategic choice of seeking a longer duration Peace Clause at the earliest, instead of living to fight the battle another day.[80] This is in sharp contrast to Maran's strategy at the final stages of the Doha Ministerial Conference, when he decided to compromise and left some battles to be fought another day.

India's officials also made an assessment of the needs of the developed countries. Their conclusion was that the USA was extremely keen, even desperate, to seal the deal on trade facilitation.[81] This provided the opening for India to aggressively push for its interest on food security.

9.11.1.3 Managing domestic constituencies

Having blocked the TFA Protocol, India's Department of Commerce had to rally other ministries to support this decision. Within a few days of taking this decision, India's Prime Minister Modi convened a meeting of the key ministers. During the meeting, the Department of Commerce explained to other ministries the reasons why India had taken the seemingly unpopular step of blocking the TFA Protocol. In particular, the risk of the public stockholding programme getting unravelled, if India did not succeed in securing a longer duration of the Bali Peace Clause, was repeatedly emphasized.[82] This point struck home. This crucial meeting was instrumental in ensuring that the entire government spoke in one voice on this issue, including in discussions with other countries at the political and official level.

How did the government deal with the strong criticism triggered by its decision on the TFA Protocol? Some officials of the Department of Commerce were candid in admitting their apprehensions that in the face of severe indictment in the media, the government might not remain firm in its decision to oppose the TFA Protocol.[83] To prevent any back-sliding, the Department of Commerce spared no efforts in reiterating the risk to India's public stockholding programme if the TFA Protocol was allowed to proceed ahead.[84] This strengthened the resolve of the government to stand firm in its opposition to the TFA, despite the adverse reaction from many countries.

There was another dimension to the problem of managing domestic constituencies, which can often pose forbidding challenges for trade negotiators. This can become a particularly difficult task, if one group of domestic stakeholders stand to benefit from a potential agreement, while another set of stakeholders would be adversely affected by it. There was no clear reason why an agreement on public stockholding for food security purposes per se would adversely affect the interests of key players in India's industrial sector. However, these stakeholders were critical of the government for blocking the TFA. Apparently, they had completely, and uncritically, swallowed the narrative of the TFA creating '$1 trillion gains' for the global economy. This was the main ground for their dissatisfaction with the government's decision to bend in favour of food security. Keeping the larger interest of food security in view, the Department of Commerce did not attach much importance to the criticism emerging from the industry in the country.[85]

9.11.2 Setting the Agenda at WTO Through Bilateral Talks

Agenda setting essentially involves jointly identifying the issues that would be discussed in greater detail during the subsequent phases of the negotiation. After India started seeking a peace clause with a duration longer than four years, the USA stopped engaging with it on the issue of food security. At the Bali Ministerial Conference, there was very little direct negotiation between these two countries on this issue. This was perhaps aimed at compelling India into folding on food security. The strategy of the USA was very clear—bury the issue by not engaging.

In the post-Bali phase, the real challenge before India was how to get the USA to start engaging constructively on this issue. India succeeded in this objective by first indulging in brinkmanship by blocking the TFA Protocol, and thereafter leveraging the bilateral summit between Prime Minister Modi and President Obama to get this issue back on the radar of the US trade negotiators. What factors played a role in deciding the strategy of using the bilateral meeting to resolve an irritant between the two countries at the WTO? Indian officials seem to have correctly guessed that in his quest for deepening political ties with the newly elected government in India, President Obama might be amenable to directing his trade negotiators to engage constructively with India on the issue of food security. Further, the keen interest of the USA in taking the TFA to its logical conclusion played an important part in India's calculus. India's officials also derived some assurance from the country's diplomats in Washington, who were confident that they had some leverage to get the officials of USTR back on to the negotiating table. In light of these factors, the key officials in the Department of Commerce decided that the only way to break the deadlock on food security was to get Prime Minister Modi to convey the importance of this issue for India directly to the US president in their bilateral summit meeting held in September 2014.[86] As has already been recounted, this approach worked.

9.11.3 Framing Issues and Creating a Favourable Narrative

How a problem is framed by a party at the negotiating table, and also outside it, can influence how it is perceived by others. The technical issues behind the problem of public stockholding were fairly complex. As mentioned earlier, even T.N. Srinivasan, who was otherwise a brilliant economist, had failed to correctly grasp its basic details. Framing the issue in a manner that could be easily understood by political functionaries, researchers, and the media, was a challenge. India adopted the simple strategy of focusing on the core of the problem—fighting hunger, ensuring food security, and protecting livelihood of farmers. Thus framed, India's approach to the problem of public stockholding became easy to understand. This played a crucial role in countering pressures from some domestic constituencies, who were unhappy that the country had blocked a '$1 trillion trade deal' on trade facilitation. Further, the focus on food security proved to be instrumental in helping the CSOs in India, particularly those who were active in the areas of international trade and right to food, to raise awareness about this issue among certain key political leaders in India during the few crucial days preceding the Bali Ministerial Conference.

While the government was successful in framing the issue to make it easily comprehensible to even lay persons, on one aspect it fell a bit short. Despite the bad press that the government received on its approach to the TFA during July–November 2014, little attempt was made by it to put across its side of the story. It was only towards the end of August that the government started actively engaging with the media for explaining its point of view. Perhaps the government was too busy with parliamentary matters and coordinating its position with other countries, to bother about countering the highly critical narrative that had emerged in the media. An opportunity of putting the record straight and creating a narrative in favour of India's position on food security was lost.

9.11.4 Coalition Building

The entire episode of food security highlights the difficulties confronted by a country if it is compelled to pursue its negotiating objective almost single-handedly. Without the open backing of some developing countries, India's political weight at the negotiating table was a bit diminished. This was particularly evident during the negotiations in Geneva during the last few weeks preceding the Bali Ministerial Conference and at the Ministerial Conference itself. It is an irony that G-33, the coalition of developing countries active on issues related to food security and livelihood, failed to function as a cohesive unit when it was most required. The reasons for this could have been manifold.

First, some countries may have been reluctant to face the wrath of the USA by coming out openly in support of India. Second, a few others may not have felt the need to openly support India, as their calculation was that India would fight hard on its own on the issue of food security. At the same time, some countries were not confident that in the face of the strong negative response from the USA, India would be able to persist with its firm stand on this issue. Third, it is also likely that some countries were not fully aware that their public stockholding schemes were already in breach of the subsidy limit under the Agreement on Agriculture. Fourth, some countries within the G-33 perceived that their export interest in rice would be adversely affected if India secured a peace clause with a duration longer than four years. Fifth, Indonesia, the coordinator of G-33, remained mostly silent during the negotiations in Geneva and subsequently at Bali. The imperative of ensuring a 'successful outcome' of the Bali Ministerial Conference appears to have muted the voice of the host country in the negotiation on public stockholding. Sixth, some countries within the G-33 were of the view that India was being selfish in aggressively pushing for its interest on food security without being mindful about the impact of its actions on the overall multilateral trading system. Thus, despite its efforts at reaching out to the G-33 and other like-minded countries, India was almost left alone to fight the battle, whose outcome would have benefited many other developing countries.

In contrast to the period October–December 2013, during August–October 2014 India was more successful in its efforts at securing the support of some developing countries. The economist at the Centre for WTO Studies, whom the Department of Commerce closely involved in the developments on food security in the post-Bali phase, identified about a dozen developing countries that were implementing public stockholding programmes for food security purposes. He undertook a detailed calculation of the support provided by these countries through such schemes.[87] His research pointed out that the following countries were already breaching, or were likely to breach the WTO-mandated subsidy limits within a few years: China, Egypt, India, Indonesia, Jordan, Kenya, Pakistan, Tunisia, Zambia, and Zimbabwe. India used this research to approach many of these countries and seek their support. India also provided overwhelming evidence that could not be disputed by these countries. Perhaps they were convinced that their existing needs converged with those of India. The power of persuasive capacity, based on well-grounded research, was evidently at work.

Further, India blocking the movement on trade facilitation would have erased any lingering doubts in the minds of some countries that eventually India would back down. This, too, would have contributed to India's credibility with other developing countries. It is, therefore, not surprising that India received a positive response from most of them. Only if this support had come earlier, say at Bali Ministerial Conference, the path to an effective peace clause with a longer duration might have been less fraught with difficulties.

A final word on effectiveness, or lack of it, of coalitions is in order. The contrast between how the G-20 functioned relatively effectively, as already examined in detail in Chapter 8, while the G-33 almost withered away when the crunch time came, is really stark. What makes the contrast more telling is that the G-20 had to grapple with the diverse interests of Brazil and India on some issues. On the other hand, on the issue of food security the interests of the G-33 constituents appeared to almost converge and there was no obvious fault line. Perhaps at crucial junctures the G-33 could have benefited from the guiding hand of a minister such as Celso Amorim, seasoned in dynamics at the negotiating table, on top of technical details of the issues, persuasive in articulation and having the wisdom to strike compromises for the sake of retaining the cohesion of the coalition.

9.11.5 Leveraging Issue-Linkage

We now come to one of the two key aspects of India's strategy on public stockholding issue—issue-linkage. The relevance and utility of linking different issues to create leverage at the negotiating table has been discussed multiple times in earlier chapters of the book. During 2012–2014, India's fortunes on the issue of food security closely mirrored the 'strength' of the linkage between the TFA and food security. Let us see how this linkage evolved, and what were its consequences at the negotiating table.

The genesis of linkage between food security and the trade facilitation arose from an apprehension among India and a few other developing countries in 2012 that after the TFA had been harvested, the Doha Round would be declared to have been concluded. This apprehension triggered the tentative and informal link between the two separate issues. In order to keep the negotiations on trade facilitation on track, the developed countries started engaging on food security. Consequently, the latter issue witnessed some progress. However, during May–October 2013, mainly on account of larger geo-political considerations, India started stressing on the internal balance within the TFA. Not much was heard about linking the progress on this issue with that on food security. This period almost coincided with hardening of the US position on food security at the negotiating table, initially in Geneva and subsequently during the early days of the Bali Ministerial Conference. It would not be incorrect to conclude that, after June 2013, the zone of possible agreement on the issue of food security had considerably shrunk.

At the Bali Ministerial Conference, the developed countries had no incentive to accommodate India beyond the bare minimum that would allow it to save face on food security, while keeping it hooked at the negotiating table on trade facilitation. This was clearly reflected in the attitude of the USA, which refused to agree to an unambiguous language that could have provided assurance to India that the peace clause would be available even after four years, in case a permanent solution was not agreed by the XI Ministerial Conference of the WTO. The USA had correctly calculated that despite the ambiguous language on the duration of the peace clause, India would not block the finalization of the TFA at the Bali Ministerial Conference.

In the post-Bali phase, India's officials realized that they would be left with no bargaining chip for securing their negotiating objectives on food security, if the TFA Protocol were to be approved. This bargaining power had to be exercised while it existed. India managed to create a small window for addressing food security, after its statement during the meeting of the PCTF held on 2 July 2014 explicitly linked the two issues. Let us recall what India said in this meeting: 'Till we have an assurance that members will engage in negotiations in good faith for finding a permanent solution on public stockholding and other deliverables, especially those for the LDCs, India will find it difficult to join the consensus on the Protocol of Amendment.'[88] In order to prevent the deal on the TFA from slipping through its grasp, the USA was induced to get back to the negotiating table and adopt a more accommodative approach on the issue of public stockholding for food security.

Was issue-linkage at the end stage of the negotiations sufficient to help India obtain satisfaction on food security? There is no straightforward answer to this question. However, it is clear that issue-linkage was a necessary condition for India to secure its objectives on food security. Much of the progress that was witnessed on this issue at the negotiating table during 2012–13 was mainly on account of linkage of food security with trade facilitation. Further, during the crucial bilateral meeting between Prime Minister Modi and President Obama on 30 September 2014, the need for resolving the impasse at the WTO appears to have motivated Obama to soften the US opposition to India's stand on food security. Obama's approach went against the grain of the consistent stand of US trade negotiators during October 2013–July 2014, which can be pithily summarized as avoiding any constructive engagement on this issue. Had India not formally created the link between the two issues in July 2014, it is uncertain whether Obama would have been inclined to accommodate India's interest on food security.

While issue-linkage may have been a necessary condition, it was perhaps not a sufficient condition for India to obtain satisfaction on the public stockholding issue. In fact, the move to untie the negotiating knot commenced only after India suggested that the two sides meet in Geneva in October 2014. Had issue linkage been a sufficient condition for India's eventual success on the public stockholding issue, the deadlock would have elicited some offer from the USA for addressing the problem at the negotiating table. No such offer was forthcoming from the USA after India blocked the TFA Protocol on 2 July 2014. Thus, it may not be inaccurate to conclude that it was issue-linkage, in conjunction with other factors, which facilitated India in securing its negotiating objectives on the issue of public stockholding. But it is also a reality that without issue-linkage, the weight of the other factors might not have been sufficient to compel the USA to change its behaviour at the negotiating table and resolve the deadlock in India's favour.

9.11.6 Engaging at the Negotiating Table: Resorting to Brinkmanship

In addition to issue-linkage, the second key element of India's strategy on the public stockholding issue in the post-Bali phase was resorting to brinkmanship. By not engaging constructively in the negotiations on public stockholding issue during the post-Bali phase, the USA had burnt bridges behind India. Consequently, India was confronted with a likely scenario that its scheme of procuring food grains for public stockholding purposes might get unravelled a few years down the line. With the USA in no mood to address its concerns, India was left with no option other than resorting to brinkmanship. What exactly is brinkmanship?

Brinkmanship refers to the strategy of 'taking your opponent to the brink of disaster and compelling him to pull back'.[89] It essentially involves 'deliberately creating and manipulating the risk of mutually bad outcome in order to induce the other party to compromise'.[90] However, for brinkmanship to have the desired impact, the following conditions must be fulfilled: first, the threat must be perceived to be credible by the other party; second, the threatened party must be able to reduce the risk of the threat by agreeing to the terms of the brinkman; and third, both the parties must have the confidence that the other will comply with its side of the deal in order that they get off the brink. We discuss each of these three aspects below.

9.11.6.1 India establishes credibility of its stand

In the context of a strategy centred around brinkmanship, in order for the threat to be credible, other parties must have reasons to believe that the brinkman would follow it through. Otherwise, its action would fail to bring the desired result. More credible the perception of threat, more effective it will be in changing the behaviour of the opponents. If there is any dissonance between further actions and the threat, others may quickly call the bluff, thereby rendering the threat ineffective. By not supporting the TFA Protocol, India deliberately created the risk of the TFA falling apart. This was perhaps intolerable to the USA, which was eventually induced to change its behaviour. This change would have been unlikely if India had not been taken seriously by the USA and other countries. What enabled India to establish and maintain the credibility of its threat to prevent the TFA from becoming a multilateral agreement at the WTO during July–November 2014?

On multiple occasions after 2 July 2014, at important forums, both international and domestic, India made its stand on the TFA-food security issue amply clear. During the BRICS Trade Ministers meeting in Brazil on 14 July 2014 and at the G-20 Trade Ministers meeting in Sydney on 19 July 2014, India emphasized that it was seeking 'an equal level of commitment and progress'[91] on the two issues. Further, India refused to dilute its stand during the meetings held in New Delhi by John Kerry, the US Secretary of State, and Penny Pritzker, the US Commerce Secretary, with key Indian ministers in the last week of July 2014.

Credibility of India's stand got further bolstered when Nirmala Sitharaman made a detailed statement on the TFA-Food security logjam in the two houses of the Indian Parliament. Following extracts from her statement in the lower house of the Indian Parliament are instructive: 'The Bali outcomes were negotiated as package and must be concluded as such . . . A permanent solution on food security is a must for us and we cannot wait endlessly in a state of uncertainty while the WTO engages in an academic debate on the subject of food security which is what some developed countries seem to be suggesting before they are ready to engage on this important issue . . . India stood firm on its demand despite immense pressure. The Government of India is committed to protecting the interests of our farmers against all odds.'[92] By publicly committing the country to a particular course of action on the TFA-food security deadlock, she had bound herself from backsliding in future. If, after issuing the threat, India had backed off without achieving its objectives on the public stockholding issue, not only would there have been an uproar in the Indian Parliament, the country would also have lost on the following three counts: first, it would have lost the opportunity of securing any further gains on the food security issue; second, its credibility in the future would have taken a serious hit; and third, it would have suffered serious reputational damage. Declaring its inflexible position in the parliament should be viewed as a strategy of India to maintain the credibility of its threat to prevent the TFA from coming into force.

9.11.6.2 USA reduces the risk by agreeing to India's core concern

For brinkmanship to be effective, it is important that the threatened party reduces the risk of falling off the brink by agreeing to the brinkman's wishes. We have already discussed how in a bilateral meeting between India and the USA in Geneva in October 2014, it took less than forty-five minutes for the deadlock to get resolved. In this meeting, in almost no time the USA agreed to India's core demand that the Bali Peace Clause should remain valid even beyond four years, if a permanent solution is not found by the XI Ministerial Conference of the WTO. After the meeting, India would have perceived the first whiff of success resulting from its brinkmanship. However, the final step remained to be taken, before the two countries could back off from the brink and the deadlock considered to have been finally resolved.

9.11.6.3 Ensuring that both parties comply with their side of the deal

After India and the USA agreed to the Permanent Peace Clause on the issue of public stockholding for food security purposes, India had no reason to oppose the TFA Protocol. The way forward required two separate decisions—one on the Perpetual Peace Clause and the other on the TFA Protocol—being adopted by the General Council of the WTO. However, the WTO members were confronted with two tricky problems—between food security and the TFA Protocol, on which issue should the decision be adopted first; and how would it be ensured that after the decision on the first issue had been adopted there would be no opposition to the adoption of the decision on the second issue?

At the crux of the two problems was how to reduce mutual suspicion between India and the USA and avoid unravelling of trust between them.

What might have helped both sides in upholding their side of the deal was the realization that the cost of reneging on the commitments would be very high for the country reckless enough to indulge in it. The two countries found an innovative solution to the problem. In the first step, the Chairman of the General Council drew the attention of the WTO Members to the proposed decisions on the two issues. Thereafter, as part of the formal action by the General Council, he proposed simultaneous adoption of the decisions on public stockholding for food security purposes and the TFA Protocol. Through this carefully choreographed set of actions, he ended the high drama triggered by India's resort to brinkmanship.

9.12 Conclusions

Success in negotiation is about changing the behaviour of a party who has something that another party desires. As discussed in detail in this chapter, what India sought was the flexibility to insulate its scheme of public stockholding for food security purposes from legal challenges by other WTO members. Further, it was not in its interest that the flexibility be limited to merely four years. It required this flexibility for a longer period, particularly when the subsidy on account of procurement of rice would exceed the 10 per cent limit, as mandated by the AOA. The ambiguous language on the duration of the Bali Peace Clause did not provide it the assurance that the flexibility would be available when it would be needed. As events turned out, it was in 2020 that India was required to invoke the Permanent Peace Clause,[93] at a time when the four-year peace clause might not have been in force.

At the negotiating table, for almost two years, the USA refused to agree to India's demand on this issue. With India pushed into a corner, and the risk of the scheme of procurement of food grains for public stockholding purposes getting unravelled within a few years, the audacious twin strategies involving issue-linkage and brinkmanship emerged. These strategies, in conjunction with certain propitious political circumstances, helped India succeed in securing its negotiating objectives on the issue of public stockholding for food security purposes. By increasing the cost for the USA of not engaging constructively at the negotiation on public stockholding issue, India was able to get its way. Many lessons on negotiating strategy stand out from this episode.

First, this episode demonstrates the crucial role of suitable strategies in determining the outcomes at the negotiating table. Initially, India gainfully deployed the strategy of issue-linkage to advance its interests on food security. However, some time towards June 2013, India unwittingly abandoned this strategy and consequently lost its way at the negotiating table. After it resorted to this strategy again in July 2014, it succeeded in securing some of its negotiating objectives.

Second, India's success crucially hinged on a calculated resort to brinkmanship. India took the first step in pursuance of this strategy, when it opposed the adoption of the TFA Protocol in July 2014. At that stage, its negotiators did not have a detailed game plan for the next steps in this strategy. Planning and implementation of the strategy evolved during the subsequent few weeks after the first step was taken. While conventional wisdom would suggest that a party should be ready with a detailed blueprint of action before implementing a strategy as risky as brinkmanship, India went against the grain and yet it succeeded.

Third, the most audacious strategies emerge when a party finds itself pushed into a corner. There are two important lessons from this. For the course of negotiations to run without bumps and deadlocks, it is in the overall interest of the parties at the negotiating table not to ignore specific interests of another party that are sensitive to a large segment of its domestic constituency. Further, if a party is pushed into a corner, others at the negotiating table must be prepared for the former to respond with a daring counter-move, which might even wreck the chances of a deal.

Fourth, a window of opportunity does not last forever. It must be seized as expeditiously as possible. After the bilateral meeting between Prime Minister Modi and President Obama had created a window of opportunity on food security, India's Ministry of External Affairs gave succinct advice to the country's trade negotiators—seize the moment and strike the deal within a month. If the problem had festered for too long, there was a risk that the goodwill created between the leaders of the two countries might not have been enough to overcome the opposition to the deal from the powerful agriculture lobby in the USA. In retrospect, a quick deal might have prevented the domestic agriculture lobby from fully exerting its influence on the White House. This is not idle speculation. The former US ambassador to the WTO, Michael Punke, is supposed to have confessed that the agriculture stakeholders in the USA had not forgiven the government for conceding too much to India on the issue of food security.[94]

Fifth, how the dilemma faced by negotiators—when to resist and when to yield—was resolved, holds important lessons. During the negotiations in Geneva on the issue of public stockholdings, held during October–November 2013, India was confronted with a difficult choice. It could have either completely rejected the text, which had proposed a peace clause for four years; or accepted the text with some reservation. India decided not to resist on this issue and instead chose to yield. If India had rejected the text, there was a risk that the issue might not even have remained at the negotiating table during the Bali Ministerial Conference. Thus, the narrow window of opportunity for striking a deal would have been lost. India chose to yield prior to the Bali meeting, and thereby provided itself an opportunity of living to fight another day.

Another crucial occasion when India's trade negotiators were confronted with the resisting versus yielding dilemma, but with a slight variation, was during the negotiations in Geneva during October–November 2014. Apart from seeking to remove the ambiguity about the duration of the Bali Peace Clause, India's negotiators had a few additional demands on this issue. However, after addressing India's core concern on the duration of the Bali Peace Clause, the USA was completely reluctant to provide any satisfaction to India on the other issues. The choice before India's negotiators was to continue to push the envelope further on the other issues, or remain satisfied with the success on its core demand. Given the imperative to wrap up the deal quickly, India chose not to push its interest on the other issues.

Overall, during July–October 2014 India took considerable risk and refused to move ahead on trade facilitation until it had secured clarity that the Bali Peace Clause would be available beyond four years, in case a permanent solution was not finalized by XI Ministerial Conference of the WTO. It ran the risk of being blamed for rocking the unsteady boat of multilateral trade negotiations. By resorting to brinkmanship, India broke ranks with other countries and rewrote the script. Consequently, it succeeded in securing the rules which it had desired for fighting hunger and poverty. After being at the receiving end of the criticism in July 2014 that it had flipped the lights at the WTO back to dark, the outcome of India's subsequent actions would have lit the lives of millions of people surviving in hunger and poverty.

Notes

1. Interview with J.S. Deepak, a former senior official of India's Department of Commerce, July 2021.
2. Interview with J.S. Deepak, a former senior official of India's Department of Commerce, July 2021.
3. Interview with J.S. Deepak, a former senior official of India's Department of Commerce, July 2021.
4. Interview with J.S. Deepak, a former senior official of India's Department of Commerce, July 2021.
5. This quote is popularly attributed to Mahatma Gandhi.
6. Revised US notification to the Committee on Agriculture, WTO document G/AG/N/USA/51/Rev.1 dated 28 January 2009.
7. US notification to the Committee on Agriculture, WTO document G/AG/N/USA/169 dated 29 August 2023.
8. Olivier De Schutter, 'The Power of Procurement. Public Purchasing in the Service of Realising the Right to Food', 2014. De Schotter was the United Nations Special Rapporteur on the Right to Food.
9. Sachin K. Sharma, *The WTO and Food Security Implications for Developing Countries* (Singapore: Springer, 2016), 12–13.
10. See paragraph 4 of Annex 2 of the Agreement on Agriculture.
11. Article 20 of the AOA provided a mandate for negotiations for continuing the reform process of agriculture.
12. Submission by India to the Committee on Agriculture Special Session, Negotiations on WTO Agreement on Agriculture, proposals by India in the areas of: (i) Food Security, (ii) Market Access, (iii) Domestic Support, and (iv) Export Competition, WTO document G/AG/NG/W/102, dated 15 January 2001.
13. Paragraph 13 of the Doha ministerial Declaration, adopted on 13 November 2001, WTO document WT/MIN(01)/DEC/1 dated 20 November 2001.
14. Doha Work Programme, Decision Adopted by the General Council on 1 August 2004 paragraph 39, WTO Document WT/L/579 dated 2 August 2004.
15. Submission by the African Group to the Committee on Agriculture Special Sessions, Special and differential treatment for developing countries, WTO document JOB (02)/187.
16. WTO document TN/AG/W/4/Rev.4 dated 6 December 2008.

17. Interview with a former high-level trade negotiator of India, April 2020.
18. Interview with Jayant Dasgupta, former ambassador of India to the WTO, July 2020.
19. Interview with Jayant Dasgupta, former ambassador of India to the WTO, July 2020.
20. The G-33 coalition of developing countries sought to protect food security, farm livelihoods, and rural development in the Doha Round negotiations.
21. G-33 Submission to the Committee on Agriculture Special Sessions titled Proposal on some elements of TN/AG/W/4/Rev.4 for early agreement to address food security issues, WTO document JOB/AG/22 dated 13 November 2012.
22. Interview with Jayant Dasgupta, former ambassador of India to the WTO, July 2020.
23. Interview with Jayant Dasgupta, former ambassador of India to the WTO, July 2020.
24. Interview with Jayant Dasgupta, former ambassador of India to the WTO, July 2020.
25. Interview with a former high-level trade negotiator of India, April 2020.
26. Interview with a former high-level trade negotiator of India, April 2020.
27. Interview with a former senior official in India's Department of Commerce, October 2021.
28. Interview with a former high-level trade negotiator of India, April 2020.
29. Interview with a former Indian ambassador to the WTO, April 2020.
30. G-33 Submission to the Committee on Agriculture Special Sessions, WTO document JOB/AG/25 dated 3 October 2013.
31. Interview with a former senior official of India's Department of Commerce, October 2021.
32. Trade Negotiations Committee document, Public Stockholding for food security purposes, WTO document JOB/TNC/29, dated 25 November 2013.
33. Interviews with Devinder Sharma and other representatives of civil society organizations in India working in the areas of international trade and food security, January–June 2021.
34. This assessment of the civil society organizations and farmers' groups proved to accurate. India would eventually need to invoke the Bali Peace Clause in March 2020, a few years beyond the four-year period that was mandated by the provisional peace clause agreed in Geneva a few days prior to the Bali Ministerial Conference.
35. Interview with Devinder Sharma, a prominent representative of civil society organization in India working in the area of international trade and agriculture, February 2021.
36. Letter no. BA/ARD/2013 dated 22 November 2013 from Basudev Acharia, Chairman of the Committee on Agriculture (Lok Sabha), addressed to Dr. Manmohan Singh, Prime Minister of India. Copy of the letter is in the possession of the author.

37. Letter dated 23 November 2013 from Shanta Kumar, Chairman of the Parliamentary Standing Committee on Commerce, addressed to Dr. Manmohan Singh, Prime Minister of India. Letter in the possession of the author.
38. Interview with a representative of civil society organization in India working in the area of international trade, January 2021.
39. Interview with Biraj Patnaik, a prominent representative of civil society organizations in India and formerly the Principal Advisor to the Commissioners of the Indian Supreme Court in the right to food case, June 2021.
40. Interview with a former trade negotiator from a developing country, September 2020.
41. Interview with a former high-level trade negotiator of India, April 2020.
42. Interview with a former high-level trade negotiator of India, April 2020.
43. Interview with a former trade negotiator from a developing country, September 2020.
44. This episode is based on interview with Rob Davies, former Minister of Trade and Industry South Africa, January 2021.
45. Interview with Rajeev Kher, a former senior official in India's Department of Commerce, December 2021.
46. Interview with Rajeev Kher, a former senior official in India's Department of Commerce, December 2021.
47. Interview with Rajeev Kher, a former senior official in India's Department of Commerce, December 2021.
48. WTO Ministerial Decision of 7 December 201, Public Stockholding for Food Security Purposes, WTO document WT/MIN(13)/38 dated 11 December 2013.
49. WTO Ministerial Decision of 7 December 2013, Agreement on Trade Facilitation, WTO document WT/MIN(13)/36 dated 11 December 2013.
50. Interview with J.S. Deepak, a former senior official in India's Department of Commerce, July 2021.
51. Communication from the USA to the Committee on Agriculture, Elements for a Work Program on Food Security dated 15 July 2014, WTO document G/AG/W/134.
52. See for example Christian Haberli, 'After Bali: WTO Rules Applying to Public Food Reserves', FAO Commodity and Trade Policy Research Working Paper no. 46, 2014.
53. Interview with J.S. Deepak, a former senior official of India's Department of Commerce, July 2021.
54. Interview with a former official of India's Department of Commerce, September 2021.
55. Interview with a former senior official in India's Department of Commerce with the author.
56. Interview with a former official of India's Department of Commerce, September 2021.

57. Interview with a former official of India's Department of Commerce, September 2021.
58. Interview with Rajeev Kher, a former Commerce Secretary of India, December 2021.
59. Statement by India at the meeting of WTO Preparatory Committee on Trade Facilitation held on 2 July 2014, in the author's possession.
60. Kanaga Raja, 'General Council Suspended, Lack of Consensus on TF Protocol', *SUNS- South North Development Monitor* No. 7853, 28 July 2014.
61. Interview with a former senior official of India's Department of Commerce, October 2021.
62. Interview with a former senior official of India's Department of Commerce, October 2021.
63. Interview with a former senior official of India's Department of Commerce, October 2021.
64. Interview with an official of a prominent industry advocacy group in India, September 2020.
65. International Chamber of Commerce, Payoff from the World Trade Agenda, Gary C. Gary Hufbauer and Jeffrey Schott, Washington D.C.: *Peterson Institute for International Economics*, 2013.
66. Surjit Bhalla, 'A Principled Congress Stance at the WTO?' *The Indian Express*, 29 July 2014; and Surjit Bhalla, 'In the Name of India, Why?' *The Indian Express*, 31 July 2014.
67. The methodology adopted by Surjit Bhalla for concluding that India's food production policies were not WTO compliant was at complete variance with what has been mandated in the AOA.
68. Interview with Sachin Sharma, Associate Professor at the Centre for WTO Studies, who was present in this meeting, July 2023.
69. The author was present in this meeting and witnessed its deliberations.
70. Interview with an Indian government official involved in agriculture negotiations, May 2020.
71. Interview with a former senior official of India's Department of Commerce, October 2021.
72. US-India Joint Statement dated 30 September 2014.
73. Interview with a former senior official of India's Department of Commerce, October 2021.
74. This paragraph is based on interview with J.S. Deepak, a former senior official of India's Department of Commerce, July 2021.
75. Interview with a former official in India's Department of Commerce, October 2020.
76. Public Stockholding for Food Security Purposes, Decision of 27 November 2014 adopted by the General Council, WTO document WT/L/939 dated 28 November 2014.
77. Dr Sachin Kumar Sharma, Associate Professor at the Centre for WTO Studies.

78. Anuradha R.V., Partner, Clarus Law Associates.
79. Interview with J.S. Deepak, a former senior official of India's Department of Commerce, July 2021.
80. Interview with J.S. Deepak, a former senior official of India's Department of Commerce, July 2021.
81. Interview with J.S. Deepak, a former senior official of India's Department of Commerce, July 2021.
82. Interview with a former senior official in India's Department of Commerce, November 2021
83. Interview with a former senior official in India's Department of Commerce, November 2021.
84. Interview with a former senior official in India's Department of Commerce, November 2021.
85. Interview with a former senior official in India's Department of Commerce, November 2021.
86. Paragraph is based on interview with a former senior official of India's Department of Commerce, October 2021.
87. The research was subsequently published in the following book: Sharma, *The WTO and Food Security.*
88. Statement by India at the meeting of WTO Preparatory Committee on Trade Facilitation held on 2 July 2014, available with the author.
89. Avinash K. Dixit and Barry J. Nalebuff, *Thinking Strategically: The Competitive Edge in Business, Politics, and Everyday Life* (New York and London: W.W. Norton and Company, 1991), 205.
90. Dixit and Nalebuff, *Thinking Strategically*, 206.
91. Statement by Nirmala Sitharaman in Lok Sabha regarding India's stand in the WTO, 5 August 2014.
92. Statement by Nirmala Sitharaman in Lok Sabha regarding India's stand in the WTO, 5 August 2014.
93. See India's notification to WTO Committee on Agriculture invoking the Permanent Peace Clause for the year 2018–2019, WTO document G/AG/N/IND/18 dated 31 March 2020.
94. Interview with a former senior official of India's Department of Commerce, October 2021.

10
Concluding Thoughts on Negotiating Strategies

10.1 Introduction

Despite the attempt of this book to simplify strategies in GATT and WTO negotiations and analyse them in a systematic manner, what emerges is a complicated picture. It is not always easy to identify which specific strategy was deployed in a particular setting. With countries deploying multiple strategies simultaneously for securing their objectives, disentangling the strategies can prove to be a challenge. What confounds the analysis is the reality that resort to a particular strategy, say divide and prosper, may require a country to deploy many secondary strategies, such as making side payments or using the carrot-and-stick strategy. To add another layer of difficulty, deployment of certain strategies, such as the Quisling strategy, may be so well concealed that it becomes hard to discern their existence. Further, it may not always be possible to attribute the success of a country at the negotiating table exclusively to a specific strategy. As seen in the episode related to food security, it was the twin strategy of issue linkage and brinkmanship, in conjunction with propitious external circumstances, that created the grounds for success in negotiations. What could constitute the 'propitious external circumstances' for a strategy to succeed may be hard to predict.

Notwithstanding the complications in analysing strategies, in the concluding chapter we discuss some implications for practice and theory of the negotiating episodes discussed in the book. Without any formal training in negotiations, most trade diplomats in developing countries

Strategies in GATT and WTO Negotiations. Abhijit Das, Oxford University Press. © Abhijit Das 2025.
DOI: 10.1093/9780198934431.003.0010

have to rely on their inherent skills, and on-the-job learning. An understanding of negotiating dynamics and strategies will help make negotiators more effective at the negotiating table. This book can prove to be a valuable resource for trade diplomats. Further, limitations of formal theories at the abstract level get revealed when confronted with the realities in some of the negotiating episodes analysed in this book. This could provide important clues to academics for revising some of the theoretical frameworks related to negotiations.

The subsequent sections of this chapter proceed as follows. Section 10.2 makes the basic point that choosing the appropriate strategy matters in GATT/WTO negotiations. The effectiveness of strategies is likely to be context-specific; the same strategy used in different stages of a negotiation might not yield similar outcomes. Relying on strategies suggested by ancient scholars in the context of wars between kingdoms, Section 10.3 provides an overview of the key points a strategic trade negotiator should keep in mind. Among the various strategies analysed in this book, two stand out. First, the role of coalition among some developing countries in countering the asymmetry in economic and political power at the negotiating table is well documented in academic literature. Section 10.4 briefly discusses a comprehensive theory explaining the effectiveness of coalitions. Based on the experience of the G-20 coalition in Agriculture negotiations, coalition against the Singapore Issues and the coalition on the TRIPS waiver, this section proposes ways to bridge a crucial gap in the theory. Second, as discussed in Chapter 4, in recent years forum shifting has emerged as the core strategy of the developed countries to meet their objectives in non-trade areas, such as labour and environment. This strategy also appears to be effective in countering coalitions and opposition of developing countries in non-trade areas. Academic literature on this strategy is rather limited — much of what is available centres around the two broad forms of forum shifting, horizontal and vertical forum shifting. These forms of forum shifting have been examined mainly in the context of norm setting for protection of intellectual property rights. Section 10.5 discusses some of the emerging trends in forum shifting, which need to be taken into account for developing a comprehensive theory on this issue in the future. Subsequently, Section 10.6 provides some overall conclusions.

10.2 Choice of Strategy Matters

The various negotiating episodes discussed in the book highlight the role of strategy in countries securing their objectives in GATT and WTO negotiations. While strategy matters in negotiations, the wisdom to choose the strategy which is most suited to the state of play at the negotiating table is equally important. A strategy that results in success at a particular stage of a negotiation may prove to be counter-productive at another stage. In the episode related to the food security issue, as discussed in Chapter 9, India resorted to brinkmanship in July 2014, which was almost the final stage of the negotiations. Had it resorted to brinkmanship at an earlier stage, say during 2013 when the Trade Facilitation Agreement (TFA) was not close to finalization, it is unlikely that the country could have created the leverage for achieving satisfaction on food security. The possibility cannot be ruled out that India's action would have been dismissed by others at the negotiating table as being petulant and not worthy of serious consideration. Further, resort to brinkmanship at a premature stage would not have provided any assurance that India would achieve its negotiating objectives on food security at a later stage. It was only after the TFA had reached the final stages that the USA and other developed countries became almost desperate to take this agreement to its logical conclusion. As this desperation is likely to have been less at the earlier stages of the negotiations on trade facilitation, brinkmanship would have not brought any significant results for India.

A strategy that may be useful in one context might not yield the desired result in another context. As discussed in Chapter 8, the G-20 took the strategic decision to actively engage on agriculture issues at the negotiating table. This was in sharp contrast to Maran's strategic choice of not engaging with the developed countries on the four Singapore Issues, a theme of discussion in Chapter 7. Both the strategies proved to be very effective for the concerned developing countries. The explanation of success of the two divergent strategies lies in the fact that while reduction of domestic support in the Agriculture negotiations was part of the positive agenda of G-20 where the USA-EU would have had to make concessions, Maran had completely defensive concerns on Singapore Issues. Just as Maran would have been happy in seeing no forward movement on Singapore Issues, the duo of the developed countries would have been satisfied with a mere cosmetic movement on agriculture domestic support. Opposite interests in the two situations demanded strategies at the extreme ends of the negotiating spectrum. Thus, which strategy to deploy when should be an important consideration for trade negotiators.

10.3 Learning from Ancient Wisdom on Strategies Related to War

What are some of the key lessons on strategies for trade negotiators? This section seeks to provide an answer to this question by drawing on the wisdom of ancient scholars, offered primarily in the context of war, and melding it with the experience at the GATT/WTO negotiating table. The role of strategy in warfare was recognized by the Chinese scholar Sun Tzu who observed that the general who wins a battle makes many calculations in his mind before the battle is fought, while the general who loses a battle makes but few calculations beforehand. Thus, by paying attention to the calculations made prior to the battle it can be foreseen who is likely to win or lose.[1] It is interesting to note that winning a battle by using appropriate strategies and without losing a single man has been considered to be superior to winning by fighting.[2] This highlights the importance of strategy in warfare. Kautilya, the ancient Indian savant of statecraft identified four broad strategies in warfare—saam (to convince and conciliate with reasons), daam (to placate with gifts), dand (to threaten with punishment), and bhed (divide and conquer).[3] These are also at the core of most of the strategies used in multilateral trade negotiations at the GATT and the WTO.

Undertaking detailed preparation prior to a negotiation is an important part of any negotiating strategy. What should be the fundamental elements of the preparation? Military strategy provides us an answer. If a general knows the enemy and himself, he need not fear the result of a hundred battles; a general will suffer defeat in every battle if he knows neither himself nor the enemy.[4] This rings true in the context of multilateral trade negotiations. A negotiator should have adequate technical knowledge of the issues at the table and their implications for his country, as well as a deep understanding of his country's positive interest and defensive agenda in the negotiations. Further, the negotiator must have a grasp of the political dynamics of the negotiations and should anticipate problems and be ready with solutions even before a contingency arises. A good illustration of this aspect of preparation for negotiations is how India's Commerce Minister, Murasoli Maran, anticipated that the developed countries would seek to undermine his tough stance on Singapore Issues by approaching India's prime minister, and the actions taken by him to preserve the country's negotiating position on these issues. In addition, the negotiator should have a reasonable understanding of the interests and strategies of other key players in the negotiation. Thus, a negotiator who undertakes a systematic and reasonable assessment of needs, stands a greater chance of success.

An important question that confronts a trade negotiator is whether to make a move or wait for others to move first. By making the first move a negotiator seeks to anchor the negotiations around her proposal. However, in order to make the first move, the negotiator must have clarity about her objectives in the negotiation, urgency to achieve the objectives and the technical capacity to put its point across. In this context, warfare strategy offers the following pithy advice: 'If it is to your advantage, make a forward move; if not, stay where you are.'[5] This advice is relevant not only for making a negotiating proposal, but also in situations of deadlocks at the negotiating table. In such situations, in order to take the negotiations forward, it is not uncommon for some developing countries to grant one-sided concessions. Often this leads to demands for more concessions and does not help these countries in securing their negotiating objectives. By paying heed to this pithy advice, on many occasions trade negotiators can prevent unfavourable drift in the negotiations on issues of their interest.

When should a negotiator dig in her heels and continue to resist? When should she yield and compromise? Trade negotiators have to frequently grapple with this dilemma. There are no easy answers to these questions. Resisting too long runs the risk of the country getting ignored and having to live with the worst possible outcome. Yielding early may diminish the possibility of raising the stakes and striking a more favourable bargain at a later stage. While grappling with similar questions, Kautilya had the following suggestion, which is relevant for trade negotiators: 'One should neither submit spinelessly nor sacrifice oneself in foolhardy valour. It is better to adopt such policies as would enable one to survive and live to fight another day.'[6] While in certain situations compromise may be preferable, the savant has the following piece of advice that is relevant for continuing to resist: 'If benefits accruing to kings under a treaty, irrespective of their status as the weaker, equal or stronger king, is fair to each one, peace by agreement shall be the preferred course; if the benefits are to be distributed unfairly, war is preferable.'[7] On the resist versus yield question, Sun Tzu's insight that the general, who knows when to fight and when not to fight, will win, is also applicable to GATT and WTO negotiations.[8]

How does a powerful country keep reluctant countries hooked to the negotiating table, particularly if concessions have to be extracted from the latter? Kautilya recommends that a king should consider accepting 'a small immediate gain for the sake of a large future benefit in order to prevent the success of the enemy's undertakings.'[9] The declaration on access to affordable medicines,[10] an issue of perceived benefit for a large number of developing countries, was the bait which prevented India from walking from the negotiating table and became an important factor in India's decision to withdraw its reservations to the launch of the Doha Round of multilateral trade negotiations in November 2001. By granting a victory to the developing countries on the issue of access to medicine, the developed countries hoped for a large future benefit from the Doha Round. This issue has been discussed in considerable detail in Chapter 7.

How can a weaker country extract concessions from the powerful? Issue linkage is one of the strategies commonly used by many developing countries to secure their negotiating objectives. The reader may recall how India secured satisfaction on the issue of food security by explicitly linking it with the issue of trade facilitation. Wisdom contained in the advice to the military general to seize something which the enemy holds dear in order to make it amenable to the general's designs appears equally relevant for trade negotiators.[11]

Forming coalitions with like-minded countries is another strategy used by many developing countries to promote their interests in the GATT and the WTO negotiations. How should countries choose partners for creating effective coalitions at the negotiating table? Kautilya offers the following simple, but highly pertinent, suggestion regarding the qualities of an ideal ally: a friend of the family for a long time, constant, amenable to control, powerful in his support, sharing a common interest, able to mobilize his forces quickly, and not a man who double-crosses his friends.[12] Viewed from a contemporary lens, a potential coalition partner must have amicable political ties for many years with the prime movers of the coalition, should lend a sympathetic ear to the concerns of the coalition and have common interests in the negotiation, be willing to subject itself to the disciplines of the coalition, possess technical skills to support the coalition, provide unstinting support to it and not defect to the other side at the first sight of inducement. The last point is particularly relevant, as the experience of many coalitions at the GATT and the WTO, including the G-20 coalition in Agriculture negotiations, suggests that the developed countries have not been hesitant in breaking coalitions arrayed against them by either using coercive strategies or by making side payments in the form of negotiating free trade agreements with the countries who abandon a coalition. The strategy of breaking coalitions, as well as the divide and prosper strategy, are in line with the advice provided by Sun Tzu to separate the enemy's forces and split them into factions, if they are united,[13] drive a wedge between the enemy's front and rear,[14] and to prevent the enemy from joining forces.[15]

Trade negotiators need to be nimble-footed in changing their strategy in accordance with the developments and dynamics at the negotiating table—so aptly demonstrated by India's Maran at the Doha Ministerial Conference. After having doggedly resisted the launch of negotiations on the four Singapore Issues, Maran changed his strategy and decided to compromise. But even while compromising at the last stage, he extracted concessions that proved to be crucial in securing his negotiating objectives two years down the line. What do strategies on warfare have to say on this issue? Sun Tzu uses the analogy of water not retaining a constant shape, but shaping its course according to the nature of the ground over which it flows, and makes the point that the general who modifies his tactics in relation to his opponent will succeed in winning.[16]

A final point on strategy in trade negotiations—the need for negotiators to have the right advisors. In the context of warfare, Kautilya considers the three components of power—enthusiasm and morale of the fighting forces; military might; and the power of good counsel and correct judgement—to be in ascending order of importance.[17] Based on good counsel, a king can arrive at the best judgement on the means and strategies to defeat kings who are mightier than him and whose forces are more enthusiastic than his men. Following this approach, a high-level negotiator should not hesitate in seeking advice from a few credible persons from outside the government who, by virtue of possessing detailed knowledge relevant for the negotiation, can provide independent counsel to the government. These individuals should not have any personal interest in the outcome of the negotiation. In order to help the trade minister/chief negotiator to weigh their independent advice, they must always be asked to provide detailed reasons for their views and opinions. Subsequently, their advice should be factored in the overall negotiating strategy and negotiating positions.

10.4 Understanding Why Some Coalitions Are More Effective than Others

Given the asymmetry in economic and political power among countries in international negotiations, coalitions have been recognized to 'provide developing countries with a critical instrument for expanding their bargaining power'.[18] As only some coalitions of developing countries at the GATT/WTO have been successful, it is relevant to understand the factors that might enable a coalition to be effective. Based on a comparative case study of coalitions of developing countries in the GATT/WTO, Narlikar proposes two necessary conditions that coalitions must fulfil before they can engage in bargaining with countries outside their fold. First, the coalition must enjoy internal coherence based on an internally consistent agenda; and second, the coalition must collectively constitute a substantial external weight. She also proposes the following seven strategies to enhance the legitimacy and effectiveness of a coalition: first, role of a sustained process that allows coalition partners to meet frequently and revise their agenda; second, importance of having a positive agenda, as opposed to a merely blocking objective; third, research-based agenda formulation, especially in the pre-negotiation phase for lending substance and legitimacy to the demands of the coalition; fourth, flexibility of agenda and negotiating space; fifth, importance of framing demands in the language of liberalization rather than protectionism or unilateral concessions; sixth, engaging with other coalitions, including through information exchange and position coordination; and seventh, engaging with non-governmental organizations and other inter-governmental organizations.[19]

Earlier chapters of the book have discussed a number of coalitions of developing countries in recent years in WTO negotiations. Here we analyse three specific coalitions from the perspective of Narlikar's theory. As discussed in detail in Chapter 7, India and Malaysia were instrumental in establishing a coalition of 52 developing countries, whose sole objective and narrow focus was to block negotiations on the four Singapore Issues during the Doha Round. Established at the Cancun Ministerial Conference of the WTO held in 2003, the efforts of the coalition resulted in the removal of three out of the four Singapore Issues from the negotiating agenda of the Doha Round. Chapter 8 has described how the G-20 coalition was created in August 2003, with Argentina, Brazil, India and South Africa as its main proponents. During 2003–2008, the coalition succeeded in preventing the Agriculture negotiations under the Doha Round from getting anchored around proposals made by the EU-USA combine and decisively changed the course of negotiations on almost all agriculture-related issues. The third coalition (referred to as the TRIPS waiver coalition) was spearheaded by India and South Africa. It was established in October 2020 and remained active until June 2022. The single focus of the coalition, which comprised 62 countries by May 2021, was to seek a temporary suspension of rules in respect of copyrights, industrial designs, patents and protection of undisclosed information in relation to diagnostics, therapeutics, etc. for the prevention, treatment, or containment of Covid-19. The eventual decision of the WTO Members on this issue—which came about twenty months after the initial proposal of the coalition—had almost no resemblance to what the coalition had proposed.[20] By that time, the decision was of very little practical utility in combating Covid-19. It may, thus, not be incorrect to conclude that the coalition failed to secure its negotiating objective. How does the theoretical framework regarding coalitions and their effectiveness, as proposed by Narlikar, explain the success of the coalition on Singapore Issues and the G-20, and the lack of success of the TRIPS waiver coalition?

First, the coalitions on Singapore Issues, and the TRIPS waiver were focused on a single issue, or a narrow range of them. The interests of the constituent countries appeared to converge. It may, therefore, not be incorrect to conclude that there was internal coherence in their objective and agenda. In contrast, the internal coherence of the G-20 was severely challenged on account of the coalition being required to balance the export aspirations of Argentina and Brazil with protectionist inclinations of India and Indonesia. Second, to a varying degree, the three coalitions can be said to have possessed substantial external weight at critical junctures of the negotiations. The coalition on Singapore Issues comprised 52 WTO members, which represented more than one third of the membership. Its members constituted 63 per cent of the population and around 10 per cent of the GDP of the entire WTO membership at the time of the Cancun Ministerial Conference in September 2003. At this meeting, the G-20 constituent countries comprised 13 per cent of the WTO membership. However, they wielded considerable heft by representing 65 per cent of the population and 13 per cent of the GDP of the WTO membership. Finally, the TRIPS waiver coalition can be treated as possessing impressive external weight. By May 2021, its negotiating proposal had garnered the direct support of 62 members, which represented 39 per cent of the WTO membership. These countries accounted for 48 per cent by population and 10 per cent by GDP of the entire WTO membership. The actual external weight of this coalition was far more, as an additional 30–35 WTO members supported the coalition, without formally signing on to its negotiating proposals. Overall, the three coalitions substantially fulfilled the requirement of possessing external weight and internal coherence.[21]

Turning to an analysis of the strategies for enhancing the effectiveness of coalitions, it is reasonable to assume that a coalition may not be in a position to implement all the strategies identified in Narlikar's theoretical framework. Based on this assumption, the three coalitions show a mixed picture in terms of the strategies adopted and their effectiveness. Although the G-20 coalition made technically sound proposals to carry forward the negotiations, its main objective was to block the EU-USA proposals from becoming the basis of a negotiated outcome. Further, the coalition was not hesitant in striking compromises, provided the core interests of the coalition was protected. Its negotiating agenda could be considered to be a blend of liberalization by the developed countries along with some degree of protection for farmers in developing countries. It is relevant to note that the large number of issues in the Agriculture negotiations allowed the G-20 to seek trade-offs and engage in meaningful bargaining, instead of pitching for unilateral concessions. Finally, it interacted effectively with other coalitions, such as the G-33 and Cotton 4, and non-governmental organizations—Oxfam being a good illustration—for garnering support at the negotiating table and also for creating narratives to promote its negotiating objectives. Overall, the strategies deployed by the G-20 for enhancing its effectiveness and resulting in eventual success are closely aligned with Narlikar's theory.

In contrast to the G-20, the coalition on Singapore Issues succeeded despite adopting strategies that were at considerable variance with Narlikar's prescription. As the basic objective of the coalition was to block the negotiations on the four Singapore Issues, it lacked a positive agenda. Further, its overall approach can be considered to be inflexible and lacking in negotiating space. While some of the coalition partners might have been happy with the removal of just two of these issues, it would have been divisive if the constituent countries had sought to create a consensus on which two issues to drop. Some members of the coalition were opposed to retaining even a single Singapore Issue in the negotiating agenda of the Doha Round. The coalition chose to limit its negotiating space by not unbundling the four issues. As the coalition had little to offer in return for getting these issues off the agenda, its approach was aimed at seeking unilateral concessions.

The TRIPS waiver coalition failed to secure its negotiating objectives, despite implementing strategies that were similar to those advocated by Narlikar. The coalition sought to temporarily set aside some rules of the TRIPS agreement for ramping up production and enhancing the availability of health products and technologies for the prevention, treatment, or containment of Covid-19.[22] Thus, it had a positive agenda. Further, its technically sound proposal and detailed responses to the questions posed by many countries points to the role of background research in underpinning the coalition's engagement at the negotiating table.[23] It showed some flexibility in its negotiating position, as evident from its initial negotiating proposal in October 2020[24] and its revision in May 2021[25]. Viewed from the narrow perspective of its own proposal, the coalition sought unilateral concessions. But examined in the larger context of the dynamics prevailing at the WTO during 2021–2022, the coalition was in a position to engage in trade-offs involving the TRIPS waiver and a parallel initiative aimed at a more comprehensive response to the pandemic, commonly referred to as the Walker Process. The coalition appears to have explicitly created a linkage between these two negotiations, as 'No Waiver, No Walker' was articulated by many developing countries' diplomats in Geneva.[26]

A particularly strong point of the coalition was the groundswell of support that it received from a large number of organizations and prominent personalities all over the world. To illustrate, in April 2021 388 Members of the European Parliament and of European National Parliaments urged the European Union and its Member States to support a TRIPS waiver.[27] In June 2021, fifteen of the UK's Nobel Prize-winning scientists, economists, and peace activists addressed an open letter to the British prime minister strongly urging him to 'do everything in your power to serve all of humanity and announce the UK's support for an intellectual property waiver on Covid-19 vaccines and treatments'.[28] In addition, 27 international civil society organizations, academics, and activists including ActionAid International, Amnesty International, Médecins Sans Frontières (MSF) Access Campaign, Norwegian People's Aid, Oxfam, and Public Citizen USA, addressed a letter to heads of State, requesting them to 'immediately support the proposal' made by India and South Africa.[29] Further in September 2021, 78 Nobel Prize Laureates and 67 former heads of State and Government (including from many developed countries such as Canada, France, Ireland, Latvia, New Zealand, Norway, Spain, Switzerland, and UK) wrote an open letter to the candidates to be the next German Chancellor expressing deep concern at Germany's continued opposition to the TRIPS waiver and urged the next German Government to 'support a wide and comprehensive waiver of intellectual property rules on all Covid-19-related technologies at the WTO'.[30] This issue did not go unnoticed even by the Pope, who mentioned the following sentence in his Christmas address in 2020: ' I cannot place myself ahead of others, letting the law of the marketplace and patents take precedence over the law of love and the health of humanity.'[31] Despite the overwhelming support and the moral force behind the TRIPS waiver proposal, the coalition failed to achieve what it had set out to do.

How can Narlikar's theoretical framework be extended to account for the success of the coalition against the four Singapore Issues and the failure of the TRIPS waiver coalition? An important variable missing from the framework is the extent of active participation, particularly through lobbying, by the relevant stakeholders in the developed countries to promote their interests on the issue being pushed by the developing country coalition. If this crucial aspect is taken into consideration, it may be less difficult to explain the contrasting outcomes of the two coalitions.

It is quite likely that binding rules on cross-border investment, particularly if it had accorded substantial protection to the interests of foreign investors in host countries, could have been of substantial commercial interest to the investors in the developed countries. In addition, commercial gains for firms in the developed countries would have been enhanced if transparency in government procurement had created new market access opportunities for them in the developing countries. However, no specific lobby group appears to have been active in pushing the commercial interests of these firms with the governments in the developed countries. Further, some longstanding experts on international trade and GATT/WTO are of the view that EU's push for initiating negotiations on the Singapore Issues was merely a ploy to delay negotiations on agriculture—an issue on which it would have found it difficult to make concessions.[32] In the absence of a well-mobilized interest group pushing for a negotiated outcome on these issues in line with its interest, the task for the developing country coalition against it became less difficult.

In contrast, the efforts of the coalition on TRIPS waiver faced an extremely daunting and formidable challenge from the multiple lobby groups active on behalf of the pharmaceutical industry in the USA, UK, and the EU. As described in Chapter 3, lobbying by the pharmaceutical industry based in the developed countries was influential in the negotiations on IPRs during the Uruguay Round. In its quest for further promoting its commercial interests, the industry continues to lobby hard for seeking more stringent standards for IPR protection in FTA negotiations. In parallel, it lobbies aggressively to prevent countries from making rightful use of the flexibilities contained in the TRIPS agreement.[33] Any policy intervention, which can even remotely have an adverse impact on its windfall profits, is quickly on the radar screen of the pharmaceutical industry. The proposal pioneered by India and South Africa for a TRIPS waiver posed a potent and immediate threat to the huge profits of companies that were involved in developing vaccines during the Covid-19 pandemic. In the long term, the proposal put at risk the core of the business model of the developed countries' pharmaceutical industry. It is no surprise that the industry lobbied hard against the proposal. During 2020–2022, coinciding with the period of Covid-19, Pharmaceuticals/ Health Products industry spent nearly $1 billion in lobbying the US government, the highest amount among different industry groups.[34] The Pharmaceutical Research and Manufacturers of America (PhRMA), the industry's lead lobbying group in the USA, spent nearly $86 million on lobbying during 2020–2022, and ranked third among the top lobbying spenders in the USA.[35] According to lobby disclosure forms from the first quarter of 2021, the pharmaceutical industry mobilized over 100 lobbyists to contact lawmakers and members of the Biden administration, urging them to oppose the TRIPS waiver.[36]

An investigation carried out by Corporate Europe Observatory shows that the main pharmaceutical lobby group in Europe, the European Federation of Pharmaceutical Industries and Associations (EFPIA), spent up to €5.5 million in 2020 in lobbying.[37] Another report mentions that in the EU during 2020–2021, Covid vaccine and treatment developers and the largest pharma lobbying groups, including the EFPIA, spent at least €30 million on lobbying.[38] EFPIA lobbied for a clear EU rejection of the TRIPS waiver proposal on multiple occasions, including during a key meeting on 9 December 2020 with DG Trade, the Commission branch responsible for the WTO negotiations.[39] Top executives of the pharmaceutical industry enjoyed direct access to senior officials and politicians within the EU.[40] It is also relevant to note that US lobby groups, including the US Chamber of Commerce and PhRMA met EU officials in March 2022 and 'presented their general concerns with the waiver proposal'.[41] No doubt civil society groups, who supported the TRIPS waiver, also lobbied. But they could not match the influence wielded by the industry and their access to key officials appears to have been rather limited and more tokenistic.[42] Nothing illustrates the limited access of the supporters of the TRIPS waiver than the fact that requests for meeting by Medecins Sans Frontieres (MSF) international president Dr Christos Christou with relevant Commission officials were either turned down or not even answered.[43]

In April 2020, speaking at a WHO press conference, President of the European Commission Ursula von der Leyen had stated the following: 'We need to develop a vaccine. We need to produce it and to deploy it to every single corner of the world. And make it available at affordable prices.' She also added that the vaccine will be 'our universal, common good'.[44] However, within a few months, the Commission appears to have substantially changed its approach on the vaccine and instead aligned it more with what was being advocated by EFPIA. In the face of the strong, persistent, and aggressive lobbying by the pharmaceutical industry, the coalition on TRIPS waiver was unable to secure its negotiating objectives.

While the experience of the G-20 attests to the value of Narlikar's theory on coalitions and their effectiveness, the contrasting experience of the coalition on Singapore Issues and the TRIPS waiver coalitions can fill an important gap in the theory. The effectiveness and success of a coalition of developing countries cannot be isolated from the ability of stakeholders in the developed countries to respond decisively if their interests clash with the negotiating stance of the coalition. A coalition of developing countries would find it more difficult to secure its negotiating objectives if it is confronted with stakeholders in the developed countries who are well organized and mobilized to promote their commercial interests at the negotiating table. When can the stakeholders be considered to be well organized and mobilized? First, an organization to represent the commercial interests of the stakeholders must exist and respond expeditiously to the developments at the negotiating table. Second, the organization must have adequate financial resources and technical capacity to lobby the governments in the developed countries on the relevant issues. Third, the organization must enjoy access to high-level officials and decision makers in the developed countries on the issue concerned. Fourth, the organization must have the ability to counter the narrative of the coalition and challenge it on technical points. Fifth, it would be an additional advantage if the organization has a history of lobbying successfully in the past. Taking these elements into consideration can enhance our understanding of the effectiveness of coalitions of developing countries. Evidently, while the stakeholders in the developed countries against the TRIPS waiver were well organized and mobilized, this was missing in respect of the Singapore Issues.

10.5 Some Emerging Trends in Forum Shifting

In Section 4.2, we have discussed in detail the strategy of forum shifting resorted to by the developed countries for various reasons, including countering the opposition of many developing countries against negotiating multilateral rules on new issues not covered in the WTO. Academic literature distinguishes between vertical forum shifting and horizontal forum shifting. Vertical forum shifting refers to 'negotiating norm-setting, rule-making, implementation, and enforcement at levels below the multilateral level (e.g., plurilateral, bilateral, unilateral, and granular/local)'.[45] Unable to achieve their negotiating objectives on issues such as labour and environment at the multilateral forum of the WTO, developed countries have been engaging in vertical forum shifting by negotiating new rules on these issues in bilateral free trade agreements. Horizontal forum shifting refers to shifting negotiations from one multilateral organization to another.[46] Shifting the negotiations for legally enforceable provisions and strengthening the protection for intellectual property rights from the WIPO to the GATT, as discussed in detail in Chapter 3, provides a good illustration of horizontal forum shifting. Academic literature suggests that while vertical forum shifting favours the powerful countries, horizontal forum shifting may offer benefits to weaker parties.[47] Researchers may need to take three specific trends in WTO, FTA, and other negotiations into consideration while advancing an integrated theory on forum shifting in the future.

First, during the Uruguay Round at the GATT, through the use of 'incorporation by reference', rights and obligations contained in treaties negotiated outside the GATT became an integral part of the WTO. The most noticeable use of this strategy at the GATT/WTO has so far been in the TRIPS Agreement. Provisions of a few agreements negotiated outside GATT/WTO, but incorporated in the TRIPS agreement by reference include the following: Paris Convention for the Protection of Industrial Property; Berne Convention for the Protection of Literary and Artistic Works; International Convention for the Protection of Performers, Producers of Phonograms and Broadcasting Organizations, adopted at Rome on 26 October 1961 and Treaty on Intellectual Property in Respect of Integrated Circuits, adopted at Washington on 26 May 1989.[48] Consequently, the relevant provisions of these treaties, which were negotiated at forums outside the GATT, became legally enforceable through the Dispute Settlement Mechanism of the WTO. To give another illustration, in respect of export credits, the developed countries reached a 'gentlemen's agreement' at the OECD in the year 1979. This is commonly referred to as the international undertaking on official export credits. This international undertaking was inserted by reference in the Agreement on Subsidies and Countervailing Measures at the WTO.[49] This provision provides flexibility to the members of the undertaking—mainly developed countries—to grant export credits, which are prohibited for most countries that are not participants to the undertaking. The Agreement on Sanitary and Phyto-Sanitary Measures provides another illustration of the use of 'incorporation by reference' in some of the agreements at the WTO. Sanitary or phytosanitary measures which conform to international standards, guidelines, or recommendations shall be deemed to be necessary to protect human, animal, or plant life or health, and presumed to be consistent with the relevant provisions of this Agreement and of GATT 1994.[50] Thus, 'incorporation by reference' appears to be an important part of the strategy of forum shifting. This is likely to acquire greater prominence, as many recent FTAs of the developed countries have extensively used 'incorporation by reference' in respect of obligations related to labour, environment, and certain other issues.[51]

Second, history of the Uruguay Round negotiations on issues related to IPRs suggests that horizontal forum shifting may not be sufficient for the developed countries to meet their negotiating objectives. In their pursuit of success at the negotiating table at the WTO, the developed countries are likely to use this form of forum shifting in conjunction with vertical forum shifting and a few other strategies. The dynamics of forum shifting on IPR issues during the Uruguay Round provides pointers to how the two forms of forum shifting can be mutually reinforcing. After shifting the negotiations on IPR issues from the WIPO to the GATT, the developed countries encountered considerable opposition to their negotiating objectives from some developing countries. In order to overcome the opposition, the USA resorted to vertical forum shifting and used coercive strategies to compel the recalcitrant developing countries to fall in line with its negotiating objectives. This is likely to be the template on forum shifting in the future.

Third, in recent years, the developed countries are pushing their interests in negotiations at the WTO by leveraging another forum—the G20 platform comprising 19 countries and the European Union[52]—to pre-cook outcomes in their favour. What factors have contributed to this emerging trend? First, unlike the intensely technical negotiations at the WTO, the stress of G20 appears to be to strike political bargains. Second, G20 is yet to see effective coalitions of developing countries, which could counter-balance to some extent the power asymmetry at this platform. This is in sharp contrast to the WTO, where coalitions of many developing countries have been effective in promoting their negotiating objectives. Third, the delegates from developing countries at the G20 forum are mostly from ministries not involved in WTO negotiations, and are generally unaware of the implications if the pre-negotiated outcomes on issues related to agriculture, digital trade, and environment are sought to be used as a template for further negotiations at the WTO. Fourth, the G20 provides a platform for trading-off trade issues with larger geopolitical matters. This provides additional leverage to the developed countries to push their trade agenda at the G20. It is, therefore, not surprising that the developed countries are increasingly using the G20 as an intermediate forum for 'pre-cooking' outcomes on trade issues, which are subsequently pushed at the WTO. Box 10.1 provides a specific illustration of this strategy.

It is relevant to ask the following question: how does pre-negotiating outcomes at the G20 enable the developed countries to secure their negotiating objectives at the WTO? It is reasonable to assume that those countries which are parties to the pre-negotiated outcome at the G20 would find it difficult to oppose these outcomes when they are sought to be negotiated at the WTO. It is not uncommon for potential opponents to be confronted by the developed countries with the following question: as you have agreed to this issue at G20, why do you now oppose it at the WTO? Further, countries which are not parties to a pre-negotiated outcome may be less inclined to oppose it at the WTO, as they are likely to perceive that the outcome already has considerable support of other countries. Finally, if the pre-negotiated outcome was agreed at the level of heads of state/ heads of government, trade negotiators are unlikely to have the authority and courage to overturn it, even if the outcome was against the negotiating objectives of the country at the WTO. With the

Box 10.1 Using G20 Forum to Pre-cook Outcomes on WTO Issues

During September–October 2021, at the WTO, Members were deeply divided in their attempt at negotiating the outcome documents for the 12th Ministerial Conference of the WTO (MC12), which was scheduled to be held during 30 November–3 December 2021 (but was subsequently held in June 2022). On many issues the interests, and consequently the negotiating positions, of the developed counties on the one hand, and many developing countries, on the other hand, appeared to be at the extreme ends of the spectrum. On account of cohesion among the developing countries, the developed countries were unable to have their way at the WTO. However, at the G20 the story was entirely different.

The G20 Ministerial Statement on Trade and Investment at Sorrento (Italy) dated 12 October 2021 contained guidance for WTO Members on some of the contentious issues for MC12. This was mainly along the lines advocated by the developed countries at the WTO. Having agreed to the contentious elements in the G20 Ministerial Statement, eight months down the line India, Indonesia, and South Africa were unable to prevent these from being included in the outcome documents of WTO MC12.

Some paragraphs of the G20 Ministerial Statement, particularly paragraphs 4 and 5 on WTO reform; and paragraphs 18-21 on trade and environmental sustainability bear an uncanny resemblance to the corresponding paragraphs in the MC12 Outcome Document adopted by WTO Members on 16 June 2022.[a] Similarly paragraphs 9–10 of the G20 Ministerial statement are strikingly similar to certain paragraphs in the WTO Ministerial Declaration on WTO response to the Covid-19 pandemic.[b] The strategy of forum shifting helped the developed countries in neutralizing the opposition of some developing countries on a few key issues relevant for MC12.

Source: G20 Ministerial Statement on Trade and Investment at Sorrento (Italy) dated 12 October 2021, WTO document WT/MIN(22)/W/16/Rev.1 dated 16 June 2022 and WTO document WT/MIN(22)/W/13 dated 10 June 2022[a] MC12 Outcome Document, WTO document WT/MIN(22)/W/16/Rev.1 dated 16 June 2022.[b] Ministerial Declaration on the WTO Response to the Covid-19 Pandemic and Preparedness for Future Pandemics, WTO document WT/MIN(22)/W/13 dated 10 June 2022.

African Union joining an expanded G20, it remains to be seen whether this will help developing countries to come together and form coalitions in the expanded G20; or by virtue of its participation in the outcomes of the expanded G20, the voice of the African countries gets muted at the WTO.

Before concluding this sub-section, it should be mentioned that there have been occasions when the strategy of forum shifting did not succeed. Attempts at negotiating a multilateral agreement on investment[53] during 1990s and an agreement on Steel Subsidies[54] during 2001–2005—both at the OECD—and subsequently 'housing' them at the WTO failed. It is for researchers to comprehend the reasons for the failures and integrate it in a comprehensive theory on forum shifting.

10.6 Overall Conclusions

Trade negotiations at the WTO are a long-drawn process. A negotiator is likely to get too embroiled in technical details and lose sight of the larger picture. One way of preventing this would be to seek answers to the following questions throughout the course of multilateral trade negotiations: does the negotiating forum promote my interest; have I consulted all the stakeholders who are relevant for the issue under negotiation; do I have all the information that may be relevant for taking a decision on the negotiating issue; am I taking a decision based on facts or is the narrative spun by other countries guiding my decision; when should I speak and when should I remain silent at the negotiating table; does my negotiating team need to be reinforced by experts with skills and knowledge that are currently missing; what do I gain by resisting, or am I better off by yielding and striking a deal; with which countries should I join hands; what do I gain by agreeing to a proposal, or lose by disagreeing; what will be the reaction of other countries to my negotiating approach on an issue; how do I minimize or manage the adverse responses from other countries to my negotiating approach; am I giving some concession without gaining any commensurate benefits; how will my approach/negotiating position in one area affect my position in another area; are any of my team members attempting to strike a side deal for personal gains; while engaging at the negotiating table, have I been following the institutional procedure and guidelines; and have I understood the meaning of each and every word in the negotiating text and have I assessed its implication for my country? Answers to these questions can provide considerable guidance to trade negotiators in taking well-considered decisions in multilateral trade negotiations.

Multilateral trade negotiations at the WTO involve many complex issues, whose implications may not be readily clear. Once the rules have been negotiated and get implemented, countries may not be able to wriggle out from complying with them without paying compensation and suffering reputational damage. This underscores the importance for developing countries to acquire the agency to influence the course of negotiations and their outcomes. However, the experience of developing countries at the negotiating table suggests that on account of the entrenched power asymmetries, they face multiple challenges in negotiating rules on international trade. This book should provide considerable ground for optimism that by adopting suitable strategies, developing countries can become more influential players at the negotiating table. This would help strengthen multilateralism, and simultaneously seek to make it more responsive to development needs of a large number of countries.

Notes

1. Sun Tzu, *On the Art of War*, trans. Lionel Giles (Atlanta, GA: Dalmatian Press, 2007), 25.
2. Sun Tzu, *Art of War*, 30.
3. L.N. Rangarajan (edited, rearranged, translated and introduced), *Kautilya The Arthashastra* (Gurugram: Penguin Books, 1992), 572.
4. Sun Tzu, *Art of War*, 31.
5. Sun Tzu, *Art of War*, 65.
6. Rangarajan, *Kautilya The Arthashastra*, 508.
7. Rangarajan, *Kautilya The Arthashastra*, 505.
8. Sun Tzu, *Art of War*, 31.
9. Rangarajan, *Kautilya The Arthashastra*, 550.
10. Declaration on the TRIPS Agreement and Public Health adopted by the Doha Ministerial Conference on 14 November 2001, WTO document WT/MIN(01)/DEC/2 dated 20 November 2001.
11. Sun Tzu, *Art of War*, 58.

12. Rangarajan, *Kautilya The Arthashastra*, 99.
13. Sun Tzu, *Art of War*, 25.
14. Sun Tzu, *Art of War*, 58.
15. Sun Tzu, *Art of War*, 29.
16. Sun Tzu, *Art of War*, 41.
17. Rangarajan, *Kautilya The Arthashastra*, 589.
18. Amrita Narlikar, *International Trade and Developing Countries: Bargaining Coalitions in the GATT and WTO* (Routledge, 2005), 7.
19. Narlikar, *Bargaining Coalitions*, 196–208.
20. Ministerial Decision on the TRIPS Agreement adopted on 17 June 2022, WTO document WT/MIN(22)/30 dated 22 June 2022.
21. The number of countries in the coalition on Singapore Issues is based on the number of countries which signed the Joint Communique to H.E. Mr. Pierre S. Pierre Pettigrew, Minister of International Trade for Canada & the facilitator for Singapore Issues, at the Cancun Ministerial Conference, dated 12 September, 2003. The number of countries in the G-20 coalition is based on the countries who were the co-sponsors of the WTO document WT/MIN(03)/W/6 dated 4 September 2003. However, countries that subsequently left this coalition have been removed, while a few other countries that joined the G-20 have been included. The number of countries in the TRIPS waiver coalition is based on co-sponsors of the WTO Document IP/C/W/669/Rev.1 dated 25 May 2021. The calculations related to share population and GDP are based on the World Development Indicators.
22. Communication from African Group, the Plurinational State of Bolivia, Egypt, Eswatini, Fiji, India, Indonesia, Kenya, the LDC Group, Maldives, Mozambique, Mongolia, Namibia, Pakistan, South Africa, Vanuatu, the Bolivarian Republic of Venezuela and Zimbabwe, Waiver from certain Provisions of the TRIPS Agreement for the Prevention, Containment and Treatment of Covid-19, Revised Decision Text, WTO Document IP/C/W/669/Rev.1 dated 25 May 2021.
23. See, for example, Communication from Plurinational State of Bolivia, Eswatini, India, Kenya, Mozambique, Mongolia, Pakistan, South Africa, the Bolivarian Republic of Venezuela and Zimbabwe, Waiver from certain Provisions of the TRIPS Agreement for the Prevention, Containment and Treatment of Covid-19, Responses to Questions, WTO document IP/C/W/672 dated 15 January 2021; and Communication from Plurinational State of Bolivia, Eswatini, India, Kenya, Mozambique, Mongolia, Pakistan, South Africa, the Bolivarian Republic of Venezuela and Zimbabwe, Responses to Questions on Intellectual-Property Challenges Experienced by Members in Relation to Covid-19 in Document IP/C/W/671, WTO document IP/C/W/673 dated 15 January 2021.
24. Communication from India and South Africa, Waiver from certain Provisions of the TRIPS Agreement for the Prevention, Containment and Treatment of Covid-19, WTO Document IP/C/W/669 dated 2 October 2020.
25. Revised TRIPS Waiver proposal.

26. Priti Patnaik, *The TRIPS Waiver Negotiations at the World Trade Organization October 2020 – June 2022: A Reportage From Geneva Health Files*, Geneva: Geneva Health Files, 2022.
27. Joint Appeal by Members of the European Parliament and of European National Parliaments Urging the EU and its Member States to Support a TRIPS Waiver. Text available on Joint-MP-MEP-Appeal-TRIPS-waiver-EN-FR-DE-ES-IT-April-2021.pdf (haiweb.org). Accessed on 20 May 2024.
28. British Nobel laureates call on Prime Minister to waive vaccine intellectual property at G7. 8 June 2021. Available on the following weblink: https://peoplesvaccinealliance.medium.com/british-nobel-laureates-call-on-prime-minister-to-waive-vaccine-intellectual-property-at-g7-922b297d1481
29. Letter for Heads of State calling for a sea-change in the Covid-19 pandemic response at the Vaccine Summit. 22 September 2021. People's Vaccine Alliance. Available on the following weblink: https://peoplesvaccinealliance.medium.com/letter-for-heads-of-state-calling-for-a-sea-change-in-the-covid-19-pandemic-response-at-the-vaccine-67f7d8edff20
30. Letter from Former Heads of State and Nobel Laureates Call on Candidates for German Chancellor To Waive Intellectual Property Rules for COVID Vaccines. 13 September 2021. People's Vaccine Alliance. Available on the following weblink: https://peoplesvaccinealliance.medium.com/former-heads-of-state-and-nobel-laureates-call-on-candidates-for-german-chancellor-to-waive-655daad6bf52.
31. 'URBI ET ORBI' Message of His Holiness Pope Francis, Christmas 2020, Benediction Hall. 25 December 2020. Available on the following weblink: https://www.vatican.va/content/francesco/en/messages/urbi/documents/papa-francesco_20201225_urbi-et-orbi-natale.html. Accessed on 4 January 2022.
32. Jacob Kol and Alan Winters, 'The EU after Cancún: Can the Leopard Change Its Spots?' *European Foreign Affairs Review* 9(2004): 1–25.
33. An investigation by Truthout has revealed that an aggressive lobbying effort by pharmaceutical interests pushed Congress and the White House to put mounting pressure on India to change its patent laws. See Ludwig, Mike, 10 October 2014, Big Pharma Lobbies Hard to End India's Distribution of Affordable Generic Drugs available on http://www.truth-out.org/news/item/26721-big-pharma-lobbies-hard-to-end-india-s-distribution-of-affordable-generic-drugs. Last visited on 4 June 2016.
34. https://www.opensecrets.org/federal-lobbying/industries?cycle=2022. Last visited on 20 May 2023.
35. Calculations based on data available at https://www.opensecrets.org/federal-lobbying/top-spenders?cycle=2021 Accessed on 15 April 2024.
36. Lee Fang, 'Pharmaceutical Industry Dispatches Army of Lobbyists to Block Generic Covid-19 Vaccines', *The Intercept*, 23 April 2021. Available on https://theintercept.com/2021/04/23/covid-vaccine-ip-waiver-lobbying.

37. Corporate Europe Observatory, 'Big Pharma Lobby's Self-Serving Claims Block Global Access to Vaccines', 19 April 2021. Available on https://corporateeurope.org/en/2021/04/big-pharma-lobbys-self-serving-claims-block-global-access-vaccines. Accessed on 20 May 2024.
38. A Furlong, S.A. Aarup, and Samuel Horti, 'Who Killed the COVID Vaccine Waiver?' *Politico*, 10 November 2022. Available on https://www.politico.eu/article/covid-vaccine-poor-countries-waiver-killed. Accessed on 20 May 2024.
39. Furlong, Aarup, and Horti, 'Who Killed Vaccine Waiver?'
40. Furlong, Aarup, and Horti, 'Who Killed Vaccine Waiver?'
41. Furlong, Aarup, and Horti, 'Who Killed Vaccine Waiver?'
42. Furlong, Aarup, and Horti, 'Who Killed Vaccine Waiver?'
43. Corporate Europe Observatory, 'The Commission's Pharma Echo Chamber', 7 May 2021. Available on https://corporateeurope.org/en/2021/05/commissions-pharma-echo-chamber. Accessed on 20 May 2024.
44. 'Von der Leyen Announces Global Response and Calls for United World Front Against Coronavirus', Brussels, 24 April 2020. European Commission—Announcement. Available on https://ec.europa.eu/commission/presscorner/api/files/document/print/ro/ac_20_749/AC_20_749_EN.pdf Accessed on 20 May 2024.
45. Susan K. Sell, 'TRIPS Was Never Enough: Vertical Forum Shifting, FTAS, ACTA, and TTP', 18 J. INTELL. PROP. L. 447 (2011). Available at: https://digitalcommons.law.uga.edu/jipl/vol18/iss2/5.
46. Susan Sell, 'TRIPS Was Never Enough'.
47. Susan Sell, 'TRIPS Was Never Enough'.
48. Footnote 2 of the TRIPS agreement.
49. Proviso to Item (k) of Annex I to the Agreement on Subsidies and Countervailing Measures.
50. Article 3.2 of the Agreement on the Application of Sanitary and Phyto Sanitary Measures.
51. See, for example, Article 14.5 on Electronic Commerce, Article 19.3 on Labour issues, Article 20.4 on Environment issues and Article 26.6 on Anti-Corruption in the Trans-Pacific Partnership Agreement; Article 12 on Trade and Sustainability in the EU Singapore FTA.
52. The African Union was admitted as a new member of the G20 in September 2023.
53. See, for example, Charan Devereaux, Robert Z. Lawrence, and Michael D. Watkins, *Case Studies in US Trade Negotiation Vol 1: Making the Rules* (Washington D.C.: Institute for International Economics, 2006), 135–186.
54. See, for example, Fabrizio Pagani, *The OECD Steel and Shipbuilding Subsidy Negotiations: Text and Legal Analysis* (Cameron May, 2008).

Bibliography

Amorim, Celso. *Acting Globally, Memoirs of Brazil's Assertive Foreign Policy*. Translated by Michael Marsden. Maryland, MD: Hamilton Books, 2017.

Bagchi, Sanjoy. *International Trade Policy in Textiles: Fifty Years of Protectionism*. Geneva: International Textiles and Clothing Bureau, 2001.

Banga, Rashmi, and Richard Kozul-Wright. *Moratorium on Electronic Transmission: Fiscal Implication and Way Forward*. UNCTAD Research Paper no. 47, 2020.

Bansal, Rohit. 'India Inc Gives Maran 10/10 on Doha Performance'. 16 November 2001. http://www.financialexpress.com/old/wto/news39.html. Last accessed 14 January 2013.

Beeson, Mark, and Stephen Bell. 'The G-20 and International Economic Governance: Hegemony, Collectivism, or Both'. *Global Governance* 15 (2009): 67.

Bhalla, Surjit. 'A "Principled" Congress Stance at the WTO?' *The Indian Express*, dated 29 July 2014.

Bhalla, Surjit. 'In the Name of India, Why?' *The Indian Express*, dated 31 July 2014.

Blustein, Paul. *Misadventures of the Most Favoured Nations*. New York: Public Affairs, 2009.

Business Ready Methodology Handbook. World Bank, 2023.

Callières, François de. *On the Manner of Negotiating With Princes; On the Uses of Diplomacy; the Choice of Ministers and Envoys; and the Personal Qualities Necessary for Success in Missions Abroad*. 1716. Translated by A.F. Whyte. Boston, MA and New York: Houghton Mifflin Co., 1919.

Capaldo, Jeronim. *Trade Hallucination: Risks of Trade Facilitation and Suggestions for Implementation. Global Development and Environment Institute*, Tufts University, USA. Working Paper No. 14-02, 2014.

Chandrasekhar, K.M. *As Good as My Word: A Memoir*. Gurugram: HarperCollins Publishers, 2022.

Chang, Ha-Joon. *Kicking Away the Ladder: Development Strategy in Historical Perspective*. London: Anthem Press, 2002.

Charlotte Denny. 'Developed World Accused of Bully-Boy Tactics at WTO.' *The Guardian*. 12 November 2001.

Cooper, Andrew, and Daniel Schwanen. 'CIGI Special G20 Report: Flashpoints for the Pittsburgh Summit. Waterloo'. Waterloo: Centre for International Governance Innovation, 2009.

Corporate Europe Observatory. 'Big pharma lobby's self-serving claims block global access to vaccines'. 19 April 2021. Available on https://corporateeurope.org/en/2021/04/big-pharma-lobbys-self-serving-claims-block-global-access-vaccines. Accessed on 20 May 2024.

Corporate Europe Observatory. The Commission's Pharma Echo Chamber. 7 May, 2021. Available on https://corporateeurope.org/en/2021/05/commissions-pharma-echo-chamber. Accessed on 20 May 2024.

Croome, John. *Reshaping the World Trading System: A History of the Uruguay Round.* The Hague: Kluwer Law International, 1996.

Dam, Kenneth. *The GATT—Law and International Economic Organization.* Chicago and London: University of Chicago Press, 1970.

Das, Bhagirath Lal. *The WTO Agreements: Deficiencies, Imbalances and Required Changes.* London and New York: Zed Books, and Penang: Third World Network, 1998.

Das, Bhagirath Lal. 'South Needs to Change Strategies in WTO'. *SUNS- South North Development Monitor,* 9 December 1998.

Das, Bhagirath Lal. *The World Trade Organisation: A Guide to the Framework for International Trade.* Penang: Third World Network, 1999.

Das, Bhagirath Lal. *The WTO and Multilateral Trading System: Past, Present and Future.* London and New York: Zed Books, and Penang: Third World Network, 2003.

Davis, Christina L. 'International Institutions and Issue-Linkage: Building Support for Agricultural Trade'. *American Political Science Review* 98, 1 (2004): 153–69.

De Schutter, Olivier. 'The Power of Procurement. Public Purchasing in the Service of Realising the Right to Food'. United Nations Special Rapporteur on the Right to Food, 2014.

Devereaux, Charan, Robert Z. Lawrence, and Michael D. Watkins. *Case Studies in US Trade Negotiation Vol 1: Making the Rules.* Washington D.C.: Institute for International Economics, 2006.

Dixit, Avinash K., and Barry J. Nalebuff. *Thinking Strategically: The Competitive Edge in Business, Politics, and Everyday Life.* New York and London: W.W. Norton and Company, 1991.

Drahos, Peter. 'When the Weak Bargain with the Strong: Negotiations in the WTO'. *International Negotiation* 8, 1 (2003): 79–109.

Druckman, Daniel. 'Situational Levers of Position Change.' *American Academy of Political and Social Science Annals,* 542 (November 1995): 61–80.

Egan, Timothy. 'Failing Farmers Learn to Profit from Federal Aid.' *New York Times.* 24 December 2000. Quoted in *Das, Bhagirath L. The WTO and the Multilateral Trading System: Past Present and Future.* Penang: Third World Network.

Elms, Deborah. 'The Origins and Evolution of the Trans-pacific Partnership (TPP) Trade Negotiations'. Asian Trade Centre Working paper, Asian Trade Centre, Singapore, 2015.

Emmott, Bill. *Rivals: How the Power Struggle Between China, India and Japan Will Shape Our Next Decade.* New York: Harcourt, 2008.

Epstein, Susan B. *GATT: The Uruguay Round Agreement and Developing Countries.* Washington, DC: Foreign Affairs and National Defense Division, 1995.

Fang, Lee. 'Pharmaceutical Industry Dispatches Army of Lobbyists to Block Generic Covid-19 Vaccines'. *The Intercept.* 23 April 2021. Available on https://theintercept.com/2021/04/23/covid-vaccine-ip-waiver-lobbying.

Furlong A., Aarup, S.A., and Samuel Horti. 'Who Killed the COVID Vaccine Waiver?' Politico. 10 November 2022. Available on https://www.politico.eu/article/covid-vaccine-poor-countries-waiver-killed. Accessed on 20 May 2024.

Ganesan, A.V. 'Negotiating for India'. In Jayashree Watal and Antony Taubman (eds), *The Making of the TRIPS Agreement: Personal Insights from the Uruguay Round Negotiators*. Geneva: World Trade Organization, 2015.

GATT Contracting Parties, Third Session, Summary record of the twenty-second meeting. GATT/CP.3/SR.22 dated 8 June 1949.

GATT document Basic Instruments and Selected Documents 9S/28. 18 November 1960.

GATT Document L/315 dated 28 January 1995. United States request for waiver in connection with Section 22 of the Agriculture Adjustment Act.

GATT document MIN.DEC dated 20 September 1986. Ministerial Declaration on the Uruguay Round.

GATT document MTN.GNG/MA/W/24 dated 20 December 1993. Modalities for the Establishment of Specific Binding Commitments Under the Reform Programme, Note by the Chairman of the Market Access Group.

GATT document MTN.TNC/11 dated 21 April 1989. Mid-term Review, Multilateral Trade Negotiations Uruguay Round, Trade Negotiating Committee.

GATT document MTN:TNC/MIN(94)/ST/38 dated 13 April 1994.

GATT document MTN.TNC/W/FA dated 20 December 1991. Draft Final Act embodying the results of the Uruguay Round of multilateral trade negotiations.

Grieco, Joseph M. 'Between Dependency and Autonomy: India's Experience with the International Computer Industry'. *International Organization* 36 (Summer 1982): 609–632.

Guzman, Martin, and Joseph E. Stiglitz. 'Post-neoliberal globalization: International Trade Rules for Global Prosperity'. *Oxford Review of Economic Policy* 40 (2024): 282–306.

Haberli, Christian. 'After Bali: WTO Rules Applying to Public Food Reserves'. FAO Commodity and Trade Policy Research Working Paper no. 46. Food and Agriculture Organization of the United Nations, Rome, 2014.

Harrison, Geoffrey W. In *Successful Negotiation: Trieste 1954*, edited by John C. Campbell, 62. Princeton, NJ: Princeton University Press, 1976.

Heilperin, Michael A. Elephant traps on the World Trade Charter. American Affairs, July 1950. Quoted in Slobodian, Quinn. 2018. *Globalists—The End of Empire and the Birth of Neoliberalisim*. Cambridge, MA and London: Harvard University Press.

Hopewell, Kristen. 'Different Paths to Power: The Rise of Brazil, India and China at the WTO'. *Review of International Political Economy* 22, 6 (2015): 1128–1158.

Human Development Report. Millennium Development Goals: A Compact among Nations to End Human Poverty. UNDP, 2003.

Hurrell, Andrew. 'Hegemony, Liberalism and World Order: What Space for Would-be Great Powers?' *International Affairs* 82, 1 (2006): 1–19.

India & the WTO, May 2003. Vol. 5 . No. 5. New Delhi: Monthly Newsletter of the Ministry of Commerce and Industry.

International Chamber of Commerce. Payoff from the World Trade Agenda by Hufbauer, Gary Clyde, and Jeffrey Schott. Washington D.C.: Peterson Institute for International Economics, 2013.

Irwin, Douglas A., Petros C. Mavroidis, and Alan O. Sykes. *The Genesis of the GATT*. New York: Cambridge University Press, 2008.

Joekes, Susan, and Rohinton Medhora. *Trade Policies in Developing Countries: What Role for Capacity Building and Research?* Ottawa: IDRC, 2001.

Joint Communique to H.E. Mr. Pierre S. Pettigrew. Minister of International Trade for Canada & the Facilitator for Singapore Issues, at the Cancun Ministerial Conference, dated 12 September 2003. India & the WTO, September 2003. New Delhi: Monthly Newsletter of the Ministry of Commerce and Industry.

Kennedy, Paul. *The Rise and Fall of the Great Powers: Economic Change and Military Conflict from 1500 to 2000*. New York: Random House, 1987.

Keynote address of Arun Jaitley at FICCI-UNCTAD Seminar on Reflections on post-Cancun Agenda—the way ahead, organised in New Delhi on 22 October 2003. India & the WTO, Vol. 5 No. 10–11, October–November 2003. Monthly Newsletter of the Ministry of Commerce and Industry, New Delhi.

Khor, Martin. 'G-17 Get Broad Developing Country Support, Attacked by EC'. *SUNS- South North Development Monitor*, No. 5402 dated 22 August 2003.

Kol, Jacob, and L. Alan Winters. 'The EU after Cancún: Can the Leopard Change Its Spots?' *European Foreign Affairs Review* 9 (2004): 1–25.

Krasner, Stephen D. *Defending the National Interest: Raw Materials Investments and US Foreign Policy*. Princeton, NJ: Princeton University Press, 1978.

Kumar, Mohan. *Negotiation Dynamics of the WTO: An Insider's Account*. Singapore: Palgrave Macmillan, 2019.

Kumar, Mohan. *India's Moment*. Gurugram: HarperCollins Publishers, 2023.

Lax, David A., and James K. Sebenius. 'The Power of Alternatives or the Limits to Negotiation.' *Negotiation Journal* (April 1985): 163–179.

Lilja, Jannie. 'Domestic-Level Factors and Negotiation (In)Flexibility in the WTO'. *International Negotiation* 17, 1 (2012): 115–138.

Marceau Gabrielle. From the GATT to the WTO: The Expanding Duties of the Legal Affairs Division in Non-panel matters. In Marceau, *A History of Law and Lawyers in the GATT/WTO*. Cambridge, U.K.: Cambridge University Press, 2015.

Mavroidis, Petros C., George A. Berman, and Mark Wu. *The Law of the World Trade Organization (WTO) Documents, Cases and Analysis*. West, 2010.

Mazzucato, Mariana. *The Entrepreneurial State: Debunking Public vs. Private Sector Myths*. Penguin Books, 2018.

McKenzie, Francine. *GATT and Global Order in the Postwar Era*. Cambridge, U.K.: Cambridge University Press, 2020.

Mittal Anuradha 'Giving Away the Farm: the 2002 Farm Bill'. *Backgrounder, Oakland, Food First* 8, 3 (Summer 2002).

Nachiappan, Karthik. *Does India Negotiate?* Oxford and New Delhi: Oxford University Press, 2019.

Narlikar, Amrita. *International Trade and Developing Countries: Bargaining Coalitions in the GATT and WTO*. London: Routledge, 2003.

Odell, John S. 'The Outcomes of International Trade Conflicts: The US and South Korea, 1960–1981.' *International Studies Quarterly* 29 (1985): 263–286.

Odell, John S. 'From London to Bretton Woods: Sources of Change in Bargaining Strategies and Outcomes.' *Journal of Public Policy* 8, 3/4 (1990): 287–315.

Odell, John S. *International Trade Bargaining under Uncertainty: Cognitive Hypotheses and Evidence.* University of Southern California, 1993.

Odell, John S. *Negotiating the World Economy.* Ithaca, NY: Cornell University Press, 2000.

Odell, John S. 'Chairing a WTO Negotiation.' *Journal of International Economic Law* 8, 2 (June 2005): 425–448.

Organski, A.F.K. *World Politics.* New York: Knopf, 1968.

Pagani, Fabrizio. *The OECD Steel and Shipbuilding Subsidy Negotiations: Text and Legal Analysis.* Cameron May, 2008.

Patnaik, Priti. *The TRIPS Waiver Negotiations at the World Trade Organization October 2020–June 2022: A Reportage from Geneva Health Files*, Geneva: Geneva Health Files, 2022.

Peter J. Katzenstein, ed. *Between Power and Plenty: Foreign Economic Policies of Advanced Industrial States.* Madison, WI: University of Wisconsin Press, 1978.

Putnam, Robert. 'Diplomacy and Domestic Politics: The Logic of Two-Level Games.' *International Organization* 42, 3 (1988): 427–460.

Raghavan, Chakravarthi. 'GATT Council Recommends Declaration for Ministers.' *SUNS–South North Development Monitor*, 18 November 1982.

Raiffa, Howard. *The Art and Science of Negotiation.* Cambridge, MA: Harvard University Press, 1982.

Raja, Kanaga. 'G20 to Present Its Own Figures in Agriculture Talks.' *SUNS–South North Development Monitor* no. 5893 dated 13 October 2005.

Raja, Kanaga. 'Agreement needed by 31 October or no Hong Kong deal.' *SUNS- South North Development Monitor* no. 5901 dated 25 October 2005.

Raja, Kanaga. 'G33 Criticizes World Bank Paper on Special Products.' *SUNS–South North Development Monitor* no. 6170, 17 January 2007.

Raja, Kanaga. 'General Council suspended, lack of consensus on TF Protocol.' *SUNS-South North Development Monitor* no. 7853 dated 28 July 2014.

Rajya Sabha Secretariat. Department-related Parliamentary Standing Committee on Commerce, Thirty fifth report on India and WTO, December 1998.

Rangarajan, L.N. (edited, rearranged, translated and introduced). *Kautilya the Arthashastra.* Gurugram: Penguin Books, 1992.

Rapp, Richard T., and Richard P. Rozek. 'Benefits and Costs of Intellectual Property Protection in Developing Countries.' *Journal of World Trade* (October 1990): 75, 77–81.

Ratna, Rajan S., Das, Abhijit, and Sachin K. Sharma. *Doha Development Agenda for Developed Nations: Carve Outs in Recent Agriculture Negotiations.* New Delhi: Centre for WTO Studies Discussion Paper No.8, 2011.

Reagan. Charging Patent Piracy, Imposes Sanctions on $39 Million of Brazilian Goods, 5 Int'l Trade Rep. (BNA) No. 42, 1415 (26 October 1988) (reporting on comments from foreign relations officials in Brazil).

Saner, Raymond. *The Expert Negotiator.* Leiden/ Boston: Martinus Nijhoff Publishers, 2012.

Sanoussi, Bilal, Philippe De Lombaerde, and Diana Tussie, eds. *Asymmetric Trade Negotiations.* London and New York: Routledge Taylor and Francis Group, 2011.

Schelling, Thomas C. *The Strategy of Conflict.* Cambridge, MA: Harvard University Press, 1960.

Sebenius, James K. 'Negotiation Arithmetic: Adding and Subtracting Issues and Parties'. *International Organization* 37, 2 (Spring 1983): 281–316.

Sell, Susan, K. 'Intellectual Property Protection and Antitrust in the Developing World: Crisis, Coercion, and Choice.' *International Organization* 49 (1995): 315–149.

Sell, Susan K. *Private Power, Public Law: The Globalization of Intellectual Property Rights.* Cambridge: Cambridge University Press, 2003.

Sell, Susan K. TRIPS Was Never Enough: Vertical Forum Shifting, FTAS, ACTA, and TTP.' 18 J. INTELL. PROP. L. 447 (2011). Available at: https://digitalcommons.law.uga.edu/jipl/vol18/iss2/5.

Sell, Susan K, and Assem Prakash. 'Using Ideas Strategically,' *International Studies Quarterly* 48 (2004): 143–175.

Sharma, Sachin K. *The WTO and Food Security Implications for Developing Countries.* Singapore: Springer, 2016.

Shukla, Shrirang P. 'From GATT to WTO and Beyond.' WIDER Working Papers (1986–2000) 2000/195. Helsinki: UNU-WIDER.

Singh, J.P. 'Negotiating the Global Information Economy Weak Powers and Globalism: The Impact of Plurality on Weak-Strong Negotiations in the International Economy.' *International Negotiation* 5 (2000): 449–484.

Singh, J.P. 'Weak Powers and Globalism: The Impact of Plurality on Weak-Strong Negotiations in the International Economy'. *International Negotiation* 5 (2000): 449–484.

Singh, J.P. 'Diffusion of Power and Diplomacy: New Meanings, Problem Solving, and Deadlocks in Multilateral Negotiations'. *International Negotiation* 20 (2015): 73–88.

Singh J.P. *Sweet Talk: Paternalism and Collective Action in North-South Trade Relations.* Stanford, CA: Stanford University Press, 2017.

Slobodian, Quinn. *Globalists—The End of Empire and the Birth of Neoliberalisim.* Cambridge, MA and London: Harvard University Press, 2018.

Soares Adriano Campolina de Oliveira. 'G-20: Origin, Meaning, and Implications for Brazilian Trade Policy.' Rio de Janeiro: CPDA/UFRRJ, Masters Thesis, 2004.

Solomon Richard and Nigel Quinney. Foreword by Madeline Albright to *American negotiating behavior: Wheeler-dealers, Legal Eagles, Bullies and Preachers.* Washington, D.C.: United States Institute of Peace, 2010.

Stein Janice G., ed. *Getting to the Table: The Processes of International Prenegotiation.* Baltimore, MD: Johns Hopkins University Press, 1989.

Stephen, Matthew D. 'Rising Regional Powers and International Institutions: The Foreign Policy Orientations of India, Brazil and South Africa.' *Global Society* 26, 3 (2012): 289–309.

Stiglitz Joseph and Andrew Charlton. *Free Trade for All: How Trade Can Promote Development.* Oxford and New York: Oxford University Press, 2005.

Strauss Robert S., 'Foreword,' in Joan E. Twiggs (ed.), *The Tokyo Round of Multilateral Trade Negotiations: A Case Study in Building Domestic Support for Diplomacy.* Washington, DC: Georgetown University Institute for the Study of Diplomacy, 1987.

Subramanian, T.S.R. *Journeys Through Babudom and Netaland: Governance in India.* New Delhi: Rupa publisher, 2004.

Sun Tzu. *On the Art of War.* Translated by Lionel Giles. Atlanta, GA: Dalmatian Press, 2007.

Tolstoy, Leo. *War and Peace.* Translated by Anthony Briggs. Penguin Books, 2009.

Tussie Diana (ed). *The Politics of Trade: The Role of Research in Trade Policy and Negotiation.* Dordrecht, Leiden and Boston: Republic of Letters Publishing BV, 2009.

UNDP. Human Development Report 1997. New York and London: Oxford University Press, 1997.

UNECOSOC document no. E/PC/T/W.14 dated 21 October 1946 Government of India, Department of Commerce. Submission to the Preparatory Committee of the International Conference on Trade and Employment. Comments on US proposals for expansion of world trade and employment.

Veiga, Pedro da Motta. 'Brazil and the G-20 Group of Developing Countries'. Available on https://www.wto.org/english/res_e/booksp_e/casestudies_e/case7_e.htm. Last accessed 23 May 2020.

Wade, Robert H. 'Emerging World Order? From Multipolarity to Multilateralism in the G20, the World Bank, and the IMF.' *Politics & Society* 39, 3 (2011): 347–378.

Walton, Richard E., and Robert B. McKersie. *A Behavioral Theory of Labor Negotiations.* New York: McGraw-Hill Book Company, 1965.

Washington Trade Daily. Linking AGOA with TFA. Vol. 23 No. 154, 5 August 2014.

Wilkinson, Rorden, and James Scott. 'Developing Country Participation in the GATT: A Reassessment'. *World Trade Review* 7, 3 (2008): 473–510.

William Wallace. 'Atlantic Relations: Policy Coordination and Conflict.' *International Affairs*, 52 (April 1976): 16.

WTO document WT/MIN(03)/W/19 dated 12 September 2003. Position of the African Union, Least-Developed Countries, Caribbean and Pacific Countries on the new (Singapore) Issues.

WTO document G/AG/N/IND/18 dated 31 March 2020. India's notification to WTO Committee on Agriculture invoking the Permanent Peace Clause for the year 2018–19.

WTO document G/AG/N/USA/169 dated 29 August 2023. US notification to the Committee on Agriculture.

WTO document G/AG/N/USA/51/Rev.1 dated 28 January 2009. Revised US notification to the Committee on Agriculture.

WTO document G/AG/NG/W/102, dated 15 January 2001. Submission by India to the Committee on Agriculture Special Session. Negotiations on WTO Agreement on Agriculture, Proposals by India in the areas of: (i) Food Security, (ii) Market Access, (iii) Domestic Support, and (iv) Export Competition.

WTO document G/AG/W/134 dated 15 July 2014. Communication from the USA to the Committee on Agriculture titled Elements for a Work Program on Food Security.

WTO document G/SCM/W/462 dated 3 September 2001. Implementation-related issues referred to the Committee at the request of the chairman of the General Council on 31 July 2001.

WTO Document IP/C/W/669 dated 2 October 2020. Communication from India and South Africa titled Waiver from certain Provisions of the TRIPS Agreement for the Prevention, Containment and Treatment of Covid-19.

WTO Document IP/C/W/669/Rev.1 dated 25 May 2021. Waiver from certain Provisions of the TRIPS Agreement for the Prevention, Containment and Treatment of Covid-19. Revised Decision Text.

WTO document IP/C/W/672 dated 15 January 2021. Waiver from certain Provisions of the TRIPS Agreement for the Prevention, Containment and Treatment of Covid-19 - Responses to Questions.

WTO document JOB (03)/157 (restricted), circulated on 13 August, 2003.

WTO document JOB(01)/140 dated 26 September 2001.

WTO document JOB(01)/140/Rev.1 dated 27 October 2001.

WTO document JOB(01)/140/Rev.2 dated 13 November 2001.

WTO document JOB(01)/140/Rev.2 dated 13 November 2001. Paragraph 32(ii).

WTO document JOB(03)/150/Rev.1 dated 24 August 2003.

WTO document JOB(03)/150/Rev.2 dated 13 September 2003.

WTO document JOB(03)/162 dated 20 August 2003.

WTO document JOB/AG/22 dated 13 November 2012. G-33 Submission to the Committee on Agriculture Special Sessions titled Proposal on some elements of TN/AG/W/4/Rev.4 for early agreement to address food security issues.

WTO document JOB/AG/25 dated 3 October 2013. G-33 Submission to the Committee on Agriculture Special Sessions titled G-33 Non-paper.

WTO document JOB/TNC/29, dated 25 November 2013. Trade Negotiations Committee document titled Public Stockholding for food security purposes.

WTO Document no. WT/L/579 dated 2 August 2004. Decision Adopted by the General Council on 1 August 2004 on Doha Work Programme.

WTO document no. WT/L/939 dated 28 November 2014. Public Stockholding for Food Security Purposes, Decision of 27 November 2014 adopted by the General Council.

WTO document TN/AG/GEN/9 dated 7 May 2004.Communication from the G-20.

WTO document TN/AG/W/4/Rev.4 dated 6 December 2008.

WTO document TN/C/1 dated 4 February 2002.

WTO document TN/RL/W/213 dated 30 November 2007. Paragraph 2.4.3 of the text of the Anti-dumping Agreement.

WTO document TN/RL/W/278 dated 12 April 2024. Additional Provisions on Fisheries Subsidies. Draft Text.

WTO document WT/DS486/AB/R dated 16 May 2018. Report of the WTO Appellate Body in the dispute EU- Countervailing Measures on certain Polyethylene Terephthalate from Pakistan.

WTO document WT/DS486/R dated 6 July 2017. Report of the WTO panel in the dispute EU- Countervailing Measures on certain Polyethylene Terephthalate from Pakistan.

WTO document WT/GC/M/71 dated 13 December 2001. Minutes of the meeting of the General Council held on 31 October and 1 November 2001.

WTO document WT/GC/W/78 dated 9 February 1998. Global Electronic Commerce, Proposal by the United States.

WTO document WT/L/579 dated 2 August 2004. Decision Adopted by the General Council on 1 August 2004 on Doha Work Programme.

WTO document WT/L/579 dated 2 August 2004. Doha Work Programme Decision Adopted by the General Council on 1 August 2004.

WTO document WT/MIN(01)/DEC/1 dated 20 November 2001. Ministerial Declaration adopted on 14 November 2001.

WTO document WT/MIN(01)/DEC/2 dated 20 November 2001. Declaration on the TRIPS Agreement and Public Health adopted by the Doha Ministerial Conference on 14 November 2001.

WTO document WT/MIN(01)/ST/10 dated 10 November 2001. Statement by the Honourable Murasoli Maran, Minister of Commerce and Industry, India, at the Plenary Session of WTO Ministerial Conference at Doha.

WTO document WT/MIN(01)/ST/4 dated 10 November 2001. Statement by H.E. Mr. Robert B. Zoellick, United States Trade Representative. WTO Doha Ministerial Conference.

WTO document WT/MIN(01)/ST/4 dated 10 November 2001. Statement by Mr Pascal Lamy, Commissioner for Trade, European Communities. WTO Doha Ministerial Conference.

WTO document WT/MIN(03)/6 dated 29 August 2003. Caribbean Declaration on the Fifth Ministerial Conference of the WTO, Communication from Jamaica.

WTO document WT/MIN(05)/DEC dated 22 December 2005. Paragraph 7 of the Hong Kong Ministerial Declaration adopted on 18 December 2005.

WTO document WT/MIN(13)/36 dated 11 December 2013. WTO Ministerial Decision of 7 December 2013 on Agreement on Trade Facilitation.

WTO document WT/MIN(13)/38 dated 11 December 2013. WTO Ministerial Decision of 7 December 2013 on Public Stockholding for Food Security Purposes.

WTO document WT/MIN(13)/ST/108 dated 10 February 2014. Statement by Hon. Andrew Robb, Minister for Trade and Investment, Australia at the Bali Ministerial Conference held during 3–6 December 2013.

WTO document WT/MIN(15)/43 dated 21 December 2015. Ministerial Decision of 19 December 2015 on Special Safeguard Mechanism for Developing Country Members.

WTO document WT/MIN(15)/44 dated 21 December 2015. Ministerial Decision of 19 December 2015 on Public Stockholding for Food Security Purposes.

WTO document WT/MIN(15)/45 dated 21 December 2015. Export Competition, Ministerial Decision of 19 December 2015.

WTO document WT/MIN(15)/DEC dated 21 December 2015.

WTO document WT/MIN(17)/59 dated 13 December 2017. Paragraph 4 of the Joint Ministerial Statement on Investment Facilitation for development.

WTO document WT/MIN(17)/60 dated 13 December 2017. Joint Statement on Electronic Commerce.

WTO document WT/MIN(21)/6/Rev.1 dated 3 December 2021. Ministerial Statement on Trade and Environmental Sustainability, Trade and Environmental Sustainability Structured Discussions (TESSD).

WTO document WT/MIN(22)/30 dated 22 June 2022. Ministerial Decision on the TRIPS Agreement adopted on 17 June 2022.

WTO document WT/MIN(22)/W/13 dated 10 June 2022. Ministerial Declaration on the WTO Response to the Covid-19 Pandemic and Preparedness for Future Pandemics.

WTO document WT/MIN(22)/W/16/Rev.1 dated 16 June 2022. MC12 Outcome Document.

WTO document WT/MIN(22)/W/22 dated 17 June 2022. Agreement on Fisheries Subsidies. Draft Ministerial Decision of 17 June 2022.

WTO document WT/MIN(24)/W/25 dated 29 February 2024. Draft Ministerial Decision on Adding the Investment Facilitation for Development Agreement to Annex IV of the WTO Agreement.

WTO Document WT/MIN(96)/DEC dated 18 December 1996. Paragraph 20 of the Singapore Ministerial Declaration adopted on 13 December 1996.

WTO document WT/MIN(96)/DEC dated 18 December 1996. Singapore Ministerial Declaration adopted on 13 December 1996.

WTO document WT/MIN(98)/DEC/2. Declaration on global electronic commerce adopted on 20 May 1998.

WTO document WT/MIN96)/16 dated 13 December 1996. Ministerial Declaration on Trade in Information Technology Products.

WTO document WTO WT/TPR/S/161996. United States Trade Policy Review, Report by the Secretariat.

WTO Members Fail to Make Progress at Mini-Ministerial. *Bridges* 7, 23 (25 June 2003).

Yanai, Akiko.2000. 'APEC and the WTO: Seeking Opportunities for Cooperation'. IDE APEC Study Centre Working Paper Series 99/00 No.2, Institute of Developing Economies, Chiba.

Yoffie, David B. *Power and Protectionism: Strategies of the Newly Industrializing Countries*. New York: Columbia University Press, 1983.

Zahrnt, Valentin. 'Domestic Constituents and the Formulation of the WTO Negotiating Positions'. *World Trade Review* 7, 2 (2008): 393–421.

Zartman, I. William. *The Politics of Trade Negotiations between Africa and the European Economic Community: The Weak Confront the Strong*. Princeton, NJ: Princeton University Press, 1971.

Zartman, I.William, ed. *Positive Sum: Improving North-South Negotiations*. New Brunswick, NJ: Transaction Books, 1987.

Index

For the benefit of digital users, indexed terms that span two pages (e.g., 52–53) may, on occasion, appear on only one of those pages.

Boxes are indicated by an italic *b* following the page number.